W9-AYF-945

THE BEST HOME BUSINESSES FOR THE 90s

▪ ▪

Other Books by Paul and Sarah Edwards

Getting Business to Come to You
Making It on Your Own
Making Money with Your Computer at Home
Working from Home

THE BEST
HOME
BUSINESSES
FOR THE 90s

THE INSIDE INFORMATION
YOU NEED TO KNOW TO SELECT A
HOME-BASED BUSINESS THAT'S
RIGHT FOR YOU

PAUL and SARAH EDWARDS

A JEREMY P. TARCHER / PUTNAM BOOK

published by
G. P. Putnam's Sons
New York

Most Tarcher/Putnam books are available at special quantity discounts for
bulk purchases for sales promotions, premiums, fund-raising, and educational needs. Special books, or book excerpts, can also be created to fit
specific needs.
For details, write or telephone Special Markets, Putnam Publishing Group,
200 Madison Avenue, New York, NY 10016. (212) 951-8891.

A Jeremy P. Tarcher/Putnam Book
Published by G. P. Putnam's Sons
Publishers Since 1838
200 Madison Avenue
New York, NY 10016
http://www.putnam.com/putnam

Copyright © 1994 by Paul and Sarah Edwards

All rights reserved. This book, or parts thereof,
may not be reproduced in any form without permission.
Published simultaneously in Canada

Library of Congress Cataloging-in-Publication Data

Edwards, Paul, date.
The best home businesses for the 90s : the inside information you
need to know to select a home-based business that's right for you /
Paul and Sarah Edwards. — Rev. and expanded.
p.   cm.
"A Jeremy P. Tarcher/Putnam book."
ISBN 0-87477-784-4
1. Home-based businesses.   2. Home-based businesses—Management.
I. Edwards, Sarah (Sarah A.)   II. Title.
HD2333.F34   1995   94-32124   CIP
658'.041—dc20

Design by Irving Perkins Associates
Cover design by Susan Shankin
Printed in the United States of America
11 12 13 14 15 16 17 18 19 20

This book is printed on acid-free paper.

CONTENTS

■■■■■■■■■■■■■■■■■■■■■■■■■■■

* *Note:* Italics refer to related businesses.

v

II: The Rest of the Best   357

INTRODUCTION

■■■■■■■■■■■■■■■■■■■■■■■■■■

Finding the Best Business for You

Our purpose in writing this book is to point you toward the most viable options for joining the over 20 million Americans making money from their homes so you can enjoy the freedom of being your own boss. Whether you're looking for new ideas or already have some idea of what you'd like to do, this book is designed to help you narrow down the many possibilities and find a business that's right both for you and for the economic climate of the 1990s.

There are literally hundreds of possible home-based businesses. And you'll find many books filled with interesting, ingenious ideas about businesses you could start. But haven't you ever wondered if many people are really making money in those businesses? We certainly have. The fact that something is a clever idea that could be done at home doesn't mean people can make money doing it.

In fact, the people we talk with want to know which businesses are truly viable. They've heard about work-at-home scams; they've heard stories about businesses that fail. So they want to know:

- which businesses are actually succeeding
- who can succeed in these businesses
- how much it costs to start them
- how much money you can actually make from them
- will there be a market for this business in the future

We wanted to be able to answer these questions with confidence, so we set out to identify what we consider to be the best home-based businesses to start, given the realities of this decade. Before we introduce you to the businesses we've identified and outline what's involved in operating them, we'd like you to know how we went about picking them.

When we began research on this book, we felt somewhat humbled by the task of selecting what we think will be the best home businesses for the 1990s, especially in providing specific information about their viability. We decided, however, to set specific criteria and make sure the businesses we chose would live up to their reputations.

First, we drew on our own experience. We've been working from home ourselves since 1974, and ever since we began writing our book *Working from Home* in 1980, we've been tracking which businesses people have been running successfully from home. Through the *Working from Home Forum* we operate on CompuServe Information Service, the many seminars we teach on operating a home-based business, and the call-ins we've had from "The Working From Home Show," which we host on the Business Radio Network, as well as the questions we receive for our column in *Home Office Computing* magazine, we have developed a sense for which businesses are doing well.

For this edition of the book, we have had the opportunity to hear back from people over a three-year period. We also have done research described under the new heading *Best Home Businesses* Estimate of Market Potential.

To project what people *will* be doing successfully is a somewhat different task, however, from describing what people have been and are doing now. Fortunately, we've always been future oriented. We began reading the World Future Society's *Futurist* magazine in 1970, and forecasts from pundits like John Naisbitt, Alvin Toffler, and Faith Popcorn have stimulated us to think about what their projections mean for home businesses.

In addition, we were engaged by At Home Professions to research which home-based businesses would be the best ones for which to develop training programs. From this research, we identified specific businesses that are more in demand and easier to access than others.

To screen our selections, we also went to the Bureau of Labor Statistics in Washington, D.C., where we examined the job projections this government office develops and interviewed the experts who synthesize the information that forms the basis for the bureau's projections. Although these projections focus on outside jobs, we find that their work is relevant to home businesses as well. For example, growth in certain job categories may signal other business opportunities, and sometimes the shrinkage of jobs in a category is compensated for by the emergence of small businesses that can be operated from home.

Once we identified businesses that seemed to have a good future, we had to address the issue of what qualifies a business as the *best*. Income possibility was certainly one criterion. We also considered other issues like lifestyle considerations, since today people want more than money from their work. In sum, to be one of our best, a business had to meet a variety of criteria, including the following:

Real Businesses with a Successful At-Home Track Record

Too many people fall prey to an endless stream of scams disguised as business opportunities promising that you can make thousands of dollars a week starting immediately working from home with no background or experience. Unfortunately, such offers look too good to be true because they are too good to be true.

If such schemes were valid businesses, wouldn't everyone be doing them? Wouldn't you meet lots of people who have become wealthy in such businesses? In fact, if these so-called opportunities were real, wouldn't most people on your block be self-employed and doing one of them, and wouldn't you all be driving Mercedeses? But when you think about it, have you ever met anyone who is making good money from one of these schemes? We haven't. After all the years we've been in this field, we haven't met a single person who is making a lot of money from a get-rich-quick scheme.

We have, however, met tens of thousands of people who are working from home successfully year after year, and every one of them is earning a living by using his or her own talents, skills, and experience. The businesses we've selected for this book are the types of businesses these successful people are running. They are *businesses*; not *business opportunities*. In fact, we hesitate to put the words *business* and *opportunities* together anymore because too often the combined term has come to refer to mythical businesses anyone can start tomorrow and make a fortune from.

The home businesses in this book do not pretend to be such opportunities. Not just anybody can start many of the businesses we've identified immediately. Truly profitable businesses are not like unskilled jobs on an assembly line. They require a combination of interests, skills, aptitudes, background, knowledge, and contacts that meet real needs people have. But everyone has some interests, talents, skills, aptitudes, and background. Therefore, in describing each business, we have attempted to honestly portray what's required and what you can expect, so you can objectively and realistically match your own strengths to a truly doable home business.

Good Income Potential

We have selected only businesses that can and are producing a sufficient income for people to support themselves in a reasonable lifestyle. Living at the poverty line is not our idea of a good life. So missing from our list of the best are businesses like astrology, handicrafts, and pet breeding, from which it's difficult for *most* people to make more than a part-time income. While such pursuits are popular and many people are doing them at home, we have included a business only if it has the potential to produce a good, steady, full-time income.

We recognize that what constitutes a good income is highly subjective.

What for some would be ample would for others be insufficient, so we've been as specific as we can be about potential earnings.

To make sure that people are in fact making money in the businesses we've selected, we conducted interviews with professional and trade-association executives from each field whenever possible. We also did in-depth interviews with owners of the businesses that were likely candidates for our list. In addition to determining whether people are making an adequate living from these businesses, we also wanted to know what they are able to charge and how they go about getting business.

We decided to drop some businesses from this edition. The 900 number business, which was a *Rest of the Best* in the first edition, is gone. Changes in regulations that raise the cost of doing this business and declining public use and respect caused us to drop it. Likewise we found that the changed economy of the 90s has impacted on the legal business in a way that makes becoming an independent paralegal fresh from paralegal training a possibility for fewer people. So we dropped this business as well.

We pondered dropping several other businesses: medical billing because so many vendors are selling it as a business-in-the-box and some markets are saturated; the gift basket business because many people find it hard to make enough income from it; and bill-auditing services because we got reports that some communities were saturated due to the number of training programs setting people up as utility rate auditors. But we also got enough positive feedback on these businesses—and, in the case of medical billing, were allowed to see the results of a national survey of doctors—that we decided to continue profiling them as viable businesses.

We also have upgraded three businesses (manufacturer's agent, meeting planner, and newsletter publisher) from the *Rest of the Best* in the last edition to the *Best of the Best* in this edition. In doing this, we added more detailed information. In addition, we have identified and profiled as either a *Best of the Best* or a *Rest of the Best* business fourteen new businesses. As we did in the first edition, we bundle kindred businesses under one category, such as editing, indexing, and proofreading under editorial services. In nine cases, we identify distinct businesses as *Related Businesses* such as directory publisher, exposition manager, manual writer, and shareware developer.

Nonetheless, although all the businesses we describe can provide what many people find to be adequate full-time incomes, we still suggest that, in selecting the best business for you, you carefully consider how much income you need and want and the demand in your own community or market.

Reasonable Ease of Entry

While we have found that many professionals like accountants, software engineers, and psychotherapists are doing well working on their own from home, we have excluded any business that requires a specific college degree. We consider this important because as corporations continue to reduce the number of people they employ and as jobs go out of existence, many people need to do something other than what they were originally trained to do or have had previous experience in. Few people have the time and resources to go back to school full-time to prepare for a new profession, although in today's world education is not a one-time event.

Some of the businesses we've chosen can be operated with any general background. Your existing skills, aptitudes, and experience may ideally qualify you for many of them. Some businesses, however, require certain skills and experience that you may need to pick up by taking some course work or working for a period of time in a particular field. Should you not have the required background for the businesses that interest you the most, you will find specific steps outlined for how you can gain whatever background you need.

So while some of the businesses you'll find most appealing may require that you take time to gain certain skills or experience, keep in mind that the best investment you can make is an investment in yourself. An investment in building experience, education, and training is never wasted. Even if preparing yourself for your chosen home business would take a year or more, that period of time will most certainly pass whether you pursue the needed preparation or not. So if you start now, you'll be ready to succeed that much sooner.

In fact, a Canadian study of entrepreneurs showed that those who succeed are the ones who have prepared themselves prior to starting their business so that they have the necessary skills and expertise to make it. The successful ones begin with realistic expectations for how much they can earn and then do their homework for at least six to nine months—taking courses and calling on experts, for example.

What we can assure you is that the businesses described in this book do not require that you be without a job while you prepare yourself for them. In fact, for some of the best businesses, like being a private detective, the ideal way to learn is to first take a job working for someone else in that business. While you may have to take a pay cut at first in order to do this, you can think of it as a way to get paid for on-the-job training.

Also keep in mind that even if a business requires no prior experience, if it is in a field you know well, getting started will be much easier. You will be able to use contacts you already have, and your reputation in the field could be valuable in qualifying you. The greater your experience in a field, the shorter and less challenging your learning curve will be once you get out on your own.

Low or Modest Start-up Costs

We have also selected businesses that do not require tens of thousands of dollars to get under way. Some businesses, like cleaning services, can be started for as little as a few hundred dollars, while others, like a desktop video business, require sophisticated computer technology and an initial investment of over $10,000.

In calculating start-up costs, we're assuming that you will be starting your business in a home office space other than on the kitchen table. People have started successful businesses from kitchen tables, but by setting up a specific desk and office area devoted to your business, not only will you avoid unnecessary backaches and eyestrain, but you'll be able to work more productively, and you and your customers, family, and friends will also be more likely to take your new business seriously.

The fact that you will be working from your home without the overhead of office or storefront rent means you will be able to start most of the businesses we've selected for this book on a part-time basis while you still have a job. We think starting out while you have the security and cash flow of a job is the safest way to finance a home-business start-up and to carry you through the months it takes to launch a business.

In addition, as soon as you start your own business, whether full- or part-time, you can convert some of your costs of living into tax-deductible business expenses (which as a salaried employee you're not eligible for) thereby reducing your annual federal and state income taxes. By starting your business while you still have a job, you can actually use the federal tax system to help fund your start-up costs. Doing this involves changing the number of allowances you claim on your W-4 so that you have several hundred additional dollars each month in take-home pay. Before doing that, however, we recommend seeing a tax consultant to make sure that you set up your home office so that such expenses are deductible.

Ability to Operate from Home

Not all businesses can be run from home profitably. In fact, we found that upon close scrutiny several businesses that you might think would be good home-based candidates are really not best suited to be operated from home. Auto brokering, with its state licensing requirements, was one such business.

All the businesses in this book can be operated successfully from home without employees. Most of them, however, can also be expanded by hiring employees or using subcontractors who may either work on your premises or from their own homes. Such expansion is not necessary, however, in order to earn a decent living.

In fact, we've talked with many people who expanded their home business only to find that while adding employees increased their gross revenues, once they paid for salaries, fringe benefits, and insurance, they decreased their net income. What's more, some people who expanded by adding personnel also found that they had to work longer hours and contend with more aggravation. By cutting back to what they could handle themselves, they ended up netting more income with greater satisfaction.

So for each of these businesses, growth is an option, not a prerequisite to success.

Variety: Something for Everyone

The businesses we selected are varied enough that virtually everyone can find something to do from home. Whether you prefer to be outdoors or at a desk, work with people or manipulate information, use your hands or your head, be alone or with others, get involved with computers or stay away from technology altogether—whatever your interests, hobbies, talents, experience, and preferences, you should be able to find a business in this book that's suited to you.

Sometimes when we talk about these businesses, someone will say, "Who would ever want to do that?" But we've learned that there is someone who can find satisfaction in doing virtually any task imaginable. There are people whose brain endorphins start to flow when they're busy cleaning things, and they're perfectly happy running a cleaning service or auto-detailing business. For others who are turned on by doing highly detailed work, a business like bookkeeping or medical transcription is enjoyable.

Still others enjoy the thrill and challenge of standing in front of an audience, even though most people list public speaking as their greatest or second-greatest fear. For them, employee training may be a perfect match. Someone who loves helping people solve problems might relish running a collection business. Should nurturing others be your passion, becoming a facialist could meet your needs. Ultimately, enjoyable work is in the *brain* of the beholder!

What the Business Profiles Will Tell You (And What They Won't)

In describing the businesses we've selected, our objective is to give you the best possible information we could obtain so that you can make a true comparison and a well-informed choice among the businesses we believe offer the best potential in these nervous 90s. The first sixty businesses are what we consider to be the *Best of the Best*. These businesses have an established track record of success and a strong continuing demand.

The *Rest of the Best*, which follow, are businesses that are sometimes less well known and at this time less common. They are being done successfully, though, and are well suited to grow and flourish in this decade. Some of the Rest of the Best are so new that it was hard to discover much about them, in which case we have included as much information as we could find.

Each Best of the Best profile begins with a general description of the business, the types of customers and clients it serves, and what makes it a good business for the 90s. We then go on to address the following issues.

☑ Knowledge and Skills You Need to Have

This section lists what you need to know and be able to do in order to operate this business, as well as any special training or licenses you may need. Here we also highlight the aptitudes, preferences, talents, and tolerances each business demands, as identified by people we've interviewed who have enjoyed and succeeded at doing it, as well as people who have not done well or enjoyed the business.

In short, this section of the profile gives you the opportunity to determine whether you already have or would be willing to acquire the needed capabilities and competencies the business requires. Sometimes the businesses of most interest to you will be a perfect match. You'll say, "Hey, I could do that right now!" At other times, however, you'll find that you have *some* of what it takes but need to develop additional skills and talents. For example, you might be able to start a business doing professional-practice management for chiropractors by taking on a relative as your first client, but you may need to develop your knowledge of billing procedures. Or you may have the expertise but not the interest or the contacts.

Not only can reviewing these profiles help you make sure you are qualified to start a given business; it can also help you avoid the mistake of focusing only on the potential opportunities a business provides. One person who came to one of our seminars learned this lesson the hard way. He decided to start a medical-transcription business because he knew there was a high demand for it and it paid well. And indeed, when we met him he was making $60,000 a year. But, not being someone who enjoys sitting still, he said the work was driving him crazy. So he was attending our seminar to find a business he would enjoy more.

The special training some of the businesses require may be acquired through community colleges, trade schools, and professional associations, or by working for/apprenticing with an existing business in the field.

Reputable trade schools will readily provide information on attrition and graduation rates as well as references. Some industries provide on-the-job apprentice programs through trade and professional associations.

We are increasingly convinced of the value of apprenticing and specifically recommend it in a number of profiles as a *First Step*. Apprenticing may mean working as an employee for the type of business you wish to enter, or it may mean literally following in the footsteps of someone in the business and assisting them for a week or several weeks. Doing this can be so worthwhile; it may even be worth paying for the privilege of assisting. You are not just reading about theory when you're out with someone actually calling on their customers, seeing and hearing how they handle problems, and enjoying the rewards of the business. Even in businesses where we do not specifically mention it, finding an apprenticing situation is worth considering.

Internships are another possible way to gain needed experience. *Internships 1995*, available through Peterson's (Princeton, N.J.; [800] 338-3282) lists

35,000 internship opportunities and provides guidance about how to apply for and get these coveted experiences, both paid and unpaid.

Where there are specific training programs available for a particular business well suited to people wanting to learn at home, we've listed these resources in the section titled "Where to Turn for Information and Help."

🐄 Start-up Costs

This section indicates what someone starting each business can expect to spend in order to get the business under way. Each item will usually have a low and high figure. The low figure is for what we consider to be a minimally equipped office; the high figure is for the optimally equipped office. Prices are as of mid-1994.

To be competitive today, most businesses require an adequate investment in office furniture; business cards, letterhead, and envelopes; and a computer of some kind. While these start-up expenses add up to a minimum of around $2,000, do not let this amount deter you. You may have some of the needed items already. You may be able to delay some purchases until your business produces the income to buy them. You can buy used equipment and furniture. You may be able to lease items, although leasing is more expensive than buying, even if you finance your purchases.

You may notice that some of our start-up costs appear somewhat higher than those you might read about in other publications. The reason for this is that while we heartily recommend that people bootstrap their business, we don't recommend trying to limp by with less than a minimally professional setup. So although you might be able to forego some of the items we recommend initially, these are the expenditures you should anticipate and plan for.

Office Furniture.   Unless the business requires something special, we have calculated standard office furniture to run around $600 at the low end and $800 at the high. This range is based on the following: a standard four-drawer filing cabinet at $150, a desk at $200 (with $200 you can buy a new economical steel desk, a used wooden desk, or a hollow-framed door placed upon two two-drawer filing cabinets), a basic ergonomically designed chair at between $200 to $400 (to keep your costs at the low end of that range, name-brand chairs can be purchased used), a printer table or stand for $100, and $50 for office supplies and accessories.

Computer hardware and software.   Unless the business requires a higher-performance computer, our estimates for computer costs are based on your buying an IBM compatible 486 computer, costing around $1,000, including monitor. In the first five months of 1994 computer prices decreased almost 25 percent, which means it's entirely possible that you'll even be able to get a more powerful 586 or a Macintosh within this budget. Software prices are based on discounts widely available by mail or in stores that heavily discount software. Under printer prices, where we think an ink jet printer is adequate, we have indicated a price of $300. Where we think a printer producing a higher-quality image is important, we have specified a laser printer available now at beginning under $600. A low-budget solution for obtaining word-processing software is to use an integrated program, such as *Microsoft Works*, *Lotus Works*, or *Claris Works*, that includes basic spreadsheet, database, and communications functions as well. Suites of the best full-powered programs (word processing, spreadsheet, database, and presentation graphics) are also now available for about $250 from Microsoft, Lotus, and Borland. In the past, any one of these programs might have cost $300 to $500.

The Five Basic Skills Required for All Businesses

There are five basic skills we believe anyone must have to run any kind of business. Although they are required for *all* the businesses in this book, we don't repeat them in each business profile. And while we don't discuss these skills in the book, the other books in our series of Working from Home Guides do. So if you are lacking in any of these vital areas of expertise, we have indicated throughout this chapter when you can turn to the other books in our series for help.

1. Basic money-management skills. While you don't need to have a lot of money to start a business successfully, you do need the ability to make the most of the money you have. Being able to focus on the bottom line and pay attention to the numbers is as essential as the ability to price your products and services, manage your cash flow, and make sure you collect payment for the work you do. If you are lacking in these skills you can get training in business courses, books, and so forth.

2. A marketing mindset. You aren't truly in business until you have business. No matter how much your product or service is in demand or how great a job you do, if people don't know about you, you won't have much business. You must be able to make your business visible to the people who need it, and this means understanding marketing.

3. Self-management skills. To make it on your own, you must become a goal-directed and self-motivated individual. You must be able to get yourself started each day, stick to business, and close the door on work at the day's end.

4. Time-management skills. In your home business, you will need to wear many hats, from chief executive officer to janitor. You'll have to do the business, get the business, and run the business. This means you'll need to manage your time effectively to make sure the most important and urgent things get done in a timely fashion.

5. Basic office organization. Since one of the roles you will probably play is that of your own office administrator, you will need to be able to organize, equip, and manage your office space so that you can work effectively in it, having a place for everything and keeping everything in its place so that you can find it easily when you need it.

For more information on mastering these five basic skills, refer to the other books in our series: *Working from Home, Getting Business to Come to You* (with Laura Clampitt Douglas), *Making It on Your Own*, and *Making Money with Your Computer at Home*.

Business cards, logo, stationery, brochures. We've generally indicated $200 at the low end to cover business cards, stationery, and so forth. However, we've found that by using a home-based desktop-publishing service that has an arrangement with a print shop, you can get a high-quality designed logo, 1,000 business cards, letterhead, and envelopes for around $600, and the extra expenditure can greatly enhance your image.

Still another alternative after you've made an investment in a computer and a printer capable of printing good quality, you can use attractive pre-printed papers from companies like Avery-Dennison, Paper Direct, and Staples with desktop publishing software or the desktop publishing capabilities of full-power word processing programs to create and produce your own cards, stationery, and brochures. To make this easier, you can get software templates designed to match the specific papers. Then you can experiment with and test the look you want for your business, how you describe it, and even your company name. The cost of doing this is mere pennies per item instead of hundreds of dollars for comparable offset printing. For example, you can create five hundred brochures for about $100. With this same capability you can also individualize your message to particular prospective customers or clients.

In fact, business consultant Alan Gregerman, president of Venture Works, in Silver Spring, Maryland, recommends that many businesses use what he calls a customized brochure. Using your computer with word-processing or desktop-publishing software and a laser printer, you can create a basic format for your brochure and then tailor the content for each person or company to whom you send it. In such cases your brochure becomes a custom-made proposal at a fraction of the cost of a standard printed brochure. Gregerman finds that such a brochure has great impact.

Organizational dues. Because making business contacts through formal or informal networking is one of the most effective methods for home businesses to get business and because feeling a sense of isolation from one's peers is one concern people have about leaving the traditional office setting, we have included $250 in start-up expenses for joining one or more professional, trade, or business organizations.

Special expenses. Beyond the basic costs listed above, we have also included any expenses that are particular to a business. Some businesses, for example, demand specialized equipment, more sophisticated computer technology, or specific software. An export agent or publicist, for example, must have a fax machine. An errand service needs a radio pager or cellular phone. Some businesses, like association management, require that you join organizations in order to market or establish yourself.

In some cases, you'll be able to postpone buying more costly equipment by leasing it or by contracting out for services. Few desktop publishers, for example, have equipment capable of producing printouts at 1,200 dots per inch, so they use service bureaus when they need to provide that level of clarity. Buying used equipment will also cut down on your initial costs.

Costs not included. Our start-up estimates do not include the costs of an answering machine, telephone equipment, or telephone services because there is a wide range of options available for meeting these needs, including converting your existing equipment, using an outside service, and so forth. At the minimum, however, you will need one separate business telephone line and either an answering machine, an answering service, or voice mail for taking calls when you are not in your office. These costs should be added to the start-up estimates you'll find in this book.

Other than the cost of initial organizational dues or brochures, our estimates of start-up expenses do not include the costs of marketing your business. Such costs are reflected instead as part of overhead estimates, which we've put in the section titled "Potential Earnings." Nor do our estimates include what you will need to cover initial operating expenses or your living expenses. If you have a job or your spouse has a job, you may be able to cover your ongoing expenses in that way until your business begins to generate income sufficient to support your lifestyle. Otherwise you should have some other plan to cover your living expenses and overhead for at least three, and preferably six to nine, months while you get your business under way.

Later in this chapter you will find a list of the five most common plans used to finance home-business start-ups.

⬇ ⬆ Advantages and Disadvantages of Each Business

Selecting a business is always a matter of balancing the best aspects with those that are least desirable. Every business has its pros and cons. These two entries will help you identify businesses that may be especially appealing to you as well as those with characteristics that you would find disagreeable.

They are intended to help you avoid businesses that won't be of interest to you and businesses you would only abandon later.

If you hate to work under the pressure of deadlines, for example, you won't want to consider technical writing or book indexing. But if you want to be in a business that holds the potential for establishing a steady stream of repeat business, being a facialist or running a mailing-list service could fill the bill.

$ Pricing

This section in the profiles answers one of the most common questions people starting a home-based business ask. In most cases, we give a range of fees or prices. These ranges are based on several variables.

First, unless otherwise indicated, the prices stated are typical for urban areas. Also local prices can vary substantially from one part of the country to another and competition in a given community may push prices downward or drive the rate higher. For example, we found desktop publishing to be a particularly competitive business. The hourly desktop-publishing prices ranged from $20 to $25 an hour when offered by a word-processing firm, but as high as $100 by a desktop publishing firm. We believe, however, that the more typical rate is around $40 an hour.

The prices you can charge are also affected by your particular background, skills, and contacts and by the type of clients you decide to serve. For example, nonprofit organizations typically operate on tighter budgets than marketing departments for large corporations. They therefore are likely to hire people who will charge less for the same service a corporation might be paying more for. Student and educational markets also pay a lower range of fees.

In setting your own prices, you should make calls to comparable businesses in your area to find out what the going rate is for the business you are considering. If you charge too much, you're apt to wait a long time for that first customer; but if you charge too little, colleagues and prospective customers may very well question your capability. So do check local prices before setting yours, and remember that what other people charge should be only one factor in determining your prices. In *Working from Home*, we have a chapter (chapter 22) on various pricing strategies and the procedures for setting your prices.

▣ Potential Earnings

The figures stated in this section are based on estimates of what you can earn from operating the business full-time without employees. By working full-time, we mean spending forty hours a week or more doing work for which you are paid, as well as marketing and administering your business. For many of the businesses, the income estimates are based on being able to bill twenty hours per week (1,000 billable hours per year). Some occupations such as bookkeeping and word processing, however, can bill out closer to the standard forty hours per week. In still other businesses, like corporate training and wedding planning, we presume you are billing a certain number of days or events each week.

Typical annual gross revenue for a programmer, for example, is $50,000. This figure is based on billing twenty hours per week, fifty weeks a year (1,000 hours a year) at $50 an hour. Many programmers, however, are able to bill in excess of forty hours a week and earn up to $100,000 per year.

We have attempted to be conservative in our income estimates, as research has shown that having realistic expectations of what you can earn is an important criterion for business success. Our figures do presume, however, that the business owner is successful in effectively marketing the business and therefore has ample business coming in.

For most of these businesses, you can exceed these projections by hiring an employee or using subcontractors. This is especially true when the business involves selling your time as the only or the principal source of revenue, as is the case with word processing or transcribing court reporters' notes. There are only 174 hours in each week, and producing revenue in more than 25 to 30 of these hours is difficult when you must not only *do the business* but also *get the business* and *run the business*.

Overhead.   In calculating overhead, which covers the basic costs of being in business (like marketing, telephone, business taxes, insurance, postage, printing, supplies, subscriptions, and so forth), we indicate whether the overhead for this business is high, moderate, or low. These estimates are based on information gathered directly from successful business owners and, whenever possible, from reports by national trade associations such as the Professional Association of Innkeepers International and the American Society for Training and Development.

We consider low operating expenses to be 20 percent or less of your gross income, moderate to be 25 to 40 percent, and high to be greater than 40 percent. We have used these estimated ranges for several reasons. First, we find that most home-based business owners do not know exactly what it costs them to operate, beyond the calculations they do for income-tax purposes. But the tax system is designed to collect taxes, not to serve as an information system for financial planning. While how much you can deduct from your taxes does reflect your business expenses, the amount you deduct depends on how disciplined you are in keeping records of things like automobile usage for business purposes and how well you engineer social engagements to make them tax deductible. Therefore, actual expenses and deducted expenses can often vary. In our estimate of overhead, no allowance is made for using your home or automobile unless this is a significant part of operating your business (for example, a bed-and-breakfast inn or an errand service).

Second, many home businesses have wide latitude in what they must spend for overhead. Furniture used in the home office may be a $500 Steelcase chair, or it may be an "early relative" dining-room captain's chair that costs nothing.

⍰ *Best Home Businesses* Estimate of Market Potential

For this edition we wanted to give you more of an idea about how open the market is for a particular business. So to the extent a business we write about has established an identity sufficient to have a yellow-page listing, a trade association that calculates its potential membership, or a commercially available mailing list of people in that business, we consulted those. Then we went a step further. Based on research by the phone companies and our analysis of sample calls to home business listings from the telephone directories of twenty-five of the largest cities in the U.S., we were able to estimate how many of a particular type of home-based businesses there are nationally even though most home-based businesses do not have yellow-page listings or appear on anyone's mailing list. These estimates are a unique source of information about the potential demand for the businesses we've profiled. When available, the national estimate for a business is summarized under the heading *Best Home Businesses* Estimate of Market Potential.

Because many of the businesses we've included don't yet have a sufficient identity to be picked up in any of these ways, we do not have estimates for every business. But where we can calculate how many businesses there are in a category, that information can give you an idea of how big the market is for a particular business and how open it might be. You can relate the national estimate to the possible number of businesses in your community. For example, if there are 10 collection agencies locally (18,761 nationally) and 100 local bookkeeping services (31,780 nationally), that tells you that the 1:10 ratio in your community is less than the somewhat more than 1:2 ratio we found nationally. Unless there is a reason a particular business does not thrive in your area, it would be reasonable to conclude that there's room for you. On the other hand, if you find there are many of a particular business in your community, perhaps there's a need for a referral service to help direct customers to companies needing them. It also tells you how important it is for you to specialize, preferably doing something or caring for customers others in that field are not doing or serving. We hope to take this information further in future editions and welcome your feedback on how useful it is to you.

We've also included some usually brief comments about the forces affecting the potential for each business. Someone in a growing community like Austin, Las Vegas, Orlando, Tucson, Provo, or Salt Lake City is apt to find more demand than in the older cities. A businessperson in Boise, Idaho, for example, told us that someone starting any one of the businesses we profiled in the first edition could be making a profit within six months. He attributed this to the numbers of people moving in from the coasts who expect big-city services that were not available. But will a county that is growing because of its attractiveness for recreation or retirement necessarily support a business that is needed in a big city? Maybe. Maybe not.

Keep in mind, too, that while most rural counties are growing, reversing a long period of declining populations, living in the country or a small town may not be for you. Most people who move to small-town and rural "paradises" discover they don't like it as much as they thought they would or find their new neighbors unwelcoming. One study found that 50 percent of people moving to a small city or town moved elsewhere after two years; the figure was 90 percent after five years. So consider well before heading off to unfamiliar locales. Many small towns don't readily welcome strangers; in some places, anyone who hasn't lived in a town for three generations is considered a stranger. So you see that picking a best business to start in a new community is more than a matter of the seeming demand.

▣ Best Ways to Get Business

When we ask operators of successful home businesses to tell us the best way to get business, over and over again they tell us the same thing:

The best source of business is referrals from satisfied customers. In fact, they tell us that once a home business is established, most business comes from word of mouth. For example, Steve Burt, a résumé writer in Gainesville, Florida, put it this way: "If you do a good job for someone, take a little extra time to talk with them, or give a client something extra. I guarantee you'll get referral business."

But, of course, you can't get referral business until you have business. So to avoid the proverbial chicken-or-the-egg dilemma we have limited our list of best ways to get business to those that can help you get your initial clients and customers. In this category, you'll find the most likely and cost-effective ways to market each business based on our interviews with people who have successfully established these businesses.

We've included this information for two reasons. First, you're not *in business* until you *have business*, so it's crucial in selecting a business to know that there are identifiable methods others have used and found reliable for bringing in business. Second, in your own business you may spend up to 40 percent of your time marketing, so it's important to select a business for which the most reliable marketing methods are ones that you feel comfortable doing. Therefore, in reviewing the businesses, we suggest considering this section as another important way to judge which businesses are best suited to your talents, interests, and personality.

In general, we have usually not listed advertising because, for a home business being started with limited capital, it can be costly. In the process of writing our book *Getting Business to Come to You* with marketing expert Laura Clampitt Douglas, we interviewed over one hundred successful home-based businesses earning over $60,000 a year and discovered that the most successful marketing methods for home-based business are often the least expensive ones. The most successful home-business owners use their time and energy, not their money, to market themselves.

Finding the best marketing method is always an experiment, so you can use our list as a starting point to test various methods until you find the ones that will actually be the most effective in your community with your prospective clients and customers. The fact that a method does not appear on our list does not mean it will not work for you. What's most important is whether you're comfortable with using a method and whether it is effective in reaching the people you need to reach.

For step-by-step information about how to use these methods, refer to our book *Getting Business to Come to You*. It also includes recommendations for how to name your business to achieve maximum marketing effectiveness, proven start-up strategies, instant business-getting techniques, and methods for getting repeat business.

Ann McIndoo, successful computer tutor whose business, Computer Training Systems, is located in Diamond Bar, California, offers this marketing suggestion for whatever business you are in: Build a client and prospect database of everyone whom you could work with, and then whenever you aren't busy, make unbillable moments productive by giving them a call. She finds it always generates work.

✚ Related Businesses

This section provides the names of other businesses that are related in terms of the type of work done, skills required, or markets served.

▰ Franchises

Where appropriate, we have included a section with the names and addresses of franchises that are available for starting the business being profiled. We have discovered a growing number of franchises that can be operated from home. Buying a franchise instead of starting a business from scratch has advantages in that a proven franchise provides a tested formula for starting a business that has worked for others. It can save you from making costly errors, shorten your learning curve, and help you make a profit more quickly. There are trade-offs in buying franchises, however: start-up costs are often higher, and franchising organizations require that you follow their procedures instead of doing it your own way.

▮ First Steps

If you decide you would like to pursue a given business, this section provides suggestions on how to obtain the knowledge and skills you will need, as well as ideas for getting your business under way. To gather this information we asked people who are in the field what advice they would give to someone wanting to start this business.

Where to Turn for Information and Help

Here we list books, trade associations and professional organizations, special training programs, and magazines and newsletters recommended by people in the field that can be of value to someone starting out in each business. For products over $50, we have indicated the current price.

How to Choose a Business That's Right for You

Selecting a business from among the many that are viable requires finding a match between two things: (1) your particular interests and capabilities, and (2) what people will pay for in your community. Finding this match is vital to your success, and this book is designed to help you find the best possible match. As you read through the businesses we've profiled, you can begin by making a list of those that hold the greatest appeal to you and in which you believe you could do well.

Finding Something You Want to Do That You Do Well

Being able to do a good job is a must in any business. A poor or even mediocre job usually guarantees that you won't have return customers, but that's not all. Sometimes clients and customers will refuse to pay for inferior work, and worse yet, an unhappy client usually tells at least seven other people what poor service he or she received. So first and foremost, you must be confident that you will be able to do a satisfactory—if not superior—job in whatever business you select.

Obviously, having a background in the business and a track record of success would therefore be ideal. For example, if you have worked as an employee for a florist doing gift baskets and have received rave reviews on your work, you're in a position to feel confident about your ability to do a good job in your own gift-basket business. Or if you've been doing bookkeeping on a salary for several years and your clients respect you and refer others to you, you're certainly well positioned to start a bookkeeping service.

But what if you don't like what you've been doing? What if you're looking for a change or if what you've been doing can't be done from home? You still have many options. You can look for a business in another field that utilizes skills similar to those you've acquired. For example, if you're good at bookkeeping but want to do something different, you could look for businesses that involve financial management, attention to detail, or record keeping.

If you are seeking a complete change, you can turn to hobbies or other interests and talents you have. When work repairing televisions dried up for

Ted Laux, for example, his wife pointed out that he had years of experience cataloguing and indexing his extensive record collection and therefore might enjoy starting a book-indexing business. She was right. That's exactly what he did.

In fact, while being good at your business is essential, our research shows it's not sufficient. You also need to enjoy it. We think it's profoundly sad that so many people feel they're squandering the precious moments of their lives doing work they dislike. We also believe that a hefty percentage of business failures, physical illnesses, and addictions of mankind can be traced to choosing the wrong job or business.

And most important, succeeding as your own boss is almost always a matter of taking the initiative and going the extra mile despite the stresses that accompany any business. Picking a business you like and that likes you is essential to staying motivated through the ups and downs of being on your own. It could even mean your business or personal survival.

Besides, it feels good to wake up in the morning eager to get to work because you like your work so much. We believe one's work should be stimulating, exciting, enjoyable, interesting, and fulfilling. And since your work is likely to be one of the primary ways you express what you have to contribute to life, your work should also be a platform through which you can give the best you have.

Therefore, in selecting a business, use your interests, talents, and likes and dislikes as a filter through which to examine the businesses we've profiled. If you are not fully confident about your ability to do a particularly appealing business, you can take the time to build your skills through practice, attending courses, or even apprenticing for a while before going out on your own.

What follows is a series of worksheets designed to help you identify what you are most interested in doing. If you already have a good idea of what type of business you want to do, you may wish to skip these next few pages. Before you do so, however, consider that it could be useful to compare your intended choice with other possibilities before you fully commit to it.

Determining If There's a Need

Once you've identified two or three businesses you think you would enjoy and do well at, we suggest that you invest a few weeks, even a few months, to test out whether you are likely to find ample customers for these businesses in your local community.

The fact that a business appears in this book means that people are succeeding at running this business from home. Clients and customers in many parts of the country are willing to pay for what these businesses offer. The market looks good for others to succeed in this business. But as we said before, the demand for a business varies from community to community. A community can become oversaturated with a particular business or otherwise not have much need for it.

In fact, we found that while many people were succeeding in these businesses, in all cases there were others who were not. Therefore, before you invest time and money in starting a particular business, it is crucial that you determine if you will be able to find enough people who are willing to pay you when you open such a business in your community. Here are several ways you can go about checking out the actual need for a business in your community.

1. Look in the yellow pages and/or other directories where such a business might be listed and see if there are other such businesses. How many listings are there? If there are a number of similar businesses, this is a good sign that there's a strong market for the business, but you will need to determine whether they are doing well and whether the market can support yet another one. Should the market be oversaturated, only the best are going to survive.

Questionnaire 1
Questions to Ask Yourself in Choosing a Business

1. Based on your education, your current or past jobs, and any special interests and hobbies, what three things do you know the most about? This expertise could be the basis for a business.

2. What other experiences in your background could you draw upon for a business?

3. What do people tell you that you do well? Think about the times you've heard someone say, "You know, you really ought to start a such-and-such, you're so good at that." Maybe they're right. And maybe they would be your first customer.

4. What things do you like doing most? Think, for example, about these questions.

> What do you like to do on your day off?
> What kinds of things do you leap out of bed for?
> What magazines, newsletters, and books do you enjoy reading?
> What headlines catch your eye?
> What things did you love doing most when you were a child?
> What is it you've always said you were going to do someday?

If this were the last day of your life, as you looked back on your life what would you say you wished you had done?

5. How much do you want to be involved with people? All the time? Sometimes? From a distance? Not at all? The answers can help you rule in or out businesses that have a lot of or very little people contact.

6. How many hours a week are you willing to invest in your business? Do you want a full-time or a part-time business? Be realistic about this. The amount of

time you're willing to invest is what separates full-time from part-time and profits from losses.

7. How much money do you need to make? How much money do you want to make? Each week? Each month? Each year? You'll notice that some of the businesses can charge considerably more than others, so choose a business that will produce the income you want and need.

8. What resources do you have available to you in terms of property, equipment, and know-how? These resources could become the basis of a business. If you look around your home, you may have many untapped resources right under your nose such as a personal computer, a van, a spare room, an automobile, a camcorder, your kitchen stove, vacuum sweeper, backyard, or mailbox.

9. Do you want to start a business from scratch, or would you prefer a franchise or direct-selling organization such as Amway or Avon that will train you in what to do?

Questionnaire 2
What Do You Like and Do Best?

Circle the work activities on this list that you like to do, and use the list to help stimulate your thinking as you complete Questionnaire 3.

Information-Oriented Work	People-Oriented Work	Thing-Oriented Work
Working with words	Advising	Cleaning
Working with numbers	Caring	Making
Analyzing	Communicating	Organizing
Compiling	Helping	Repairing
Creating	Informing	Working with animals
Evaluating	Organizing	Working with food
Finding	Negotiating	Working with plants
Keyboarding	Performing	Working with tools
Organizing	Persuading	
Synthesizing	Planning events	
	Teaching	

If you discover there are no such businesses in your area, this could mean that there's an unmet need and the community is ripe for such a business—or it could mean that there is not enough need to support such a business. You'll need to investigate further.

2. Call your competition.   Find out what services they actually offer and whom they serve. You might be able to specialize in some aspect of the work that they do not provide, or you might offer your services to a market they are not serving. Let them know you are thinking of starting a similar business and ask if they ever need to refer out overload or if there is a type of clientele they cannot or don't wish to serve and therefore are turning away. Also, find out how long they've been in business. This will give you an idea of how persistent a need there is for this business.

In a good market, while there may always be one or two people who fear competition, the majority of competitors will tend to be forthcoming with information and even glad that others are joining the field. Some will even offer to help you. But if you find that all or most of the people you talk to are consistently closed-mouthed or are complaining about business, this could mean there's not enough business to go around.

Questionnaire 3
Business Selection Worksheet

Your Long List

List your six best or strongest skills, talents, abilities, capabilities, or aptitudes.

1. _____

2. _____

3. _____

4. _____

5. _____

6. _____

List the six subjects or fields you know the most about, are the most competent in, or have the most experience and expertise in.

1. _____

2. _____

3. _____

4. _____

5. _____

6. _____

3. Read business, trade, and professional journals related to your field. These periodicals, especially local ones, can provide a wealth of information about the demand for a business. Sometimes they list new businesses and bankruptcies, track sales volumes, cover booms and busts by region or area, and feature success and comeback stories. Also read the trade journals your potential clients read to see what their concerns are and to follow emerging trends.

4. Attend local business, trade, and professional meetings. Follow the topics addressed at these meetings and listen to the table talk. Are people singing the blues or whistling "Dixie"?

5. Talk directly to potential customers. Locate and contact potential clients to find out how they are currently being served and if they are happy. Listen to what they complain about. See if you can identify how you could provide faster, cheaper, or better service.

Your Short List

Now narrow the long list down to the three skills and subjects that you like most, in rank order.

Skills   Subjects

1. _____   1. _____

2. _____   2. _____

3. _____   3. _____

With this short list in mind, you can look through the profiles for the businesses that best correspond to what you know about, what you're good at, and what you enjoy.

Some people also find it useful to make a list of the things they dislike doing, because a negative filter can prevent you from entering into a business that has a fatal flaw for you. If a business is otherwise appealing to you, however, consider the possibilities of working with someone else who would do those aspects that for you are disagreeable. That person might be a partner, a subcontractor, or an employee. For example, a desktop publisher who isn't an especially fast typist can subcontract with a word-processing service to do text entry. Many partnerships form because one person is good at being the *inside* person, handling production and administration, while the other is the *outside* person, handling sales and customer contact.

6. Talk with the chamber of commerce and local government planning agencies about the size of your market and community developments that will affect your business potential.

7. Analyze the marketing literature of your competitors to see how they are addressing the market and what they are and are not offering.

Check Your Zoning

Zoning regulations vary from community to community, so another important step in determining which business is best suited to you is to determine what restrictions, if any, have been placed on the type of work you can do from home.

Zoning regulations typically divide communities into residential, commercial, industrial, and agricultural zones, with subdivisions within these categories. Even in residential areas, many zoning regulations allow so-called home occupations. But some communities prohibit working from home altogether in residential zones, or allow certain activities but not others. In some locales, for example, you can't have clients coming to your home. In others, you can't have employees, use your address in advertising, or sell retail.

Questionnaire 4
Other Criteria for Selecting the Right Business

Circle the answer that best describes the business you want.

Income Potential

How much money you think you need to:
- survive? How much do you need to get by?
  Under $25,000 $25,000 to $50,000   Over $50,000
- thrive? What do you need to meet or exceed the standard of living afforded by your job?
  Under $25,000 $25,000 to $50,000   Over $50,000
- get rich? How much money would you really like to make?
  Under $25,000 $25,000 to $50,000   Over $50,000

Where You Want to Work

Work at home   Work from home

Amount of People Contact

Mostly working with people   Some work with people   Not a people business

What's Required

A business I'm already prepared to enter.
Something that will require me to learn new talents and skills.

Start-up Money Needed

Low—under $2,500   Moderate—$2,500–$7,500   High—over $7,500

Therefore, it's important to find out specifically how your home is zoned and what business activities can and cannot be legally carried out on your premises. To determine if your home can be used for business purposes, you will need to check the zoning ordinances at either your city hall or your county courthouse. To know whether you need to check with the city or the county, a general rule of thumb is that if you would call the police for an emergency, you are governed by city zoning; if you would phone the sheriff's office, you deal with the county.

For more information about zoning and specifically what you can do if you are not zoned to do the types of businesses you wish to do from home, refer to chapter 9 of *Working from Home*.

Choosing One and Only One

Once you've gathered the needed information and weighed what you've discovered, we urge you to settle upon one *single* business to pursue. We think it's an error to diffuse your efforts by trying to start up several businesses at once. Instead, we urge you to focus your energy on one undertaking. This will greatly maximize your chances for success.

Focusing on only one business will enable you to be sure that the message you deliver to other people about what you do in your business is clear. We know too well the glazed look that comes across people's faces when they hear someone go into describing three or more things he or she can do for them.

In the 90s people want to trust their business to experts; they want to do business with people who are specialists. And few people will believe that you can be an expert in multiple fields. There is rarely enough time to do all that needs to be done in one business, let alone in multiple businesses. So select the *one* business you want to pursue and develop a plan for how you will proceed.

Tailoring a Business to Get the Right Fit

If you don't immediately find a business profiled in this book that suits your needs and those of your community, don't despair. Having read about the types of businesses that are doing well and the kind of skills and background you need to do them, you can use this information to create a unique business tailored to you and your community. Many of the most successful home businesses we discovered came about in just that way. Of course we could not include those businesses in this book, because very few people would be able to build such unique enterprises, but here are a few examples.

PHIL ABLIN of Rockport, Texas, had been a securities broker for sixteen years and was looking for a change. His hobby was fixing things around the house, but instead of simply becoming a general repairman he created a unique repair business based on his personal experience of living in a resort area. He returned to the community where he was raised and became the House Doctor, doing maintenance and repair for absentee home owners on Key Allagro Island, a resort area on the Gulf Coast of Texas. Although his first job was weeding a flower bed for $3.75 an hour, he now grosses $150,000 a year.

DAVID ELIASON had been a radio news director in Dubuque, Iowa, for three years when his job was eliminated. He decided that rather than leaving town to find a similar position, he'd stay in Dubuque and do something he really enjoyed. He turned his hobby of dabbling with electronics into a home-based business called Professional Audio. He designs and installs sound systems for churches, auditoriums, racetracks, office buildings, and theaters and grosses $200,000 a year.

RITA TATEEL of Los Angeles may be the ultimate proof of how with ingenuity you can turn even the most unlikely interests into a business. Instead of matching specialists with businesses who need them, she matches celebrities with events that need them. Burned out from her social-welfare career, she created Celebrity Source, which provides celebrities for fund-raising events. She says of her business, "Ninety percent of what I enjoy outside of work is an element of my work, even watching TV and going to parties."

We know hundreds of stories such as these, so use the businesses in this book as a springboard to create a business that is perfect for you.

Preparing a Business Plan

The profiles in this book should not be confused with a business plan. This book is intended to stimulate your thinking and provide information to help you choose the best business. If you've done the things we suggested above, however, you will be well along the way to gathering the information you'll need to prepare a solid plan.

A business plan is simply a road map. It sets out your goals. It outlines where you're going with your business and how you plan to get there. As a home-based business you will probably not be seeking investors or getting a loan to start your business, so preparing a business plan is not for someone else's benefit. It's for you—so you'll know *what* you're doing and *how* you're doing at each step along the way. Having such an operating plan to guide your daily activities can prevent you from making costly mistakes.

There are three key parts to such a business plan:

1. Three descriptions of your business. Three brief statements, one of 25 words, one of 65 words, and one of 125 words, that describe what your business is, whom you serve, and what benefits you provide will help you know precisely what you intend to do and will enable you to talk successfully about it with business contacts, potential customers, and clients.

You can use the 25-word description as part of your standard introduction of yourself and who you are. The 65-word description is the answer you can give to the question, "What do you do?" or your reply to the statement "Tell me more about your business." The 125-word description can be used as the basis for writing proposals and advertising and brochure copy describing your business.

2. A plan for how you intend to market your business. Identifying as thoroughly as possible the people who need what your business has to offer and how you will let them know about your business can help you select the best marketing methods to make sure you have enough business. In this portion of your plan you should:

- define exactly who your customers or clients are
- identify who your competition is
- clarify what advantages you have over your competition in terms of price, service, quality, variety, ease of use, and so forth
- determine how big your market is and if there are enough buyers for you to reach the level of income you desire or need
- identify how you will let the people who need your product or service know about what you have to offer

3. Financial projections. Identifying how much you need to earn in order to survive and thrive, and then checking out the going prices in your community, can help you know what you will need to charge and how many clients or customers you will need to have each month to reach your income goals. You should also identify which start-up expenses you will have and identify how long you will need to supplement your income before your business can support you. Keep in mind that a business can take anywhere from three months to over a year to turn a profit. So you should have a plan for how you will cover your living and operating expenses during that period. Some people advise that to be on the safe side you should double the time you think it will take you to break even. With careful planning, however, most home businesses are basically able to finance their start-ups themselves. (In chapter 3 of *Working from Home*, we have listed many ideas and variables to consider in starting up your business, including five ways to finance your venture.)

Opening Your Business

Once you know what you want to do and have a solid business plan, there are a number of important details you must take care of to actually set yourself up in business, such as selecting which form of business you wish to operate, getting the necessary licenses and permits, setting up and equipping your office, opening your business bank account, setting up an easy-to-follow record-keeping system, and having your letterhead and stationery printed. In this country, however, taking care of these details is the easiest part of starting a business. Let's go through them one by one.

Dealing with Legalities

In operating on your own, you must choose one of three forms of business. Your business can become a sole proprietorship, a partnership, or a corporation. We recommend beginning as a sole proprietorship unless your business faces the danger of being sued for damages, needs to establish independent contractor status with companies that require it, or you will be working with a partner, in which case you will probably want to incorporate. You should consult an attorney and an accountant, however, in selecting the best form for your business.

The name you select for your business is one of the most important decisions you will make, so once you've selected your name, you will need to register and protect it.

If you are a sole proprietorship and use a name for your business other than your own, you will need to register the fictitious business name with your county clerk or secretary of state. Specific requirements vary by state. If your business is a corporation, you will need to reserve the name with the secretary of state.

You may wish to trademark your name to protect it from use by others. You do this through your state; if you meet the qualifications, you may also register it with the U.S. Patent Office in Washington, D.C. Federal registration takes about one year to eighteen months and currently costs several hundred dollars.

Because state, county, and local regulations vary from place to place, you will need to determine whether your business requires any of several licenses and permits. These could include a city or county license, a state sales permit if you need to charge sales tax, a federal employer's identification number, and any other special licenses.

Setting up Your Financial System

When you open your business you should set up a separate business checking account. We recommend selecting a small or local neighborhood bank where your business will be noticed and valued.

If you're happy with your existing bank, you may want to open your business account there because they already know you. Find out what the

---

Five Home-Business Start-up Steps

Check off each step as you complete it.

_____ **1. Deal with the legalities.** Determine the form of your business. Select and register your business name. Obtain and file needed licenses, permits, and registrations.

_____ **2. Create a financial system.** Establish a bank account and your credit. Set up your bookkeeping and accounting system. Get needed insurance.

_____ **3. Set up your office space.** Select an adequate location for your home office. Get needed equipment, furniture, and supplies. Establish your telephone service. Set up your mail service.

_____ **4. Develop your business identity** on your logo, cards, and stationery.

_____ **5. Establish your work schedule** and start getting business.

---

bank's policy is on holding checks deposited for collection, however. Some banks won't credit your account for checks over a certain amount until the checks have cleared. This could cause cash-flow problems for you, so accept only immediate access to your funds.

Cash flow is the lifeblood of being self-employed. Making sure you collect what you are owed is like making sure you get your paycheck. The best strategy for having ample cash on hand, of course, is to make sure you have plenty of business. But you also have to make sure you get the money you're owed in a timely fashion. To keep your cash flowing, get money up front, take deposits, get retainers, and require partial or progress payments. Request payment in cash at the time of sale or delivery of your service. Take bank cards instead of extending credit. Experts claim that offering MasterCard or Visa can increase your business 10 to 50 percent. Unfortunately, most banks will not offer MasterCard or Visa merchant accounts to home-based businesses. In chapter 14 of *Working from Home*, however, you will find a list of sources through which you can obtain merchant status.

If you must bill your clients or customers, always bill promptly instead of waiting until the end of the month. Also offer discounts of 2 to 5 percent if payment is made within ten days from the date of the invoice. And be sure to act promptly on any overdue account.

One of the best ways to make the most of your money is to keep careful track of it, so set up a reliable bookkeeping and accounting system right from the beginning. The purpose of keeping good records is to enable you to know how your business is doing. With good records, you'll know where you're making a profit and where you aren't. You'll know what your costs have been, where you can cut expenses, and in which ways you'll need to modify your plans and projections. Good records also will enable you to take the greatest advantage of allowable tax deductions and will protect you should you be audited.

Today the easiest way to keep simple, accurate records is to use a computer with software like *Quicken* or *One Write Plus*. Such programs keep your bank balance for you and can quickly print out income and expense reports.

To help make sure you get the basic insurance you need to protect your home office and your business, refer to chapter 11 in *Working from Home* in which we discuss which types of insurance you might need and under what circumstances you need it.

Setting up Your Home Office

Where you locate your home office and how you set it up are two of the most important factors in determining whether you'll be able to run a business successfully at home. Many people are concerned about interruptions from family or distractions from household activity; others worry that they'll feel compelled to work morning, noon, and night, because their work is always there. Where you put your office and how you set it up can protect you from these potential problems. For a full treatment of this topic (including claiming your tax benefits) see chapters 5–8, 10, and 17–19 in *Working from Home*.

Developing Your Business Identity

Selecting the right name for your business may be one of the most important business decisions you make. If your name is memorable, distinctive, pronounceable, and understandable, it can be a valuable sales tool. On the other hand, if your name is hard to pronounce, confusing, and difficult to spell, it can actually cost you business.

In chapter 4 of our book *Getting Business to Come to You*, you'll find a list of rules for naming your business and the pros and cons of the five most common strategies for choosing a business name. We suggest that you follow these guidelines to select several possible names for your business. Then list your top choices on a sheet of paper and ask several potential customers which company they would be most inclined to contact and why.

Once you've selected your name, you need to create a graphic image for your business cards and stationery. Now that you're in business, your cards and stationery are more than paper you use for correspondence. You should think of them as miniature billboards for your business. They create a first impression for people with whom you don't have face-to-face contact. Some of the people you do business with may know you only through your stationery.

So think about your graphic image as part of your promotion and sales effort. Design your logo, cards, and stationery to make a statement about your business. Make sure they convey the image you want to create. For example, if you are a computer consultant, you might want to project a modern, high-tech look, so you could use a paper, type style, and design that convey a clean, sleek, and forward-looking image. On the other hand, if you are an errand service, you might want to convey a warmth and friendliness, in which case you may choose a paper, type style, and design that are rounded, warm, soft, and reminiscent of the familiar past.

Don't leave these important decisions up to the standard format at your print shop. In chapter 4 of *Getting Business to Come to You* we outline how to create a business image that sells itself.

Establishing Your Work Schedule

Even though as your own boss you are free to work when and if you want to, we urge you to set up a work schedule. A schedule not only will help you organize your work, but will also help your family and friends know when they can and cannot interrupt you. Business contacts will know when they can best reach you. A schedule will even help you to avoid having your work take over your life, because it will tell you not only when it's time to start working, but also when it's time to stop.

If you are operating a part-time business, we suggest that you make a commitment to work at least eight hours a week in your business. And don't plan to squeeze all eight hours in on Saturday. Spread the eight hours throughout the week, so that you'll be sure to get some work done even when things you want to do come up on the weekends. In Part II of *Making It on Your Own*, we provide guidelines for managing your time so you can balance the three principal aspects of being your own boss: getting the business, doing the business, and running the business.

Having completed these five basic start-up steps, not only will you be in business, but you will be in position to make sure that you have business.

Using the Resources in This Book

At the end of each profile, we have listed resources that can be useful to you in learning about or actually operating each business. This information is intended as a starting point. Most of the resources are not specifically about how to start such a business.

So, unless otherwise indicated, DO NOT phone these resources, especially the associations and organizations, expecting that they will help you get started in a business. Some may provide you with general information and others may be useful for networking, but unless indicated, none are in the franchising business or offer actual business plans to get you started.

PART I

■ ■

The Best of the Best

■ ■ ■ ■ ■

ABSTRACTING SERVICE

If you like to read and have a special expertise or affinity for technical subjects, an abstracting business may interest you. The main job of an abstracting service is to read articles from journals and magazines of all kinds and condense them into a brief synopsis of ten to fifteen sentences for computer storage and retrieval. In some cases, the articles are indexed instead of, or in addition to, being abstracted. Indexing means that the abstractor creates a list of key words based on the article or selects terms from a controlled vocabulary list so that a computer can locate an article quickly.

Free-lance abstracting and indexing services may work for any of the 6,000+ database producers (such as Chemical Abstracts Service, Information Access Company, and Dow Jones) that provide on-line information to businesses, researchers, and professionals around the world. Many of these database producers specialize in areas such as law, medicine, engineering, science, and other technical fields.

In addition to such database applications, abstracting and indexing services also may work for corporations, creating summaries of books and articles of interest to the company's executives, technical people, or clients. Some large corporations make extensive use of abstracting and indexing to stay up-to-date and competitive in today's world of rapidly changing information.

☑ Knowledge and Skills You Need to Have

- You need to have sufficient knowledge in the subject areas in which you are abstracting or indexing—or a broad-enough general knowledge and interest—to be able to ferret out central ideas and relevant information from printed materials on a wide range of topics. Subject specialists are generally more valuable.

■ You must have the ability to synthesize and consolidate information. This requires learning how to read an article or book differently than you normally would. You need to be able to skim through and pick out key points, condense the points into the required number of lines, and pick out key words that someone would use to search for that information.

■ You need excellent writing skills and the ability to communicate the material you're abstracting clearly and concisely.

■ You need to have a familiarity with database services, CD-ROM publishers, and other companies that supply or deal with information.

■ Start-up Costs

	Low	High
Computer with hard disk and modem	$1,000	$3,000
Fax machine	300	900
Printer	300	1,600
Suite software (mostly word processing)	250	400
Office furniture, especially ergonomic chair	400	1,000
Business cards, letterhead, envelopes	100	600
Reference books and dictionaries	100	300
Total	$2,450	$7,800

■ Advantages

■ The work can be interesting and intellectually stimulating.

■ You learn constantly about a variety of subjects and can keep abreast of significant changes in many fields.

■ You may have a great amount of flexibility in choosing your working hours: days, evenings, weekends, etc.

■ The kind of writing you do for abstracting—in which you focus and summarize in a clear and concise manner—is valuable for doing other kinds of writing.

■ The business is a good add-on business to an editorial service, indexing service, or technical writing service.

■ Disadvantages

■ In some cases, you may have tight deadlines and turnaround times; some articles must be completed within a few days.

■ The work is highly detailed and requires intense concentration, precision, and careful organization.

💲 Pricing

$5 to $15 per article for doing a full abstract with index. Specialists can charge more.

🖳 Potential Earnings

TYPICAL ANNUAL GROSS REVENUES: $30,000 based on billing thirty hours per week, fifty weeks per year, averaging $20 per hour.

OVERHEAD: low (20 percent or less).

📈 *Best Home Businesses* Estimate of Market Potential

Total number of abstracting services in the United States, including home-based businesses: 4,279. Because of the continuing growth of information, we anticipate the market for abstracting services to grow.

📇 Best Ways to Get Business

- Directly soliciting database publishers by sending samples you have written along with your résumé emphasizing any relevant background you may have.

  - Since many types of database producers hire local freelancers, in order to find database publishers in your area, decide which type of database you want to work with and search a directory like *Ebsco Index and Abstract Directory* or *Gale Directory of Online Databases* to identify publishers in that field by address. You can find these directories in many large public and academic libraries.

  - To get corporate work, contact corporate librarians and the department responsible for technical writing.

  - Responding to occasional newspaper classified want ads.

If you have writing experience or a technical skill but you do not have specific experience abstracting articles, you should create a portfolio of samples to show prospective clients. Then call several database publishers in your local area and try to set up an appointment to discuss their needs and your qualifications to work for them.

📕 Where to Turn for Information and Help

ORGANIZATIONS

National Federation of Abstracting and Information Services (NFAIS), 1518 Walnut Street, Suite 307, Philadelphia, PA 19102; (215) 893-1561, fax (215) 893-1564. This organization offers information, conferences/workshops, a monthly newsletter, and a variety of books on topics of interest to abstractors and information professionals.

BOOKS

Guide to Careers in Abstracting and Indexing, Ann Marie Cunningham and
   Wendy Wicks, National Federation of Abstracting and Information Services. See address above.

The Information Broker's Handbook, Sue Rugge and Alfred Glossbrenner,
   New York: Windcrest/McGraw Hill, 1992. A good overview of abstracting, databases, and the electronic information industry.

■ ■ ■ ■ ■

ADVERTISING AGENCY

Economic changes in the 1990s have altered the rules of the advertising
business in ways no one could have imagined five or ten years ago. Larger
companies that once dominated the market have lost clients to smaller,
upstart agencies; clients are cutting their spending on advertising; and marketers are reducing their television, radio, and print advertising in favor of
direct mail and other less-traditional forms of promotion. The very center of
gravity of the business has shifted from New York and Los Angeles to San
Francisco, Minneapolis, Boston, Portland, Ore., and Richmond, Va.

In short, the industry is more competitive than ever, which means new
opportunities for the creative advertising professional who may be home
based. While home-based ad agencies aren't likely to wrest the million-dollar
corporate accounts from the majors, there are a lot of different ways to split
the $138 billion U.S. advertising pie. Using a computer, some specialized
software, and a high-resolution printer, someone with experience in the
business who has the necessary skills can make a good living running an ad
agency from home. After all, bright ideas can germinate and flourish anywhere. You can choose to specialize in one particular type of product or
service, or in one specific medium (TV, radio, or print).

Steve Shoe runs a home-based advertising agency in Denver, Colorado, called
Railroad Promotions. After many years in the business, Shoe finally realized
that the overhead on his office was draining his resources, so he decided to take
a few of his steady clients and move his office into his house. A model railroad
hobbyist, Shoe was approached by a local rail line to do ads for them. He agreed
to represent the company "if it didn't ruin my hobby." That was ten years ago,
and he's still going strong. In fact, he now has an employee who works with
him in his home. Shoe's decision to specialize helped him establish a name for
himself. It built his reputation as someone with expertise in the field and also
gave him easy access to potential clients in professional and amateur groups.
Some of his current clients include the Colorado Railroad Museum, the Model
Railroad Association, and Craig Thorpe, an artist who photographs and paints
trains (he did a calendar for Amtrak). He has also pitched his services to a
construction company that manufactures nothing but railroads.

"Are we making a fortune? Living high on the hog? No," says Shoe. "But we're doing something we feel good about, something we like, and making all the bills."

Shoe recommends a similar course of action for someone who is just starting out. "Pick something you like—a hobby." Possible clients include a local hobby shop, a magazine dealing with the topic, a specialty bookstore, and other things related to the hobby. Shoe says for ethical reasons it's best not to solicit businesses that are in direct competition with each other, such as two model railroad shops in the same city. He points out a benefit of focusing on one of your hobbies: you already know what the people you'll be dealing with are like, because you're one of them. Chances are that you also have some ideas about which advertising approaches would appeal to hobbyists, have contacts in the field, read the literature, and know when and where the trade shows and conferences are held.

If you have been in the field for a while and have developed some expertise, you can make extra money by teaching at local colleges and adult schools.

✔ Knowledge and Skills You Need to Have

- You need to know basic principles of design, layout, and typography.
- You must be good at writing copy that conveys your client's message in a catchy, appealing, and memorable way.
- You should have a portfolio of your best work in order to get new business.
- There is no substitute for experience in this field. Steve Shoe thinks it inadvisable to go into advertising if you don't know anything at all about it, but if you have some experience you may be able to hone your skills by working with an acquaintance and/or by reading extensively.

🐷 Start-up Costs

	Low	High
Computer with hard disk and modem	$1,000	$3,000
High-resolution laser printer	1,500	3,000
Presentations, desktop publishing and photo software	1,000	2,000
Scanner	1,000	2,500
CD-ROM	150	500
Fax	300	900
Office furniture, especially an ergonomic chair	400	1,000
Copy machine	400	1,200
Business cards, letterhead, envelopes	100	600
Organizational dues	250	250
Total	$6,100	$14,950

◨ Advantages

- Advertising is a creative endeavor. You get to use both your verbal skills and your artistic talents.
- You can specialize in a field you enjoy, which means you get paid to do the things you like best.
- You get to meet a lot of interesting, colorful, and knowledgeable people.
- Loyal clients will give you repeat business—and referrals.

◨ Disadvantages

- You are often working on tight deadlines.
- There is a lot of competition in this field. Many of the people who have lost jobs at major advertising agencies over the past few years have gone out on their own.
- You have to know how to do a broad range of things, including pasting up ads, writing press releases, putting an ad campaign together, etc.—or at least know where to go to find other people who can do those things for a reasonable price.

$ Pricing

Most advertisers charge by the hour or by the project. Sometimes they have a monthly or six-month contract. Average hourly fees for small home-based agencies run from $35 to $75 per hour.

▣ Potential Earnings

TYPICAL ANNUAL GROSS REVENUES: $35,000 to $75,000, based on billing twenty hours a week at $35 to $75 an hour, fifty weeks a year. According to *The Writer's Market 1994*, ad copywriting earns between $20 and $100 per hour, $250 and up per day, $500 and up per week, or $1,000 to $2,000 as a monthly retainer. Rates will vary depending on region of the country, whether you are in a major metropolitan area, the type of client you're servicing, and the medium you're working in (TV, radio, or print).

OVERHEAD: moderate (20 to 40 percent).

◨ *Best Home Businesses* Estimate of Market Potential

The trend toward boutique advertising agencies favors home-based work and independent contractors.

◨ Best Ways to Get Business

- Networking with other people in the advertising field, going to ad club meetings.

- Networking with your contacts in clubs and hobby groups.
- Advertising in a trade publication where professionals who might need your services will see your ad.
- Teaching at a community college or adult school.

◻ Where to Turn for Information and Help

ORGANIZATIONS

American Advertising Federation, 1101 Vermont Avenue, N.W., Suite 500, Washington, DC 20005; (202) 898-0089, fax (202) 898-0159. Parent organization for many local ad clubs or ad federations. Look in your telephone directory for your local affiliate; sponsors meetings, workshops, and competitions.

International Association of Business Communicators, 1 Hallidie Plaza, Suite 600, San Francisco, CA 94102; (415) 433-3400.

BOOKS

How to Start and Run Your Own Advertising Agency, Allan Krieff, New York: McGraw-Hill, 1992.

The Twenty-Two Immutable Laws of Marketing, Al Ries and Jack Trout, New York: Harper Business, 1993. Al Ries and Jack Trout have written a number of books that are marketing classics, including *Positioning: The Battle for Your Mind, Marketing Warfare,* and *Bottom-Up Marketing.* All were published by McGraw-Hill.

NEWSLETTERS

Creative Business, 275 Newbury Street, Boston, MA 02116; (617) 424-1368. Published ten times per year, this newsletter is directed at copywriters, designers, art directors, and principals of creative businesses. Subscribers also receive free unlimited telephone consultation. It was founded by Cameron Foote, who also gives Creative Business Workshops around the country for people in creative businesses.

DIRECTORIES

Standard Directory of Advertising Agencies, 3004 Glenview Road, Wilamette, IL 60091.

MAGAZINES

Advertising Age, Crain Communications, 220 E. 42nd Street, New York, NY 10017; (212) 210-0170; subscriber service (800) 678-9595; 740 N. Rush, Chicago, IL 60611-2590; (312) 649-5200.

Adweek, 1515 Broadway, New York, NY 10036; (212) 536-5336; (800) 722-6658.

Folio, Cowles Business Media, P.O. Box 4949, Stamford, CT 06907-0949.

Presentations, Maclean Hunter Company, 50 S. 9th Street, Minneapolis, MN 55402. Covers high technology used in professional presentations.

Target Marketing Magazine, North American Publishing Company, 401 N. Broad Street, Philadelphia, PA 19108. Covers direct marketing, telemarketing, use of catalogues, etc.

■ ■ ■ ■ ■

ASSOCIATION MANAGEMENT SERVICE

Organizations of all types, especially professional and trade groups, often need someone to manage and administer their operations. Since many organizations have grown beyond the size that volunteer officers can effectively manage, but are not large enough to justify renting office space and hiring employees, they turn instead to people who make a living administering professional and trade associations on a contractual basis.

The association manager provides a cost-effective solution to staff an organization. He or she also enables the organization's volunteer leadership to concentrate on program and policy issues rather than administrative tasks and provides the organization with continuity during leadership changes.

Actually, association management services, also called *executive director services*, have existed for over one hundred years. What association managers specifically do depends on which functions their clients want them to handle. However, to serve clients well, they need to be prepared to do just about everything an organization needs to have done. They may keep membership lists, write and publish the association's newsletter, answer phone calls, handle incoming mail, mail out information about the organization, keep the financial records, collect dues, pay bills, make arrangements and take reservations for membership meetings and events, help raise funds, and book speakers for meetings as well as national conventions. They may also get involved in membership development, professional education, lobbying, and marketing. With today's office technology, all the tasks involved, however, can be done from someone's home.

There are literally thousands of associations from which your clients can come, and new ones form every year. Some associations are national trade associations (for manufacturers) such as the Model Railroad Trade Association, managed by Steve Shoe (who got into the position from an advertising background), and the Windsurfing Association, managed by Scott Sea (formerly a Wall Street broker who decided to leave his high-pressure job to enjoy working full time with his hobby). Other associations may be state and local professional associations or hobbyist organizations like the Lake Amphibian Flyers Club, a group of 400 individuals worldwide who pilot Amphibian aircraft on lakes. One association manager, Bill Goddard, also finds churches to be in the market for executive director services, because they often have many administrative needs but not the budget to hire full-time staff.

Many people get into this business by first working for an association as a volunteer. Other people find their first clients through a want ad in a newspaper or magazine and convince the association to let them work from home. Some managers manage just one association; others work with two or more at a time.

Another alternative is simply to start your own association. For example, consider starting one based on your own profession, hobby, or special interest. Or while it's best to start an association around something you know and care about, there are many businesses that lack an association, and this provides opportunities. For example, in researching this edition of this book, we could find no associations serving bill auditing service operators, business network organizers, business plan writers, computer repair and maintenance service operators, computer tutors and trainers, desktop videographers, errand service operators, expert brokers, export agents, mailing list service operators, calendar service operators, disc jockeys (defunct organization), duplicating services, home tutors, leak detection services, plant caregivers, proposal and grant writers, referral services, restoration services, and several of the specialties in the travel group of businesses. Whether these are viable as organizations we can't predict, but the possibility is there.

Starting your own association is doubly profitable, since you can obtain a fee for managing the association as well as take a profit on your annual convention or any advertising you can get for your association's newsletter. It may be organized as a nonprofit or a for-profit venture.

☑ Knowledge and Skills You Need to Have

- You need to be good at organizing paper, information, and people. You'll be handling lots of details and administrativia and making sure that everything runs smoothly and that everyone is taken care of.

- You need to be able to manage an office at the secretarial level or higher. You will probably also need a personal computer and be able to type to do mailing lists, memos, and bookkeeping.

- You need good people skills to deal with the constantly changing board of directors and officers of the associations you manage and their goals. It helps to have a modicum of political savvy to handle personality and ego conflicts that arise within the association.

- You may need to be a good writer, because you may compose press releases, newsletters, and correspondence on behalf of your organization.

- You'll need sensitivity to motivate and guide volunteers, most of whom are involved with the association as a labor of love or for personal development, and who generally respond better to persuasion than to commands.

- You should have marketing skills in order to bring in new members.

🐷 Start-up Costs*

	Low	High
Computer with hard disk	$1,000	$3,000
Ink-jet or laser printer	300	1,600
Fax machine	300	900
Copier	300	800
Suite software	250	400
Office furniture, especially an ergonomic chair	400	1,000
Brochure	100	1,000
Business cards, letterhead, envelopes	100	600
Total	$2,750	$9,300

* In some cases, the organization you represent may pay for your equipment and supplies.

🔼 Advantages

- Association work offers ample variety to keep almost anyone from being bored.

- You get to attend and possibly travel to many interesting meetings and conventions, with the costs paid for by your clients. Some of your other travel can be tax-deductible.

- This business provides a lot of visibility. You can meet many interesting people, often some who are leaders in their industry.

- When you do your job well, your efforts will be greatly appreciated.

- Some people can build their business extensively, taking on more and more associations and hiring employees to handle the clerical work.

🔽 Disadvantages

- Navigating organizational politics can be tricky. You must watch out not to insult an important member of the association or to step on anyone's toes in the line of your work. Your job could suddenly end if a new officer decides to hire someone else.

- You're on call. You need to be available when your clients need you. So sometimes you will be extremely busy.

- Organizational meetings are often held in the evenings or on weekends.
- Except for associations organized around hobbies and avocations, which typically don't operate on rigid time lines, you're apt to find that there will always be some big event or project in the works, so your vacations and time off will be pretty much confined to December and August.

💲 Pricing

Professional association managers usually operate on a monthly or yearly retainer. The amount of the retainer depends on what functions you perform for the association and the amount of time you spend on the job. You therefore need to estimate how much of your time the tasks will take each month and negotiate a fixed monthly fee. Average monthly rates range from $2,000 to $4,000 per month.

🔳 Potential Earnings

TYPICAL ANNUAL GROSS REVENUES:

- For managing other associations: $24,000 to $48,000, based on a monthly retainer of $2,000 to $4,000.
- For running your own association: $20,000 to $40,000, based on an organization with 400 members, each of whom pays $35 to $100 a year for dues. Conference fees can greatly increase your income.

OVERHEAD: low (20 percent or less).

✅ *Best Home Businesses* Estimate of Market Potential

Total number of association management firms in the United States, including home-based businesses: 2,357. Occupational and business specialties are growing and with them can be expected to grow associations suited to management and organization by people able to operate from home.

📩 Best Ways to Get Business

For engaging existing associations as your clients:

- Contact the presidents of professional and trade associations directly. Refer to the *Encyclopedia of Associations*, published by Gale Research, which is available in most libraries.
- Subscribe to *ASAE Career Ops*, a newsletter published by the American Society of Association Executives, listed below. Call (202) 408-7900 for more information.
- Respond to the occasional classified ads in newspapers for associations seeking managers.

- Network with professional, trade, or industry groups to learn about potential openings.
- Volunteer to do seminars on administration and management for association leadership teams.

For starting your own organization:

- Mail a brochure to a list of potential new members.
- Get some publicity for your organization or advertise in the publications your audience likely reads.
- Get a board of directors for your association and ask them to network to find members.

⬛ First Steps

- If you don't have any administrative experience, you might volunteer to administer a group to which you belong or another association that needs help. Or you could get elected to office in an organization to gain the experience of running an organization.
- If you already have business administrative experience, find a niche you could serve, such as medical associations or professional organizations. Survey the officers of such potential clientele regarding their likes and dislikes in administering their organizations, and see if you can locate one that would need your services.
- In either case, join ASAE (see below) or network with other independent association managers to learn more about their work.

⬛ Where to Turn for Information and Help

ORGANIZATIONS

American Society of Association Executives, 1575 I Street, N.W., Washington, DC 20005; (202) 626-2723. The main organization for this profession, ASAE has many useful publications, books, and local chapters for independent association managers. They also publish a newsletter listing job openings, *ASAE Career Ops*, to which you may wish to subscribe.

The Society for Nonprofit Organizations, 6314 Odana Road, Suite 1, Madison, WI 53719; (800) 424-7367 or (608) 274-9777. A resource center for nonprofit organizations of all types, including associations, throughout the country.

Many states also have regional organizations of independent association executives. Check your yellow pages.

BOOKS

Encyclopedia of Associations: Regional, State, and Local Organizations, Detroit: Gale Research describes over 50,000 trade associations, professional societies, labor organizations, fraternal, sporting, patriotic, and charitable organizations.

Principles of Association Management, Henry Ernstthal and Vivian Jefferson, Washington, DC: American Society of Association Executives, 1988.

■ ■ ■ ■ ■

BED-AND-BREAKFAST INN

A bed-and-breakfast inn is truly a *home* business, because your home becomes the business. Once upon a time, when homeowners had more space than they needed, they took in boarders. Today's version of this long-lost practice is a bed-and-breakfast inn, which offers travelers the comfort of a home environment, sometimes at a cost less than what a hotel would charge for a comparable room.

The idea of bed-and-breakfast inns developed in the 1980s. Although at this writing they represent less than 1 percent of the hotel industry, they are a well-established option for today's travelers. Whereas there were only 400 bed-and-breakfast inns in the United States in 1975, today there are more than 20,000, half of which are in private homes. And Pat Hardy, codirector of the Professional Association of Innkeepers International, foresees continued growth for B&B inns during the 90s.

Pat points out that with their emphasis on service, bed-and-breakfast inns have influenced the traditional hotel industry to offer new services to their guests, such as concierge floors and complimentary breakfasts. Pat, who is also a coauthor of the book *So You Want to Be an Innkeeper*, predicts that urban inns and small executive retreats will do particularly well in the 90s.

This is an ideal business for someone who loves to have house guests, decorate, and keep a beautiful home. The location of a bed-and-breakfast inn is of particular importance, however. You need to live in a desirable area that draws travelers who are interested in staying at such an establishment. Inns are commonly located in areas that attract tourists or business travelers who want a small, more private and personal overnight experience.

The business encompasses every type of proprietor and establishment. You can make innkeeping your full-time profession and run a fully licensed inn or manage a B&B as a part-time venture, occasionally renting out three or fewer rooms for extra income. However, if you hope to make a good profit, the more rooms you have available to convert into guest rooms the better. Profitability with fewer than six guest rooms is difficult, according to a national study by the Professional Association of Innkeepers International.

Smaller inns with a higher occupancy rate can make money, as can those located in the West, where the weather is more suitable for year-round travel.

This business provides many perks. Expenses such as interest on your home, the cost of operating your car, your insurance, eating out, magazines, cleaning supplies, and even travel may be tax deductible, but be aware that the IRS is increasingly auditing B&Bs.

Start-up Costs

Acquisition cost. If you are converting your existing home, you will not have any acquisition costs; however, if you're buying an inn, you can expect to pay $15,000 to $50,000 per guest room, depending on the area.

Renovation cost. If you are converting your existing home into a fully licensed inn, you can expect to spend $15,000 to $40,000 per guest room, depending on the locale and your taste.

Working capital. To open an inn in your home you should allow for $10,000 per room up-front to cover the costs of utilities, insurance, marketing, maintenance, supplies (towels and linens), and so forth. New businesses need additional capital in the initial years.

Advantages

- You can live in a desirable location in the country or city.
- Almost any life experience, from housework to marketing, can be effectively applied to operating an inn. Other skills needed can be learned, such as business planning.
- Operating an inn provides an increased opportunity to enjoy family life. This business can be an opportunity for couples to work together. Also, this is a business in which your teenagers can easily get involved working for you. (Having young children around is more difficult.)
- Being an innkeeper is a way to earn an income while your property appreciates in value.

Disadvantages

- Your income is limited to the number of rooms you have.
- As an innkeeper, you need to be at home most of the time, and you're often tied to the telephone.
- With small properties in particular, you are on the job seven days a week. You have few weekends off.
- Even small inns are subject to food, health, fire, and building codes. Meeting such regulations involves a degree of red tape, as well as higher

costs for making sure your home adheres to the more demanding standards these laws require.

■ You need special insurance, in addition to regular homeowners' insurance.

💲 Pricing*

Average Fee per Room in 1993	Standard Rate	Corporate Rate
Northeast	$105	$94
South/Southeast	$ 91	$76
Midwest	$ 87	$72
West	$101	$95

* Data provided by the Professional Association of Innkeepers International.

🖩 Potential Earnings

1992	Net Operating Income*	Occupancy Rate	Gross Income
1 to 4 rooms	$ 4,611	43%	$ 39,408
5 to 8 rooms	$34,628	45%	$ 99,099
9 to 12 rooms	$78,939	45%	$209,575

* Does not include debt service (mortgage) costs or depreciation.

OVERHEAD
1 to 4 rooms	86%*
5 to 8 rooms	64%*
9 to 12 rooms	56%*

AVERAGE OCCUPANCY RATES
National (1992)	50%
Northeast	47%
South	50%
West	57%
Rural	45%
Village	51%
Urban	53%

📝 *Best Home Businesses* Estimate of Market Potential

Total number of bed-and-breakfast inns in the United States: 20,258. The personalized service afforded by inns is increasingly being adopted by the hotel industry, testifying to the success of the inn concept. We believe the popularity of inns will continue.

📬 Best Ways to Get Business

■ The most effective way to get business is getting your inn listed in travel and guide books.

- Happy guests will generate referrals, so one of the best business-getting strategies is to provide a good-quality room, spectacular breakfasts, and some other distinguishing service.

- Travel sections of newspapers and magazines, even TV news and talk shows, sometimes do feature stories on unique, charming, and colorful inns, so sending out news releases can lead to valuable visibility.

- To get repeat business, do regular mailings to your former guests announcing special services, offering special discounts, and informing them of upcoming events or activities in your community.

- Cooperative marketing through your state or regional inn association, chamber of commerce, or state division of tourism.

- Reservation services in your community or region can refer business to you for a percentage of the fee you receive, usually between 10 and 35 percent. You can find reservation agents in your local yellow pages or through the national association for such agencies, listed below.

First Steps

1. Be a guest at a bed and breakfast inn yourself, particularly one listed in books for tourists. Read critiques to see what's recommended and what's not.

2. Obtain information from the associations listed below, and attend any workshops offered in your area.

3. To gain experience, consider taking work as an inn sitter for vacationing inn owners.

Where to Turn for Information and Help

ORGANIZATIONS

American Bed & Breakfast Association, 10800 Midlothian Turnpike, Suite 254, Richmond, VA 23235; (800) 769-2468 or (804) 379-2222. Offers an inn-rating program to open inns and a list of resources for aspiring owners.

Bed and Breakfast National Network, Box 4616, Springfield, MA 01101; (800) 884-4288. An organization of bed and breakfast reservation services. It will send you a list of reservation agencies with which you might want your inn to be listed.

Lanier's Inn Forum on CompuServe Information Service (GO INN-FORUM) has a message topic and library for those in the inn business. Active topics of discussion range from the merits of software for operating an inn to recipes for pleasing guests.

National Bed and Breakfast Association, P.O. Box 332, Norwalk, CT

06852; (203) 847-6196. Publishes a guide on starting a bed and breakfast and offers seminars and one-on-one advice.

Professional Association of Innkeepers International (PAII, pronounced "pie"), Box 90710, Santa Barbara, CA 93190; (805) 569-1853, fax (805) 682-1016. Offers a free kit for people interested in running an inn, called the *Aspirers Intro Package*, which includes a catalogue of books, software, and other materials of use to those seeking to become innkeepers.

Books

Bed and Breakfast USA, edited by Betty Rundback, New York: E. P. Dutton. Published annually.

How to Start and Run Your Own Bed and Breakfast Inn, Ripley Hotch and Carl Glassman, Harrisburg, PA: Hackpole Books, 1992.

Marketing Handbook for Bed and Breakfast/Country Innkeepers, prepared by PAII and updated frequently. Available from PAII, listed above.

Open Your Own Bed and Breakfast, Barbara Notarius and Gail Sforza Breuer, New York: Wiley, 1992.

Owning and Managing a Bed and Breakfast, Lisa Angowski Rogak, Dover, NH: Upstart Press, 1994.

The Romance of Country Inns: A Decorating Book for Your Home, Gail Greco, Nashville, TN: Rutledge Hill Press, 1993.

So You Want to Be an Innkeeper, Mary F. Davies, Pat Hardy, Joanne M. Bell, and Susan Brown, San Francisco: Chronicle Books, 1990.

Newsletters

Innkeeping, Box 90710, Santa Barbara, CA 93190; (805) 569-1853, fax (805) 682-1016. Monthly, $65 a year.

■ ■ ■ ■ ■

BILL-AUDITING SERVICE

Companies spend a lot of money on gas, electricity, water, sewer, telephone, insurance, freight, and a wide variety of other goods and services they purchase from other businesses. The bills they receive are often difficult to understand, especially utility bills because they are among the most complicated. Nevertheless, most companies simply pay these bills without verifying their accuracy. But sometimes meters are misread, miscalibrated, broken, or the data have been entered or calculated incorrectly; decimal points can be misplaced; discounts overlooked; and alternative services or rates not known.

Often lots of money can be recouped by carefully checking utility bills or by switching phone services. And that's what a bill-auditing service does.

Also called an *overcharge collection service*, an auditing service verifies bills against purchase orders; checks to see that goods have been delivered; compares charges against what the laws, tariffs, or contracts allow; and checks the math, the billing rate, and other classifications to make sure their clients have not been overcharged. When overcharging is found, the auditor negotiates a refund covering the period in error, then splits the savings of past overcharges with the client. In some cases, auditors may also have as part of their contract that if they can save the client money in the future by getting a better rate or switching services, they will be entitled to one half of those savings as well for anywhere from one to two years.

Auditors can also save their clients money by figuring out more economical ways to obtain service. For example, a company that has multiple water meters that are being separately billed might save hundreds or thousands of dollars by something as simple as combining these meters so that the readings are reflected in one bill. A savings of $300 a month over twelve months for three years comes to $10,800 and represents a $5,400 fee for the auditor.

Bill auditing is growing especially fast because many companies are simply not able to keep up with their bill paying and just pay bills without double-checking them. Many auditors therefore focus their services on commercial and industrial clients who have utility or other bills amounting to at least $2,000 to $3,000 each month, where the profit potential is greatest. And with over five million business establishments in the United States, there is an abundant number of prospective clients among schools, colleges, government agencies, churches, hospitals, retail stores, hotels and motels, grocery stores that stay open all night, nursing homes, auto dealers, and even cities and towns that use a lot of electricity, water, or phone service. One auditor saved a city over $6 million dollars in utility bills and profited nicely from his diligence. In addition, the 1992 Energy Policy Act requires that new homes be rated for energy efficiency, and this means that a residential market will also be opening up to rate the utility usage of new homes. In Colorado and California, for example, the state governments are licensing people to do energy ratings.

Another big area for auditing is telephone systems—helping clients choose the specific equipment and the calling plans that best suit their needs and budget. Many who choose this specialty work closely with the phone companies and are aware of programs with lower rates. Other areas offering opportunities for auditing are freight services, insurance, credit card charges, and workers' compensation.

✔ Knowledge and Skills You Need to Have

- You need to learn the applicable laws, tariffs, and regulations well enough to spot errors in utility bills. If you are doing telephone auditing, you need to be familiar with the programs offered by a multitude of phone services in your area.

- You need to be able to do basic math and use a calculator accurately.
- Essentially, auditors find errors, so you need some analytical ability. You need to have an eye for money in the way that an editor has an eye for words.
- You need to have the instincts of a detective and the creativity of a budget-stretching parent of ten children in finding ways to save your clients' money. This is a very detail-oriented business. You must have a penchant for minute facts and correctness, and persistence to keep trying to locate errors.
- It helps to be creative. Although much of your job involves looking for billing errors, you can also save your clients money by offering suggestions on how to use utilities more economically.
- You must have good communication and people skills, as you will be marketing your services to company presidents and high-level managers. Although one might think this is a business that sells itself, one needs the ability to get in the door and make a sales presentation.

■ Start-up Costs

	Low	High
Calculator	$ 50	$ 150
Computer	1,000	3,000
Ink-jet or laser printer	300	1,600
Suite software	250	400
Office furniture, especially an ergonomic chair	400	1,000
Business cards, letterhead, envelopes, contracts, agreements	100	600
Brochure	100	1,000
Total	$2,200	$7,750

■ Advantages

- Auditing is a business that does not require that you collect money as part of making a sale. Customers pay only for savings you obtain for them.
- It is a year-round and recession-proof business. Companies always welcome an infusion of cash and the prospect of future reduced overhead.
- The business can offer more than a one-shot service. Clients can be sold on paying for savings over a three-year period.
- The income potential is excellent, with the possibility of large sums of passive income from future savings for which you do no additional work.
- Competition may be relatively low.

🔁 Disadvantages

- There is often a sixty- to ninety-day lag between when you make a claim for an error and when you get payment from the utility.
- You are paid only if you find savings.
- The utility tariffs in some states, such as New York, do not provide many opportunities for savings.

💲 Pricing

Auditors often charge 50 percent of past savings and sometimes for future savings for one to two years. Average fees run $500 to $3,000 on utility refunds. Because you may negotiate a contract in which your client business agrees to pay you for savings it will realize over the next two years, your income from that client may also continue for years without additional effort by you.

🖩 Potential Earnings

Once seasoned, an auditor can do one to two claims a day; a slow rate is two to three claims a week.

A claim that takes you eight to twelve hours to do manually in the beginning can be done in twenty minutes once you develop an eye for what you're looking for. Many auditors typically have one or two very large cases in a year that may net them $20,000 to $50,000.

TYPICAL ANNUAL GROSS REVENUES: $50,000 to $200,000 a year, according to estimates by companies involved in the business. For example, you may review five companies per month, file claims on two of them producing $1,000 to $15,000, and then one or two large claims a year for $20,000 or more.

OVERHEAD: low (20 percent or less).

📈 *Best Home Businesses* Estimate of Market Potential

Although we get reports of saturation of utility bill auditing from some metropolitan areas, growth for auditing services as a whole is good.

📇 Best Ways to Get Business

- Direct solicitation of businesses that are likely users of large amounts of energy, such as stores that stay open all night, restaurants, dry cleaners, or coin laundries.
- Using direct mail followed up with telephone calls. Start by making at least fifty calls.

- Networking and personal contacts in business organizations.
- Serving on fund-raising committees of causes and organizations.
- Contacting gatekeepers (influential individuals) such as accountants, business consultants, lawyers, bankers, and bankruptcy trustees who can refer clients to you.
- Giving speeches on how much money can be saved by auditing.
- Getting publicity for your work in newspapers and trade papers.
- Working with real estate agents to do audits on homes for utility usage and energy efficiency.

First Steps

The easiest way to acquire the knowledge you need for this business is by working for a company or utility such as a phone company, an insurance company, a government regulatory agency, and so forth. If you don't have such experience, however, you need to learn the laws, regulations, tariffs, and billing procedures of the type of audits you plan to do. (Training programs that provide this information are listed below.) You can expect a three- to six-month learning curve. An alternative is to start this business part-time.

Related Business

Expense Reduction Service. Similar to a bill-auditing service, this business focuses on more than utility, telephone, and freight bills in helping a company save money. The central concept of this business is helping companies reduce cash outflow in every possible way. Your service might evaluate all purchasing decisions by a business, including office supplies, overnight mail carriers, printing, insurance, photocopying—everything the company does. Your market includes many small and mid-size businesses, retail stores, schools, and so on. Some services even pool the office supply orders from among their clients, then purchase the supplies at a discount and keep a small percentage of the savings.

Property Tax Reduction Service. Either in conjunction with a bill-auditing service or as a stand-alone service, this business focuses on helping businesses and residential property owners lower their property taxes by appealing the tax assessment rate applied by the owner's county or city. Because of vast fluctuations in the market value of property and, in the case of office buildings, the rental ratio that may determine the income potential for a property, many properties are assessed at too high a rate, and the owners are consequently paying too much property tax. Like bill auditing, a property tax reduction service usually keeps 50 percent of any savings achieved.

▣ Where to Turn for Information and Help

TRAINING PROGRAMS

There are many companies offering training manuals and instruction in utility bill auditing, property tax reduction, and related auditing services. Prices for such training run from $995 to $10,000, so you should be sure to do some research to find a program that fulfills your needs while fitting your budget. Four such companies are:

Auditel, 233 Springfield Avenue, Joliet, IL 60435; (800) 551-9282 or (815) 741-5555. Offers two days of classroom training plus one year of consultation afterward for $9,900. However, members of the Auditing Services section of the Working From Home Forum have reported negotiating a lower price. The company has been in business for fifteen years. The company also operates ARM Consultants International, Inc. and Freight Audit International ([800] 841-4402).

Institute of Consulting Careers, Inc., 222 S.E. 16th Street, Portland, OR 97214; (800) 696-4594; (503) 240-0931. Offers a training course covering bill auditing for utilities, phone, cellular, water, sewer, and waste management.

Public Utility Consultants, 25800 Ward Avenue, P.O. Box 2029, Fort Bragg, CA 95437-2029; (800) 833-2998 or (707) 964-0100. Offers a training program with manuals and software for $995 and live class training for an additional fee.

Utility and Tax Reduction Consultants (UTRC), 1240 Iroquois Drive, Suite 106, Naperville, IL 60563; (800) 321-7872 or (708) 369-3072. UTRC offers a three-day, seven-manual training course for $3,995 in the fundamentals of utility auditing including electric, telephone, leases, expense reduction, property taxes, and other areas. Fee includes software.

BOOKS

The Business Environmental Handbook, Martin Westerman, Grant Pass, OR: The Oasis Press, 1993.

The Consumer Guide to Home Energy Savings, Alex Wilson and John Morrill, Berkeley, Calif.: American Council for Energy Efficient Economy (ACEEE), 2140 Shattuck Avenue #202, Berkeley, CA 94704.

How to Earn Money on Your Utility Bills, Jim Meyers, P.O. Box 3477, Littleton, CO 80161-3477; (303) 770-7453.

■ ■ ■ ■ ■

BOOKKEEPING SERVICE

The mushrooming number of small businesses is good for bookkeeping services because entrepreneurs often need assistance in understanding the ins and outs of financial record keeping. As Chellie Campbell, of Cameron Diversified Services, points out, "While doing business is getting more complex, people are not getting better at handling their money. Today virtually everybody needs some professional guidance."

Also, as the complexity of doing business and the intricacy of tax laws increase, fewer small-business owners have the time or the ability to do the necessary financial record keeping themselves, yet many can't hire full-time personnel to carry out these functions. As a result, bookkeeping is a good business year in and year out. Bookkeeping services do well even during difficult economic times because at such times businesses are especially careful about their money.

Every business performs some aspects of its bookkeeping, so what you do for your clients depends upon which services they need and which services you wish to provide. Bookkeeping services range from making deposits, reconciling bank statements, and recording transactions to doing payroll, billing, managing accounts receivable and payable, and preparing financial reports for tax or accounting purposes. Accounting, which is not in the purview of the bookkeeper, involves interpreting the financial statements (income statement, balance sheet, profit and loss) and determining how best to use that information in business and tax planning. Sometimes people confuse bookkeeping with accounting, especially since software manufacturers refer to their products as accounting software when in fact this software simply helps keep track of information and does not interpret it. Bookkeepers keep the records; accountants audit and analyze them.

Bookkeeping is a business you can start with a personal computer. Although computer experience is not necessarily needed, using the computer and an accounting software package are absolute necessities for a bookkeeping service today.

Bookkeeping services can be conducted from your home office, although you do have to go to your clients' offices periodically. Mobile bookkeeping services have also become popular. A mobile bookkeeper can travel to an office with a laptop computer and software or use a van equipped with computer, printer, and electrical generator as a traveling office. Bookkeeping services may choose to specialize in the type of businesses they handle or serve a variety of clients.

☑ Knowledge and Skills You Need to Have

■ You must know how to do bookkeeping accurately and reliably. This includes knowing basic principles of bookkeeping and what types of information must be kept in what form for legal and tax purposes.

- You must feel comfortable using a computer, since most of your work will require the use of accounting and sometimes spreadsheet software.
- You need a clear, logical mind and enough real-world experience that you recognize whether your client's numbers make sense when they're tallied.
- You need to be thorough, dependable, and accurate.
- You need to enjoy paying attention to details.
- You need sufficient communications skills to handle people who become emotional about money matters.
- You need honesty and integrity. If you would go along with a client who asks you not to report or to hide income, it's in your interest to find a business that is less apt to compromise your integrity and get you in trouble. Also, a client who will ask you to use questionable practices may have no compunction about not paying your bill.

🐖 Start-up Costs

	Low	High
Personal computer with hard disk	$1,000	$3,000
Printer	300	1,600
Financial calculator	50	150
Accounting software	50	350
Office furniture, especially an ergonomic chair	400	1,000
Business cards, letterhead, envelopes	100	600
Organizational dues	100	250
Total	$2,150	$9,100

- Add $4,000 to $12,000 to buy a used van if you want to be a mobile bookkeeping service.

📖 Advantages

- Bookkeeping is an essential, not discretionary, business activity; therefore it is generally recession resistant.
- Bookkeeping is not hard to sell because all businesses know they need it.
- This career allows you to learn a lot about business in general and about many specific kinds of businesses.
- If you like numbers, the work is challenging and fun—like solving puzzles.

📖 Disadvantages

- Bookkeeping is very technical and demands careful attention to detail Mistakes can result in your clients' facing substantial interest assessments on late payments or penalties from the government.

- People get very emotional if they're not satisfied with their results and tend to blame the bookkeeper when the message is bad news.
- Collections can be a problem unless you use retainers and refuse to work when clients get behind.
- You need to keep current about tax-law changes relative to payroll and record keeping.
- Using easy-to-use software, many businesses that might have outsourced it in the past are doing their bookkeeping in-house. However, because mistakes and errors inevitably are made, opportunities arise and even specialized practices can be built around straightening out messes companies have made of their books.

$ Pricing

Charges range from $15 to $35 an hour, depending on locale; higher-end fees are paid for preparing a company's financial statements (balance sheet, income statement, profit and loss), analyzing the balance sheet, and tax preparation, particularly corporate tax returns. Some bookkeepers can also charge for travel time to clients' offices.

Some bookkeeping services charge a flat fee per month rather than hourly. The fees range from $150 to $600 for small businesses, depending on the complexity of their accounts and the number of checks they write per month.

Potential Earnings

TYPICAL ANNUAL GROSS REVENUES: $22,500 to $52,500, based on working 1,500 hours a year (or 30 billable hours a week) at $20 to $35 an hour. Some people are able to bill more hours per week if they have steady clients.

OVERHEAD: low (20 percent or less).

Best Home Businesses Estimate of Market Potential

Total number of bookkeeping services in the United States, including home-based businesses: 31,780. Growing at the rate of several new businesses every minute, the demand for bookkeeping services is fed by nearly thirty million small businesses of fewer than one hundred employees. In addition, not-for-profit organizations add to this demand.

Best Ways to Get Business

- Focused advertising and promotional efforts to retail stores and services within a twenty- to thirty-minute drive from your home.
- Your own personal contacts with small businesses in your community.
- Networking in business and trade organizations such as the chamber of commerce.

- Advertising in the yellow pages.
- Obtaining overload or referral business from CPA firms, other bookkeeping firms, and financial planners.
- Making speeches and offering workshops on financial topics.

✚ Related Businesses

Bill-paying service. Many people need or want help taking care of their finances. That's what a bill-paying service provides. You create a budget for each client and then pay the monthly bills. Bill-paying services are usually an add-on service to another business, such as bookkeeping or professional organizing. *See also:*

- Bill-Auditing Service
- Tax Preparation Service

▦ Franchises

General Business Services, 8320 Guilford Road, Suite A, Columbia, MD 21046; (800) 583-9100. Requires a business and management background. You provide financial management and tax-planning services to small businesses. The minimum franchise fee is $15,000.

⚑ First Steps

If you have no prior background in bookkeeping, you can learn this skill from community-college courses, books, or on-the-job experience. If you have a background already, your first steps might be talking with other bookkeeping services, selecting and learning to use the software, and identifying potential clients.

◻ Where to Turn for Information and Help

ORGANIZATIONS

The American Institute of Professional Bookkeepers, 6001 Montrose Road, Suite 207, Rockville, MD 20852; (800) 622-0121, fax (800) 541-0066. Current membership includes 40,000 employed, part-time, and independent bookkeepers. Membership is currently $39 per year. Benefits include reports and monthly newsletters containing updates about tax laws and other key information, a telephone hotline, free federal and state tax forms, and discounts on Airborne Express delivery.

BOOKS

Bookkeeping on Your Home-Based PC, Linda Stern, New York: Windcrest/McGraw-Hill, 1993.

The Encyclopedia of Journal Entries. Published by the American Institute of Professional Bookkeepers. All entries conform to FASB, APB, and other GAAP standards. $77.

Keeping the Books: Basic Record Keeping and Accounting for the Small Business, Linda Pinson and Jerry Jinnett, Dover, NH: Upstart Press, 1994.

Simplified Accounting for Non-Accountants, Rick Stephan Hayes and C. Richard Baker, New York: John Wiley and Sons, 1986.

Small Business Accounting Handbook, Small Business Association Publications, Box 15434, Fort Worth, TX 76119. The SBA also has many other free or low-cost publications, such as *Keeping Records for Small Business* and *A Handbook of Small Business Finance.* Write for a list of publications.

Magazines and Newsletters

Journal of Accounting, Taxation, and Finance for Business, The American Institute of Professional Bookkeepers, 6001 Montrose Road, Suite 207, Rockville, MD 20852; (800) 622-0121. Four quarterly issues of approximately ninety pages each. $69 a year.

Practical Accountant, Faulkner & Gray, 11 Penn Plaza, 17th Floor, New York, NY 10001; (212) 967-7000.

Government Resources

The Internal Revenue Service offers seminars on federal taxes. State and municipal tax offices are a source for information about rules for sales taxes and local income taxes.

Courses

The American Institute of Professional Bookkeepers offers self-teaching courses on basic bookkeeping, payroll, adjusting entries, depreciation, inventory, financial statement analysis, completing the four basic business tax forms, and more. Each course, $39. (800) 622-0121.

McGraw-Hill's NRI Schools offer a course in bookkeeping and accounting. McGraw-Hill Continuing Education Center, 4401 Connecticut Avenue, N.W., Washington, DC 20008; (202) 244-1600.

Prentice Hall offers a thirty-six-hour accounting course. Often available at your local library.

United States Department of Agriculture Graduate School offers reasonably priced correspondence courses in accounting. Write for a catalogue: Correspondence Program, Graduate School, USDA AG Box 9911, Washington, DC 20250. Or call to speak with a counselor at (202) 720-7123 or (202) 447-2187.

■ ■ ■ ■ ■

BUSINESS BROKER

Business brokers bring together a client who wants to sell a business with someone who wants to buy a business. They generally focus on businesses with a price of under $500,000, exclusive of any real estate the business owns. Business brokers function much like real estate brokers; in fact, in twenty states, business brokers are required to have a real estate license; some states require a business broker's license as well.

Business brokerage is a growing home-based business. According to the International Business Brokers' Association, 10 percent of its 3,000 members in the U.S. work from home. The U.S. Department of Commerce estimates that there are sixteen to eighteen million businesses in this country and that 20 percent change hands every year. Fortunately, 90 percent of these are priced under $500,000, so there are plenty of opportunities for business brokers. One reason for the high turnover of businesses, according to *Inc.* magazine, is that more people prefer to buy an ongoing business because failure rates for businesses that are bought are lower than those for businesses started from scratch or even franchises.

Because they often operate under real estate laws, brokers must represent one side or the other. Ninety-nine percent of business brokers choose to represent those who are selling a business. The most successful home-based brokers specialize in selling a particular size or type of business, such as restaurants, bowling centers, medical practices, or businesses in a particular geographic area.

Home-based business brokers can make a profit with a relatively small number of sales per year. Whereas a small two-to-three-person brokerage might need to make two hundred sales annually in order to stay afloat, a home-based solo broker probably can manage quite well with between ten and twenty sales per year because of lower operating expenses.

Finding people who want to buy a business is not difficult. Brokers tell us that advertising in the business-opportunities sections of newspapers draws six to twelve inquiries per ad. Nine out of ten people who buy businesses are first-time buyers. Tom West, owner of the Business Brokerage Press, says business brokers spend about 40 percent of their business time out of the office calling on sellers to get listings; 40 percent dealing with buyers; 10 percent working with outside professionals such as attorneys and bankers; and 10 percent doing analysis.

☑ Knowledge and Skills You Need to Have

- Because of the complexity of brokerage transactions and the significant assets at stake, it is essential for a business broker to have a solid business and legal grounding. Brokers need to have the ability to read and evaluate financial reports such as profit-and-loss statements to be able to represent their clients honestly and effectively. You also need to be familiar with the legal aspects of selling a business.

▪ This business requires considerable perseverance and patience to get listings and to find the right match between buyers and sellers. While some sales happen quickly, most take several months or even a year between getting the listing and closing a sale.

▪ Brokers must have good sales skills. First you must convince an owner to sell and have you represent him or her. Then you must sell buyers on the merits of the businesses you represent.

▪ A broker needs to have good communication and interpersonal skills to build a strong relationship with both buyers and sellers. You must be able to listen and empathize in order to structure deals that are satisfactory to both parties. And you must be able to negotiate successfully with buyers, attorneys, accountants, and sellers.

▪ You should have a conference area or separate office space in your home for meeting with people who are interested in the businesses you represent.

▪ A real estate broker's license is currently required to sell a business (or to get paid for selling one) in the following states: Alaska, Arizona, California, Colorado, Florida, Georgia, Idaho, Iowa, Michigan, Minnesota, Nebraska, Nevada, Oregon, South Carolina, South Dakota, Texas, Utah, Washington, and Wisconsin. However, there is always change, so you should check with your state's real estate commission and with other brokers in your area.

Start-up Costs

	Low	High
Computer with hard disk	$1,000	$3,000
Printer	300	1,600
Suite Software	250	400
Accounting software and special software for evaluating businesses	50	350
Office furniture, especially an ergonomic chair	400	1,000
Business cards, letterhead, envelopes, and listing forms	100	600
Telephone system with two lines with "hold" and "trip" features to handle many calls	125	250
Answering machine or voice mail	100	200
Total	$2,325	$7,400

Advantages

▪ Being able to serve your clients well is easy because buyers will come to you. Brokers fail only if they don't get listings.

▪ The costs of starting this business are minimal and expenses are low.

- You are like a matchmaker. When you do your job well, everyone is happy.
- Fees are high; overhead is low.
- There's little to lose if this business isn't right for you; you should know this within six months.

🏳 Disadvantages

- Getting businesses for sales is just plain hard work. You will probably need to specialize to succeed.
- You don't make any money until the sale is complete.
- You may not have the patience, persistence, and interpersonal skills necessary to enjoy this business, but you won't know until you try.

💲 Pricing

Ten to 12 percent of a business's selling price, with a $10,000 minimum, is the standard fee.

🖳 Potential Earnings

TYPICAL ANNUAL GROSS REVENUES: $100,000, based on one sale a month for ten months of the year at a minimum fee of $10,000 each. Some brokers earn much, much more. As Tom West says, "With a $10,000 minimum, it's all up to you."

OVERHEAD: low (20 percent or less). Note: A good answering service is necessary. You need to have a live person answering your phone. To get premium service, voluntarily pay the answering service $50 more a month.

📈 *Best Home Businesses* Estimate of Market Potential

Total number of business brokers in the United States, including home-based businesses: 8,487. The growing numbers of small businesses should translate into a demand for business brokers.

📭 Best Ways to Get Business

- Contacting business owners directly by phone, mail, or in person.
- Soliciting listings by going up and down the street talking to business owners.
- Networking in associations if you're specializing in some industry, or in other organizations of business owners.
- Getting referrals from lawyers, accountants, and bankers.
- Purchasing lists of names of franchises and private companies for sale all over the country.

✚ Related Businesses

Venture-Capital Broker. This form of business brokering matches owners of undercapitalized businesses with sources of money. In return the venture-capital broker receives a percentage of the money raised and sometimes an equity position in the venture. Four hundred thousand of the 600,000 new businesses starting up every year need additional funds. But according to venture-capital broker André Brady, only one in 1,000 will get funded using only venture capital. By using creative financing, however, like various forms of leasing, bridge loans, second mortgages, accounts-receivable financing, and real estate loans, the broker can improve the odds of finding other sources of funding for one in twenty businesses. An excellent resource to learn more about creative financing is *Guerilla Financing*, by Bruce Blechman and Jay Conrad Levinson (Boston: Houghton Mifflin, 1991).

First Steps

- If a real estate broker license is required in your state, contact the state agency responsible for licensing realtors for the procedures necessary to become licensed.
- To gain experience in this business, you might begin by working for an established broker.
- If you have no experience with analyzing financial statements, take a community-college class or other adult-education course in basic business finance.
- Talk with other business brokers.

▢ Where to Turn for Information and Help

ORGANIZATIONS

Institute of Certified Business Counselors, 3485 West First Avenue, Eugene, OR 97402; (503) 345-8064.

International Business Brokers Association, Box 704, Concord, MA 01742; (508) 369-2490. A professional organization for business brokers, with over eight hundred members. It offers a certification program and regular conferences.

BOOKS

The Business Brokerage Press offers many books of critical importance to those interested in this field. They can be reached at Box 247, Concord, MA 01742; (508) 369-5254. A few of their titles include:

Business Brokers Reference Guide, updated annually. Contains latest court cases, rent guidelines, price comparisons, pricing rules, and other valuable information. $62.

Business Brokerage: Managing for Profit, Tom West. $92.

MAGAZINES AND NEWSLETTERS

The Business Broker, Business Brokerage Press, Box 247, Concord, MA 01742; (508) 369-5254.

SOFTWARE

ValuSource, 7222 Commerce Center Drive, Suite 210, Colorado Springs, CO 80919; (800) 825-8763. Offers two choices: *Value Express* for businesses under $300,000 and *ValuSource* for larger businesses.

MANUALS

30 Days to a Successful Brokerage, Business Brokerage Press, Box 247, Concord, MA 01742; (508) 369-5254. $90; if purchased together with *Video Training Program,* $215.

VIDEOS

Video Training Program, featuring Tom West. Four-part, two-and-a-half-hour video training program. Business Brokerage Press, P.O. Box 247, Concord, MA 01742; (508) 369-5254. Cost: $150; if purchased together with *30 Days to Successful Business Brokerage,* $215.

REFERRAL SERVICES

Two services to help you find buyers and sellers are:

Franchise Broker Network, 3617A Silverside Road, Wilmington, DE 19810; (302) 478-0200.

Nation-List Headquarters, 1660 South Albion Street, No. 407, Denver, CO 80222; (800) 525-9559; (303) 759-5267.

■ ■ ■ ■ ■

BUSINESS NETWORK ORGANIZER

A business network organizer solves two of the most common problems small-business owners face: (1) marketing their business, and (2) finding time to exchange information with other small-business owners in their community. A network organizer sets up groups of small-business owners to meet regularly, usually weekly, in order to give one another business referrals and to help one another get business. Each group or club has only one person from any particular business or profession, so there's no competition among the members of the group. Such networking organizations are a structured way for professionals and business owners to refer clients and customers to one another.

Also called word-of-mouth marketing, getting business through referrals from other people has been a common practice for a long time. Increasingly, however, the traditional service and fraternal organizations such as Rotary, Eagles, Elks, Lions, and Moose are not appealing to small-business owners who need more focused networking organizations, sometimes referred to as leads clubs or networking groups.

That's where the business network organizer steps in. Rather than people joining loose networking groups that often turn into coffee klatches and social gatherings, the networking organizer helps business owners form a more formal group that follows specific procedures to get business from one another and from outside the group. Members pay a fee to the organizer who conducts their meetings, establishes procedures, and ensures that the group is networking smoothly.

There are two ways to become a network organizer: start one or more groups yourself, or purchase a franchise from one of the companies already established that teaches you how to run your business. For example, one franchise organization, Business Network Intl., founded in 1985 by Ivan Misner, Ph.D., offers a two-hundred-page manual for network organizers to learn the business along with a solid training program and direct experience.

While some critics believe that networking is a fad, Misner says, "Networking has proven to be as much of a fad as having a sale." In fact, Tom Peters, coauthor of *In Search of Excellence* and *Thriving on Chaos,* advises small businesses to devote 75 percent of their marketing time and money to developing a structured word-of-mouth network. Networking is, as it always has been, the most reliable and cost-effective way for a small business to make sure that it has business.

☑ Knowledge and Skills You Need to Have

- You need to have an outgoing personality.
- You need to be comfortable speaking in front of groups and able to speak well extemporaneously.
- You must be able to motivate, lead, and educate people in the skill of networking.
- You have to be able to set up and run an organization.

▲ Advantages

- The market for networking organizations is expanding.
- Running a networking group provides an excellent opportunity to market another business or profession you may have.
- You may make valuable contacts and friends throughout the business community.

🔁 Disadvantages

- Unless you run multiple chapters, a networking organization will not provide a full-time income. But it can be a route to expanding another business.
- Networking means constantly attending early-morning meetings.
- Members who don't use what the organization teaches about effective networking techniques may blame you or the organization for not providing them with enough business leads.

🐷 Start-up Costs

	Low	High
Computer with hard disk	$1,000	$3,000
Fax machine	300	900
Printer	300	1,600
Copy machine	300	900
Suite software (mostly word processing)	250	400
Desktop publishing software (to do your own news-letters)	50	250
Office furniture, especially ergonomic chair	400	1,000
Business cards, letterhead, envelopes	100	600
Total	$2,700	$8,650

Note: the above figures are for starting your own business; add franchise fees if you decide to purchase a franchise.

💲 Pricing

Members pay from $200 to $1,500 per year to be in your groups.

🖥 Potential Earnings

- Most new organizers run only a few groups in their first one or two years as they build up their own network of clients. Projected earnings for four groups with twenty members in each who pay $250 per year are thus $16,000.
- With experience and time, a leader can run ten to twenty groups, each with twenty-five or more members. Projected earnings for a leader running twenty groups, each with twenty-five members paying $250 per year, are $125,000.

OVERHEAD: high (over 40 percent: includes room rentals, promotional materials, and mailings).

📈 *Best Home Businesses* Estimate of Market Potential

As trend forecaster John Naisbitt predicted, we have seen a relationship between the growth of *high tech* and *high touch*. Business networking has grown dramatically right along with the dramatic use of technology in business. As the use of technology continues to expand, we expect to see a continuing growth in the role of business networking.

The Best Ways to Get Business

- Personal contacts (your own word of mouth, of course).
- Referrals from current group members.
- Attending and exhibiting at local trade shows.
- Using direct-mail advertising to small businesses and professionals.

Franchises

Business Network Intl., 268 South Bucknell Avenue, Claremont, CA 91711; (800) 825-8286 (for southern California, call [909] 624-2227). In business since 1985, Business Network Intl. has over 300 chapters in twenty-five states at the time of this writing. To become a franchisee, you must begin as a regional director for six months, which is a paid position giving you the chance to learn the ropes and see if you enjoy the business. The franchise fee includes several days of on-site training and a two-hundred-page operating manual. If your chapter does well and the relationship is mutually satisfactory, there is an opportunity to franchise. The fee is $5,000.

First Steps

If you've had experience networking and getting business through word-of-mouth marketing, develop procedures for running your network. Then begin recruiting a membership. Don't start a networking group until you have at least twenty paid members. To recruit members, invite people to free meetings at which you describe the organization and demonstrate the process; then follow up by phone with those who are seriously interested. Don't begin a second chapter until your first one is thriving.

If you have had no experience with networking, your first step should be to join a network or two and become familiar with what works and what doesn't. You may wish to consider one of the franchise opportunities listed above that can accelerate getting your business off the ground.

🔲 Where to Turn for Information and Help

BOOKS

How to Work a Room, Susan Rowane, New York: Warner Books, 1988.

Is Your "Net" Working? Ann Boe and Betty Young, New York: Wiley, 1989.

The World's Best Known Marketing Secret: Building Your Business with Word-of-Mouth Marketing, Ivan Misner, Austin, Texas: Bard Productions. Available from BNI Products; (800) 688-9394.

NATIONAL NETWORKING ORGANIZATIONS

In addition to the franchise organizations above, which are also networking groups you can join, call the following organizations for additional information:

LEADS, P.O. Box 279, Carlsbad, CA 92018; (619) 434-3761; (800) 783-3761.

LeTip International, 4926 Savannah Street, Suite 175, San Diego, CA 92110; (800) 255-3847.

The National Association of Women Business Owners, 1377 K Street N.W., #637, Washington, DC 20005; (301) 608-2590.

■■■■■

BUSINESS PLAN WRITER

If you've ever thought about starting your own business, you've probably heard the old adage "Write a business plan." The problem is, most people don't know how to write a business plan, which opens up a huge market for specialized business writers who can help companies of all sizes create a business plan for their future.

A business plan is like a road map. It shows entrepreneurs where they're headed, gives insights into whether their product or service is feasible, and lays out estimates and projections of expenses and revenues. While most businesses start out without a formal business plan, research shows that those with a good business plan increase their likelihood of success. And as a business grows, a formal business plan is needed to seek loans or outside financing, attract investors, get acquired, or franchise their operation.

The market for business plan writers is best in regions where businesses are starting up or expanding. Linda Elkins, who makes a full-time living writing business plans in Mechanicsville, Maryland, finds she gets most of her business from companies that are just beginning, followed by those seeking second-round financing. Linda points out that in this business, "you are basically a translator. You listen to your client's ideas, review their financial data and the other information they have gathered, and then put this information into the clearest, most direct format possible." Sometimes your job is also to point out additional information the client needs to gather in order to formulate a good plan.

Several software programs are available to make writing business plans easier, quicker, and more professional. These programs also make it easy to examine and present alternative scenarios for a business, using spreadsheets and what-if scenarios. But as Marcia Layton, a business plan writer in Rochester, New York, adds, "Owning the software does not make you a business plan writer; if it were that easy, businesses wouldn't need you either." You also need to have a good sense of business and finance and be able to work with your clients to help them gather information on markets, sales potential, and income projections. "All in all," says Marcia, "it's an exciting field" that nevertheless demands a combination of writing skill, business expertise, and creativity.

✔ Knowledge and Skills You Need to Have

- You need to have a general business background (accounting, bookkeeping, and marketing) and familiarity with financial statements, business jargon, and your local business community.
- You should have already written a few business plans so you know how to put one together and what issues are most important to owners and/or financing sources.
- You need to have the ability to see a business situation from the viewpoint both of the owners and of potential funding sources.
- Good business-writing, grammar, and organizational skills are required.
- You need the ability to present yourself professionally and credibly as an expert who can be relied upon.
- You need the ability to motivate and inspire cooperation from your clients.

🐾 Start-up Costs

	Low	High
Computer with hard disk	$1,000	$3,000
Fax machine	300	900
Printer	300	1,600
Suite software	250	400
Additional business-planning software	100	250
Office furniture, especially ergonomic chair	400	1,000
Business cards, letterhead, envelopes	100	600
Brochures	100	1,000
Organizational dues for networking	250	500
Total	$2,800	$9,250

⏸ Advantages

- The work is challenging and varied. Each business situation is different.
- You have the opportunity to learn about new people and new business ideas.
- It can be very rewarding to assist others in achieving success.
- If you take an equity interest in a client's business as part of your fee, you have the potential to strike it rich.

⏸ Disadvantages

- Business start-ups and expansions are sensitive to economic cycles, so your client base may fluctuate and you may be subject to feast-or-famine cycles.
- Because you are often working with new or changing businesses, you may encounter clients who have collection or legal problems.
- You must continuously market to find new clients; once you work with a company to write their plan, it does not usually generate repeat business for several years.

💲 Pricing

Fees range from $2,000 to $5,000 for each business plan, depending on the time it takes to write it (generally two to four weeks) and the amount of research you may need to obtain financial data, analyze the competition, and develop sample marketing plans. Proven consultants can charge as much as $25,000 working on a major plan for a corporation seeking new financing. Many writers charge a flat fee such as $5,000 to work with a company until the client is satisfied.

Business plan writers can also get business editing and rewriting business plans already developed by a client. Fees for this kind of work may be based on an hourly rate such as $100 per hour or a flat fee such as $500 to review and edit a business plan.

🖥 Potential Earnings

TYPICAL ANNUAL GROSS REVENUES: $20,000 to $100,000. An example is a writer who creates ten plans per year at an average of $5,000 each, plus edits ten plans at $500 each, generating $55,000 in gross revenues.

OVERHEAD: low (20 percent or less).

📝 *Best Home Businesses* Estimate of Market Potential

Many of the well over 500,000 new small businesses that form each year will expand. As they do, they require business plans for obtaining loans and capital. While business plan software is fully able to help someone develop a business plan for his or her own use, experience suggests that highly individualized plans are necessary to get outside money. We rate business plan writing as one of *the best of the best* home businesses.

▣ Best Ways to Get Business

- Teaching courses at local colleges and extension schools in writing business plans and small-business development. Your students are likely to be entrepreneurs who may hire you to help them write their plans.

- Networking through personal contacts at organizations such as trade shows and business associations for those industries or fields in which you have experience. You should join at least two organizations and become active in both.

- Making contacts with bankers, lawyers, venture capitalists, and other gatekeepers at universities or organizations that might run new-business incubator workshops, offer mentor programs, or have an entrepreneurship center.

- Writing articles in the local press about the value of business plans.

- Advertising in local business newsletters and getting publicity about your work in the business media in your area.

▣ First Steps

- If you have some business background, begin by doing a few plans without fee to gain experience and develop a portfolio of work to show to prospective clients.

- Read and study business-planning guides and learn to use business-planning and spreadsheet software. *Caveat*: Buying a business-planning software package with prewritten templates does not automatically transform you into a business plan writer. You need to custom-tailor each plan you write to your clients and not produce a "plan in a can."

▣ Where to Turn for Information and Help

BOOKS

The Business Plan: A State of the Art Guide, Michael O'Donnell, Lord Publishing, 14 Los Monteros Drive, Dana Point, CA 92629, 1988; (800) 525-5673 or (714) 240-7090.

Business Plans That Raise Dollars, Stanley R. Rich and David E. Gumpert, New York: Harper and Row, 1985.

The Business Plan Writing Handbook, Linda Elkins, Business Plan Writing, Mechanicsville, MD; (301) 373-3745.

The Complete Handbook for the Entrepreneur, Gary Brenner, Joel Ewan, and Henry Custer, Englewood Cliffs, NJ: Prentice Hall, 1990.

The Do-It-Yourself Guide to Writing a Business Plan, Marcia Layton, Layton & Co., 36 Oakbrier Court, Penfield, NY 14526. Order by calling (716) 377-4960 or fax to (716) 377-2915.

How to Prepare and Present a Business Plan, Joe Mancuso, Englewood Cliffs, NJ: Prentice Hall, 1983.

COURSES

Many colleges, universities, and extension schools offer courses in writing business plans. These are targeted to entrepreneurs starting a business but are equally useful to the person starting a business-plan-writing business. Other courses include:

American Woman's Economic Development Corporation offers a course for women on how to put together a successful business plan; 71 Vanderbilt Avenue, Suite 320, New York, NY 10169; (212) 692-9100.

GOVERNMENT RESOURCES

Small Business Development Centers are located throughout the United States. They are affiliated with educational institutions and sometimes chambers of commerce. The centers tend to specialize in particular types or sizes of small business. Contact the nearest office of the Small Business Administration for the Small Business Development Centers in your area.

SOFTWARE

Software such as the following packages can take you and your clients step-by-step through developing a business plan.

BizPlan Builder, Jian Tools for Sales, 1975 West El Camino Real, Suite 301, Mountainview, CA 94040; (800) 346-5426; (415) 941-9191. This software is a working business plan outline on disk, including prewritten portions and spreadsheet files you fill in. Available for both PC and Macintosh computers. Requires coordination with standard word processor and spreadsheet programs.

Ronstadt's Financials, Lord Publishing, 14 Los Monteros Drive, Dana Point, CA 92629; (800) 525-5673 or (714) 240-7090. Enables nonexperts to generate the financial projections necessary to do "pro formas."

Success Inc., Dynamic Pathways, 180 Newport Center Drive, Suite 100, Newport Beach, CA 92660; (800) 543-7788; (714) 720-8462.

Tim Berry's Business Plan Toolkit, Palo Alto Software, 144 East 14th Avenue, Eugene, OR 97401; (800) 229-7526. DOS, Windows, or Mac versions available.

Venture and *B-Tools,* Star Software, Suite 404, 363 Van Ness Way, Torrance, CA 90501; (800) 242-7827; (310) 533-1190.

∎ ∎ ∎ ∎ ∎

CATERER

Catering once again has become a viable, profitable, and enjoyable enterprise for the person with the right mix of cooking knowledge, business acumen, and people skills. In fact, revenues from social catering (that is, weddings, bar mitzvahs, and other special events handled by independent caterers as opposed to restaurants) topped $2.6 billion in 1992, the latest year for which figures are available. One reason for the growth in the catering industry is the increase in food delivery—especially lunches—to offices and corporations. The growth is partly the result of economic shifts that have put pressure on workers to spend more hours on the job and eat at their desks, and partly the result of changes in the tax laws that have created incentives for businesses to feed clients and employees in-house (fully tax deductible), instead of dining out (partially deductible).

We are told that most catering services begin at home because whether specializing in social catering or office delivery, start-up does not require years of training, expensive equipment, or capital investment. Initial costs are relatively low, and you can pass along many of those savings to your clients. Particularly in the case of social catering, you can launch the business in your spare time, since most special events take place in the evenings or on weekends. Starting the business on a part-time basis gives you considerable flexibility and lets you "test-market" your product with a minimum of risk. And you can earn handsome profits—generally ranging between 10 percent and 20 percent of the price of the event.

Many home-based caterers begin by whipping up confections in their kitchens at home. But experts generally advise against that practice, because in most states it is illegal to sell food to the public that has been prepared in a home kitchen. In calculating your start-up costs, therefore, you need to figure in the cost of renting a commercial kitchen (renting a church kitchen is often an inexpensive way to start). You can cut costs by sharing kitchen rental expenses with other caterers, a practice that is becoming more and more common. Another alternative, though one that is relatively expensive, is to install a commercial kitchen in your home. This, however, also requires zoning that will allow you to have a commercial kitchen.

Besides office delivery and social catering, there are a number of other catering opportunities for home-based entrepreneurs. According to Denise Vivaldo, owner of a food styling and consulting firm, and author of *How to Open and Operate a Home-Based Catering Business: An Unabridged Guide*, the possibilities include preparing private banquets at hotels, furnishing meals to airlines, cooking for parties aboard chartered yachts, supervising supermarket takeout counters, catering for department stores, or serving as an executive chef in a company dining room or in someone's home. Caterers are also in demand on movie and TV sets, and even at events such as art auctions and local charity fund-raisers. Vivaldo suggests getting a foot in the door by offering a gourmet specialty—fancy cookies or muffins, for example—to an established supplier, and then building on your reputation. Suzan Schatz of Tulsa specializes in gourmet wedding cakes in the commercial kitchen she created adjacent to her home, and her customers include other caterers. Arlene Breskin in Westchester County, New York, caters from the commercial kitchen she has built into her basement producing "cookie bouquets." Dinnerworks in Ottawa, Canada, shops for and prepares two weeks of meals for clients in their kitchens.

Caterers must scrupulously observe health, safety, zoning, product liability, labor, workers' compensation, and other laws and regulations. Violations can be more than merely costly; they can put you out of business. So it makes sense to hire a good attorney at the outset to help you comply with all pertinent government codes. You also need to keep detailed records of your income and expenses, as well as your inventory of food, equipment, and supplies; your employees; your clients; your jobs; and the like. There are several inexpensive computer programs available that can simplify much of this record keeping, although some caterers prefer to hire a bookkeeper.

☑ Knowledge and Skills You Need to Have

- Although you don't necessarily have to be a gourmet cook, you should have a good level of cooking experience and enjoy experimenting with new recipes, preparing food, and planning menus. And it goes without saying that you should find entertaining pleasurable.

- You must be a people person, someone who can get along well with clients, staff, suppliers, bureaucrats, and others—and keep them all happy. You need to be pleasant, courteous, and tactful, even when problems develop.

- You should have a manager's mentality, meaning that you are well organized, because catering involves lots of little details and costs. Without controlling these, you cannot make a profit or be successful. You also need to know how to write up a good contract for your jobs.

- You need to be assertive enough to market your services actively. It is a competitive business in which getting a regular client is hard, and keeping one is tough.

- You must be knowledgeable about sanitation, safe and proper food preparation, and storage techniques. In addition, you need to develop many contacts among suppliers so that you can find top-quality ingredients at good prices.

▣ Start-up Costs

	Low	High
Kitchen rental*	$8,000	$12,000
Equipment (pots, pans, etc.)	500	1,000
Insurance	1,000	2,000
Legal and professional fees	1,000	3,000
License		
Brochures/advertising/promotion	1,000	5,000
Total	$10,500	$23,000

* Based on $100 to $150 per day × 2 days per week × 40 weeks per year. Price reflects average rental rates for a major city in mid-1994. Denise Vivaldo recommends that people starting catering businesses cut costs by sharing the rental of a commercial kitchen and using it on different days.

You will probably also need a delivery vehicle such as a van or truck.

▣ Advantages

- Cooking is one of the most natural and pleasant experiences for people who enjoy food. You get to do something creative that also makes people happy.

- You can work as much or as little as you like. How much you earn depends in part on how much you choose to work.

- As Denise Vivaldo points out, you'll never starve or not be unwanted in the kitchen at parties.

▣ Disadvantages

- Successful catering takes a tremendous amount of work and careful long-range planning. The highest rate of failure among new businesses is among people involved in restaurants and other food businesses.

- Many jobs require that you spend time meeting with clients to learn about their needs, and then you must prepare a competitive bid or proposal, without a guarantee that you will get the contract.

- Social catering involves working evenings and weekends, which takes away from personal/family time. Catering is also often a seasonal business if you are specializing in weddings (June, July) or parties (November–January).

- Besides the menu planning and cooking, you also have to do serving and cleanup, unless you hire people to do those things for you.

- You need to find excellent help. The success of your events depends in large part on other people, including your staff such as servers or bartenders.

💲 Pricing

Caterers try to price events so that food costs run between 28 percent and 35 percent of the total fee. In other words, as a general rule, you should charge about three to four times what you pay for food to cover your time and profit. For example, a sandwich costing you $1.50 is priced at $5.25; a dinner costing $8 is priced at $28 per person.

But every job is different: preparation time, the number of guests, the elaborateness of the menu and the decor all should figure into your pricing calculations. Remember, too, that there are other costs that you may or may not want to charge separately for: china, silver, linens, glasses, tables, chairs, serving staff. Some caterers add a built-in gratuity. The goal is to factor in all your costs—food, labor, overhead, etc.—and leave yourself some profit. When you are just starting out, it is helpful to find out what your competition charges, so you don't stray too far from the norm.

🔢 Potential Earnings

TYPICAL ANNUAL GROSS REVENUES: $30,000 to $50,000 for a home-based caterer averaging $500 to $1,000 per week. Energetic caterers with extensive networks of contacts can make up $70,000 to $80,000, but only after many years in the business once they have built a reputation and steady list of clients.

OVERHEAD: high—greater than 30 or 40 percent.

📝 *Best Home Businesses* Estimate of Market Potential

Total number of catering firms in the United States, including home-based businesses: 48,262. Catering, though subject to fluctuations of the economy, will grow—particularly in parts of the U.S. experiencing substantial population and economic growth.

📇 Best Ways to Get Business

- Networking among wedding planners, bakeries, bridal shops, florists, cooking stores, and others who might be willing to refer clients to you who are in need of catering services. Contact business associations and your local chamber of commerce to get a list of professional associations in your community with whom you can make contact to discuss your services.

- Leave business cards and sample menus at churches, synagogues, reception halls, and country clubs.

- Send press kits to newspapers and radio and television stations.

- Write articles for the food sections of local papers or give speeches to civic and business groups.

- Send out menu postcards, preferably once a month, to previous and prospective clients.

- Volunteer your catering services to a charity to develop some word-of-mouth business.

First Steps

1. Start by volunteering to do a couple of parties to get exposure, to see if you like the business and to find out if you're any good at it. Organize an event for your child's school, for a local scouting group, or for your friends or neighbors.

2. Network within your community to learn about the potential need for your services. Do "informational" interviews with your own colleagues, businesses, and companies to see if they are interested in a new catering service.

3. Join the professional organizations (see below).

Where to Turn for Information and Help

ORGANIZATIONS

American Culinary Federation, P.O. Box 3466, St. Augustine, FL 32085; (904) 824-4468. Offers accreditation to experienced chefs.

American Institute of Wine and Food, 1550 Bryant Street, 7th Floor, San Francisco, CA 94103; (800) 274-AIWF; (415) 255-3000. A national nonprofit organization founded by Julia Child, Robert Mondavi, and others. Holds monthly meetings and periodic fund-raisers. Local chapters in many cities.

International Association of Cooking Professionals, 304 W. Liberty Street, Suite 301, Louisville, KY 40202; (502) 583-3783. National networking group made up of chefs, food stylists, Inn Forum cooking instructors, and food writers.

National Association of Catering Executives (NACE), 304 West Liberty, Suite 201, Louisville, KY 40202; (502) 583-3783.

National Association for the Specialty Food Trade, 1270 Avenue of the Americas, New York, NY 10020; (212) 921-1690. Membership includes, among other things, entree to NASFT's Fancy Food and Confection shows.

The National Restaurant Association, 1200 Seventeenth Street, N.W., Washington, DC 20036; (800) 424-5156. Keeps members updated on relevant national and state legislation and maintains a library for members. The group's Educational Foundation cosponsors restaurant shows around the country.

Books

The Culinary and Hospitality Industry Publications Services (CHIPS) sells a number of books of interest to caterers, including *Art of the Party* (Reynolds), *Buffets: A Guide for Professionals* (St. Laurent), *Catering Menu Management* (Scanlon), *Complete Guide to Special Event Management* (Young), *Complete Off-Premise Caterer* (Lieberman), *Food Presentation and Display* (Pegler), *Party Food* (Kafka), *Special Events: Art & Science of Celebration* (Goldman), *Successful Buffet Management* (Yudd), and *Successful Catering* (Splaver). For more information or to place an order, contact **Culinary & Hospitality Industry Publications Services (CHIPS),** 1307 Golden Bear Lane, Kingwood, TX 77339-3017; (713) 359-2270, fax (713) 359-2277. Some other useful books are listed below.

Freelance Foodcrafting, by Janet Shown, Boulder, Colo.: Live Oak Publications, 1983.

The Guide to Cooking Schools, Doris Shaw. Shaw Associates, Publishers, 625 Biltmore Way, Suite 1406, Coral Gables, FL 33134; (305) 446-8888. Also available directly from Book Passage, Corte Madera, CA; (800) 321-9785.

How to Open and Operate a Home-Based Catering Business: An Unabridged Guide, Denise Vivaldo, Old Saybrook, Conn.: The Globe Pequot Press, 1993.

Kitchen Science, by Howard Hillman, Boston: Houghton Mifflin, 1989.

Start and Run a Profitable Catering Business, George Erdosh, North Vancouver, B.C.: International Self-Counsel Press Ltd., 1994.

Bookstores for Cooks

The Cook's Library, 8373 W. Third Street, Los Angeles, CA 90048; (213) 655-3141.

Kitchen Arts and Letters, 1435 Lexington Avenue, New York, NY 10128; (212) 876-5550.

Magazines

Bon Appetit, Knapp Communications Corporation, 6300 Wilshire Blvd., Los Angeles, CA 90018-5202; (213) 965-3600.

Food & Wine, American Express Publishing Corp., 1120 Avenue of the Americas, New York, NY 10036; (212) 382-5618.

Food Arts: The Magazine for Professionals, Food Arts Publishing, Inc., M. Shanken, Publishers, 387 Park Avenue South, New York, NY 10016; (212) 684-4224. For restaurateurs and caterers.

Special Events Magazine, Miramar Publishing, P.O. Box 3640, Culver City, CA 90231-3640; (800) 543-4116. Covers party trends and offers tips for making parties extraspecial.

CaterMate, 100 Franklin Avenue, Nutley, NJ 07110; (201) 284-0052. The company has the same name as their event-planning software. It can be used in conjunction with *Food Track* from System Concepts, Inc., 6560 N. Scottsdale Rd., Building H, 2nd Floor, Scottsdale, AZ 85253; (602) 951-8011 or (800) 553-2438, which offers sophisticated abilities to manage food and beverages.

Recipe Writer Pro, Sales Analysis Pro, and *Inventory Pro,* At-Your-Service Software, Inc., 450 Bronxville Road, Bronxville, NY 10708; (914) 337-9030. Recipe Writer Pro performs quantity conversions, calculates your expenses and profits by plate and by ingredient, and lets you write recipes and make notes about clients' preferences. Sales Analysis Pro tallies your best- and worst-selling items. Inventory Pro helps you itemize and keep track of your supplies.

■ ■ ■ ■ ■

CLEANING SERVICES

Modern life leaves most of us with very little time for cleaning up. According to studies reported in *American Demographics* magazine, most people today feel like they're having to squeeze more and more into less and less free time. And it's no wonder. Over half of all households consist of two-career couples. More than 40 percent of all households consist of a single person. Almost a quarter of all families today have only one parent. Almost every sixth person in the workforce works more than one job.

So who has time to clean? And who wants to anyway? Housecleaning ranks as American's most disliked daily task, even less popular than grocery shopping, cooking, and going to work. According to a survey by Spiffits (manufacturers of premoistened towels), 13 percent of us hate cleaning and 66 percent merely tolerate it. A survey by *Family Circle* magazine of 35,000 working women and homemakers shows that 42 percent end up ignoring household chores. And a *Good Housekeeping* survey shows that two-thirds of women are unhappy with the way they keep house because they can't keep up with the standards by which they were raised.

It's just this type of dilemma that has made residential and commercial cleaning services one of the fastest-growing segments of the economy, with the number of such companies more than doubling in the last five years. Home cleaning alone is a $92-million-a-year industry. The Bureau of Labor Statistics says there will be more than half a million people cleaning things for others by the year 2000.

There's a new twist to cleaning services as well that makes them growing businesses: environmentalism and a growing awareness of health issues in both businesses and homes. Respiratory illness has now been increasingly linked to air pollution and molds in air ducts and air filters. "Sick" buildings and homes have become accepted terms. As a result more and more people want to live in a clean environment not for cosmetic reasons but for health reasons. At the same time, consumers are looking for "green" cleaning products that don't use toxic chemicals or cause environmental harm.

As a result, the cleaning industry provides many opportunities, and cleaning businesses are among the easiest businesses to start profitably from home. The standard cleaning or janitorial service is the most common. You can serve either residential or commercial clients. Specializing in cleaning tasks that the general services don't provide is also a profitable way to start a cleaning service. Examples of specialties are apartment preparation, auto detailing, carpet cleaning, floor cleaning, ceiling cleaning, drapery and upholstery cleaning, window cleaning, venetian-blind cleaning, air-duct cleaning, pool cleaning, drain cleaning, chimney cleaning, and yard and lawn services, which are a form of cleaning, too.

All these businesses can be run from home, although, of course, the cleaning is done on the customer's premises. You can do this business alone or as a family, or, if you choose, you can hire employees to do the actual cleaning. In some communities you can earn a good living specializing in offering only one type of cleaning service. In other communities you will need to offer a combination of services in order to make a good living throughout the year. Just how good an opportunity cleaning services can be is evidenced by the large number of franchises and training and licensing programs available to help you set them up. Further information follows about each of the various types of cleaning services.

✔ Knowledge and Skills

One of the greatest advantages of starting a cleaning service is that there is very little formal knowledge or experience needed. You simply need:

- the appropriate equipment and supplies, including "green" products
- knowledge of how to use them
- the willingness to work hard and produce superior results
- a growing awareness of health and safety

🔧 Advantages

- Generally start-up costs and overhead for all types of cleaning services are low.
- The business can easily be started as part-time or sideline business.
- You can get free technical expertise from janitorial supply houses and product manufacturers.
- Usually there are ample customers who need these services.

- By adding crews of workers, your business can grow very large and still be home based.

- You can build a base of regular clients who will use your services repeatedly.

- Some types of cleaning services, such as auto detailing, allow you to work outdoors.

▣ Disadvantages

- In general, most types of cleaning businesses have a low-status image, which must be overcome by creating a very clean, neat, and professional identity.

- Cleaning is hard, dirty work. You'll have to be willing to roll up your sleeves and get your hands and clothes dirty.

- Some cleaning is seasonal or periodic in nature, or subject to weather conditions.

- Unless you hire employees, your income is limited by the number of hours you can work in a day. And when you hire crews, you will need to bill, which can lead to collection problems.

$ ▣ Pricing and Potential Earnings

See the individual cleaning businesses described below.

Best Home Businesses Estimate of Market Potential

Cleaning and janitorial services are another business that benefits from the time crunch that individuals feel and from the increasing use by businesses of outside contractors. Surveys repeatedly show that as individuals have less discretionary time, cleaning is one of the first things to go. Turning to enterprises that do cleaning and janitorial work of all kinds is part of the continuing changes in the way we manage our lives and businesses.

▣ Best Ways to Get Business

- Taking out classified ads in weekly community newspapers. This is one home business for which advertising works very well. Find the local paper that produces the best results and advertise there indefinitely.

- Listing in the yellow pages. Find a way to distinguish your service from others.

- Distributing flyers in neighborhoods or business districts.

- Calling directly on businesses that could use your services.

- Sending direct mail offering some type of introductory discount, and then turning each customer you get into a regular weekly or monthly account.

■ For more periodic types of services, keeping names of past clients in a computer database and calling them periodically.

First Steps

■ Take advantage of free training and expertise from janitorial supply houses.

■ Wait until you see what character your service takes before you invest in significant amounts of supplies and equipment.

■ If you do commercial cleaning, you can start as a sideline business because you are usually working evenings and weekends. In contrast, residential customers expect cleaning to be done during weekday hours.

■ Residential cleaning costs less to start because commercial services are often required to have a bond and the equipment needed is larger and more expensive.

■ For equipment you use infrequently, rent rather than buy.

■ Offer to help out other services on days you don't have business. You can learn from them and they can help you in return when you get busy.

■ Carry a pager or use an answering service to make sure you don't miss calls while you are working. Consider purchasing a cellular phone.

Additional Information

Contact *Cleaning Consultants, Inc.*, 1512 Western Ave., P.O. Box 1273, Seattle, WA 98111; (800) 622-4221; (206) 682-9748. Publishers of *Cleaning Business Magazine* and dozens of books on cleaning and restoration services.

Air-Duct Cleaning

Cleaning heating and air-conditioning ducts involves using vacuums and other equipment to remove dust and debris from the ducts in commercial or residential buildings. This is actually an environmentally oriented business, because inefficient heating systems can waste 50 percent of the energy they generate, and clogged air-conditioning systems waste electricity. And it's a year-round business: air-conditioning in the summer; heating in the winter.

Duct cleaning has traditionally been done using a truck-mounted super-powered vacuum. Such equipment, however, runs from $25,000 to $50,000 and may leave much of the finer debris. Air-Care, however, has developed a system that is totally portable and removes not only the heavy buildup and debris but also the finer dust that increases growth of bacteria, mold, and mildew. Air-Care's program is not a franchise; it's a dealer program in which for a $15,000 fee they provide all the equipment, training, and promotional materials for you to use their methods in your business.

Using this system, people can charge an average of $500 per job and do two jobs a day. Therefore, if you specialize in air-duct cleaning and work four days a week, fifty weeks a year, you can gross $200,000 per year. Air-duct cleaning can also be an adjunct to general cleaning, chimney cleaning, or carpet cleaning. For more information contact Air-Care, Air Duct Decontamination Division, DPL Enterprises, 5115 South Industrial Road, Suite 506, Las Vegas, NV 89118; (800) 322-9919.

NRI Schools, McGraw-Hill Continuing Education Center (4401 Connecticut Avenue, Washington, DC 20008), offers a home-study course in air-conditioning, heating, and refrigeration. And International Correspondence Schools (925 Oak Street, Scranton, PA 18540), offers a career diploma program in air-conditioning and refrigeration.

Auto Detailing

Auto detailing is a growing cleaning business, given American's love affair with cars. There are now more than 120 million cars on the road in the country and about 16,000 auto-detailing businesses. And with the average price of a car now hovering around $18,000, more and more people want to keep their cars in tiptop shape.

Home-based auto detailing goes beyond what a car wash can do to make an automobile look and feel like new. Auto detailers work on their client's premises where they polish and clean a car inside and out, right down to the finest detail. It takes about three hours to thoroughly detail a car. So if you work quickly, you can do two to three cars a day. In addition to working for individuals, you can also work for used-car dealers or companies with fleets of cars that routinely need to be detailed.

Start-up costs for an auto-detailing business range from $2,000 to $4,000, excluding the cost of a minivan or station wagon to carry your equipment and supplies. You will need portable water-supply equipment; a professional waxer/polisher; an air washer; a wet-dry vacuum; a portable generator; and an assortment of soft brushes, cleaners, waxes, and towels. Overhead for each car averages $5 to $10 in supplies.

The price you can charge depends greatly on your clientele. Detailing for private individuals ranges from $100 to $300 per vehicle; detailing wholesale to car dealers and fleet owners averages $50 to $60 per vehicle. Some detailers charge by the hour at rates of $25 and up. With a fifty-week work-year, if you detail fifteen cars per week at a wholesale price of $55, your potential gross revenues are $37,500; detailing twelve cars per week retail at $100 per vehicle would earn you $60,000 per year. Some detailers also run a complementary business doing auto paint touch-ups.

The best ways to get business as an auto detailer include directly soliciting corporations, rental car agencies, funeral homes, limo companies, car dealers, and others who operate fleets of cars; networking in associations and business groups of executives; taking out a yellow-page listing; and even approaching upscale car owners as they park their cars in parking lots and handing out your business card, flyer, or brochure.

ORGANIZATIONS

The Curtis System Advanced Automotive Care, 55 Hercules Drive, Colchester, VT 05446; (800) 334-3395. They are a training company that sells a system (for $1,895 to $4,450) to start and run an auto-detailing business. The program is not a franchise; you pay only the one-time fee and for additional supplies as you need them.

Color Tech Systems, 479 Interstate Court, Sarasota, FL 34240; (813) 378-1193. Offers a paint touch-up business.

CLEANING PRODUCTS

Cyclo, 1438 South Cherokee Street, Denver, CO 80223; (800) 525-0701. Also provides information about pricing and other facts about starting an auto-detailing business.

Glo-Shield Glass, 3060 Whitestone Expressway, Flushing, NY 11354; (718) 463-1035.

Production Car Care Products, 1000 East Channel Street, Stockton, CA 95205; (209) 943-7337.

Carpet Cleaning

Carpet-cleaning services can serve both residential and commercial clients and can be easily started on a part-time basis. Wall-to-wall carpeting is commonplace in both homes and offices, but since cleaning carpets requires special equipment, most people hire someone instead of trying to do it themselves. Carpet-cleaning methods today include steam, dry extraction, and carbonation. Some carpet cleaners also clean draperies and upholstery.

Costs for start-up run around $3,000 to $4,000 depending on the type of equipment you buy. You should also have a station wagon or van, because equipment does not fit well into a regular car. When you're first starting you can rent machines by the day. You can charge a flat fee such as $150 per job, or you can charge by the square foot (preferred) or by the room. Prices range from 10 to 25 cents a square foot depending on how much carpet there is, how dirty the carpet is, and whether it can be done by machine or must be done by hand. You can also charge for such extras as preconditioning, stain removal, and stain guarding. Usually this works out to be somewhere between $25 to $60 an hour, for an annual gross income of $30,000 to $60,000.

No real background is required, but you do have to have good equipment and know how to use it. Edward Svadlenka, who owns Mighty Clean Enterprises, finds that there's plenty of business. Repeat customers are particularly important to reduce marketing time and overhead.

ORGANIZATIONS

The Carpet and Rug Cleaning Institute, P.O. Box 2048, Dalton, GA 30722; (706) 278-3176. A trade organization for rug manufacturers that has information about types of carpets and carpet care.

MAGAZINES

Cleaning Business Magazine, Cleaning Consultant Services, Box 1273, Seattle, WA 98111; (800) 622-4221; (206) 682-9748. Covers how to start a home cleaning/window-washing service and offers referrals. Quarterly, $20.

TRAINING PROGRAMS AND FRANCHISES

If you're interested in this business but don't want to go it alone, here are four companies you can affiliate with that will teach you the ropes.

Chem-Dry Carpet Cleaning, 1530 N 1000 West, Logan, UT 84321; (800) 841-6583. Offers its franchisees a patented carpet-cleaning method that uses carbonation. This method has two major benefits: lack of environmentally toxic chemicals and quicker drying time. The franchise fee is $14,950 plus a flat $175 monthly royalty. In business since 1975.

Host, 16th Street, Box 1648, Racine, WI 53401; (800) 558-9439. Offers a free or very low cost three-hour training program in its dry-extraction carpet-cleaning system, available through local janitorial-supply distributors. Host equipment and products can be purchased for around $2,000; once you have purchased the system you can attend the three-day Host School in Racine, Wisconsin, for free.

Rug Doctor Pro, 2788 North Larkin Avenue, Suite 5A, Fresno, CA; (800) 678-7844. Offers a franchise as a carpet, upholstery, drapery, and ceiling- and wall-cleaning service for residential and commercial customers. In business for eighteen years. The minimum franchise fee is $5,000, and start-up costs run from $10,000 to $20,000, depending on the equipment needed. Financing is available.

Von Schrader Company, 1600 Junction Avenue, Racine, WI 53403; (800) 626-6916. Will provide training, equipment, and uniforms for room, carpet, upholstery, and wall cleaning. The fee is $2,995. This is not a franchise.

BOOKS

Cleaning Up for a Living, Don Aslett and Mark Browing, Whitehall, Va.: Betterway Publications, 1988.

Ceiling Cleaning

Although most commercial facilities need to have acoustical ceilings cleaned, most cleaning services don't provide this, so there is a need. You can buy one of the many chemical cleaning packages available from ceiling-cleaning distributors, who will instruct you in how to use them. Or you can tie in with a company like Ceiltech, which offers a start-up ceiling-cleaning program for $3,500. This includes equipment, marketing materials, and solutions. Ceiltech estimates that you can earn $150 an hour using its system to clean ceilings. Or ceiling cleaning can be an add-on service to a general or carpet-cleaning service. For more information you can contact Ceiltech at 825 Gatepark Drive, #3, Daytona Beach, FL 32114; (800) 662-9299 or (904) 239-9426.

Air-Care also has a ceiling-cleaning system. When you become an Air-Care dealer, the company provides all the equipment, training, and promotional materials for $12,500. Contact Air-Care, Air Duct Decontamination Division, DPL Enterprises, 5115 South Industrial Road, Suite 506, Las Vegas, NV 89118; (800) 322-9919.

See also Rug Doctor Pro (under Carpet Cleaning) and Steamatic (under Residential and Commercial Cleaning) for ceiling-cleaning franchise opportunities.

Chimney Cleaning

Did you know there are 25 million fireplaces in the United States and sooner or later they all need cleaning? In fact, failing to clean a chimney that's being used regularly can cause a serious fire hazard, and in some states there are now laws about the level of pollutants emerging from chimneys. So if you live in a climate and community where people burn wood in their fireplaces regularly, you can earn up to $400 a day as a chimney sweep. This is a low-overhead business. All the equipment you need fits easily into a car. In addition to a specialized vacuum and a set of tools, you need a ladder and the knowledge of how to do the work.

Gary Trotter was working in a grocery store when he started a part-time business as a chimney sweep. Within five months he had made more money than he earned in a year at his grocery job. He knew it was time to become his own boss, full-time. His business, Thee Chimney Sweep, is now available as a franchise. It offers a comprehensive three-week training program and all needed equipment. The franchise fee is $7,500, and there is no royalty. Contact Thee Chimney Sweep, 36 Vernon Road, NE, Rome, GA 30165-8999; (706) 232-5261.

Floor Cleaning and Refinishing

In his book *Cleaning Up for a Living*, Don Aslett says there are few good floor-care professionals, and yet stripping, waxing, sanding, and refinishing hardwood floors is certainly a service needed by homeowners and business establishments like restaurants. The necessary equipment can be purchased from a wholesale janitorial service for less than $2,000. And you can charge considerably more per hour than a general housecleaning service.

Mobile Power Washing

Using a truck equipped with a tank that holds hundreds of gallons of hot water that is propelled through high-pressure hoses, mobile power washers go where large things need cleaning. They clean construction sites; aluminum siding; old brick, cement, and marble on buildings being restored; farm, industrial, and construction equipment; garbage trucks, airplanes, and boats; parking lots; restaurant freezers and vent hoods; awnings and signs; air-conditioning units, phone booths, shopping carts, and hotel dumpsters. They also travel to residences to clean driveways, patios, kitchen floors, siding, basements, pool decks, and mobile homes.

When Greg Souser bought power cleaning equipment he thought he would use it to bring in some extra income each month. Little did he know his home-based company, Tri-State Mobile Power Wash, would become a $100,000-a-year business. Souser borrowed $10,000 from the bank to launch the business. He works with a partner and spends 50 percent of his time cleaning, 30 percent selling, and 20 percent administering. He likes the regularity of working with his monthly accounts. His company motto is We Wash Anything, Anywhere, Anytime.

The equipment runs from $800 to $10,000, depending on how much water pressure it has, how many gallons per minute it produces, and whether it has hot and cold water. It is available through industrial steam-cleaning equipment suppliers, which can be found in the yellow pages.

TRAINING PROGRAMS AND FRANCHISES

Sparkle International, 26851 Richmond Road, Cleveland, OH 44146; (800) 321-0770; (216) 464-4212. Offers a franchise that includes a customized van with the mobile cleaning unit installed. All training, chemicals, and equipment are included, along with marketing and sales information. Franchise fees run from $7,500 to $45,000, and you can get a protected territory. In business for twenty-six years.

Silva-Craft, Inc., 90 Curtwright #3, Amherst, NY, 14221; (800) 661-1696; (416) 466-4164. Provides a start-up package for a mobile car/boat/plane wash. The package, which costs from $1,095 to $1,595, includes supplies, training, and a cleaning system.

Wash on Wheels Marine Clean, 5401 South Bryant Avenue, Sanford, FL 32773; (800) 345-1969; (407) 321-4010. Although Wash on Wheels also offers franchise opportunities for outdoor and indoor pressure-cleaning services, their Marine Clean franchise is a boat-and-yacht cleaning service. The down payment is $7,900 and includes the franchise fee, training, and equipment.

Pool Cleaning

If you live in a community where many homes have year-round swimming pools, pool cleaning can be a way to earn a steady, regular income working out-of-doors. As anyone who has a swimming pool knows, pools have to be cleaned properly and on schedule or you've got trouble. Therefore, most pool owners turn this task over to someone they can rely on to make sure it gets done right.

You do need to learn how to do this business, because it involves using various hazardous chemicals, which must be used in the proper ways. If you don't have any experience, chemical manufacturers provide some training, as do stores that sell spa and swimming-pool equipment. The best route, however, would be to work for a time as an assistant to someone in the business.

Start-up costs, including equipment and supplies, run from $500 to $1,000. You can earn $50,000 or more a year.

Residential and Commercial Cleaning

You can start a residential cleaning service by investing $1,000 in basic professional cleaning supplies and equipment. For start-up on a shoestring, you can use the supplies and equipment on the premises of your clients or you can use your household equipment until you have enough income from the business to purchase additional equipment. Fees for general housecleaning run from $50 to $75 a day or $10 to $20 per hour for the average home, depending on the going rates in the community. Income from working full-time by yourself can be $20,000 to $30,000 a year. You can earn more if you work as a husband-and-wife team or hire teams of individuals to work for you.

Commercial cleaning services are also in demand. Although large office buildings contract with janitorial services that provide crews to clean all the offices each night, smaller buildings and small retailers also need cleaning services. These contracts can become a steady, reliable source of business. Commercial janitorial services can charge more than residential services, and a one-person service can earn about $50,000 a year. A profitable specialty can be preparing homes and apartments for new owners and tenants, particularly in growing areas of the country.

One way to learn how to run a cleaning service is to work briefly for an established service. In addition, here are several resources you can use to learn about starting a cleaning or janitorial service.

ORGANIZATIONS

Building Service Contractors Association International, 10201 Lee Highway, Suite 225, Fairfax, VA 22030; (800) 368-3414. Trade association for commercial cleaning companies. Offers educational programs, printed materials, and networking for members.

FRANCHISES

There are many franchises that will help you get started in this business. The following ones encourage you or allow you to operate from home.

Classy Maids, Box 160879, Altamonte Springs, FL 32716-0879; (800) 445-5238. In business since 1980; franchise fee is from $5,900 to $9,500, which includes the cost of supplies, uniforms, and so on. Financing is available for half the fee over four years.

Jani-King, 4950 Keller Springs Road, Suite 190, Dallas, TX 75248; (800) 552-5264; in Texas, (800) 533-9406. Specializes in commercial cleaning. In business since 1969. Variable franchise fee.

ServiceMaster, 855 Ridge Lake Boulevard, Memphis, TN 38119; (800) 338-6833. In business since 1947, one of the oldest home-based franchises and the biggest such business in the world, with 4,029 franchises. The franchise fee ranges from $8,700 to $19,700; financing is available for up to 65 percent of the total cost.

Steamatic, Inc., 1320 South University Drive, Fort Worth, TX 76107; (800) 527-1295. Specializes in commercial and residential cleaning services, working primarily with insurance companies on settling claims for fire and water damage from accidents or natural disasters. In business since 1946. In addition to general cleaning, Steamatic franchisees learn how to clean carpets, upholstery, draperies, electronics, and air ducts, as well as how to do wood restorations and fire and flood repair. Steamatic is also heavily involved in environmental cleaning. Franchise fee ranges from $5,000 to $18,000, and financing is available.

BOOKS AND MANUALS

Cleaning Up for a Living: Everything You Need to Know to Become a Successful Building Service Contractor, Don Aslett and Mark Browning, Crozet, VA: Betterway Publications, 1991.

Comprehensive Custodial Training Program: Instructor's Guide, William Friggin, Cleaning Consultant Services, Box 1273, Seattle, WA 98111; (206) 682-9748. A comprehensive guide to training employees.

Everything You Need to Know to Start a Housecleaning Service, Mary Pat Johnson. Cleaning Consultant Services, Box 1273, Seattle, WA 98111; (206) 682-9748.

Is There Life after Housework?, Don Aslett, Cincinnati: Writer's Digest Books, 1980. Step-by-step instructions for cleaning every area of the home in 75 percent less time. Includes sample contracts.

VIDEOS

Home Care Series, 2 vols., Don Aslett, Article One Publishing, Box 1682, Pocatello, ID 83204. These videos demonstrate professional housecleaning methods. Although they are designed for people to use in cleaning their own homes, you can also use them to learn cleaning methods for starting a business.

Cleaning Business Magazine, Cleaning Consultant Services, Box 1273, Seattle, WA 98111; (206) 682-9748. Covers material on how to start a home-cleaning or window-washing service and offers referrals. Quarterly, $20.

Window Cleaning

You've undoubtedly heard the saying *We don't do windows.* But virtually every residence and business establishment in the country has windows, and someone has to clean them periodically. This demand has led to specialized window-cleaning services.

Clean windows are particularly important to retail shops, which count on a clear view of their merchandise. And retailers make good clients because they need their windows cleaned frequently and regularly. Although you actually charge per pane, per side, or per story, you can earn what amounts to $15 to $25 an hour for residential clients and $20 to $35 an hour for commercial clients. And since there's plenty of work, you can work a full forty hours a week and earn about $50,000 a year.

One advantage of this business is that you are working outdoors. Dan Rastorfer, of Silverstreak Services, tells us the work doesn't need to be boring because you can work while listening to a radio or tape headset and you meet a lot of interesting people. Start-up costs can be as low as $200 for a pail, a bucket, squeegees, and ladders. You need average motor abilities, and it helps to be somewhat ambidextrous and have no fear of heights.

You do need to have health insurance, however, because there is a risk of injury. You should also have liability insurance, which runs about $2,500 a year (more if you have employees). A related service is removing window paint from store windows after holidays and sales.

How to Start a Window Cleaning Business: A Guide to Sales, Procedures and Operations, Judy Suval, Cleaning Consultant Services, Box 1273, Seattle, WA 98111; (206) 682-9748.

American Window Cleaner, 27 Oak Creek Road, El Sobrante, CA 94803; (510) 222-7080. "The voice of the professional window cleaner."

Window-Blind Cleaning

Miniblinds, vertical blinds, and venetian blinds adorn the windows in millions of households and office buildings across America. But if you've ever tried to clean these blinds, you know why most cleaning services not only don't do windows, but don't do blinds, either. A blind-cleaning service, however, can make up to several hundred dollars per job. Start-up costs and overhead can be very low. And little specialized skill is required.

You can buy specialized equipment to clean the blinds faster and more efficiently. This equipment runs from $500 to $20,000, and you can find out about it through cleaning and janitorial supply houses.

S. Morantz, Inc., has created a specialized blind-cleaning machine. The Morantz family has been in the blind-cleaning business for sixty years. They provide you with the special equipment they've developed, teach you how to use it, and support you in developing your business for a fee that ranges from $10,000 to $20,000. Contact S. Morantz, Inc., 9984 Gantry Road, Philadelphia, PA 19115; (215) 969-0266. (Morantz also sells screen-printing, drapery, and swag-making business information and training.)

■ ■ ■ ■ ■

COLLECTION AGENCY

There's nothing new about the idea that businesses often need help in collecting money owed to them. For many years, businesses have hired agencies to collect on delinquent accounts. But home-based collection services are taking an ever-larger and more-profitable share of the market by carving out a niche for themselves. There are currently about 5,900 home-based collection agencies nationwide.

Large collection agencies tend to focus on the most cost-effective cases—those involving substantial sums of money and where recovery is likely with a minimum of effort. Most of the collectors work on commission, handle multiple accounts, and are under tremendous pressure to produce. Although the agencies often make good profits, the collectors themselves seldom do.

Smaller, home-based agencies offer collectors a higher earnings potential, with significantly lower stress. Most small agencies actually outperform the larger agencies. On average, big agencies succeed in collecting money owed in about 20 percent of all cases, while small agencies have an average success rate of about 30 percent. The difference is attributable mainly to the fact that small agencies devote a greater portion of their resources to the toughest (and most time-consuming) 10 percent of cases, which primarily involve "skips," debtors with hidden assets, people who must be sued, and other stubborn types. With fewer accounts and less pressure from supervisors, collectors are able to take a more patient, low-key approach which usually nets better results. In general, they are also better paid than people doing the same work in large agencies.

Statistics show that 20 percent of people who are delinquent on their accounts will pay after receiving only one dun notice in the mail. The big agencies generally make no attempt to collect on smaller bills after that initial mailing, putting their people to work on collecting only the larger bills that will produce a sizable commission when paid. With lower overhead, however, a home-based collection service can afford to collect on accounts of all sizes, thereby increasing the money collected for its clients and still make sufficient money to prosper.

Using a personal computer and special collections software, a home-based collection service can become very efficient by reducing the time and labor required for handling mailings and accounting. Using on-line services can also reduce the cost of tracking down debtors.

Collecting money from people is regulated by both the Federal Fair Debt Collection Practices Act and state laws. State laws typically require people who do collections to be bonded and licensed; however, obtaining a collection agency license is usually not difficult. City and/or county business licences also may be required, however, obtaining a collection agency license usually is not difficult unless your state does not allow collection agencies to be home-based.

Some typical collection customers are grocery and department stores who got stuck with bad checks and cable-television operators and companies trying to collect from people who purchase from infomercials. In addition, there are three other specialty areas you might be able to focus on:

Health-care providers.   Today three out of every four dollars sent out for collections are for hospital and medical bills not covered by insurance. For the most part, the people who owe money for their health care will pay on these debts if dealt with appropriately.

Day-care businesses.   Collecting on unpaid bills for day care is another growing area for collections. With more women working and having to place their children in a day care that may cost as much as $125 per child a week, parents can get behind on day care as much as any other kind of debt.

Child support.   There are more than 15 million delinquent parents in this country who collectively owe roughly $24 billion in unpaid child support. The delinquency rate is estimated to be 49 percent by the Children's Defense Fund. The staggering nonwelfare caseload of 6.5 million cases of delinquent fathers has in fact overwhelmed federal and state agencies, creating an opportunity for private collection agencies. Within the last couple of years, several companies have begun to offer franchises for child-support collections with start-up costs ranging from $300 to $8,000, depending on whether you handle the collections yourself or simply sign on the clients, leaving it to the parent company to do the tracing and collections.

Infomercial purchases. Generally the cost of products sold by infomercial are less than what interests larger collection agencies. We have actually had the maker of one of the more popular infomercials on television contact us for the names of home-based collection agencies. Infomercials are becoming more and more common on television, so we can expect more of their business to be going to home-based collection agencies.

☑ Knowledge and Skills You Need to Have

- To do well in this business you need to have good communication skills. You need to be able to persuade businesses to hire you while their outstanding accounts are still young and to convince the people you contact to pay the bill you're collecting on.

- Patience is essential. You must be both firm and fair with the people who owe money. Rather than haranguing them, you need to see them not just as debtors but as people with money problems whom you can assist.

- A collector needs to have high self-esteem. You need to be able to keep your self-esteem intact in the face of rejection when people refuse to pay their bills or lie to you.

- Basic budgeting skills are needed so that you will have sufficient knowledge to advise debtors on how to begin solving their financial problems.

- You need to know about the provisions of the Federal Fair Debt Collection Practices Act and the laws in your state regarding collections.

- If you will be collecting on medical bills, you need to have an understanding of health-insurance policies and billing practices.

🐂 Start-up Costs

	Low	High
Computer with hard disk and modem	$1,000	$ 3,000
On-line services (per-year fees)	100	1,000
Fax machine	300	900
Printer	300	1,600
Word-processing and spreadsheet software	250	400
Specialized collections software	100	250
Telephone headset	40	70
Office furniture, especially ergonomic chair	400	1,000
Business cards, letterhead, envelopes	100	600
Brochures	100	1,000
Organizational dues for networking	250	500
Total	$2,940	$10,320

▣ Advantages

- This work is both challenging and rewarding. When you help make it possible for someone to pay a bill, everyone wins.
- Sometimes you're able to help people solve their financial problems and avoid having to go into bankruptcy.

▣ Disadvantages

- People may return your phone calls at all hours of the day and night.
- The standard working hours—from 10 A.M. to 8 P.M.—may be inconvenient.
- Hearing about people's financial problems all day long and having people become angry with you or lie to you can be emotionally draining.

▣ Pricing

Commissions range from 25 percent on young accounts to 50 percent on those that must go to court. For child-support collections, commissions average around 15 percent.

▣ Potential Earnings

TYPICAL ANNUAL GROSS REVENUES: $30,000 to $60,000, based on a 25 percent commission for collections of $10,0000 to $20,000 per month.

OVERHEAD: moderate (20 percent to 40 percent; includes leasing a postage meter).

▣ *Best Home Businesses* Estimate of Market Potential

Total number of collection agencies in the United States, including home-based businesses: 18,761. The markets served by home-based collection agencies are growing.

▣ Best Ways to Get Business

- Directly soliciting potential clients by phone or in person. To see doctors, find out which day of the week they see pharmaceutical salespeople and ask to be placed on that schedule.
- Networking in organizations of professionals and small-business owners.
- Writing articles for local publications that are read by your target clientele.
- Speaking and even offering seminars at meetings and trade shows attended by professionals and small-business owners.

✚ Related Business

Commercial Debt Negotiator

Negotiating commercial debts on behalf of debtors is a related business. It differs in that unlike a collection agency representing creditors, the commercial debt-negotiator represents those who owe money. Keen negotiation skills are required. One may be negotiating directly with bankers, business owners to whom money is owed, as well as attorneys, accountants, and collection agencies who represent them. As with a collection agency, one works on a commission, which may range from 10 to 30 percent of the amount saved a client. Creditors usually welcome a debtor or his representative with a cash offer to settle a delinquent account. The alternative for the creditor is to turn the debt over to an attorney, a collection agency, or go directly to court to collect the money owed. All these alternatives are expensive in terms of time and money. One gets clients either by cold-calling or from bankers who may refer customers having problems. You must check whether representing debtors in this way would be legally permissible in your state.

⏷ First Steps

If you have no background in doing collections work, a good way to gain the experience is to take a job for several months with a collection agency. If you have experience, subscribe to *Collector* magazine and join the American Collectors' Association listed below.

▢ Where to Turn for Information and Help

ORGANIZATIONS

American Collectors' Association, Box 39106, Minneapolis, MN 55439-0106; 4040 West 70th Street, Minneapolis, MN 55435; (612) 926-6547.

BOOKS

The Fair Debt Collection Practices Act, U.S. Code Annotated. St. Paul, MN: West Publishing Company. Updated annually. Available in libraries.

MAGAZINES

Collector, American Collectors' Association, Box 39106, Minneapolis, MN 55439-0106; 4040 West 70th Street, Minneapolis, MN 55435.

SOFTWARE

Debtmaster, Comtronic Systems, 205 N. Harris Avenue, Cle Elum, WA 98922; (509) 674-7000. Single-user version, $2,495.

Assistance to Parents Collecting Court-Ordered Child Support (ATPC), 709 D Street, #108, Ramona, CA 92065; (800) 995-5835. Began operations in 1991. For a license fee of $5,000 plus a monthly charge of $100 to cover dues, advertising, and technical support, franchisees receive a training course and manual; computer software and databases; contracts, powers of attorney, and other legal forms; national advertisement in women's magazines, and membership in the National Child Support Enforcement Association (NCSEA). Franchisees also have the right to use the ATPC name, although they operate independently. ATPC associates earn a commission of 20 percent of the sum collected.

Child Support Enforcement Specialists, Inc., P.O. Box 70525, Houston, TX 77270-0525; (800) 460-2737 or (713) 877-2150, fax (713) 877-2156. The company offers four different options, from a $300 arrangement whereby CSES handles collections and the agent receives 5 percent of the gross collected to an $8,000 package which includes operations manuals, literature, phone support, radio and television commercials, a two-day training session, and a "protected territory" with a population of 750,000. With the most-expensive option, agents can choose to handle collections themselves or let the company do it for them in exchange for a commission. Availability of the four programs varies from state to state.

■■■■■

COMPUTER CONSULTANT

Although some programmers call themselves computer consultants, there is a distinction between what a computer consultant does and what a programmer does. Whereas programmers are valued for their specialized know-how and are paid to write code, computer consultants take a broader view of an organization and its computer needs in an effort to help solve information-management problems of all kinds. In a sense, a computer consultant is actually a combination of hardware and software expert, programmer, technical writer, and business adviser. The consultant asks people what they want to achieve and explores possibilities for how a computer can help them accomplish it. Whereas programmers work on fixed, objective targets, consultants deal more with broader, moving targets. According to consultant Nigel Dyson-Hudson, "The programmer is like the chief scientist sitting atop a triangle of ever more highly specialized knowledge. Consultants, on the other hand, work on an inverted triangle; the more skilled they get, the broader their knowledge must become."

In general, consultants may perform many types of work. In fact, consultant coach Bill Mooney has identified thirteen different types of work that computer consultants might do:

1. business requirements analysis
2. preliminary system design
3. preliminary cost/benefit analysis
4. software analysis
5. hardware selection
6. documentation
7. implementation
8. validation
9. training
10. technical support
11. management of the system
12. maintenance of the system
13. periodic evaluations/audits

As Mooney points out, some consultants do only one of these, some do two or three, and some do a wide number of them, but many forget that they can do more. In Mooney's view, each of these tasks can be an entire field to be mined by the savvy computer consultant; or alternatively, a consultant can contract for the whole enchilada, and subcontract out the work to others such as programmers, maintenance people, and technical writers. In short, there is as wide a range of ways to conduct a computer consulting career as there is for many other kinds of consulting.

For all computer consultants, however, having a customer service orientation is a key to getting business. One rule of thumb, according to consultant expert Alan Simon, is that computer consultants must have these five nontechnical traits to get along with—and keep—their clients:

■ They must understand the client's business.
■ They must speak the language of the client, without using technical jargon.
■ They must propose sensible solutions.
■ They must appear to be businesspeople.
■ They must know the software of the business in which they work.

For additional information on this career, also read the entries Management Consultant, Computer Programmer, and Specialty Consultant.

☑ Knowledge and Skills You Need to Have

- Technical knowledge of hardware and software is a must. You need to be an expert in several technical or functional areas (databases, networking, legal software, medical software, etc.).

- In order to market yourself as a consultant, you need to have a specialty, but you must also have an overview of everything in the field so you can provide the entire solution. Once you have a client, you don't want to have to refer him or her to someone else. But you do need to know when to bring in a subcontractor and whom to choose.

- You need to be able to inspire trust in your client. You need to have the ability to communicate on the client's level and know how much information he or she really wants to have. You need to be able to convey with confidence that you understand a client's situation and can take care of it.

- You need to be good at splitting your time among your clients, your work, any team members you work with, and keeping up with the industry. Tony Camas, who has a consulting firm, Boston Automation, Inc., agrees with this analysis and finds his work consists of about 50 percent of his time interacting with clients and running his business (he has an employee now) and only about 30 percent of his time designing systems or developing programs.

⬛ Start-up Costs

	Low	High
IBM compatible or Macintosh SE computer equipped at the high end with modem, large hard disk, CD-ROM*	$2,000	$ 4,000
Laser printer	300	1,600
Copier	300	800
Fax	300	900
Suite software	250	400
Additional software (contact management, presentation software, clipart, desktop publishing, etc.) to do your own presentations, brochures, newsletters	500	1,000
On-line services access for one year	200	500
Office furniture, especially an ergonomic chair	400	1,000
Business cards, letterhead, envelopes	100	600
Brochure	100	1,000
Organizational dues	250	250
Total	$4,700	$12,050

* You need to have access to computers that are as advanced as the computer systems of your clients.

▣ Advantages

- In this business, problems are opportunities. Essentially, as a consultant, you're in the business of solving problems.

- People are grateful when you help them. You can make or break a business through your skills.

- You can often work any time of the day or night you wish as long as the job is done on time.

- If you're good at getting business, you can do this work from anywhere in America.

- You perform varied activities, and there is seldom boredom or repetition.

- The demand is high. If you're good, you don't have to be concerned about competition.

- Some contracts can last for many months or even a year, guaranteeing you steady income.

▣ Disadvantages

- At least part of the time, you may have to work under time pressures due to client deadlines.

- You must devote considerable time to keeping current in the fast-changing computer field. To stay current, computer consultants typically read ten to twenty hours a week.

- If you must work on fixed bids you have to be skillful at estimating, as project costs can easily exceed estimates.

- Cash flow can be difficult to control; you have to stay on top of your billings with clients and be sure they pay you periodically for your work.

- It can be hard to survive unless you have a few big clients or are willing to work for an agency (although agencies can provide you with a few good jobs, which can become leads to your own contracts down the road).

▣ Pricing

Computer-consulting rates typically range from $28 to $170 per hour, with an average rate around $55 to $60 per hour. Factors that influence rates include:

- Which of the thirteen types of work you are performing for the client: Design and analysis pay the highest, but you can also make good money at the maintenance or training level.

- Community size: Rates are higher in metropolitan markets.

- Client size: Rates are higher for large corporations.

- Specialization: Rates vary depending on which industries you serve and which hardware and software you work with.
- Length of project: Some consultants discount for long projects.
- Whether you work through a broker who finds the jobs for you: Brokers who refer you to or place you with clients typically take one-third of the hourly rate.

Bidding a fixed price per job is risky for an inexperienced consultant. A high bid that protects the consultant may scare off a potential client; a low bid can cause heavy losses for the consultant if the project costs exceed estimates.

▣ Potential Earnings

TYPICAL ANNUAL GROSS REVENUES: $37,500 to $75,000, based on billing 25 to 30 hours per week, fifty weeks a year (1,250 to 1,500 hours per year) at $30 to $50 an hour. Many experienced consultants can earn up to $100,000 a year and sometimes as much as $300,000 a year.

OVERHEAD: moderate (20 to 40 percent).

▣ *Best Home Businesses* Estimate of Market Potential

Total number of self-employed computer consultants and programmers in the United States, including home-based businesses: 182,960. The market for consulting services will continue to grow, but this is a competitive market.

▣ Best Ways to Get Business

- Performing market research to identify a range of clients who can use your services, based on your knowledge, expertise, and background.
- Speaking to civic, trade, and professional organizations and writing articles to attach a reputation to your name.
- Getting certified by a vendor or software publisher as an installer or trainer using their system.
- Outreach in a few voluntary activities to get your name around, such as helping people at computer and software user-group meetings and special-interest groups, without expectation of compensation, or answering questions on on-line computer services and local bulletin-board systems, or participating in conversations on on-line services.
- Joining and participating in organizations, such as trade and business associations, particularly in industries or fields in which you have experience, and letting people know what you do.
- Joining or forming a business referral group. Women's organizations can be particularly helpful.

- Going to computer shows and other places where new products are demonstrated.

- Referrals and repeat business from former clients are the best ongoing sources of business. So keeping in contact is vital. One way of accomplishing this is sending newsletters to gatekeepers and former and prospective clients.

First Steps

1. Work as an internal consultant for a large company for a period of time, or offer yourself as a subcontractor to another consultant to help build your name and reputation.

2. Start with either a cash reserve to cover you for eighteen months or a contract in hand that is large enough to cover your overhead and living expenses to the extent that you do not have reserves or a spouse's income.

3. Identify a niche or specialty. Ask yourself, What kinds of problems can I solve, for whom can I solve them, and what platform can I work in (hardware, software, system, function)?

4. Join the Independent Computer Consultants' Association, especially a local chapter. Through contacts there you may be able to get subcontracts or referrals if you have a specialty.

Where to Turn for Information and Help

In addition to the resources below, see also those listed under Computer Programmer and Management Consultant.

ORGANIZATIONS

In addition to the following computer groups (and dozens of others that are local in every state or region), you should also join the associations of the fields in which you work (legal, medical, banking, etc.).

Association of Personal Computer User Groups (APCUG), 1730 M Street, N.W., Suite 700, Washington, DC 20036. To locate a group near you, call (914) 876-6678.

CompuServe, Computer Consultants' Forum. CompuServe, 5000 Arlington Centre Boulevard, P.O. Box 20212, Columbus, OH 43220; (800) 848-8990 or (614) 457-8650; once on-line, type GO CONSULT.

Independent Computer Consultants' Association, 933 Gardenview Office Parkway, St. Louis, MO 63141; (800) 774-4222. The ICCA sponsors the Consult Forum on CompuServe Information Service. The Independent Computer Consultants' Association estimates that there are more than 5,000 home-based computer consultants in this country, with specialties more or less evenly divided among the major subfields.

National Association of Computer Consultant Businesses, 1250 Connecticut Avenue, N.W., Suite 700, Washington, DC 20036; (202) 637-6483.

Institute for Certification of Computer Professionals, 2200 E. Devon Avenue, Suite 268; Des Plaines, IL 60018; (708) 299-4227.

PC or MAC Users Groups, such as the Berkeley Macintosh Users' Group or the Boston Computer Society or the San Francisco PC Users' Group. APCUG (above) can help you locate a PC Users' Group in your city or town; User Group Connection (below) can help you find a MAC group.

Software Publishers Association, 1730 M Street, N.W., #700, Washington, DC 20036-4510; (202) 452-1600.

User Group Connection, P.O. Box 67249, Scott Valley, CA 95067; (408) 461-5700. To locate a nearby MAC users' group, call (800) 538-9696, ext. 500.

NEWSLETTERS

The Consultant and Contractor's Newsletter, 105 N. Main Street, Boonton, NJ 07005; (201) 299-1535.

Khera Business Report, P.O. Box 8043, Gaithersburg, MD 20898-8043; (301) 309-0969. Reports on issues of interest to computer consultants and publishes an annual salary survey.

BOOKS

Computer Consulting on Your Home-Based PC, Herman Holtz, New York: Windcrest/McGraw-Hill, 1993.

The Computer Consultant's Guide: Real Life Strategies for Building a Successful Consulting Career, Janet Ruhl, New York: John Wiley, 1994.

Contract and Fee Setting Guide for Consultants and Professionals, Howard Shenson, New York: John Wiley, 1990.

Diary of a Successful Computer Consultant, Benjamin A. Aminnia, Pointer Corp., 5660 Etiwande Avenue, #5, Tarzana, CA 91356; (800) 468-4322.

Exploring Requirements: Quality Before Design, Donald Gause and Gerald M. Weinberg, New York: Dorset House, 1989.

Handbook of Walkthroughs, Inspections, and Technical Reviews, Daniel P. Freedman and Gerald M. Weinberg, New York: Dorset House, 1990.

How to Be a Successful Computer Consultant, Alan R. Simon, New York: McGraw-Hill, 1990.

Million-Dollar Consulting, Alan Weiss, New York: McGraw-Hill, 1994.

Peopleware: Productive Projects and Teams, Tom DeMarco and Tim Lister, New York: Dorset House, 1987.

The Secrets of Consulting: A Guide to Giving and Getting Advice Successfully,
Gerald M. Weinberg, New York: Dorset House, 1985.

SEMINARS

**How to Start and Build a Profitable Full-time or Part-time Computer
Consulting Business,** one-day seminar offered around the country by
the Center for Consulting and Professional Practices, Division of William Mooney Associates, 19401 South Vermont Avenue, Suite K100,
P.O. Box 6159, Torrance, CA 90504; (213) 321-9342. Bill also provides
one-on-one coaching to help independent consultants attract more and
better clients.

■ ■ ■ ■ ■

COMPUTER PROGRAMMER

Programmers earn their livelihoods preparing step-by-step instructions—
called programs, or software—that a computer follows in order to perform
tasks. Programmers are divided into two categories:

- systems programmers who write programs that tell the computer how to
  carry out its own internal instructions, and
- applications programmers who write programs that solve problems and
  carry out the daily activities of businesses and people, like record keeping
  (databases), word processing, billing, invoicing, flow charting, and a
  wealth of other tasks.

The Bureau of Labor Statistics has identified programming as one of the
fastest-growing occupations. The number of programmers is expected to
grow by 45 percent between 1990 and 2000, amounting to about 250,000
new programmers. And much of this work is going to freelance programmers
because of the downsizing within companies and also the proliferation in the
past ten years of personal computers and off-the-shelf software. Twenty years
ago, in the era of large mainframes, it took a staff of programmers to put
together an application, but today, many jobs can be handled by small one- or
two-person home-based companies that specialize in personal computing
applications programming. In fact, according to Glenn Casteran of Laguna
Vista Systems in Newport Beach, California, much of programming today is
applications programming performed for companies that need to adapt a
commercial package or develop a customized program around the specific
ways their business works.

A programmer will begin much as a consultant (see entry for Computer
Consultant) does, assessing the client's needs and getting an understanding of

the tasks that the client wants the computer to perform. Once the programmer has a full understanding of what has to be done, he or she may have to design, write original code, or modify an existing program to do the job desired. Glenn Casteran points out that many applications today are written using the macro programming languages of either Access, dBase, or FoxPro.

After writing a program and loading it into the client's system, the programmer must also test and implement the program. Programs seldom work the first time, and it can often take hours of trials and analysis to figure out how to make them work without any bugs. In fact, David Lake of Boulder, Colorado, who has been an independent programmer for the past fifteen years, says, "I spend two hours of my time testing for every hour of programming. I hire people to try to break my programs. If they do, I fix it."

It is expected that programming will remain a good business for quite a long time, as the computerization of every aspect of our society has become a de facto standard. Each day brings a new wave of products, devices, and concepts that use computers, and each must be controlled by some kind of program. Dave Bennett, a San Diego programmer, has written dozens of applications over the past few years. He says of this field, "The work is growing more challenging and complex. Windows, Unix, Macintosh, LANs, and OS/2 programming are taking us a geometric step beyond DOS programming."

☑ Knowledge and Skills You Need to Have

- First you need to be able to do computer programming. How much knowledge you need depends on whether you will work with clients who have problems for which you must design solutions or clients who already have solutions in mind and want you to program their solutions. Some routine applications programming can be performed by workers with a high-school education. However, most companies would expect applications programmers, particularly independents, to have some college training or vocational school background. Systems programmers usually have a college degree and a strong knowledge of the computers they work with.

- Working as an independent programmer requires more expertise than you will be able to develop by simply taking a community college course on programming. You need to be able to do more than write code. Most programmers find they must be familiar with the operations of a wide range of hardware and software.

- In addition, Glenn Casteran points out that it helps to have a background in databases, accounting, and general business because so much of a programmer's potential business will revolve around one of these fields. Your business knowledge should also cover the fields in which you are working (medical, legal, industrial, etc.). You must know the procedures of that business and speak the "lingo" so that clients will feel that you understand their needs.

- Ideally you should have two to five years of programming experience so that you know how long it takes to complete jobs and thus tell clients with confidence what you will charge for a finished project.
- Working as an independent programmer requires that you have excellent communication skills and customer service skills. Programmers may be very good, but unless they can speak to their clients in ordinary language, they will not be hired or rehired. You must also know how to treat the client with respect. As Glenn Casteran says, "Don't argue with the client."
- You must be willing to sell yourself and do regular marketing—skills that are sometimes lacking in a computer programmer.
- Finally, you must learn quickly and be ready to keep learning because the computer industry changes very quickly and new technologies (hardware and software) are constantly emerging that you need to know.

■ Start-up Costs

	Low	High
Computer (486 or better) with 8 meg of RAM, large hard disk, and a modem	$1,000	$ 3,000
Network system file server set for at least two computers		3,000
Printer	300	1,600
Communications, compiler, and miscellaneous software	1,700	2,500
On-line services	200	500
Errors and omissions insurance	200	500
Office furniture, especially ergonomic chair	400	1,000
Business cards, letterhead, envelopes	100	600
Magazines, books, and ongoing courses	300	1,000
Total	$3,200	$13,700

■ Advantages

- Programming for personal computers is one of the fastest-growing occupations. Programmers are in demand and are respected as experts.
- You can work your own hours, choose your own projects, and work in a wide variety of fields.
- Programming is a challenge, and it can feel very satisfying to develop a program that makes an entire business work.

■ Disadvantages

- You are often under pressure. As software becomes more powerful, the inherent difficulty of directing computers shifts to programmers, not the user.

- Although it's necessary to specialize in a particular platform (the hardware or operating system that computers run on), uncertainty as to which platforms will be in future demand heightens the risk of your skills becoming obsolete.
- Sometimes the more interesting projects are not the most profitable ones.
- The IRS often regards independent programmers who work on large projects that take months or years to be employees rather than independent contractors. The IRS position has grave tax repercussions for both you and the company that hires you unless you fulfill all requirements to be considered an independent contractor (see our book *Working From Home*, fourth edition).
- As the price of commercial software has come down, many clients experience sticker shock at the cost of custom programming, and so charging what you are worth can cause arguments.
- Some clients will keep changing their minds about how they want the software to work, and so you must make sure your contracts are specific about the design and payments for work. It is best to get "milestone" payments so that a client does not end up owing you thousands of dollars at the end of the project (and not paying it if he or she doesn't like your work).
- You need to market continuously to keep projects coming into your shop.

$ Pricing

According to the Khera Business Report, programming rates range from $25 per hour to $125 per hour, with an average of $54 per hour. Variables include which platform you are working on, the type of work you are doing, and the location.

▣ Potential Earnings

TYPICAL ANNUAL GROSS REVENUES: $50,000 based on billing 1,000 hours (twenty hours per week times fifty weeks per year). Many programmers are able to bill in excess of $100,000 per year.

OVERHEAD: moderate (20 to 40 percent). As a home-based programmer, you need constantly to update your skills through courses and books, as well as by purchasing new hardware items and software products.

▨ *Best Home Businesses* Estimate of Market Potential

Total number of self-employed computer consultants and programmers in the United States, including home-based businesses: 182,960. The market for programmers is good but true self-employment opportunities are clouded by federal and state efforts to classify programmers and other technical personnel as common-law employees instead of independent contractors.

▣ Best Ways to Get Business

- Turning your former employer into a client.
- Assisting people at computer and software user-group meetings and special-interest group sessions, and answering questions on on-line computer services and local bulletin-board systems.
- Making personal contacts in trade and business associations and other organizations, particularly in industries in which you have experience.
- Joining or forming a business referral group.
- Getting referrals from other professional contacts such as business consultants and accountants.
- Teaching classes on programming for businesspeople.
- Getting listed as a consultant for referrals with companies with whose software you work.
- Writing articles or columns about how a computer can make a business more productive.
- Contacting computer stores about what you do. Retail computer stores can be a great source of business. A customer who has taken the initiative to go to a computer retailer is already sold on using a computer but may need custom software (or software customization like spreadsheet models, database applications, and so forth).
- Checking bulletin boards at colleges and universities for companies seeking help.

▣ First Steps

Computer courses are available at most universities and community colleges. There are also many commercial trade schools that teach computer programming. To develop your skills you might consider doing temporary work through technical job shops until you feel you can take on clients on your own. To develop the social skills you need and to market yourself, Dave Bennett suggests you "learn to play golf and then get out on the course with business men and women."

▣ Where to Turn for Information and Help

ORGANIZATIONS

Association of Shareware Professionals, 545 Grover Road, Muskegon, MI 49442.

CompuServe Information Service, 5000 Arlington Centre Boulevard, Columbus, OH 43220; (800) 848-8199. Many forums focus on specific hardware platforms or software applications.

Independent Computer Consultants Association (ICCA), 933 Gardenview Office Parkway, St. Louis, MO 63141; (800) GET-ICCA.

Society for Technical Communications, 901 North Stuart Street, Suite 304, Arlington, VA 22203; (703) 522-4114. The society has local chapters.

Software Management Association, P.O. Box 12004, #297, Vallejo, CA 94590; (707) 643-4423. Association for programmers who do maintenance programming.

Software Publishers Association, 1703 M Street, N.W., #700, Washington DC 20036; (202) 452-1600. If you write software, you may be eligible for membership.

BOOKS

How to Copyright Software, M. J. Salone, Berkeley: Nolo Press, 1990.

The Programmer's Survival Guide, Janet Ruhl, Englewood Cliffs, NJ: Prentice Hall, 1989.

Programming Productivity, Capers Jones, New York: McGraw-Hill, 1990.

The Shareware Book, Robert Schenot, from Compass/New England, P.O. Box 117, Portsmouth, NH 03802-0117.

MAGAZINES AND NEWSLETTERS

Databased Advisor, Clipper Advisor, FoxPro Advisor, Access Advisor, and dBase Advisor, all available from Databased Solutions, 4010 Morene Boulevard, #200, San Diego, CA 92117; (800) 336-6060; (619) 483-6400.

PC Techniques, Coriolis Group, 7721 East Gray Road, #204, Scottsdale, AZ 85260; (800) 410-0192; (602) 483-0192.

✚ Related Business

Shareware Developer

As PC sales mushroomed in the past decade, a new breed of software developer emerged, people who developed utility programs, games, amusements, and even full-scale business software that was distributed at very low cost through third-party distributors and/or over on-line services. Called shareware, this breed of software would usually arrive for free or only a few dollars, and if the user liked the program after thirty days, he or she was requested to mail in $10 to $50 to pay for the program. Shareware was a bargain compared to commercial software. A few shareware programs hit the big time, however, and made their programmers millionaires. Today, as the price of commercial software has dropped, shareware no longer appears to be a huge bargain, but there is still plenty of room in the market for innovative and creative programmers to develop their own games, utilities, and business applications to sell via a number of big shareware distributors, or in retail chains like K-Mart and Wal-Mart, and even via CD-ROM disks. The most lucrative market, according to the Association of Shareware Professionals, is games. This is because programmers give away part of a game at low cost, then withhold the ending or other levels hoping that users will buy the additional programs.

■ ■ ■ ■ ■

COMPUTER REPAIR AND MAINTENANCE

There are over 100 million computers installed in businesses and homes across the United States and Canada. Perhaps the only common fact that applies to every one of them is that they all eventually get dirty and need cleaning. As much as computer owners hate to admit it, our machines simply cannot keep functioning efficiently and without risk unless they are cleaned once or twice per year, or sometimes more often if they are located in a dusty or high-traffic environment. Cleaning actually prolongs the life of a computer, preventing overheating from a malfunctioning fan and dusty disk drives that lose their ability to read or write to diskettes. In some businesses, an uncleaned computer can crash after one or two years, but cleaning could make it survive for five years or more.

Unlike knowing where to take a car for simple maintenance, few computer owners know where to go or how to get their computers repaired or cleaned; and even for those who do know of places to have this work done, it's plainly not convenient to carry or ship a desktop or printer somewhere. This reality is now driving a profitable new business for qualified individuals who have a basic understanding of the inner workings of computers, monitors, printers, and keyboards.

Cleaning, repairing, and maintaining computers is actually not very difficult, according to Lu Howell of *Computer Dust Busters* in Salt Lake City, Utah. The requirements include knowing how to open up the machine swap boards and spray the disk drives and cooling fan with air containing no moisture, as well as how to cleanse the keyboard, printer (laser or dot matrix), and monitor. Little in the way of tools are needed as well: a few screwdrivers, cloths, air sprays, and disk drive cleaning disks. Lu also checks the clock battery and notes down serial numbers on the drives and monitors to help clients keep track of their equipment. All in all, it takes about an hour for two people to perform a cleaning, or two hours for one person.

Despite the simplicity of the business, Howell has been able to develop a full-time business, taking care of the maintenance needs of many businesses in her area. Because Utah requires a license and a commercial storefront to do computer repair (similar to any technical license for working on televisions, VCRs, and other electronic equipment), her home-based company technically cannot do repair, nevertheless Lu finds plenty of business handling the basic needs of preventive maintenance.

In addition, Lu finds that once you are performing maintenance for a client, and they trust your service, they usually ask you to do more for them: backups, software installation, training and tutoring, and even consulting and system purchasing. As a result, some of Lu's maintenance clients have become much bigger accounts for whom she carries out a wide variety of services with larger fees charged by the hour or by the project. One client, for example, has Lu purchase his systems, configure them, and provide computer supplies that she buys at a discount and then marks up. The client is all too happy to pay a premium for Lu's work, knowing that he is getting dedicated service and knowledgeable help. She also became certified by Novell for network installations, which allows her to handle many high-paying jobs. As Lu points out, computer maintenance and repair is thus an excellent entrée into many opportunities for profit in the computer field.

☑ Knowledge and Skills

- One must become comfortable with the insides of computers, their quirks and their connections and interfaces with other computers and the telephone system.

- Being diplomatic and sympathetic with computer users in the face of irrationality is necessary and keeps people calling.

🐘 Start-up Costs

	Low	High
Computer with hard disk and modem	$1,000	$3,000
Fax machine	300	900
Printer	300	1,600
Suite software (mostly word processing)	250	400
Tools, cleaning supplies, diagnostic software	300	500
Spare parts	600	1,000
Office furniture, especially ergonomic chair	400	1,000
Business cards, letterhead, envelopes	100	600
Reference books	100	300
Total	$2,750	$9,300

🔼 Advantages

- As the amount of office technology in homes and offices grows, so does the need for its maintenance and repair.

- Not a desk job, you make money while you're on the go.
- Many problems are solved by swapping boards, so that if you have any aptitude for technical work, you will become proficient quickly.

⬆ Disadvantages

- You may feel pressure because people are apt to communicate a sense of emergency when their systems are down. On the other hand, maintenance can be done at your own pace.
- Although it's probably necessary to specialize in a particular platform or type of equipment, your business will be dependent on the technology you are serving.

⑤ Pricing

Hourly rates range from as low as $20 for beginners and smaller communities to several hundred dollars, but most rates are between $40 and $65 an hour. Some repair services charge for travel time; others do not. Those who charge for travel time either charge their hourly rate "port to port" or a flat fee for a service call. With experience in knowing how long a repair will take, it's possible to charge by the job, which is favored by many customers.

ⒸPotential Earnings

TYPICAL ANNUAL GROSS REVENUES: $75,000 based on billing thirty hours per week, fifty weeks per year, averaging $50 per hour.

OVERHEAD: low (20 percent or less).

⑦ *Best Home Businesses* **Estimate of Market Potential**

Having more technology in our homes and businesses means having more things to be maintained and repaired. Some technology, like TV sets and consumer telephones, people throw away rather than fix. But when people and businesses encounter problems with tools like computers, printers, fax machines, and copy machines, the question is more likely to be "How soon can we get this fixed?" On-site repair of customer equipment offers the advantages of timely service and convenience over taking or mailing a product in, and as long as there's a cost advantage over buying a new one, the outlook is rosy for computer repair.

🏪 Best Ways to Get Business

- The most effective method of getting business is word of mouth. The value of this kind of marketing is that maintenance is still something that many people don't think about, but all it takes is one crash or burnout for a business to realize that taking care of their computers and backing up their data are absolute requirements. Each satisfied customer is therefore a walking advertisement for you and will likely refer many others to your business.

■ To get your first customers, print up plenty of business cards and leave them in office buildings, computer stores, and other locations where businesspeople may see them.

■ Yellow-page advertising. Research shows that people needing computer repair frequently turn to the yellow pages.

■ Teach computer classes and seminars, even if for free, to enable people to become aware of your expertise. Adult-education programs, however, will usually pay you.

⊞ Related Business

Backup Service

If you are a technically oriented, computer-literate person, and especially if you already run a computer-related business such as consulting, repair, or training, you can earn extra money by running a remote backup service for your small-business clients. This means that you don't even have to go to your clients' offices. All your work is done automatically over the phone lines using the clients' computers, your computer, and modems. Such a service is usually not a stand-alone business but a profitable adjunct to an existing practice. A resource for starting a backup service is *The RBS Book: How to Start and Operate a Remote Backup Data Service,* by Rob Cosgrove, Precision Data Corporation, 654 South White Station, Memphis, TN 38117; (800) 833-4732; (901) 682-0732. This is a package that includes the software to run a backup service plus seventy shareware programs for file and network maintenance.

⊞ First Steps

The best way to get into the business is simply to gain experience maintaining computers. Once you feel comfortable and know what you are doing, you are ready to set up your business.

Determine if you need a state license. Perhaps, during the course of qualifying for a license, you can farm out business you generate to a licensed repair shop with whom you have an arrangement to share in the fees or work under its license.

▢ Where to Turn for Information and Help

BOOKS

Effective PC Networking, Steve Heath, Stoneham, MA: Butterworth-Heinemann, 1993.

Servicing Personal Computers, Michael Tooley, Stoneham, MA: Butterworth-Heinemann, 1993.

Repairing PCs: An Illustrated Guide, Michael F. Hordeski, Blue Ridge Summit, PA: McGraw-Hill, 1994.

Start Your Own PC Repair Business, Linda Rohrbough and Michael Hordeski, Blue Ridge Summit, PA: McGraw-Hill, 1995.

MAGAZINES

The *Computer Shopper,* 1 Park Avenue, 11th Floor, New York, NY 10016; (800) 274-6384. Filled with information on prices of computers and their components, this is a large-format publication widely available on newsstands.

Processor, P.O. Box 85518, Lincoln, NE 65801; (800) 334-7443. A traderlike magazine, it's a source for new equipment and parts. *Computer Hotline,* 15400 Knoll Trail Drive, Suite 500, Dallas, TX 75248; (800) 866-3241. Also a traderlike publication, it's helpful in finding used supplies and equipment.

Service Support Magazine, 12416 Hymeadow Drive, Austin, TX 78750; (512) 250-9023.

COURSE

McGraw-Hill, NRI Schools offers a home-study course in microcomputers and microprocessors that prepares individuals to repair computers. It includes a computer and diagnostic hardware and software. 4401 Connecticut Avenue, N.W., Washington, DC 20008; (202) 244-1600. Cost: $2595.

Upgrading and Repairing PCs Quick Reference, Scott Mueller, Carmel, IN: Que, 1994.

■ ■ ■ ■ ■

COMPUTER TUTOR

Just as driver education has become the standard way to prepare new drivers to operate motor vehicles, computer tutoring has become established as the way for people to learn how to use computers and the software programs written for them. Although there are many computer training programs available in community colleges and commercial facilities, independent computer tutors have an advantage because they can take the training to their clients and customize it to their needs. Also, many people prefer individual instruction, which allows them to learn at their own pace.

Both businesses and individuals hire computer tutors. Computer tutors generally work at the client's office or home, teaching in classroom style or doing one-on-one coaching. Sometimes they go into a company to help an entire office automate: they assist in setting up the computer systems to do what the business needs to have done and then teach the employees to use both the hardware and software. Increasingly, as companies upgrade their software or switch from one software package to another, they need computer tutors to help employees make the transition.

Some successful tutors specialize in working with particular occupations or particular software applications, such as legal or accounting programs. In these situations, tutors must have expertise in both the software itself and the ways in which the software is used in that specific occupation.

Jan Berinstein, for example, teaches WordPerfect with an emphasis on law offices and legal applications, such as formatting litigation documents. She works with both individuals and groups, offering private lessons, corporate training, and adult-education classes to legal secretaries and paralegals in the Los Angeles area. "My background in legal word processing has been a real asset," she says, "and because I have a specialty, I have a built-in market for my services." She gets much of her business through referrals, but she recommends advertising in legal newspapers, accounting journals, medical newsletters, etc. A less-expensive method of advertising is to produce a newsletter filled with tips and interesting tidbits. Berinstein periodically sends brief newsletters to everyone she can think of—business associates, existing clients, and acquaintances.

A computer tutor must be generally computer literate and highly proficient in at least one software package, such as a specific popular word-processing or spreadsheet package. A tutor must also keep up with developments in both hardware and software, and be able to communicate well with people. The latter is particularly important, Berinstein says, because "inexperienced computer users may not know how to ask a question in such a way as to elicit the information they want. If you don't listen carefully to their questions and don't take time to give thoughtful answers, they will become frustrated."

Other good markets for computer tutors include the medical field and the construction industry. Alternatively, some trainers prefer to promote themselves as generalists. They learn multiple software packages in an effort to reach as wide a client base as possible.

☑ Knowledge and Skills You Need to Have

- To be a computer tutor, you must be able to operate a personal computer and have a thorough knowledge of at least one software program that an ample number of people need to learn. Some software manufacturers will even train and certify you to teach their software. Some of these courses are free; others charge a hefty fee. Once you are certified, the software publisher may even refer business to you, so becoming certified is probably to your advantage. Also, you may be able to deduct the cost of the training from your income taxes.

- You need to be familiar with whatever field you decide to work in so that when clients ask questions about how to use the software to do their work, you will understand what they're talking about and be able to answer in a way that makes sense to them.
- Computer tutors need good communication skills in order to listen to and interpret students' needs.
- Good presentation skills and the ability to communicate directions and technical information in simple, clear, and concise language are important.
- You need to have patience with novice computer users as they learn. They may make repeated mistakes, ask obvious questions, and often need ample encouragement and reassurance.
- You should have sufficient writing skills to prepare correspondence, proposals, documentation, training materials, and curricula.

■ Start-up Costs

	Low	High
Computer with hard disk (as good a computer as clients have)	$1,500	$ 2,500
Laser printer	650	1,600
Software necessary to serve your customers' needs (some software companies will give you free software or a special discounted consultant/ trainer price)	500	2,000
Training cost to become certified for the software programs you teach	500	4,000
Modem	100	600
Fax	400	1,000
Office furniture, including a table for assembling training materials	500	800
Comb binding machine for your training materials	200	550
Business cards, letterhead, envelopes	200	600
Customized brochure and/or presentation folder	100	2,000
Organizational dues	250	250
Total	$4,200	$15,900

■ Advantages

- Responding to the varied requests of clients provides a challenge and keeps the work interesting.
- Helping people to become more productive and develop confidence in using technology is satisfying.
- You're learning all the time because you need to keep pace with the cutting edge of technology and new updates of the hardware or software you teach.

- Tutoring and training can be a good step to other forms of computer consulting and get you entrée to a larger contract doing software installations or needs analysis for a company wanting to expand its use of computers.

ⁱ⁻ Disadvantages

- You must deal with people's resistance to technology and to change.
- People's egos become involved when learning something new, so sometimes you must work with those who don't want to be in a student role and who don't like someone else telling them what to do or knowing more than they do.
- This has become a competitive business, so you must stand out and specialize.

$ Pricing

Hourly tutoring fees range from $25 to $60. Don't be surprised, however, to find hobbyists offering to tutor individuals for as low as $10 an hour. To command professional prices you must target your market and take your work and yourself seriously.

Price workshops so that clients perceive a savings in what it would cost their employees to learn on their own. A fee can be calculated at somewhat less than the employees' rate of pay multiplied by the time it takes to train them. For example, if employees earn $15 an hour and your program is four hours long, you might charge $50 per student.

▣ Potential Earnings

TYPICAL ANNUAL GROSS REVENUES: $36,750 to $63,000, based on training three days a week, fifty weeks a year, at $35 to $60 per hour ($245 to $420 per day).

OVERHEAD: low (less than 20 percent). Primary expenses are telephone and office supplies.

⁊ *Best Home Businesses* **Estimate of Market Potential**

As software prices continue to decline, software publishers are making documentation briefer and charging for customer support. Although software is becoming easier to use, we think these factors favor the continuing use of computer tutors.

ⁿ Best Ways to Get Business

- Give speeches at business meetings and associations about the benefits of computerizing using the software you are familiar with. This is the fastest, cheapest, and easiest method to help people understand how your training can help them.

- Get certified or licensed by, and listed to get referrals from, the software company whose packages you teach.

- Solicit referrals from manufacturers, resellers, suppliers, and consultants who serve the same types of companies you work with.

- Network and make personal contacts through the professional, trade, or business associations of the field in which you are specializing.

- Sometimes, as in the legal field, you cannot join the professional association and therefore you must network through civic or other business organizations. You can also network in computer and software user groups; manufacturers can direct you to user groups in your area.

- Send direct mail advertising to companies that have purchased particular software packages. Their names are sometimes available, listed by zip code, from software vendors. Without such a highly qualified list, direct mail is too expensive.

- Provide a quarterly newsletter highlighting information about software upgrades, user tips, and new equipment to past, present, and potential customers and everyone else you meet who could refer business to you.

- Ask satisfied clients for referrals to others who need training. Offer free or discounted advice to potential clients—for example, help solve people's software problems over the phone. "Creating goodwill is very important for small businesses," says Jan Berinstein. "Even if there is no immediate payoff, people remember you and eventually refer others to you."

- Advertise in computer publications or specialized trade publications for your target market, such as a legal journal or magazine.

First Steps

Doing computer tutoring is like speaking a foreign language—you can't fake it. Therefore you must have a solid knowledge of the software packages and equipment you will be training others to use. If you are a computer user now, begin by teaching the programs you know well, or spend some time polishing up and deepening your knowledge of the programs you will be teaching. Often training and licensing to teach a package are available from the software manufacturer.

Select a market that you will specialize in (for example, law firms, construction companies, small businesses, medical or dental offices). Your niche should be in a field in which you are knowledgeable and comfortable, and which you enjoy. If possible, specialize in marketing your services to a field in which you have been working. Survey that field to identify what people like and dislike about using computers.

If you must enter a field with which you are not familiar, volunteer to do a project for a company in the field of your choice in exchange for your learning the ins and outs and special needs of that field. Take ample time on that first project to learn as much as you can by observing and asking questions. If possible, join and become active in the professional or trade associations in the field and subscribe to publications in the field.

▣ Where to Turn for Information and Help

ORGANIZATIONS

Association of Personal Computer User Groups (APCUG), 1730 M Street, N.W., Suite 700, Washington, DC 20036. To locate a group near you, call (914) 876-6678.

Computer Training Forum on CompuServe. The Computer Training Forum is a special interest group of computer trainers who communicate through their computers. GO DPTRAIN is the on-line address of this forum. Contact CompuServe Information Service, 5000 Arlington Centre Boulevard, Box 20212, Columbus, OH 43220; (800) 848-8199 or (614) 457-0802.

PC or MAC Users' Groups, such as the Berkeley Macintosh Users Group, the Boston Computer Society, or the San Francisco PC Users Group. APCUG can help you locate a PC Users' Group in your city or town; A User's Group Connection can help you find a MAC group.

Ziff Institute, which offers over 140 seminars, panels, and case studies, is at 25 First Street, Cambridge, MA 02141; (800) 34-TRAIN.

BOOKS

The Computer Train Handbook: How to Teach People to Use Computers, The Masie Center, 75 Cambridge Parkway, Suite PH3, Cambridge, MA 02142; (800) 95MASIE.

Computer Training Manuals; a Researcher's Workbook: A Reference, Training Manuals, Research Division Staff, Denver: Prosperity & Profits, 1993.

See also books listed under Corporate Trainer.

NEWSLETTERS

The Micro Computer Trainer, 606 Ninth Street, Box 2487, Secaucus, NJ 07096-2487; (201) 330-8923. A monthly newsletter offering practical solutions and strategies for the microcomputer training professional.

FRANCHISES

COMPUTOTS, Box 408, Great Falls, VA 22066; (703) 759-2556. Franchisees teach computer classes to preschool children at private schools and day-care centers. In business since 1983; franchise fee is $15,000.

■ ■ ■ ■ ■

COPYWRITER

Companies, retail stores, and organizations often have a need to describe their products and services in written materials that represent them to the world. The copy in advertising, direct mail, brochures, and newsletters not only needs to be written clearly and concisely, but also must capture attention, impress, inspire trust, and motivate the reader to buy or to call for further information. Rarely do small-business owners have the time, talent, or know-how to prepare these materials themselves, however. And often they can't afford to employ a full-time copywriter to do it for them. So instead they turn to freelance professional copywriters.

Copywriters prepare copy for a wide variety of materials: ads, brochures, instruction manuals, grant proposals, press releases, media kits, feature stories, ghostwritten magazine articles, TV and radio spots, catalogues, company names and slogans, consumer-information booklets, captions for photographs, product literature, annual reports, product names and packaging labels, marketing communication plans, speeches, telemarketing scripts, video scripts, and storyboards. Their clients include major corporations, doctors and lawyers, small manufacturers, automotive dealers, retail stores, hotels, restaurants, banks, health clubs, consumer electronics firms, and direct-mail catalogues.

Versatility can be a real plus in this business, but more and more copywriters are developing their own niche. Rosalind Sedacca, for example, is a freelance copywriter based in West Palm Beach, Florida, whose business focuses on television and radio scripts, sales letters, brochures, and newsletters. Recently, she has begun to specialize further, producing marketing materials for business consultants, professional trainers, and booking agents. The sales brochures and training materials she writes help her clients land important accounts. Like many other copywriters, she works closely with graphic designers to put together a complete package that her clients can use to promote their businesses.

Bob Bly, a prolific copywriter based in New Jersey, does a variety of different works, from ads to brochures to direct-mail copy. He enjoys the writing, likes having a flexible work schedule, and earns a good living. In fact, he says he makes more money than he could make in a staff job. But he feels some pressure trying to meet deadlines—which he says are shorter today than they were ten years ago—and working on multiple projects at once. Bly, whose numerous publications include several books, reports, and monographs targeted to other writers, gets most of his business as a direct result of his books. He also does some advertising and other forms of promotion, gives seminars, and produces audiocassettes about marketing. He has this advice for people who want to start a copywriting career: "If it doesn't sound too immodest, read my book, *Secrets of a Freelance Writer*."

☑ Knowledge and Skills You Need to Have

A strong background in English and communications is necessary. In addition, the following skills are needed:

- the ability to write clear, interesting, arresting, and compelling copy.
- curiosity about how something works and a sense of what makes something appealing, unique, better, interesting, beneficial, and so on.
- creativity, and in particular, the imagination to say something in a way that hasn't been said before.
- the self-discipline to overcome writer's block and to see a project through even when ideas don't flow readily.
- the willingness to market yourself and your services by networking, by direct mail, and by writing articles about your specialty.
- a logical, organized mind that can assimilate information, synthesize it, and integrate it into a theme or message.
- the ability to visualize the layout of a printed page and work closely with graphic designers.

🐂 Start-up Costs*

	Low	High
Computer with hard disk, modem, and possibly a CD-ROM	$1,000	$3,000
Fax machine	300	900
Ink-jet or laser printer	300	1,600
Suite software with spell checking, grammar checking, and thesaurus features	250	400
Desktop publishing software	100	500
Office furniture, especially an ergonomic chair	400	1,000
Business cards, letterhead, envelopes	100	600
Dictionaries, general word books, and CD-ROM disks for reference	100	300
Total	$2,550	$8,300

* Other items you may want to have are a scanner, a small copier, and membership in a few on-line services.

📋 Advantages

- There is no fixed schedule for this work. You can do it anytime you want with the exception of meetings on clients' schedules.
- This is creative work—taking plain, even dull information and creating something original through your writing and creative talents.
- You have the opportunity to try out your ideas and discover how your work influences people.

■ This work is concrete and finite. When you finish a project, you have something in your hands that didn't exist before.

🖻 Disadvantages

■ Frequently you will need to work under the pressure of tight deadlines.

■ Nonwriters don't appreciate how long it takes to write, and so pricing your service appropriately is sometimes difficult.

■ To be successful, you have to work on and juggle several projects at once, which can be stressful.

■ The actual copywriting is something you must do alone.

■ You may come up against a wall because the subject is difficult to write about, or you cannot find a new idea to fit into your campaign.

💲 Pricing

Prices for copywriting are very regional. You can charge by the hour, by the day, or by the job.

By the hour.   Fees can range from $10 an hour for a novice to over $150 an hour for speechwriters, with average fees running from $40 to $75 an hour for professionals with some experience.

By the day.   Fees for consulting on a direct-mail project range from $1,500 to $2,000 a day.

By the job.   Fees range from $2,000 to $7,000 for a direct-mail package, $2,000 to $4,000 for a sales letter, $1,000 to $2,000 for a radio script. When you bid by the job, you work on an estimate of your total time, so to price the job you need to have records of your hours spent on projects over the years so that you will know how much time a job will take you and price it accordingly.

🖳 Potential Earnings

Robert W. Bly, the author of *The Copywriter's Handbook,* has surveyed attendees at his workshops in cities across the country. He has found that people who approach copywriting as a business typically earn:

■ $20,000 to $40,000 a year during their first two years, which he calls phase I

■ $40,000 to $80,000 a year during what he calls phase II

■ $80,000 to $175,000 a year when they become real pros during phase III, which often occurs in three to five years.

OVERHEAD: low (20 percent or less).

📈 *Best Home Businesses* Estimate of Market Potential

Copywriting is another field that should be expanding with the dramatic growth of small businesses.

📇 Best Ways to Get Business

- Talking to former clients or employers and businesspeople you know or meeting and showing them samples of your work. Send samples to them and let them know what you really do at a level they understand.
- Networking in organizations, such as trade and business associations, particularly in industries or fields in which you have experience.
- Developing affiliations with related professionals like marketing consultants, graphic designers, desktop publishers, newsletter publishers, photographers, and printers who can refer business to you.
- At the conclusion of a successful project, ask for a reference letter you can use in talking with prospective clients.
- Dropping off samples of your work at the offices of other businesses in your clients' office buildings, or business centers, indicating that you work for their neighbor and would like them to see a sample of what you do.

👣 First Steps

1. Take courses offered by local writers' groups, extension programs, colleges, and universities.
2. Join special-interest sections of writers' groups that meet to read their material to one another and compare notes.
3. Develop a look for your own business card and letterhead that is an advertisement of what you can do for others.
4. Join an organization of people who can refer you to clients—for example, printers, graphic designers, photographers, or marketing consultants. Also join associations in the fields you might typically be working in.
5. Create a portfolio of at least five samples to show clients.
6. Read books and go to writers' workshops. Never assume you're done learning.

📋 Where to Turn for Information and Help

ORGANIZATIONS

American Advertising Federation, 1101 Vermont Avenue, N.W., Suite 500, Washington DC 20005; (800) 999-2231; (202) 898-0089, fax (202) 898-0159. Parent organization for many local Ad Clubs or Ad Federations. Look in your telephone directory for your local affiliate; sponsors meetings, workshops, and competitions.

American Marketing Association, 250 South Wacker Drive, Chicago, IL 60606; (312) 648-0536.

Direct Marketing Association, 11 West 42d Street, 25th Floor, New York, NY 10036; (212) 768-7277.

Editorial Freelancers' Association, 71 West 23d Street, Suite 1504, New York NY 10010 (open 2–6 P.M., M–F); (212) 929-5400, fax (212) 929-5439. Membership organization offering a bimonthly newsletter, membership directory, rates survey, job phone, meetings, courses, a variety of publications, and insurance. Some benefits require a fee in addition to the basic membership dues.

BOOKS

Breakthrough Advertising: How to Write Ads That Shatter Traditions and Sales Records, Eugene Schwartz, New York: Boardroom Books, 1984.

The Copywriter's Handbook, Robert W. Bly, New York: Henry Holt and Company, 1990.

How to Make $50,000 a Year or More as a Free-Lance Business Writer, Paul D. Davis, Rocklin, CA: Prima Publishing, 1992.

How to Make Your Advertising Make Money, John Caples, Englewood Cliffs, NJ: Prentice Hall, 1986.

Looking Good in Print: A Guide to Basic Design for Desktop Publishing, Roger C. Parker, Chapel Hill, NC: Ventana Press, 1988.

Scientific Advertising and My Life in Advertising, Claude Hopkins, Chicago: Crane Books, 1966.

Secrets of a Freelance Writer: How to Make Eighty-five Thousand Dollars a Year, Robert W. Bly, New York: Henry Holt and Company, 1990.

Tested Advertising Methods, John Caples, Englewood Cliffs, NJ: Prentice Hall, 1986.

Words That Sell, Richard Bayan, Chicago: Contemporary Books, 1987. A classic.

Write Great Ads: A Step-by-Step Approach, Erica Levy Klein, New York: Wiley, 1990.

Writer's Profit Catalogue, 22 East Quackenbush Avenue, 3d Floor, Dumont, NJ 07628; (201) 385-1220. This catalogue is a listing of dozens of books, pamphlets, and audio tapes produced by noted copywriter Bob Bly.

MAGAZINES AND NEWSLETTERS

Creative Business, 275 Newbury Street, Boston, MA 02116; (617) 424-1368. Published ten times per year, this newsletter is directed at copywriters, designers, art directors, and principals of creative businesses. Subscribers also receive free unlimited telephone consultation. Founded by Cameron Foote, who also gives Creative Business Workshops around the country for people in creative businesses.

The Direct Response Specialist, Stilson and Stilson, Box 1075, Tarpon Springs, FL 34688; (813) 786-1411. Monthly selling by direct mail and direct-response advertising. Useful source of knowledge for writing copy that will sell.

Freelance Writer's Report, Maple Ridge Road, North Sandwich, NH 03259; (603) 284-6367. Monthly newsletter of market news and tips on marketing and managing a freelance writing business more effectively.

Writer's Digest Magazine, 1507 Dana Avenue, Cincinnati, OH 45207; (513) 531-2222.

SOFTWARE

The increasing availability of CD-ROM with reference material for writing will be a boon to writers. Writers will be able to find quotes instantly, look up rules of usage, and so forth. Software that you can run on your hard disk is already available, such as:

Writer's Dreamtools, Slippery Disks, Box 1126, Los Angeles, CA 90069. Lists by day and date thousands of birthdays and historical events, the feast days of every saint, and holidays around the world; there's also space for users to add their own information. *Clichés and Catch Phrases* lists more than 12,500 clichés and catch phrases. *Slang Thesaurus* provides words that meet all your criteria, neatly organized by part of speech. Mail order only. $35 each or $79 for all three.

■ ■ ■ ■ ■

DESKTOP PUBLISHER

"If you have a background in the design field or are willing to work hard and learn how to design using desktop publishing software on a personal computer, you can start a home-based desktop publishing business," says Heidi Waldman, a home-based desktop publisher in St. Paul, Minnesota.

Desktop publishing, often referred to as *DTP*, grew out of enhancements to word-processing software that, little by little, have made it possible for almost anyone equipped with a computer and a high-resolution laser printer to prepare professional-looking printed materials for clients of all sizes. Today desktop publishing eliminates many steps in the process of preparing printed materials; pages no longer need to be pasted up and typeset, for example. The desktop publisher uses a personal computer and desktop publishing software to replace the services once provided by a layout artist, typesetting service, color separator, and even printer.

According to Noel Ward, editor in chief of *Desktop Publishing Journal*, as of the mid-1990s there are about three million desktop publishers nationwide. That figure includes people who publish brochures and catalogues, art directors, and others. As the technology becomes more and more affordable, the number of desktop publishers will continue to grow.

The market for desktop publishing is extensive, including large companies, nonprofit organizations, government agencies, and other small home-based businesses. Organizations of all kinds need material for both their internal and their external communications, from memos and papers, to training manuals, annual reports, quarterly journals, and sales/promotional brochures and ads. Since the arrival of desktop publishing in 1985, a crudely typed and photocopied price list, contract, newsletter, or bulletin is no longer acceptable. Now proposals, flyers, forms, newsletters, reports, and presentation materials of all types are expected to look good and be produced quickly.

Desktop publishing has significant advantages over traditional publishing: production time is shortened, changes are not difficult or expensive to make, and, of course, overall cost is lower. Desktop publishing has an advantage over word processing, too. Even word-processing programs that have desktop publishing capabilities are limited in their ability to develop complex designs, and they don't have a full range of typographic controls. And simple desktop publishing software is available for as little as $50—although for professional-quality output, you will have to pay considerably more (see below).

The Aldus Corporation, producers of *Pagemaker*, one of the leading desktop publishing programs, has identified 350 different types of documents that are being created by using desktop publishing. Many desktop publishers today specialize by serving different sizes or types of clients or by offering specialized desktop publishing applications such as newsletter and directory publishing. The work can be done at home, but someone skilled in desktop publishing can also work on-site for companies.

Some desktop publishers take on any work that comes their way, but others serve only certain industries or work on selected types of documents— newsletters, proposals, books, or directories. You can specialize still further by doing only newsletters for law firms or catalogues for mail-order craft companies, for example. The possibilities are limited only by your imagination.

☑ Knowledge and Skills You Need to Have

- You need to have good computer skills and a knowledge of certain technology (like scanners) as well as the ability to learn in depth the use of desktop publishing software, which is becoming more sophisticated these days.

- You should have a feel for design and typography, plus an ability to write and edit other people's writing. Lawrence Miller, a designer who operates Daddy Desktop, points out that "too many desktop publishers can't write. They mistake typing for writing. They also can't design. They mistake the tools for the ability. It is possible, and desirable, to learn to design and write well, but you won't learn it in a software manual. It's a process of being aware of what you want to do, studying, and doing, taking courses and doing some more."

- You need to be able to read standard editing symbols, because clients may use them in marking up copy for changes and corrections.

- Good communications skills are a must, both to get business and to draw out of clients what their objectives are. Often visual concepts are difficult to articulate clearly. You must help them do that.

- You should know or be willing to learn about typesetting, layout, and printing practices and procedures. One reason for this is so that you can estimate your own time to design and lay out a piece when you bid on projects.

- Finally, you also need patience because clients often change their minds once they see something in print.

■ Start-up Costs

	Low	High
Macintosh or IBM-compatible computer with large hard disk and full-page monitor	$2,500	$ 6,000
Laser printer (high-resolution)	1,600	6,000
Desktop publishing, word-processing, and drawing software and fonts	2,000	3,500
Color scanner	400	800
Fax (required for fast turnaround approvals)	300	800
Two-line telephone	100	200
Office furniture, especially an ergonomic chair	400	1,000
Business cards, letterhead, envelopes	100	600
Direct-mail advertising followed up with telephone calls	500	2,500
Organizational dues	250	250
Total	$8,150	$21,650

■ Advantages

- The work is interesting and creative. People who dreamed of doing design work can now do it with desktop publishing.

- Desktop publishing is a rapidly growing field, and if you market aggressively, you can earn a large wage for your efforts.

- There is ample opportunity to develop new skills including newsletter publishing, copywriting, and advertising-agency and multimedia services.

Disadvantages

- The field is increasingly competitive. In order to stay profitable, you need to market your services energetically—which can be time-consuming—and find a way to distinguish yourself from your competition.
- You are often working under the pressure of deadlines, and sometimes you'll have to work nights and weekends.
- There is a constant demand to keep current with the latest advances in software.
- Unless you take necessary precautions, you risk developing repetitive-motion injuries as a result of constant keyboarding.

Pricing

Desktop publishers may charge by the hour, by the page, or by the job.

By the hour. Typical hourly prices range between $25 and $65, up to $90 for color work. Heidi Waldman points out that "in a metropolitan area, a desktop publishing business is not going to survive charging under $40 an hour."

By the page. Typical prices range between $25 and $50; again, prices are higher for color.

By the job. Pricing by the job involves estimating how many hours the job will take and allowing a fudge factor for corrections and changes. This method of pricing is popular, because many clients prefer to pay a fixed price.

In addition, some desktop publishers charge an extra fee for higher-quality output. For example, a typical charge for a 1,270-dots-per-inch Linotronic is $12 per page; for film, $15 per page.

Potential Earnings

TYPICAL ANNUAL GROSS REVENUES: $40,000 based on four billable hours a day at $40 per hour. If you are in a major metropolitan area, you can probably charge $50 per hour or more; hourly rates are normally higher for color work. Earnings may be increased by offering additional services, such as pickup and delivery, extra-fast turnaround time, high-quality printing, and a wider variety of font types.

OVERHEAD: moderate (20 to 40 percent).

⚡ *Best Home Businesses* Estimate of Market Potential

Total number of desktop publishing firms in the United States, including home-based businesses: 23,176. Desktop publishing is past its period of rapid expansion. We project future growth in specialty areas and in parts of the country where people from urban areas are relocating.

📖 Best Ways to Get Business

- Directly soliciting print shops, small service and retail businesses, professional practices, and nonprofit organizations with a portfolio of your work.

- Networking in publishing and desktop publishing organizations, as well as leads from clubs and chambers of commerce. Contact mail list services too, as they often have stores that want to do mailings but do not have the ability to produce a nice flyer or brochure.

- Using direct mail in the form of a letter, a sales flyer, or an introductory brochure sent to a specific market in larger cities or, in smaller communities, to businesses that advertise in the yellow pages and in newspapers.

- Following up these mailings with a personal phone call in which you ask for an appointment, to which you bring samples, perhaps customized for the prospective customer's business.

- Phoning and then writing companies that have placed help-wanted ads seeking graphic-arts personnel to do their backup or overflow work.

- Advertising in the yellow pages.

- Placing three- to five-line ads in local publications, particularly computer publications, in which you provide specific information about your operation such as the software you use, the output you can offer, and so forth.

- Offering a discount with the first job—for instance, one hour free with a minimum two-hour job.

🕐 First Steps

1. If you have no experience in the graphic-design field, you need to take several courses in design, such as those available from continuing-education programs, community colleges, colleges and universities, and art schools.

2. Learn about working with service bureaus and printers.

3. Learn to use desktop publishing software and relating drawing programs. Courses are available from computer schools, continuing-education programs, and desktop publishing divisions of art schools.

4. If you have experience, do market research to find a specialty market not being served before you acquire the expensive software and equipment needed for desktop publishing.

🖸 Where to Turn for Information and Help

ORGANIZATIONS

Association of Desktop Publishers, 4507 30th Street, Suite 800, San Diego, CA 92116; (619) 563-9714. International association; publishes a newsletter, reviews hardware and software and negotiates discounts for its members. Membership: $125 per year.

Desktop Publishing Forum, CompuServe Information Service, 5000 Arlington Centre Blvd., Columbus, OH 43220; (800) 848-8199. Once online, enter "GO DTPFORUM."

Graphic Artists Guild, 11 West 20th Street, New York, NY 10011; (212) 463-7759.

National Association of Desktop Publishers, 462 Old Boston Street, Topsfield, MA 01983; (508) 887-7900. Publishes a monthly magazine. To join, call (508) 887-2246.

Special-interest groups of computer and software users in your area can be of value also.

BOOKS

Create Your Own Desktop Publishing System, Harley Bjelland, New York: Windcrest/McGraw-Hill, 1994; (800) 822-8158. Provides help in selecting hardware components of a desktop publishing system.

Desktop Publishing as a Business, Heidi Waldman, White Bird Press, Box 11881, St. Paul, MN 55111.

Desktop Publishing by Design, Ronnie Shusan and Don Wright, Redmond, WA: Microsoft Press, 1989. Available in both Pagemaker and Ventura editions.

Desktop Publishing: Dollars and Sense, Scott R. Anderson. Hillsboro, OR: Blue Heron Publishing, 1992.

Desktop Publishing Success, Felix Kramer and Maggie Lovaas. Homewood, IL: Business One Irwin, 1991.

Handbook of Pricing and Ethical Guidelines, Graphic Artists Guild. North Light Books, 1507 Dana Avenue, Cincinnati, OH 45207-1056; (513) 531-2222; 1987.

No Sweat Desktop Publishing, Steve Morgenstern, New York: AMACOM Books, 1992.

Owning and Managing a Desktop Publishing Business, Dan Ramsey, Dover, NH: Upstart Press, 1994.

Pricing Guide for Desktop Publishing Services, Brenner Information Group, 9282 Samantha Court, San Diego, CA 92129. $49 plus $3 shipping and handling.

Roger Black's Desktop Design Power, Roger Black. New York: Bantam, 1991.

If you're interested in adding to your library regularly, there is a Graphic Artist's Book Club, P.O. Box 12526, Cincinnati, OH 45212-0526; (800) 937-0963.

MAGAZINES

Adobe Font and Function. Call (800) 83-FONTS for a subscription. Free.

How Magazine, F&W Publications, 1507 Dana Avenue, Cincinnati, OH 45207; (513) 531-2222. Emphasizes business aspects of graphic design.

Personal Publishing, The Renegade Company, Box 390, Itasca, IL 60143.

Publish! PC World Communications, 501 Second Street, San Francisco, CA 94107; (800) 234-3498; (415) 243-0500.

Step by Step, Dynamic Graphics, 6000 North Forest Park Drive, Peoria, IL 61614.

NEWSLETTERS

Before and After, Pagelab, 331 J Street, Suite 150, Sacramento, CA 95814. Tips on designing newsletters.

COURSES

Desktop Publishing and Design, NRI School of Home-Based Businesses, McGraw-Hill Continuing Education, 4401 Connecticut Avenue, N.W., Washington, DC 20008. This at-home study course includes a computer, software, mouse, printer, and lessons in both design and operating a desktop publishing business.

■ ■ ■ ■ ■

DESKTOP VIDEO

Desktop video, often called DTV, is a term that signifies the application of computers to produce video films. DTV is highly related to a multimedia service (see separate entry on Multimedia Service) but focuses more exclusively on producing videos rather than CD-ROM disks. In the same way that multimedia uses computer technology to integrate animation, photos, music, sound, and video footage, DTV pertains to similar processes for editing, animating, and creating a finished videotape.

DTV is not a single business but, in reality, three possible business opportunities:

■ Desktop editing, in which a DTV service edits video footage at much lower costs than a traditional video production studio can. DTV services can use computers to cut, paste, and edit footage in the right sequence, add sound, and perform many sophisticated editing tasks such as fades, wipes, animation overlays, and titles.

- Desktop authoring, in which a DTV service uses a special software authoring system to create an interactive presentation that combines video with sound, animation, photos, and other images. (This area is perhaps closest to multimedia, but the final product is video footage.)

- Desktop animation, in which a DTV service uses the power of computers (rather than dozens of costly animators) to create animated footage using many special software products that allow you to create graphics, draw your own artwork, "morph" photos (making an image turn into another image), and many more techniques.

Each of these businesses is distinct, but all can be applied to any number of purposes. Harvey Summers, author of **Operating a Desktop Video Service on Your Home-Based PC**, points out that the applications of DTV include:

1. *Event videographer:* This service uses camcorders to film weddings, sports events, reunions, and business meetings and applies DTV to the editing of the footage to achieve better effects at lower cost than traditional editing.

2. *Education and training:* This service can produce instructional materials for companies, businesses, and schools using inexpensive video equipment and DTV.

3. *Business proposals:* This service can be hired to produce a video or animation of how a company proposes to do a project under bid.

4. *How-to videos:* Many DTV services focus on producing commercial products that teach people how to perform a task or sport. Such products can be marketed by direct mail, or by classified ads, or sold in video stores.

5. *Marketing videos:* Many companies produce videos to sell their products, from Apple and IBM to car companies, carpet companies, and sports equipment companies. With DTV, companies of any size can afford to produce a product demo that can be mailed out to prospective clients very inexpensively.

6. *Home sales:* Many real estate agencies are using DTV to preview homes for prospective buyers. DTV thus saves them travel time and money.

7. *Video depositions:* Nearly all lawsuits and criminal cases require lawyers to interview witnesses and defendants; in the past their statements were recorded by a court reporter, but more and more lawyers are using videotape to document testimony more fully, because showing exactly how a witness appears can often help a jury decide if the person is telling

the truth. In addition, videos are being used to show how accidents happened and what a day-in-the-life of an injured plaintiff is like. These are used for both negotiations as well as in trial proceedings.

8. *Television commercials:* DTV brings the cost of producing television commercials down so far that even small businesses can afford to buy a commercial to air on cable television.

9. *Advertising agency prelims:* Most large advertising agencies spend millions of dollars creating alternative campaigns for their clients to give the client a choice of themes or concepts. In the past, showing the client these ideas required intensive storyboarding using illustrators and graphic artists. DTV is now being used by many advertising agencies actually to create a higher-quality first draft of the commercial so that a company can visualize more clearly what their ad campaign may look like.

These are just some of the applications of DTV, and there are many more. The point is, many home-based businesses can now compete in territory that was formerly restricted to large video production houses. Kevin McFarland, whose home-based company is called Desktop Video and Graphics, saves his clients two-thirds of what it would cost them to produce presentations at a studio. He points out that "there are ten million presentations made every week in the United States, and most of them use slides and flip charts. I feel like I'm on the crest of a wave." Mary Holzer has a business called Show and Tell Systems in which she uses full-motion animation to produce marketing and training videos.

One reason for the growth of DTV has been the great leaps in computer technology that allow video imaging to be transferred to digital format inside a computer. The technology that caused much of the wave was the *Video Toaster*, from NewTek. The Toaster has become synonymous with DTV, in that it represented the most efficient technology at the lowest cost for bringing video into the computer to perform editing, animations, titles, and special effects. The Toaster generates a full network-broadcast-level video signal that is of duplicatable quality. It also can produce real-time digital video effects, which means transitions need to be limited to dissolves and cuts, but can also include peels and tumbles to reveal another image. The Toaster is housed inside an Amiga computer, and the complete system can be purchased for as little as $4,000, although as we write this, the Amiga's future is uncertain. Since the Toaster, many other companies now produce the specialized hardware and software for PCs or Macintoshes.

Like multimedia services, the use of DTV is increasing and the learning curve to get into the business is shrinking because of technology like the *Toaster*. So if you are visually oriented and believe there is a George Lucas or Steven Spielberg lurking inside you, the world of DTV beckons.

✅ Knowledge and Skills You Need to Have

- You need to understand images and how they fit together. This can be acquired by studying film or video in or out of college. However, learning video production involves more than doing an apprenticeship, or working for an established professional or a cable television station that has local programs. Virtually every local cable system offers such training. A background in animation, graphic design, or cartooning is helpful.

- You need to be technically and mechanically inclined. Robert Goodman, a Philadelphia film and video producer, says that to be good at desktop video someone needs to be "an artist with a technical side or a technician with a good visual sense."

- Because this is an art form, you need to be sufficiently *right-brained* that you can work without using logic for every decision, according to Jim Mack who runs a video- and film-editing service in Michigan.

🦬 Start-up Costs

The start-up costs of a desktop video business depend on which platform (Windows/PC, Macintosh, or Amiga) you will use. For each platform, there is also a wide range of levels of sophistication that you can choose from in terms of how much equipment to buy, the quality of the equipment, and the range of services you need to offer. If you work on more than one platform, you also need additional equipment to import and translate images from one format to another.

Expenses Common to Desktop Animation, Authoring, and Editing

	Low	High
Computer with 500 megabyte hard disk	$ 1,500	$ 3,000
Ink-jet or laser printer	300	2,500
Tape drive for backup	150	1,200
Suite software	250	400
Office furniture, especially an ergonomic chair	400	1,000
Business cards, letterhead, envelopes	100	600
Subtotal	$ 2,700	$ 8,700

Desktop Animation

	Low	High
Dedicated computer with large hard disk	$ 1,500	$ 5,000
Backup power supply	80	500
Personal animation recorder (that substitutes for an NTSC video card, video recorder, and edit controller)	2,000	2,000

Expenses Common to Desktop Animation, Authoring, and Editing
(*continued*)

	Low	High
Digitizing tablet	250	800
Optical scanner		2,500
Total for desktop animation	$ 6,530	$19,500

Desktop Authoring

	Low	High
Authorware or desktop presentation software	$ 400	$ 5,000
Writable CD-ROM and software		10,000
Total for desktop authoring	$ 3,100	$23,700

Desktop Editing

	Low	High
On the low end is using a personal computer with a desktop video editing suite like *Video Machine* that has the ability to control a source deck or a combination of *Cineworks* from Touchvision and an IBM ActionMedia card. Another choice is to use an Amiga computer with a *Video Toaster* from NewTek at $5,000 equipped with a *Flyer* card at $5,000 (which substitutes for a videotape recorder and two additional decks) plus enough hard-drive capacity to store half an hour of tape and a time-based corrector at $750. The street price for a Toaster system runs between $10,000 and $13,000.	$ 1,800	$13,000
A source deck, such as a camera, that feeds in video	1,200	3,500
One to three high-quality videotape recorders. With more than one videotape recorder, you need one or more time-based correctors with Genlock at $1,000 each.	4,000	22,000*
Two color monitors or TVs with audio and video inputs	400	1,200
Total for desktop editing	$10,100	$35,400

* Not needed for the *Flyer* card.

🔧 Advantages

- DTV is an exciting field and open to many opportunities for work. Other than print, video is the most accepted medium today and has unlimited potential for personal and business use.

- The work is creative and challenging. The people you deal with are creative, and work is done in an informal manner.
- The variety of projects provides interesting problems. Your work is not routine.
- You have the chance to be in on the ground floor of a new industry and pioneer new ways of producing videos.

🖙 Disadvantages

- There is a learning curve to getting into the business unless you already have a background in video or computer hardware.
- You can spend hours on a single minute of video if you work as part of a team and people disagree about what to do or how to handle an edit.
- Video production is a highly competitive field; it helps to specialize such as training films, tutorials, how-to's, educational, corporate, product demos, etc.

💲 Pricing

Pricing varies greatly, with the rule of thumb being Get paid whatever you can get. Some DTV services charge by the hour, ranging from $50 to $150. Many prices are dependent on the nature of the task, according to Harvey Summers: for example, project proposal writing may cost $350 per day; scriptwriting $50 per minute of video time; filming $125 per hour; digitizing video $50 per hour; editing $150 per hour; and music scoring $50 per minute of video time.

🖾 Potential Earnings

TYPICAL ANNUAL GROSS REVENUES: $35,000 per year to $150,000 per year, based on billing out 1,000 hours at $35 to $150 per hour as an average rate.

OVERHEAD: moderate (20 to 40 percent).

🗹 *Best Home Businesses* Estimate of Market Potential

For those with the necessary capabilities, this is one of *the* best home businesses for the 90s.

🖎 Best Ways to Get Business

If you are producing your own videos, begin by identifying a film idea or educational product that has not yet come to market because it would have been too costly using traditional video methods. For example, one DTV service we know contacted a psychologist who had a sex-education program for couples; the service agreed to share the risk with the psychologist, and together they produced a tape marketed to other professional therapists as a training tape.

Other ways to get business include:

- Research industries or business areas in which you might get clients based on your skills, background, and interests. Identify some clients who would benefit from a product demo or training tape.
- Network and make personal contacts in user groups and other organizations such as trade or business associations. This can help you find clients for whom you can produce a tape, although they may not have thought of how you could help them at a low cost.
- Advertise in the yellow pages.
- Take contract work from other videographers who need editing services or production services you can supply.
- Send a direct-mail piece to ad agencies, video services, studios, and product designers.
- Teach classes on video production and editing.
- Place announcements on computer bulletin boards.

⬚ First steps

1. Take classes in video production. Read as much as you can about the field.
2. Apprentice at a local cable television station to learn the technical aspects of video production. If you are not technically oriented, take courses in design at community colleges or art schools.
3. Work as a volunteer to develop a reputation, or apprentice through a service bureau.
4. Create a few demo products of your own work to show to potential clients.
5. Start small; take a small job at low pay just to get some work under your belt and have a finished tape to show to larger clients.

⬚ Related Businesses

Video Data Service, 24 Grove Street, Pittsford, New York 14534; (800) 836-9461; (716) 385-4773. A videography franchise. The fee is $15,950, which includes equipment and training. The primary activities for Video Data Service franchisees are taping weddings, making film-to-tape transfers, taping legal depositions, and duplicating and editing videotapes.

🄾 Where to Turn for Information and Help

TRAINING

First Light Video Productions, 8536 Venice Blvd., Los Angeles, CA 90034; (800) 777-1576. First Light has a thirty-two-page catalogue filled with videotape-based training courses about all aspects of video production.

Graphix Zone at 800-55-GRAFX (in California, call [714] 953-7013).

Padgett Thompson, offers one- and two-day seminars on video direction; (800) 255-4141

NEWSLETTERS

Video Marketing Newsletter, Outback Group Productions; (501) 741-2566.

BOOKS

Operating a Desktop Video Service on Your Home-Based PC, Harvey Summers, Blue Ridge Summit, PA: Tab/McGraw Hill, 1994; (800) 822-8158.

MAGAZINES

There are now dozens of magazines in this field, including *AV Video, New Media, Desktop Video World, PC Presentations, Video Systems, Video Toaster User, Videography,* and *Videomaker.*

■ ■ ■ ■ ■

EDITORIAL SERVICES

There are over 20,000 book publishers in the country as well as thousands of newspapers and magazines. Most are small and many hire outside professional help in preparing their manuscripts for publication, including editors, proofreaders, and indexers. Businesses of all kinds also use editors and proofreaders in preparing reports, research papers, documents for clients, and contracts. These include hardware and software companies, high-tech manufacturers, professional training companies, trade associations that publish journals, law firms, and even typesetters and small printers.

Each editorial task encompasses a different range of duties and skills, so it is worthwhile to examine them separately.

Editing

■ Editing involves a broad range of manuscript wordsmithing activities. There are developmental editors who work with authors to develop or rework initial concepts into a logical, well-organized manuscript. These editors may help a writer plan the sequence of chapters or sections, develop ideas, do research, and even rewrite portions. When the manuscript is complete and being prepared for typesetting, copy editors check for proper grammar and clarity, make corrections and style improvements, and double-check the content and consistency.

Proofreading

■ Depending on your skills and experience, one of two types of proofreading services may suit you. Content proofreaders read word-for-word, comparing the typeset proofs against the original manuscript to check for typos, misspellings, and so forth. Design proofreaders, in addition to proofing content, check the proof for adherence to design specifications, typographical correctness, kerning, improper or excessive hyphenation, and so on, once copy has been typeset.

Indexing

■ Indexers typically work for book publishers constructing key word indices for the back of a book. Indexing is usually performed for nonfiction books, professional books, and reference materials to help readers find information quickly. Indexers must be very detail oriented and have excellent reading and analytic skills.

Some editorial services perform all three tasks, although most specialize in only one type of editing as well as in a subject area or areas such as business, science, or medicine. Indexing is the most specialized and detailed skill of the three services and may not appeal to all people.

✅ Knowledge and Skills You Need to Have

■ You need to have an excellent knowledge of grammar and punctuation. You also need to know the standard markings and procedures followed in copyediting and proofreading by publishers and typesetters.

■ Good communication skills are a must; you will be working with authors and other editors, and your notes and comments to them must be clear and written in good English.

■ You need to be detail oriented and meticuluous. Editing, proofreading, and indexing all require a high level of attention to detail.

■ You should be highly organized. Most editorial services work on more than one project at a time, often under pressure to complete the work by a deadine that cannot be missed.

■ It helps to be visually oriented, able to imagine how the printed word will look on the page in a designed piece. Some editorial work requires, in fact, the ability to fit copy into limited space when each word or page counts.

🐷 Start-up Costs

	Low	High
Computer with hard disk and modem	$1,000	$3,000
Laser printer	300	1,600
Fax machine	300	900
Suite software (mostly word processing)	250	400
Contact management software	100	300
Office furniture, especially ergonomic chair	400	1,000
Reference books (dictionaries, etc.)	200	500
Business cards, letterhead, envelopes	100	600
Total	$2,650	$8,300

👍 Advantages

- Editorial work and publishing are usually interesting, creative, and intellectually stimulating. You have a chance to read a variety of books and articles ahead of their publication.
- You can often choose your own hours in which to work: day or night.
- Editorial work can sometimes help you develop your own ideas for books and the contacts needed to get your own writing contracts.

👎 Disadvantages

- Some editing and proofreading can be tedious and repetitive.
- Unless you take precautions to prevent it, you can develop a repetitive-motion disorder from typing or retyping memos or manuscripts.
- Editorial work is usually done alone, and so you may have little socialization with other people on a regular daily basis.
- The growth of desktop publishing has somewhat reduced the need for proofreaders, due to the use of computerized spellcheckers and the greater control desktop publishers have in typesetting and layout on the computer. (Desktop publishing has not affected editing and indexing to the same degree.)

💲 Pricing

Developmental editors can earn between $25 and $50 per hour. Some charge by the manuscript, ranging from $2,000 to $4,000 to review and comment on a 400-page manuscript.

Copy editors may receive from $15 to $30 per hour, depending on the complexity of the work and the turnaround time.

Proofreaders earn anywhere from $10 to $25 an hour, depending on the field and locale. Indexers usually charge from $3 to $5 per printed book page they read to produce the index, or from $20 to $50 per hour. A service that uses computer software for indexing can receive the higher fees.

🖳 Potential Earnings

GROSS REVENUES from an editorial service range from $22,500 to $45,000, based on billing thirty hours per week, fifty weeks per year (1,500 hours per year) at $15 to $30 per hour. An enterprising editor or indexer can earn more than $50,000 with several years of experience.

OVERHEAD: low (20 percent or less).

📈 *Best Home Businesses* **Estimate of Market Potential**

Total number of editorial service firms in the United States, including home-based businesses: 4,412. The continuing increase in the number of small publishers producing information in multiple formats and media will create a continuing demand for independent providers of editorial services.

🖻 Best Ways to Get Business

- Personal contacts are the best marketing tool for editorial services. Get to know in-house editors at publishing companies, magazines, journals, and newsletters who are responsible for hiring out. Take them out to lunch to find out what kind of work they usually have available, how they decide whom to pick, and how much they typically pay. Leave your business card and stay in touch on a regular basis so that you remain foremost in their minds. If you specialize in corporate work, get to know copywriters who may be getting contracts for business brochures, annual reports, and other business documents.

- Refer to *Writer's Market* or *Literary Market Place* to locate names and addresses of publishers to whom you can send a résumé and samples of your work.

- Check the ads for freelance work that appear in two trade magazines, *Publishers Weekly* and *Library Journal*, both of which are available in many public libraries. Look also in specific trade magazines for advertisements for writers and editors who know how a specific industry works.

🖪 First Steps

Unless you have several years of editorial experience or are a published author yourself, don't expect to be hired as a developmental editor. These editors usually come from the ranks of a publishing house or magazine. Copyediting is more available, however, if you have good writing skills and an excellent command of English. Copyeditors should be prepared to pass a test by editing a passage designed for hiring editors at publishing houses. People interested in book indexing often prepare samples to send the production manager in a publishing house.

❑ Where to Turn for Information and Help

ORGANIZATIONS

American Society of Indexers, P.O. Box 386, Port Arkansas, TX 78373; (512) 749-4052, fax (512) 749-6334. Roster currently includes about 1,100 members, about one-third of whom are home based. Publishes numerous books and informational materials on a career in indexing. Call for a list of publications.

Editorial Freelancers' Association, 71 West 23rd Street, Suite 1504, New York, NY 10010; (212) 929-5400.

Freelance Editorial Association, P.O. Box 380835, Cambridge, MA 02238; (617) 729-8164.

In addition, there are many national and regional organizations for writers of all kinds that may be of interest to editors as well for purposes of networking.

COURSES

United States Department of Agriculture offers a course in indexing. For more information, contact Correspondence Study Program, Graduate School USDA, Room 1114, South Agriculture Building, 14th and Independence Ave. S.W., Washington, DC 20250; (202) 447-2187 for information; call (202) 720-7123 to speak with a counselor.

BOOKS

Education and Training in Indexing and Abstracting: A Directory of Courses and Workshops Offered in the U.S. and Canada, published by American Society of Indexers. See address above.

Freelancers on Indexing. Transcript of a panel discussion. American Society of Indexers; see address above.

A Guide to Freelance Indexing, A. Cynthia Weber, American Society of Indexers; see address above.

How to Start and Run a Writing and Editing Business, Herman Holtz, New York: John Wiley, 1992.

Literary Market Place, Bowker's. Updated yearly. Available in most public libraries.

Writer's Market, Writer's Digest Books, 1507 Dana Ave., Cincinnati, OH 45207; (800) 289-0863. Updated yearly. Writer's Digest also publishes *Children's Writer* and *Illustrator's Market, Guide to Literary Agents & Art/ Photo Reps*, and other specialized market directories.

Copy Editor, P.O. Box 604, Ansonia Station, New York, NY 10023; (212) 757-2645.

Editorial Eye, Editorial Experts, 66 Canal Center Plaza, Suite 200, Alexandria, VA 22314; (800) 683-5859, fax (703) 683-4915.

Editors Only, P.O. Box 17108, Fountain Hills, AZ 85269-7108; (800) 952-0122 or (602) 837-6492. Available on-line on Newsnet

Freelance Writer's Report, Maple Ridge Road, North Sandwich, NH 03259; (800) 351-9278; (603) 284-6367. Of interest to writers and editors alike.

Library Journal, 833 W. South Boulder Road, Lewisville, CO 80027; (800) 677-6694. Subscriptions.

Publishers Weekly, 249 W. 17th Street, New York, NY 10011; (800) 278-2991. Subscriptions.

Writer's Digest, Subscriber Service Department, P.O. Box 2124, Harlan, IA 51593-2313. Subscriptions.

■ ■ ■ ■ ■

EMPLOYEE TRAINER

As American industry and business undergo rapid change, and as our jobs demand more, workers need additional training. There's new technology to learn, new procedures to deal with increasing government regulations, new management techniques, and new methods of selling, servicing, and interacting with customers. Businesses also need to provide training to keep their employees once they've been hired, because employee turnover costs them thousands of dollars for each employee who leaves the organization. This is good news for the training industry. In fact, the American Society of Training and Development (ASTD), the world's largest professional association of trainers, estimates that as of 1993, there has been a 45 percent increase in the number of Americans who get formal training on the job, with the majority of that training occurring in manufacturing industries. Overall, 16 percent of employees now get formal training while in 1983 only 11 percent did; in addition, 15 percent of employees get informal on-the-job training. Formal training is concentrated on employees ages twenty-five to forty-four, and the most popular topics covered in such training are: team building, quality, general management skills, change management, interpersonal skills, performance management, communication, and cultural diversity.

In the past, employee training in large organizations was usually provided by an in-house staff. Today many companies no longer keep a training staff on the payroll and are forced to hire outside, freelance trainers to come in on an ad hoc basis to address the specific needs of their staff and labor force. Even companies with large training staffs use outside trainers to teach specialized skills.

Although employee training is an expense that is customarily cut during economic downturns, training programs that hold special promise during the 90s include teaching basic literacy skills (reading, math, computers, and business writing), sales training, management skills, and customer service. The need for basic literacy training is expected to grow at a rate of 17 percent a year and perhaps even more. Trainers are also called upon even in the worst of times to help a company handle particular crises and challenges.

Most corporate trainers specialize in one or two areas. Robert Johnson, of BJE Associates, in Campbell, California, for example, is a trainer who focuses on the employee development process in the sales arena. His clients include industrial organizations that are seeking greater business-to-business sales. Robert usually works with larger companies (100 to 150 people), but on occasion he also has small-to-medium-sized firms, particularly because such companies frequently employ people who have no training in phone sales or sales presentations.

Kathryn Dager, whose firm Profitity focuses on customer-service training, says of this field, "Nothing is more satisfying than working with a company and seeing the entire company become more successful as a result of the new skills its employees have mastered."

Trainers most often conduct their programs, which may range from a four-hour workshop to a five-day event, on the premises of their clients. Some trainers give workshops off-site, however, and take employees to a rented hotel conference room to avoid the distractions of their work. Trainers are usually expected to provide their own visual aids and appropriate written materials. Many trainers custom-create their own workbooks or three-ring binders to give employees as part of the package for their training, but others purchase off-the-shelf materials from any of hundreds of training suppliers and publishers.

☑ Knowledge and Skills You Need to Have

- People skills are perhaps the most important factor in being a successful trainer. You must be able to communicate with a group of employees and make their training a positive experience. This means being entertaining, informative, and definitely not bashful. On occasion, you must do role-playing to demonstrate a situation, so dramatic ability is useful.

- You must also have excellent presentation skills and/or a background in teaching so that you know how to break down information in the kind of small chunks that make learning easier.

- It's important for trainers to have resolved any personality issues they may have. Such issues easily surface when teaching before a group and not only hinder the learning process but prevent trainers from getting good evaluations from students. Training must come from the heart to be genuine; you need a sincere desire to help people learn. In some cases, you also must know how to deal diplomatically (without losing your own cool) with a difficult audience member who is demeaning the training for others.

- Sales and marketing skills are also critical; getting contracts for your own business takes time so you must be prepared to sell yourself and the value of your seminars.

- You very likely need excellent writing skills for writing proposals and a statement of your work. You may also want to write some of your own training materials or customize the off-the-shelf product you buy.

■ Start-up Costs

	Low	High
Computer with hard disk and modem	$1,000	$3,000
Fax machine	300	900
Laser printer	300	1,600
Suite software	250	400
Desktop publishing and presentation software to make your own overheads, charts, graphs, etc.	250	500
Comb-binding machine to bind your workbooks	250	500
Office furniture, especially ergonomic chair	400	1,000
Business cards, letterhead, envelopes	100	600
Reference books	100	300
Organizational dues	150	400
Total	$3,100	$9,200

■ Advantages

- Training can be intellectually stimulating and rewarding. You earn your living using your brain. Also, watching people learn new skills and become more effective is rewarding.

- You can often build a solid reputation if you are good. This means that many clients will sign up with you again and again.

- Top trainers make excellent money. Training is often a good step into other areas, such as writing and publishing your own programs, books, tapes, manuals, and other products that can earn you more money as well.

- If you like to perform, or appear before an audience, this is the right job for you other than being a stand-up comedian.

■ Disadvantages

- Training is a difficult product to sell, and it can have a long selling cycle. That is, it may take quite a while for a company to realize that it could benefit from your training. Few companies have a sense of urgency that they need you.

- Training is often perceived as being the same as buying consulting; companies feel that they are purchasing a long-term commitment, which is not actually true.

- Unless you live in a large community, you may need to travel widely to develop a large-enough client base to support yourself. In addition, you are often competing with big training companies in a competitive business; you need to find some distinguishing factors to separate your business from the crowd.

- Trainers do not command as much respect as management or marketing consultants.

- You need to make arrangements with hotels to get good deals on conference rooms, as many trainings need to be held off-site. Small companies often don't have conference rooms either. This means you also need to drag around your easels, flip charts, and presentation materials,

💲 Pricing

Most trainers charge a daily rate ranging from $600 to $2,000 per day or an hourly rate of at least $100 to $150 per hour. As you might expect, fees are higher in urban areas than in smaller communities. You can also charge higher prices to train trainers to teach what you know. When trainers work with service brokers, they may work for as little as $175 per day or give the broker a percentage of their fee.

Some consultants charge by the trainee, in which case they relate the per-person fee to the salary level of the employees. So training fees for a group of twelve people earning in the mid-twenties per year ($100 a day) are apt to be around $1,200.

🖥 Potential Earnings

TYPICAL ANNUAL GROSS REVENUES: $35,000 to $75,000 in the first year. With experience, some trainers can make $125,000 to $300,000, but realistically $100,000 is good number once you've built up a clientele. (This reflects training 100 days per year at $1,000 per day.)

OVERHEAD: low (20 percent or less).

🔎 *Best Home Businesses* Estimate of Market Potential

As we move into the last half of the 90s, at any given time, it's estimated that one in twenty-five American workers will be in a job-retraining program. Professional knowledge is now spoken of in half-lives; for example, "the half-life of an engineer's knowledge is five years." The need for lifelong learning is fueling the training industry, and the downsizing of corporations and other large organizations favors the role of independent contractors to provide this training.

⬛ Best Ways to Get Business

- Networking with and contacting local area sales managers and human resource managers. The more you get to know them and they know you, the better your chances of selling them one of your programs.
- Demonstrating what you can do by speaking before professional and trade associations in the industries in which you work. Speak also before local groups such as Kiwanis and Rotary Clubs.
- Writing articles and getting other publicity to expand your reputation and perception of expertise.
- Have a portfolio of attestations and recommendations from satisfied clients. Collect testimonial letters from all participants in workshops you have given to show to prospective clients.

⬛ First Steps

An academic degree or teaching experience is not always a prerequisite to becoming a trainer. In fact, training is very industry related, which means that you can start in a field with which you are already familiar. For example, if you used to work in banking, begin by developing seminars and workshops you can give to people in the banking field. A successful training in this area can be used as a stepping stone for another client in the same field, and eventually in other fields. Assisting a practicing trainer as an apprentice is another way of gaining know-how.

You can also learn a great deal from the resources below and by joining ASTD or attending their annual conference. Another useful resource is to take courses offered by image consultants in your area who specialize in presentation skills. (See entry on Image Consultants for information on how to contact their national association.)

Develop a step-by-step outline for what you intend to teach. Identify the specific skills and knowledge employees will gain. Develop the accompanying written material you plan to hand out during your course. Test out your training program by volunteering to do training for nonprofit organizations or by offering it by invitation to select contacts.

If you have experience doing training, you can begin by finding a niche within your industry that you feel comfortable with and enjoy. Take a video training workshop to build your presentation skills, learn as much as you can about human behavior, and observe other people's workshops. Then get out and start selling your program. If selling is new to you, take sales training courses. Don't be undercapitalized. Unless you have already lined up clients before you start, you'll need a cushion to live on for three to six months while you get your initial clients.

⬚ Where to Turn for Information and Help

ORGANIZATIONS

American Management Association (AMACOM); (800) 262-9699; (212) 903-8087. Publishes hundreds of books on training and management education.

American Society for Training and Development, 1640 King Street, Box 1443, Alexandria, VA 22313-2043; (703) 683-8100. Largest training organization with over 55,000 corporate-based professionals: managers, human-resource specialists, designers, instructors, evaluators, consultants, researchers, and educators. Offers a professional journal, local chapters, and a train-the-trainer certificate program.

National Speakers' Association, 1500 South Priest Drive, Tempe, AZ 85281; (602) 968-2552. While there are stylistic differences between speakers and trainers, many people speak professionally and train. The National Speakers' Association has a training program that it requires as a condition of membership.

Pfeiffer & Co., 8517 Production Avenue, San Diego, CA 92121-2280; (800) 274-4434; (619) 578-5900. This company publishes and distributes many books, tapes, and videos on training. It also offers seminars on training throughout the country.

BOOKS

Re-Educating the Corporation, Daniel R. Tobin, Oliver Wight Publications; (800) 343-0625.

The Trainer's Professional Development Handbook, R. Bard, C. Bell, L. Stephan, and L. Webster, San Francisco: Jossey-Bass, 1987.

Training and Development Handbook: A Guide to Human Resource Development, R. I. Craig, Oklahoma City: McGraw Hill, 1987. Considered to be the basic nuts-and-bolts how-to book for new trainers and a valued reference for experienced trainers.

Your Career in Human Resource Development: A Guide to Information and Decision, R. Stump, ASTD, Box 1443, Alexandria, VA 22313. Booklet to help readers determine whether they are suited for the human-resources field.

MAGAZINES

Training and Development Journal, ASTD, 1640 King Street, Box 1443, Alexandria, VA 22313-2043; (703) 683-8100

Training: The Magazine of Human Resource Development, Lakewood Publications, 50 South 9th Street, Minneapolis, MN 55402; (800) 707-7769; (612) 333-0471.

Butler Learning Systems, 1325 West Dorothy Lane, Dayton, OH 45409-1385; (513) 298-7462. Butler provides qualified applicants with the opportunity to become an affiliated distributorship using their programs. They provide the fundamental training tools you use in your workshops: videos, audiotapes, and workbooks, which can be sold as collateral materials. They have a national advertising program, but you negotiate and track your own clients.

■ ■ ■ ■ ■

ERRAND SERVICE

People are now trying to squeeze more into the twenty-four-hour day than at any other time in history. The reasons are many. Two-career couples now outnumber single-income families; jobs are demanding more than forty hours a week; many people spend more than an hour a day just to get to and from work. In addition, exercise and fitness, once perceived as leisure, have become must-dos for many. The result is that many people are willing to pay others to run their errands and handle life's time-consuming minutiae.

Personal errand services do the grocery shopping, pick up cleaning and laundry, take shoes in to be repaired, take care of pets, run to the post office—whatever a client needs. Sometimes called a personal shopping service, an errand service may also pick out a last-minute gift or even find a dress for that special occasion.

Cathleen Carlson, who runs an errand service in Los Angeles called Errands Unlimited, says, "As long as it's legal, we do it. However, we don't transport people and we don't pick up children. But we do take items back to stores to be returned or exchanged. We buy gifts. We take gifts to be wrapped. We make pickups and deliveries and do grocery shopping for small or new companies. For example, we deliver wedding cakes for a bakery. Hiring us is cheaper than hiring a driver and leasing a truck."

In this business, the best customers are regular ones who use the services several times a week. In addition to small companies that don't have their own delivery person on staff, your clients might include senior citizens, two-income families, single working women with children, and high-income individuals who can afford, for example, to hire someone to drive to every button shop in town to find a certain kind of button. So customers range from the extravagant to the frugal, and the work varies from the frivolous to the basic—from picking up theater tickets to getting in groceries.

Six years ago, Cathleen was working three days a week and had one client; now she has two full-time employees. She has doubled her gross every year and says she's making more money than she ever has before.

✔ Knowledge and Skills You Need to Have

- You need to like doing things for other people. A customer-service orientation is critical in this business. You must be patient as you may need to stand in lines, drive in traffic, and wait for people; the customer is always right.
- Stamina is also important. Activities like running in and out of stores, hopping in and out of the car, climbing stairs, and lugging groceries are tiring, so you need to have energy all day long.
- Organizational skills are important. You must be able to plan a route for your errands. An effective route can save you two hours a day.
- You have to be assertive to get help quickly. You have to be able to ask questions like where to find the return counter in a store and know how to cut through red tape to get to the right person.
- To get from place to place quickly and efficiently, you need to know your city and be able to read a map.
- You need to like driving.

🐂 Start-up Costs

	Low	High
Business cards, letterhead, envelopes	$ 400	$ 600
Flyer	200	500
Late-model car or van	4,000	16,000
Pager or cellular phone	100	1,000
Total	$4,700	$18,100

🖒 Advantages

- It's gratifying to know that you are saving people time and making their lives easier.
- You're not confined to an office; you're outdoors, moving around and doing lots of different things.
- There may be variety in the type of errands you do.

🖓 Disadvantages

- This business will not work in all communities. It works best in places where life seems hectic and complicated. It won't work, for example, where there is a mom-and-pop store handy on every corner or where parking is so limited that you'll spend your earnings on parking fees.
- Errand services are highly susceptible to the ups and downs of the economy. In order to keep busy, you need a few steady clients; having one major client who provides ample repeat business is essential.
- It takes a long time to build up business.

- Because you personally can run only a limited number of errands in a day, the key to earning a significant income is in having others working for you.
- Unless you can afford to hire staff, you have to handle all tasks yourself, from answering the phones to billing, banking, and running the errands. If you do have employees, however, it means you'll have to bill clients, which can cause cash-flow problems. So you have to stagger your billing in order to have money coming in every day.
- Because employees get paid on a per-job basis, rather than by the hour, you may experience high staff turnover when business is light. You are competing against hourly wage workers who are willing to do the same type of work for less money.
- The v.ork can be wearing day after day, both on you and on your motor vehicle.

$ Pricing

Hourly rates range from $10 to $25 per hour. Some services require a one- or two-hour minimum to account for driving time to and from the site, or simply to maintain a modicum of income. Having only lots of fifteen to thirty-minute jobs doesn't provide for a living.

▣ Potential Earnings

TYPICAL ANNUAL GROSS REVENUES:

- *Working by yourself:* $26,250, based on working seven hours a day, five days a week, fifty weeks a year, at $15 an hour.
- *With two employees* who will pay all their own expenses and receive 50 percent of the revenue: $52,000.

OVERHEAD: moderate (20 to 40 percent).

⚡ *Best Home Businesses* Estimate of Market Potential

The Economic Policy Institute calculates that workers have added an extra month to their annual work and commuting time since 1969. A survey found that leisure time dropped from 26.2 hours a week in 1973 to 16.6 hours in 1987. If you think about it, the more "labor-saving" appliances and tools we use, the less time we seem to have. Gone are the days when people went for drives in the park; now many people don't have time to wait in lines, pick things up, and do other chores. So a demand has been created by busy people for errand services. The rapidly growing numbers of elderly make use of errand services, too. Both physical limitations and fear of crime prompt senior citizens who can afford it to hire others to do things for them.

■ Best Ways to Get Business

- Directly soliciting business from particular groups—for example, patrons of a charity, small bakeries, or gift-wrapping services.
- Backing up your contacts with this group with direct mail. Get a mailing list from charity rosters or membership directories.
- Taking out advertising in the program booklets at charity events to attract the interest of wealthy patrons.
- Delivering flyers to homes in select neighborhoods.
- Placing classified advertising in local and community newspapers.
- Networking with groups who could use your service.
- Getting publicity about your business in newspapers and magazines.
- Requesting establishments your clients use—for example, dry cleaners, shoe shops, and so forth—to allow you to post a card or flyer.
- Yellow pages advertising under Delivery Service, Messenger Service, and/or Shopping Service.

■ Related Businesses

Additional businesses you could branch out into are:

- messenger service (regulated by state utility commissions in some states)
- firewood delivery service
- publicity escort service for authors, celebrities, and corporate spokespeople.
- hauling service (see separate entry under Rest of Best)

■ First Steps

The key to establishing this business is finding a major long-term client to keep you busy several days a week while you start building your clientele. Such a client might be a business that you will do pickup and deliveries for.

■ ■ ■ ■ ■

EXECUTIVE SEARCH

Matchmaking is an old profession that in the world of employment has become known as the search business, or *headhunting*. Companies turn to executive-search firms to match them up with top-notch personnel. Unlike an employment agency, however, which usually charges a fee to the people the agency places in jobs, executive recruiters are paid by the employer to find qualified people to fill management, professional, and technical positions. And unlike employment agencies, which are heavily regulated by state laws, recruiters are free of licensing requirements.

Because the overwhelming amount of work is done by telephone and even via E-mail, executive searchers can work from anywhere. Of the 22,000 recruitment firms, an estimated 30 percent operate from home. Some states prohibit recruiters from meeting with clients or candidates in their homes, but most business is done by phone or at trade shows.

In fact, Paul Hawkinson, editor of the *Fordyce Letter*, a newsletter for the recruitment industry, found he was more successful after he moved his executive-search firm to his home. He says, "I was running a forty-employee operation from two floors of office space. Our billings were excellent, but my accountant told me that everyone was making money except *me*. I fired everyone, closed the offices, and moved to my house. My blood pressure went down, my happiness quotient soared, and I finally started putting some money into *my* pocket."

Anthony Byrne, a consultant and trainer in the executive-search industry, says the opportunities in this field are excellent because it's one of the fastest-growing service industries in the world. In the 90s, the executive-search industry is going in two directions: toward companies with six- to fifteen-person offices which make heavy use of technology and toward small firms with a specialized niche. Successful home-based recruiters are therefore often highly specialized by industry and type of personnel they place, such as restaurant executives or chefs.

Bill Vick of Plano, Texas, a highly successful home-based recruiter, is an example of a recruiter specializing in the software industry. He makes use of computer technology and psychological profiling to find executives for the microcomputer industry. In addition, he has developed software called *SOLO* that manages the entire recruiting process. (See below, Where to Turn for Information and Help.)

Vick says, "My business is in my mind, in the information and knowledge I have and my ability to apply what I know. My office has only electronic walls. With a personal computer and a fax machine I can use as an external printer, I can conduct business from anywhere, anyplace, and at any time. I am even making use of the Internet. Occasionally I do a joint sale with another recruiter; I may have the candidate, and he has the client (the company), or vice versa."

While the telephone is a useful tool, Vick emphasizes the need to make face-to-face contacts, particularly at trade shows. Building personal relationships can be critical, he notes. He also gets business by giving speeches about technology at meetings of trade groups. Networking with other recruiters can bring in a lot of business through "splits," where one recruiter matches his or her client with another recruiter's candidate. In fact, Vick says, recruiters really have three different "customers": the client (the company seeking an executive), the candidate (the potential hire), and other recruiters with their own pool of clients and candidates.

About this business, Vick observes, "The easiest thing is finding people to fill the jobs, but the most important thing is finding the clients. By this measure recruiters should be paid for finding clients, not people. But the opposite is true."

Although Vick thinks the field is "grossly misunderstood," even by practitioners, it is a $7-billion-a-year business with excellent potential for skilled, knowledgeable recruiters.

✅ Knowledge and Skills You Need to Have

- Home-based recruiters must have knowledge of the kind of people needed in the specialized field in which they work: accountants, engineers, CEOs, and so forth.

- This is literally a people business. Recruiters must be good at meeting people, developing relationships, judging character, assessing needs, and establishing trust.

- Most successful recruiters have a sales personality. They are at ease with selling.

- Recruiters must be patient yet tenacious. You must have high self-esteem and strong self-confidence to deal effectively with rejection. You'll hear twenty *nos* for every *yes* when looking for clients.

- Home-based recruiters don't have the camaraderie of working with other recruiters to keep them motivated to work hard without a guaranteed return; therefore they must be self-motivated to keep themselves going.

- Recruiters need to have the ability and desire to read and synthesize large amounts of diverse information. For example, you should be able to read through three to five magazines a day to keep up with trends and changes in the field you're working in.

🐏 Start-up Costs

	Low	High
Computer with hard disk and modem	$1,000	$2,500
Ink-jet or laser printer	500	1,600
Database, word-processing, and communications software	700	1,000
Fax	300	600
Telephone headset	40	70
Office furniture, especially an ergonomic chair	600	800
Business cards, letterhead, envelopes	200	600
Brochure	100	2,000
Total	$3,540	$9,420

⮛ Advantages

- Start-up costs are low.
- Bringing a candidate and an employer together can be very satisfying. With a good placement, the future of both parties is enhanced from the match. A company can turn around because of a placement you've made.
- The income can be high, as fees are usually substantial.
- This business provides a great deal of flexibility. Using a computer makes your office totally portable. You can take a month to travel in Europe, and your business doesn't have to stop.

⮛ Disadvantages

- This is a high-risk business. You get paid only when you find the right person. If you miss out on finding someone, you have no income.
- The competition is stiff.
- The work has a relative lack of prestige.
- The business is stressful; there are big wins and big losses.
- Most of the work consists of making phone calls, and only highly motivated people can keep at it without colleagues and coworkers around for support.

$ Pricing

Recruiters charge 20 to 40 percent of the first year's earnings of someone they place in a position, with 30 percent the norm for the industry. However, according to Hawkinson, most home-based recruiters charge 25 percent, thereby competing in terms of price with larger office-based competitors who have higher overhead.

Most recruiters work on a contingency-fee basis. In other words, they get paid only when they locate a suitable candidate. Although the trend is toward contingent searches, some recruiters work on a retainer. With a retainer they receive 30 percent of the fee upon acceptance of the search; 30 percent at thirty days; and 30 percent at sixty days. The closure rate on such searches is about half.

▣ Potential Earnings

TYPICAL ANNUAL GROSS REVENUES: $123,000 (the industry average in 1993, according to a survey of 6,000 consultants conducted by the *Fordyce Letter*). But, according to Hawkinson, "home-based self-employed recruiters do a higher gross for lower fees with higher net earnings." Most home-based recruiters complete fifteen searches a year and average nearly $150,000.

OVERHEAD: low (20 percent or less), with expenses basically telephone and computers.

▣ *Best Home Businesses* **Estimate of Market Potential**

Total number of executive search firms in the United States, including home-based businesses: 19,927. The continuing growth of small businesses fuels Department of Labor projections of 43 percent increases in the number of executive, administrative, and managerial personnel and 37 percent increases in technical personnel between 1992 and 2005. This growth supports a sustaining demand for executive recruiters.

▣ **Best Ways to Get Business**

- Calling companies that have repeatedly advertised for a particular position in trade and professional publications. Carefully script your telephone calls, and use the same script over and over.
- Going to trade shows to make and renew contacts.
- Sending a newsletter to prospective and existing clients. Bill Vick cautions that this can be rather expensive, however.
- Speaking about recruitment issues to professional and trade associations.
- Mailing postcards advertising your business to companies that are prospective clients.

⬓ **First Steps**

Don't start out cold in this business. Go to work for an existing search firm, where you can be trained in the industry, and decide whether this is a business you will enjoy and succeed at. Spend a year or two learning the ropes. The turnover rate in the industry is high. Only two in ten stay with it after the first year, one in ten after two years.

☐ **Where to Turn for Information and Help**

ORGANIZATIONS

National Association of Executive Recruiters, 222 South Westmonte Drive, Suite 110, Box 2156, Altamonte Springs, FL 32715-2156; (800) 726-5613; (407) 774-7880. Has 2,300 members.

National Association of Personnel Services, 3133 Mt. Vernon Avenue, Alexandria, VA 22305; (703) 684-0180.

BOOKS

The Placement Strategy Handbook, Paul Hawkinson and Jeff Allen, The Kimberly Organization, Box 31011, St. Louis, MO 63131; (314) 965-3883. They also publish *Placement Management,* by the same authors.

The Directory of Executive Recruiters, Kennedy Publications, Templeton Road, Fitzwilliam, NH 03447; (800) 531-0007. Lists over 2,500 search professionals in North America indexed by specialities, geography, industries, and contact persons.

Kennedy's Pocket Guide to Working with Executive Recruiters, Kennedy Publications, Templeton Road, Fitzwilliam, NH 03447; (800) 531-0007. Thirty chapters of information on how recruiters work; includes the valuable Lexicon of Executive Recruiting.

MAGAZINES AND NEWSLETTERS

Catalog of Executive Search Books, Kennedy Publications, Templeton Road, Fitzwilliam, NH 03447; (800) 531-0007. Approximately fifty hard-to-find special reports, directories, and practice improvement titles for practitioners and users of search.

Executive Recruiter News, Jim Kennedy, Templeton Road, Fitzwilliam, NH 03447; (800) 531-0007. Trends and statistics, with emphasis on retained recruiters.

The Fordyce Letter, Box 31011, St. Louis, MO 63131; (314) 965-3883.

SOFTWARE

SOLO, available from Solo Systems for $2,500; (800) 364-8425 or through Bill Vick's Internet address: VICK@onramp.net.

■ ■ ■ ■ ■

EXPERT SERVICES BROKER

Expert services brokers find consultants, specialists, and experts of any kind for businesses who need them. This business is based on the theory of providing the missing piece to a puzzle. If, for example, a company has a problem that requires a chemical engineer to solve and they don't have one on staff, management can turn to an expert service broker who will find the person they need—someone with a chemical engineering degree who can step in on a one-shot basis and solve the problem.

Carl Kline, of National Consultant Referrals, points out that expert service brokers are not employment agencies (because they don't get the consultant a permanent job), or temporary agencies (because they don't actually hire the consultant after getting a job listing), or even brokers in the technical sense of the term (true brokers actually get a client and then subcontract out the work). Although some people continue to refer to them as brokers, he uses the term *expert referral service.*

Essentially service brokers put their clients in touch with the experts they need at the time they need them. They begin by locating a pool of reliable, highly talented and skilled experts whom they can match up with clients who need their expertise when the occasion arises. This becomes a database of experts from whom they draw to meet the needs of clients.

For example, clients may be companies needing the expertise of a direct-mail specialist, a toxic-waste manager, or market-research analyst. Or your clients may need expert advice on a particular technical, political, or marketing matter for a specific project of limited duration. Other clients for whom expert service brokers frequently work are attorneys who need to locate an expert witness for a trial.

Clients can also call on the service broker to provide them with trainers who can teach specific skills to their employees. A company might turn to a service broker, for example, to find someone to teach their staff how to set up, use, repair, and sell new technology. Laurel Garrett became a service broker when she discovered that small-business owners often need help but don't know exactly what they need or where to find it. She says, "My business is to find the most efficient, economical way of getting a job done that is beyond the range of my client's capabilities."

The demand for this business is growing for a number of reasons. First, an increasing number of corporations are cutting back their permanent staff and relying more heavily on project-by-project consultants to step in. However, there are many consultants out there, and companies often don't have time to research the qualifications of each one or even to find the closest one in their area. As a result, the service brokers fulfill a need in providing them with experts who have the skills that match their needs at the price they can pay.

As Carl Kline says of this business, "Working with someone like me is like working with a matchmaker. When a company needs an expert, they don't want to spend hours reading the yellow pages, picking out names, and calling some unknowns. They want to find someone quickly, and so I can provide them with a résumé and description very quickly so they can see who the candidate is and whether or not there might be a match."

✔ Knowledge and Skills You Need to Have

- According to Kline, it helps to know something about consulting or to have been a consultant. This allows you to be familiar with the nature of the consulting business and to understand better the expectations that a client has.

- You need to be proactive and aggressive to find both assignments for your list of experts and suitable experts for your clients. This means going to lots of meetings, making phone calls, and keeping your name in front of the business community in your area. The saying that "Success lies not in what you know but who you know" is literally true in this business.

- You must know what makes a good consultant. The experts you provide are the key to your success. If the experts you refer are not up to par, your clients will not call upon you again. So you must be able to locate, recognize, and recruit top talent.

- An expert service broker needs to be able to listen carefully to clients and help them identify precisely what they need. Often what they need may not be exactly what they say at first, so you need to have good communication skills to help people articulate their needs.

- Objectivity and a desire to serve are essential. You can't just be intent upon finding work for yourself or your friends. You aren't an agent; you are a broker. So if your friend is not the best one for the job, you have to be able to say no.

🐷 Start-up Expenses

	Low	High
Computer with hard disk and modem	$1,000	$3,000
Laser printer	500	1,600
Fax	500	1,000
Suite software	250	1,000
Database program or contact management software and bookkeeping software	100	1,000
Telephone headset	40	70
Office furniture, especially an ergonomic chair	400	1,000
Business cards, letterhead, envelopes	100	600
Brochure	1,000	2,000
Organizational dues	250	250
Total	$4,140	$11,520

📖 Advantages

- Because companies are undergoing change so rapidly and are finding it more difficult to keep in-house experts, this is a business that is responsive to a fundamental change in the economy.

- You get to meet a lot of interesting people and keep up-to-date about new technologies.

- You are providing a win/win service. When you make a good match, everyone is happy.

- The work offers a lot of variety and is intellectually stimulating because you can work with a wide range of clients and experts who are involved in solving a wide range of problems.

- This is a business that can be done from anywhere in the country. In fact, your clients need not, and probably will not, all be located in your local community.

🗂 Disadvantages

- To make money, you must spend a lot of time on the phone selling. This is a five-day-a-week job, says Kline, and that means that you cannot leave the phones for very long or hire an answering service to take messages. When clients call, they usually want to talk *now*.

- There are time pressures from clients who often wait until the last moment when they need help immediately.

- You can be deluged with people who may or may not be qualified, wanting you to find them work. You also need to keep tabs on how much your consultants are charging, because their rates must be competitive but not excessive. Companies won't continue using you if your consultants charge too much.

- It can take a year or more to develop and build your business.

💲 Pricing

The most common ways to operate this business are that the consultants for whom you find work agree to pay you 20 percent (some pay 25 percent) of the fee they negotiate with their client, excluding travel fees and other expenses that are reimbursed by the client. Kline adds that because many companies like a consultant and tend to rehire the same person over and over again, you need to have a contract that requires the consultant to pay you the 20 percent commission for any work done for a client for whom you have made the referral for up to twelve months. Expert service brokers may also charge a small fee for consultant members to become registered with their service, but too high a fee will discourage consultants from joining.

A few services operating like brokers use an alternative method of charging. They bill the clients directly and then pay the consultant a daily rate. For example, the broker gets a contract for $500 per day, then locates and pays an expert or trainer at the rate of $300 to $400 per day and pockets the remainder.

🖵 Potential Earnings

TYPICAL GROSS REVENUES: An active, ambitious broker who matches one to five consultants per week can gross $50,000 to $150,000 per year, based on commissions of $500 to $2,000 per match.

OVERHEAD: moderate, from 20 to 50 percent (biggest cost is phone bills).

📈 *Best Home Businesses* Estimate of Market Potential

The demand for specialists continues to grow in all aspects of society. This business will become increasingly international in scope.

▶ Best Ways to Get Business

- Attending business meetings, associations, trial lawyers' association meetings, and all other professional meetings as frequently as possible to meet potential clients and potential consultants.
- The most effective brokers aggressively identify the most likely clients in industries that might need consultants and get on the phone to identify their needs.
- Yellow pages advertising under the categories of Expert Referral Services or Consultants.

⏩ First Steps

- Your own contacts are a key source to start this business. Corporations will work with you only if you have some names of good people and the type of consultants they need. Qualified consultants are interested in being part of your database only if you have contacts with corporations who need them.
- Learn as much about consulting as you can. Read books on the topic (see the Management Consultant, Computer Consultant, and Specialty Consultant listings in this book). Begin signing up qualified experts and start contacting the leading companies in industries that might need their expertise. Volunteer to help them analyze what needs they have.

◻ Where to Turn for Information and Help

ORGANIZATIONS

American Association of Professional Consultants, National Bureau of Professional Consultants, 3577 Fourth Ave., San Diego 92103; (800) 543-1114; (619) 297-2207. Association for newcomers in consulting with less than five years experience. Membership costs $100 and includes a newsletter, resources, annual conference, and networking. Also allows you to take the American Management Association's self-study course that leads to a certificate in business management and consultancy, comparable to an MBA (takes about eighteen months to do). To join the AAPC, write a letter on your letterhead.

NEWSLETTERS

The Professional Consultant, edited by Paul Franklin, 123 N.W. Second Avenue, Suite 405, Portland, OR 97209; (800) 223-5085.

BOOKS

Building a Consulting Practice, Robert O. Metzger, Ph.D., Salt Lake City: Sage Publications, 1994.

Complete Guide to Consulting Success, Howard Shenson and Ted Nicolas, Dearborn Trade, 520 N. Dearborn St., Chicago, IL 60610-4354; (800) 621-9621.

FRANCHISES

Power Base, Inc., 8445 Camino Santa Fe, #207, San Diego, CA 92121; (800) 434-5200. Sells a franchise to the **National Consultant Referral, Inc.,** company for each area code in the country for $25,000 plus a yearly royalty based on gross income. Each franchisee gets the leads that are phoned in from companies seeking experts, as well as the opportunity to generate business in their own territory. All franchisees also have access to the complete database for the company and may cross-reference their consultants with clients to increase the opportunity to make a match. National Consultant Referral, Inc., currently has 4,000 consultants listed.

■ ■ ■ ■ ■

EXPORT AGENT

In most of the world, there is a hunger for American products, according to the Manufacturer's Agents National Association. There are, in fact, many new opportunities arising due to the opening up of the European Economic Community, Eastern Europe, Latin America, and the Pacific Rim. From chemicals and adhesives, to manufacturing equipment and plastics, to electronics and consumer products, many countries in the world are wide open to American products.

At the same time, as the U.S. trade deficit has caused the dollar to drop dramatically against world currencies, the United States has become a relatively low-cost place to manufacture goods. This means that many American firms are looking overseas for new markets.

Taken together, these two trends mean that exporting is a quickly emerging field for the rest of this decade. You can either export products you manufacture yourself or work with American manufacturers as an independent agent to sell their products overseas. Many smaller manufacturers need someone who can oversee export sales and establish relationships with foreign import agents who have the necessary business and political contacts.

Getting into exporting can be exciting and lucrative, but it also takes hard work, research, and money. According to John Jagoe, author of *The Export Sales and Marketing Manual,* "The secret to your success as an export sales agent will depend on the quality of your preparation. You've got to do your homework."

☑ Knowledge and Skills You Need to Have

■ You need an understanding of the basics of locating and negotiating with foreign suppliers, profits and margins in exporting, credits and risks, pricing, customs and shipping overseas, and international banking. You also need a good understanding of the various government regulations on export, paying taxes and duties, and distribution methods of the countries to which you intend to export. Many countries have distribution methods and pricing structures very different from those in the U.S.

■ You must have a knowledge of American government regulations and forms for exporting goods.

■ You need to be persistent in making contacts by telephone, letters, and announcements. You also have to be patient with the various steps in the process of exporting.

■ You need the ability and willingness to do research in the library and on the phone. Good communications skills are a must. You are talking with people from other cultures and must explain the exporting process to manufacturers.

■ The ability to maintain your composure and not be easily rattled by hassles in dealing with language barriers, other cultural habits, and red tape is necessary.

🐷 Start-up Costs

	Low	High
Computer with hard disk and modem	$1,000	$ 3,000
Ink-jet or laser printer	300	1,600
Suite software	250	400
Copier	300	800
Fax	300	900
Office furniture, especially an ergonomic chair	400	1,000
Business cards/letterhead	100	600
Brochures	100	1,000
Trade association dues to join those associations relevant to the products you sell	100	500
Reference books and publications	200	500
Total	$3,050	$10,300

📖 Advantages

■ This is a tremendous growth area of the economy, now that the European Community, Eastern Europe, and the Pacific Rim have opened up.

■ This business has opportunities for international travel.

■ You can develop loyal long-term relationships with businesspeople in other countries that lead to other opportunities, based on your providing good service.

⚁ Disadvantages

- To be truly successful, exporting requires knowledge of foreign countries and a foreign language, skills that many Americans do not have.
- Because international business transactions take longer, much patience is required. It can take months before your deals are finalized.
- There are many hassles because of the complicated nature of international transactions. Murphy's Law (anything that can go wrong will go wrong) often applies.
- Time differentials may stretch your normal working day.

⑤ Pricing

- Commissions range from 2 to 3 percent for high-volume consumer items like sports apparel to 5 to 15 percent for costly proprietary items, such as software.
- With experience and a track record of success, it becomes possible to obtain retainers. To encourage getting a retainer, offer to deduct up to 50 percent of the retainer from your initial commission.

ⓒ Potential Earnings

TYPICAL ANNUAL GROSS REVENUES: $60,000 to $100,000 within three years from start-up.

OVERHEAD: high (more than 40 percent). Overhead is high because of international communication costs, translation expenses, secretarial services for major projects, and travel. A twenty-four-hour answering service is preferable to an answering machine because calls must be taken at all hours of the day and night. Telephone costs can run from $300 to $500 a month. At this volume, however, you can expect to qualify for discounts on your long-distance service. Travel costs are high, but you should get your suppliers to share in the travel costs. Seminars to keep up on the field and to network can run $50 a month or more; entertainment, $100 a month and up.

⚁ *Best Home Businesses* Estimate of Market Potential

Total number of export agent firms in the United States, including home-based businesses: 2,922. With 50 percent of U.S. exports coming from companies with fewer than nineteen employees, there are many potential customers for export agents. The only soft spot for exporting is fluctuations in economies around the world. U.S. goods are becoming increasingly competitive, the dollar is cheap, and trade treaties are in place.

⬛ Best Ways to Get Business

- Making direct contacts with U.S. manufacturers by phone and fax to find out which are seeking to export their products; you also should make contact with importers and manufacturers in other countries to find out what they are seeking. This is a market-driven business.

- Speaking and offering seminars at meetings, trade shows, and conferences.

- Contact foreign embassies, consulates, and trade offices in Washington, D.C., and major cities. Ask their commercial officers for leads. (The State Department publishes a Diplomatic List annually, listing all foreign embassies in Washington.)

- Write to the commercial sections of U.S. embassies overseas and U.S. consulates telling them what you are looking for. Many will reply with a list of prospects.

- Read the *Journal of Commerce*, an international newspaper that lists leads for exporting obtained from the U.S. Department of Commerce's Trade Opportunity Program in which dealers and distributors worldwide contact American embassies seeking U.S. sources. Call (800)-221-3777.

⬛ First Steps

- Read about and attend seminars on export procedures. The government has many useful documents. See below.

- Identify businesses and/or industries on which you wish to concentrate and learn about the countries where such products would be well received.

- Make use of the free advice offered by experts with the state and federal governments.

- Start contacting U.S. companies you'd like to represent. It is wise to begin this step in your local area so you can keep communication and travel expenses down at first.

⬛ Where to Turn for Information and Help

ORGANIZATIONS

Federation of International Trade Associations, 1851 Alexander Bell Drive, Suite 400, Reston, VA 22091; (703) 620-1588. Can supply you with the names and addresses of local trade associations throughout the United States.

International Union of Commercial Agents and Brokers, P.O. Box 19352, 1000GJ, Amsterdam, Holland. Has up-to-date information on contracts and the laws of the land for many countries for exporting.

Manufacturers' Agents National Association (MANA), P.O. Box 3467, Laguna Hills, CA 92654-3467; (714) 859-4040. MANA is the national association for independent sales agents, including agents interested in export. They are also a member of the Intenational Union of Commercial Agents and Brokers above. Ask MANA for a reprint of their March 1994 article "64 Ways to Find Overseas Trading Partners."

BOOKS AND MANUALS

A Basic Guide to Exporting, U.S. Department of Commerce, available from the Government Printing Office. $9.50.

Export Profits: A Guide for Small Business, Jack S. Wolf, Upstart Press, 1994, Dearborn Trade, 520 N. Dearborn Street, Chicago, IL 60610-4354; (800) 621-9621.

Export Sales and Marketing Manual, John R. Jagoe, Export USA Publications, P.O. Box 39264, Minneapolis, MN 55439-0264; (800) 876-0624, fax (612) 943-1535. Provides step-by-step plans for entrepreneurs who want to start their own export business. Includes sample correspondence, contracts, pricing and budgeting worksheets, and shipping documents. Delivered current, $295. Quarterly updates, $175 a year. Mention this book to receive a 20 percent discount.

REFERENCE MATERIALS

Chambers of Commerce Worldwide, P.O. Box 455, Loveland, CO 80537. Offers a directory of overseas chambers of commerce.

The Global File, Dun and Bradstreet Information Services, provides marketing and sales information on more than 4 million businesses and 1.7 million corporate affiliations in 200 countries. You can select international prospects for direct-mail or telemarketing campaigns, pinpoint prospects, locate partners, and find selling opportunities. Call (800) 624-5669 for information.

Thomas Register of Manufacturers, Thomas Publishing Company, 5 Penn Plaza, 9th floor, New York, NY 10119; (800) 222-7900, ext. 200. Available both in print in libraries and as an on-line database (on CompuServe and Dialog). Provides the names and addresses of manufacturers and can be used as a prospect list.

Tradeshow Week Data Book, Tradeshow Week, 121 Chanlon Road, New Providence, NJ 07974; (800) 521-8110. $265. An international edition is available for $175 from R. R. Bowker, Order Department, Box 762, New York, NY 10114.

FEDERAL GOVERNMENT RESOURCES

Office of Export Licensing. For information on licensing requirments and export-control regulations and policies, contact the Office of Export Licensing voice information system at (202) 482-4811.

You can get additional information from the U.S. and Foreign Commercial Service of the International Trade Administration; call (202) 482-5777.

The Small Business Administration. SBA offers personal assistance and free advice through its Small Business Development Centers and Service Core of Retired Executives (SCORE), located throughout the country. In addition, the SBA's Office of International Trade Assistance, Office of Procurement Assistance, and Office of Minority Business Opportunities provide information and programs that may be helpful. To locate the SBA offices with these services nearest you, write to the SBA, Small Business Development Centers Headquarters, 1129 20th Street, N.W., #410, Washington, DC 20036.

U.S. Department of Commerce, 14th Street and Constitution Avenue, Washington, DC 20230. The department's experts in Washington and district offices throughout the United States have first-hand knowledge of overseas markets. They offer information on overseas trade opportunities, customs, regulations and procedures, market potential, and so forth. The Department of Commerce also offers seminars on exporting. Contact the export seminar staff at (202) 482-4811.

STATE GOVERNMENT RESOURCES

Most state governments have international trade offices to help companies within their states become successful exporters.

MAGAZINES AND NEWSLETTERS

American Australian Business, P.O. Box 280, Roseville, NSW 2069, Australia.

Business America, the Magazine of International Trade, available from Superintendent of Documents, U.S. Government Printing Office, Washington, DC 20402; (202) 512-1800. A biweekly published by the U.S. Department of Commerce. $53 per year.

Coble International, 1420 Steeple Chase Drive, Dover, PA 17315; (717) 292-5763. A newsletter that lists up to 1,000 export leads, with contact information.

Export Leads, P.O. Box 30200-L, Washington, DC 20030. Publishes hundreds of classified listings of products being sought by world importers every month.

Export Today, Trade Communications, 733 15th Street, N.W., #1100, Washington, DC 20005; (202) 737-1060.

■ ■ ■ ■ ■

FACIALIST

Facialists help their clients (men and women) take care of their skin. They work to slow down the natural aging process, avert wrinkles and skin problems, and keep the face looking as young and healthy as possible. Care of the skin is an ongoing process, so satisfied clients can become regular customers. Because skin needs taking care of between facials, facialists can sell their clients skin-care products as well.

The beauty business is a perennial one. People want to look and feel their best all year long, in good economic times as well as bad. This is especially true now that the baby-boom generation is aging. By the year 2000, over half the population will be over thirty-five years of age. As people age, they spend more money, more frequently, on skin care. In fact, throughout the 90s, it is estimated that skin-care products have been growing at the rate of better than 7 percent a year, and will continue to do so.

A facialist's clients include all occupations for which people need to present themselves at their best. Executives, performers, service personnel, professional speakers, and airline attendants are just a few of the groups of people for whom appearance is an important element. Facialists can perform several treatments for a client, too: basic, deep pore cleansing and hydrating.

Gloria Martell, a Los Angeles facialist, sees most of her regular customers about once a month. For a while, she had an assistant and was able to see between five and ten clients a day, but she emphasizes that facialists who work alone are seldom able to schedule that many clients each day, unless they herd people through. It takes awhile for the client to disrobe and dress again, and you also need to spend time counseling clients on proper follow-up care and to demonstrate and sell skin-care products—something most facialists do to make extra money. In good years, Martell has earned more than $50,000 a year working from home on her own.

☑ Knowledge and Skills You Need to Have

- Becoming a facialist requires training to become a cosmetician (about six months), and most states license facialists as cosmeticians. Some facialists also perform electrolysis, which requires a separate license.

- This business requires that you have a nurturing personality and genuinely enjoy pampering people.

- You need to feel completely comfortable touching and having close physical contact with your clients.

- You need a good understanding of hygiene because of the potential for contracting or spreading communicable diseases.

- An outgoing personality is helpful if your business also involves product sales.

🐗 Start-up Costs	Low	High
Training	$2,000	$ 2,500
Table for clients	800	2,500
Steamer	1,000	2,000
Sterilizer	600	600
Towels and miscellaneous equipment	200	400
Specialized equipment	2,000	4,000
Brochure with rate card	200	600
Business cards, letterhead, envelopes	100	600
Total*	$6,900	$13,200

* These figures do not include remodeling or decorating costs for transforming a room in your home into a treatment area.

🕮 Advantages

- The market will continue to expand as the population ages and more people want to stay young-looking.
- The work is neither stressful nor physically demanding.
- Your income potential is good if you market correctly.
- You can see clients at the hours of your choosing.
- You can build a steady, repeat clientele.

🕮 Disadvantages

- This business requires having a separate room in your home, which must be decorated, equipped, and dedicated to use as a salon.
- Clients will be coming through your home unless you have a separate entrance to your treatment room.
- Zoning may be an issue because many zoning codes do not permit a continual stream of clients and customers coming to a home business.
- You may work yourself out of business with some clients, says Gloria Martell, because people's skin improves and they feel that they no longer need your services.
- You put yourself in contact with many different people and there is the possibility of contracting an illness or disease. Rubber gloves are sometimes used to avoid direct contact.

💲 Pricing

Facialists charge by appointment. A basic facial runs from about $50 on up. Additional services increase this amount. A regular customer will come monthly, yielding an annual income per regular customer of $600 or more.

▣ Potential Earnings

TYPICAL ANNUAL GROSS REVENUES: $40,000, based on four clients a day, four days a week for fifty weeks, at $50 per session. About six appointments a day is the maximum unless you have an assistant. Appointments often take more than an hour because people sometimes have special problems that need attention, and you also have to do some consultation with the client. Earnings may be increased by selling products and teaching classes and seminars.

OVERHEAD: low (approximately 20 percent).

▨ *Best Home Businesses* Estimate of Market Potential

Total number of facialist firms in the United States, including home-based businesses: 9,556. The growing market for facialists is indicated by the many new skin-care technologies and products coming onto the market. They range from chemical processes to electrical-stimulation methods developed to serve aging baby boomers eager to maintain a youthful appearance. Looking vibrant and healthy is also part of the fitness culture that continues to be popular with a large segment of the population.

▧ Best Ways to Get Business

- Personal contacts and informal networking among friends, social organizations, and at your health club.
- Networking in professional organizations, such as "leads" clubs.
- Passing out catalogues through friends.
- Creating a newsletter to send to past and prospective clients.
- Doing direct mail featuring special prices or offering complimentary facials.
- Giving your clients complimentary gift certificates to give to their friends.
- Holding an open house at which you provide information about your services.

▧ First Steps

First you must complete your training. Training as a cosmetician can be obtained at private cosmetology schools or community colleges. You'll find cosmetology schools listed in your yellow pages. The formal training program is usually less than six months in length and leads to certification. Then, if your state requires it, you need to obtain your license. To get the information you need, look in the telephone book for your state's information number and call to find out which state agency administers the licensing exam.

Once you are trained and, if necessary, licensed, you must set up a room in your home as your salon and begin marketing your services. A good marketing technique is to offer an initial complimentary session. So, in addition to the marketing methods mentioned above, to get your business under way offer to do a session for people you know who are in a position to pay for your service if they like the experience. While doing this demonstration, educate them about their skin and tell them why regular professional care is impor-tant. Talk with them about *their* skin in particular and, using a mirror, show them the benefits they could enjoy if they had regular facials.

🔲 Where to Turn for Information and Help

ORGANIZATIONS

International Association of Aestheticians, 4447 McKinney Avenue, Dallas, TX 75205; (214) 526-0760.

MAGAZINES

Dermascope, 4447 McKinney Avenue, Dallas, TX 75205; (214) 526-0760. Bimonthly.

Skin, Inc., 362 S. Schmale Road, Carol Stream, IL 60188; (708) 653-2155, Fax (708) 653-2192.

FRANCHISES

Affiliates of these companies are not truly facialists, but selling cosmetics can be a good alternative or sideline business.

Alloette Cosmetics, 234 Lancaster Avenue, Malvern, PA 19355. Alloette is reported to be the only cosmetics franchise you don't need a storefront to operate. They've been in business since 1978, and they have 100 franchises. As an Alloette franchisee, you recruit and train beauty con-sultants, who sell skin-care products through home shows. The fran-chise fee is $80,000, part of which can be financed by Alloette. Although this fee is higher than that for most home-based businesses, the profits to be made in the beauty business are great.

A low-cost alternative is to become an Avon or Mary Kay distributor. For more information contact: **Avon Products,** 9 West 57th Street, New York, NY 10019; (800) 367-2866; (212) 546-6015. Also **Mary Kay Cosmetics,** 8787 Stemmons Freeway, Dallas, TX 75247; (800) 201-1362; (214) 630-8787.

■ ■ ■ ■ ■

FAMILY CHILD-CARE PROVIDER

The era of Ozzie and Harriet is just a memory. Women no longer work only until they have babies. Today, more than 50 percent of married women with children under six work outside the home, and a majority of divorced women with preschool-age children work. So who takes care of the infants, toddlers, and preschoolers while Mommy and Daddy are at work? Day care is the solution for nearly a third of full-time working mothers.

The Bureau of Labor Statistics reports that parents spend over $20 million on child care each year, and that figure continues to grow. Not only do two-career households need child care, but millions of working single parents are becoming a large market as well. In fact, according to a study by Dr. Kathleen Christenson of the New School for Social Research, 50 percent of women who work at home use some form of child-care help too, at least part-time.

Much of commercial day care is done in people's homes in what is called *family child care* as opposed to day care in large centers, schools, churches, and temples. A 1990 Mathematica Policy Research study estimated that there are between 550,000 and 1.1 million family child-care providers compared to 80,000 larger centers. But even this number of family child-care homes is not enough, as other studies have indicated that many communities lack sufficient resources, particularly for infants and toddlers. Many businesses as well are looking for day-care resources to offer as part of their benefits for employees, increasing the demand. Small companies that can't afford on-site day-care centers especially are potential customers for new family child-care centers.

More importantly, *good* family day care is the key to success. According to a five-year study by the Families and Work Institute, just 9 percent of family child-care providers in a sample survey were rated "good," while 56 percent were ranked only "adequate." That leaves a lot of room for new child-care centers committed to quality and excellence.

These facts bode well for someone interested in turning a love for children and play into a career. Opening your own family child care is relatively easy. Most states require a license or registration with a government agency if you intend to have more than three children. The licensing process usually requires an inspection of your home for space, cleanliness, and safety, and some states also require that you have taken a training course in CPR, emergency care, and perhaps child development.

One regulation to remember is that you will likely need approval from your zoning board to operate a home-based day-care business. Your home may be located in an area that is zoned to permit no family day care or that limits the number of children to three or six. Some zoning ordinances allow home day-care businesses only if all abutting neighbors agree to it because of the additional noise and traffic it generates.

The procedure for passing the proper zoning and licensing varies greatly by state and city, but there are strong incentives for taking these steps. First, the unzoned, unlicensed day-care operator risks being ordered to close down. Second, licensed day-care providers are eligible for food subsidies from the U.S. Department of Agriculture to help pay for breakfasts, lunches, and snacks you give to your children. Licensing is also needed for liability insurance, which anyone involved in providing care needs to have to protect his or her business in the event of an accident. Finally, being fully licensed opens up the opportunity to become accredited by the National Association for Family Day Care.

The mark of high-quality family day care, according to the Families and Work Institute, is a purposeful commitment to create home environments in which children can be nurtured and can learn. This means that you should try to have ample toys for children to play with both indoors and out that are suitable to their developmental level. You need to take every precaution to remove dangerous chemicals, cleaning fluids, and other things that could hurt children. In addition, day-care centers need to stimulate children's mental, physical, and social development by providing them with learning experiences of all kinds.

To enjoy this business, you must like children and be willing to give them warmth and attention. You also need patience and understanding because you are, in effect, a professional parent—dealing with temper tantrums, tears, and fighting.

Day care has traditionally been low paying and although it may have less income potential than most businesses described in this book, it provides a wealth of psychic rewards for someone who wants to stay at home and loves working with children.

☑ Knowledge and Skills You Need to Have

- You must like taking care of and parenting other people's children.
- You need to have an upbeat personality and not be quick to get angry, because children will test you regularly.
- A knowledge of child development and how appropriately to handle various behaviors at different ages is especially useful.
- Getting along with parents requires tact and tolerance.
- You need to be able to schedule, organize, and manage four or five things at the same time.
- Making time for the various types of developmental tasks the children need to do each day requires organizational skills.
- You need to be able to give first aid.
- You need to enjoy children's games and stories or at least be able to enjoy the children's enjoyment.

🐗 Start-up Costs

	Low	High
For Six Children		
Liability insurance*	$ 375	$ 500
Toys and equipment	1,000	2,000
Beds and cribs or playpen for children under two	350	500
Fire extinguisher	25	50

	Low	High
Smoke detectors	50	50
Children's tables and chairs	125	150
Cordless telephone (so you can continue to watch children despite inevitable phone calls)	75	125
Business cards	100	100
Brochure	100	200
Total	$2,200	$3,675

* You may be able to get umbrella coverage with your homeowner's policy. Without insurance, parents need to sign a notice in which you state that you do not have insurance.

Advantages

- If you love taking care of children, this business means you can make money doing what you love.
- You can earn a living and stay home with your own children, who become part of your career.
- Operating a home-based day-care center makes you eligible for important tax deductions. You can take deductions for the rooms you use for day care even if those rooms are used at other times for nonbusiness purposes.

Disadvantages

- You are essentially confined to your home and yard every weekday. You can't run out somewhere for lunch or for errands.
- Unless you have an assistant, you can't take a day off unexpectedly to go to the doctor or dentist or just to relax.
- You can't go to your own children's school events during daytime hours unless you make special arrangements for someone to relieve you.
- For ten hours a day your conversation is limited to talking with small children.
- Normal auto insurance doesn't cover transporting children, so unless you get special insurance coverage you may have to call an ambulance if a parent can't come to get a child in the event of illness or injury.

Pricing

Pricing varies considerably with location, age of child, and quality of care. For example, in Milwaukee a parent may pay $135 per week for full-time infant care; $175 in Washington, D.C., and $225 in San Francisco. The rate in a rural area may be $100 or less. It is therefore useful to call other day-care providers in your area to assess fees and determine your fee relative to other family day cares around you, taking into account the number of children you intend to have, whether or not you employ any staff, and the quality of the environment you can offer.

▣ Potential Earnings

Although home-based day-care centers work best both financially and psychologically when two adults are present, the calculation below is based on a one-person operation.

TYPICAL ANNUAL GROSS REVENUES: $30,000 to $45,000, plus additional revenues you can get in reimbursements from the Child Care Food Program. These figures are based on charging an average of $100 to $150 per child for six children, fifty weeks per year.

Some states will license home day care for up to twelve children; however, you must hire a helper if you have more than six children, which means paying someone else to assist you, and this may also cause a zoning problem.

OVERHEAD: high (more than 40 percent).

▨ *Best Home Businesses* **Estimate of Market Potential**

Continuing need for day care by single and dual-career couples, a shortage of day-care facilities, and growing concern about children being cared for in institutional environments all feed a strong demand for family day care into the twenty-first century.

▥ Best Ways to Get Business

- If your business is new, get a listing with a referral agency. Child Care Resource and Referral Agencies provide free services; they are funded with government grants. They may also provide loans for toys and other equipment.
- Networking with other family day-care providers and receiving their overflow.
- Putting notices on bulletin boards in supermarkets, laundries, and other retail locations.
- Advertising in local parenting newspapers and magazines.
- Contacting small businesses to locate companies that might be interested in contracting directly with you to supply day care for children of employees.
- Once your business starts, encourage referrals from your current families.

▤ Franchises

Monday Morning America, 276 White Oak Ridge Road, Bridgewater, NJ 08807; (800) 335-4MOM; (908) 685-0060. Founded by Suzanne Schmidt, who worked for twelve years as a family day-care provider herself, they offer two opportunities that could be of interest to day-care providers. The first is a family day-care management service. They train existing and new family day-care providers, who become part of their network. You set your own rates, but they screen and match you with families in need of child care and handle your collections. They also provide backup for vacations and sick leave; advertising; insurance; ongoing training classes; an equipment, toy, and book loan rotation program; and paid holidays. This service is free to the provider because the firm adds its fee to those set by the day-care provider. They also offer franchises to individuals who would like to become a family day-care management service; the franchise fee is $9,000.

First Steps

1. Check your zoning to see if you can offer day care in your home. It's a good idea to talk over your plans with neighbors to avoid their opposition, even if you don't have zoning problems.

2. Contact a child-care information agency in your area (these agencies are listed in the yellow pages under Child Care) or the local family day-care association to learn about the demand for day care in your area, licensing requirements, and sources for training, such as the Red Cross and community colleges. Elementary schools are another source of information about the need for day care in your area.

3. Apply for a license or registration, according to the requirements of your state.

4. Take classes in first aid, emergency preparation (for example, earthquakes, hurricanes, tornadoes), and operating a day-care business in your home, if available.

5. Establish your rates and written policies, including hours of operation, deposits required, late fees if children are picked up late, medical issues, holidays, notice of termination, and payment. To avoid collection problems, have parents pay on Friday prior to the next week. Never let unpaid bills go for more than one week.

6. Obtain equipment, and childproof your home. You may be able to buy used equipment and toys (wood is more durable than plastic) at garage sales and secondhand stores. You can even borrow books and sound recordings from your library.

Where to Turn for Information and Help

ORGANIZATIONS

Children's Defense Fund, 25 E Street, N.W., Washington, DC 20001; (202) 662-3547. Publishes a study of child care in the U.S.

National Association for the Education of Young Children, 1509 16th Street, N.W., Washington, DC 20036; (202) 232-8777.

National Association of Child Care Resource & Referral Agencies, NACCRRA Field Office, 2116 Campus Drive S.E., Rochester, MN 55904. Call Child Care Aware at (800) 424-2246. This association refers parents to local referral agencies that help them locate day care. Those local agencies also provide information and assistance to people interested in starting a family child-care home business.

National Association for Family Child Care, 725 15th Street, N.W., Suite 505, Washington, DC 20005; (800) 359-3817 or (202) 347-3356. The association offers accreditation to day-care providers who meet their states' requirements and have been providing care in their home for eighteen months. It annually publishes the *National Directory of Family Day Care Providers,* listing over 1,000 local support groups of day-care providers. For membership information, call (602) 838-3446.

Save the Children Child Care Support Center, 1447 Peachtree Street, N.E., Suite 700, Atlanta, GA 30309; (404) 885-1578. The center annually presents a national family-care conference. It publishes a variety of materials. Call or write to be added to the conference mailing list and/or receive a list of publications.

BOOKS

Home Child Care: The Tender Business, Ellie Roosli Peters, Greenlawn Press, 1075 Greenlawn, South Bend, IN 46617. 1990.

Negotiated Care: The Experience of Family Day Care Providers, Margaret E. Nelson, Philadelphia: Temple University Press, 1990.

Opening Your Doors to Family Child Care, Kathy Modigliani, National Association for the Education of Young Children. See address above.

Room for Loving, Room for Learning: Finding the Space You Need in Your Family Child Care Home, Hazel Osborn, St. Paul: Redleaf Press, 1994.

Setting Up for Infant Care: Guidelines for Centers and Family Day Care Homes, edited by A. Goodwin, Washington, D.C.: National Association for the Education of Young Children, 1988.

Start & Run a Profitable Home Daycare: Your Step-by-Step Business Plan, Catherine Pruissen, Bellingham, Wash.: Self-Counsel Press, 1993.

Start Your Own At-Home Child Care Business, Patricia Gallagher, Young Sparrow Press, Box 265, Worcester, PA 19490; (800) ALL-BOOK. 1994.

Toddler Day Care: A Guide to Responsive Caregiving, R. L. Leavitt and B. K. Eheart, Lexington, Mass.: Lexington Books, 1985.

Redleaf Press, 450 N. Syndicate, Suite 5, St. Paul, MN 55104-4125; (800) 423-8309. Publishes training and resource materials for family child-care providers. Call or write for a free catalogue.

At-Home Professions, 2001 Lowe St., Ft. Collins, CO 80525; (800) 359-3455. Offers a training course in starting a family day-care center.

The Windflower Institute, 815 N. Nevada Ave., Suite 1, Colorado Springs, CO 80903; (719) 520-1614. A national training, consulting, and advocacy group. Publishes a quarterly newsletter and other publications.

■■■■■

GIFT BASKET BUSINESS

If you like and are good at handicrafts and also want to find a way to make money using your creativity and design skills, a gift basket business is something to consider. With fewer hours of discretionary time for managing life's details, most people have little time to shop for gifts. What could be better than a present that seems to be custom tailored for the recipient and yet takes no time to select, wrap, and deliver? Gift baskets fill the need perfectly.

It's no wonder gift baskets continue to grow in popularity as a way for a business to say thank-you to a client or for an individual to remember a loved one at Christmas, Easter, Valentine's Day, Mother's Day, Father's Day, Secretary's Day, birthdays, graduations, weddings, anniversaries, baby showers, and other special occasions. Even death and divorce have become occasions for sending thoughtful gift baskets to cherished friends and relatives. According to an industry survey in 1992, 80 percent of gift basket entrepreneurs reported an increase in sales, and had an average annual income of $72,500.

A gift basket can be filled with traditional gourmet foods, wines, and kitchen items, or it can be a special package containing hobby items or sports gear, bath soaps and lotions, art supplies, or almost anything special. Baskets can be customized to all kinds of occupations and interests—car dealers, politicians, realtors, children at camp, chocolate lovers, and so on. By finding out about the personalities and interests of the people you're preparing baskets for, you can add a personal touch by including items they would especially enjoy.

Some people create gift baskets to serve specific markets, such as hospital patients. Boredom Baskets/Boxes makes baskets consisting of several individually wrapped packages. The baskets contain directions that a new package is to be opened each day, and the packages contain both silly and useful gifts, such as decks of Old Maid cards, puzzles, and travel toothbrushes. Romance can be packaged, too, in the form of baskets filled with items like champagne splits and glasses; audiotapes and CDs with romantic music; and fragrant soaps, sponges, and bath mitts that might be used in a shared bathing experience.

With enough ingenuity and some marketing savvy you can develop a profitable part- or full-time business with a following of grateful customers who appreciate the compliments they get when their easy-to-give personalized gift baskets arrive.

The most profitable markets are corporate buyers, followed by individuals. Gift baskets can be sold directly to businesses through personal contact, by mail, or by placing them in retail stores like hospital gift shops, nail salons, boutiques, and health-food stores. Other regular customers might include wedding planners, resort hotels, real estate agents, meeting planners, and contest operators.

Mary Ann Jacobs started a part-time gift basket business, Gifts to Go, in Tucson, Arizona, six years ago while working as an accountant. Now, she sells year-round, mainly to corporate clients. Her Southwest-style baskets—shaped like coyotes, saguaro cactus, doves, and armadillos and filled with blue corn chips, Indian red popcorn, salsa, and other goodies characteristic of that region—have a wide appeal and help promote the local economy.

Jacobs emphasizes the importance of having some kind of business background. Just being an artist isn't necessarily enough to guarantee success in this field, she says. Those who do best in the business are generally those who know something about marketing, business planning, and administration. Although she has taken marketing classes, Jacobs says she does no advertising at all. Early on, she found that advertising really wasn't cost-effective for her. Instead, she gets her business through telemarketing and referrals from satisfied clients. "You have to stay in front of the clients you already have," she advises. "Take extra-good care of them and they'll do the marketing for you" by telling other people how good you are.

☑ Knowledge and Skills You Need to Have

- Although you do not need any particular background, you must have an artistic sense and the ability to select and design baskets that are visually appealing.

- Creativity helps. You need to be able to identify unique goods to put into your baskets to distinguish your business from run-of-the-mill baskets.

- You need to know how and where to purchase supplies at a cost-effective price to maximize your profit.

- In most states, you need a liquor license in order to sell baskets containing wine or champagne. Be sure to check in advance and comply with all pertinent laws and regulations.

- You must be able to communicate effectively with customers and have sufficient enthusiasm and personality to sell your product.

- You need to be able to manage your time effectively so that you can make the most of peak seasons.

- Being good at organizing is essential, because an order for 100 baskets can take up a lot of space. And because a big order can result from just one telephone call, you need to be able to organize your work space effectively so your materials won't take over your home.

◫ Start-up Costs

	Low	High
Initial inventory of baskets, excelsior, food, and other items	$ 500	$5,000
Hot-glue gun	5	20
Shrink-wrap machine	100	400
Business cards, letterhead, envelopes, invoices	600	800
Desk, chair, assembly tables	600	800
Two-color flyer or brochure (sales go up with color brochure)	500	2,000
Organizational dues for networking	250	250
Professional portfolio of photographs of your baskets to show to prospective customers	100	500
Total*	$2,655	$9,770

* Add $1,500 to $3,000 for a computer and ink-jet printer if you want to computerize your client list and print your own brochures and advertisements.

▣ Advantages

- This is an artistic business that allows you to express your creativity and your love for beautiful things.
- People like to get gifts, so delivering them is a pleasant experience.
- You can easily start this business on a part-time basis. Start-up costs are relatively low, and it is an easy business to get into.
- You can often get free samples and other goodies from suppliers.

▣ Disadvantages

- This business can take over your home, with shredded paper and inventory everywhere. It helps to have plenty of storage space or a dry garage.
- You may have to work around the clock during holidays and other peak periods to market, make, and deliver your baskets. You may even be so busy at holidays that you miss out on celebrating them yourself with your family.
- Demand tends to be seasonal—about 50 percent of business occurs around holidays, particularly Christmas—and can be slow at other times of the year unless you are creative in lining up other types of business.
- You will do better at this business if you have at least one other person working with you.
- You are competing with larger mail-order gift basket companies.

- You may need to offer discounts to bigger customers like wedding planners, resorts, meeting planners, etc.

$ Pricing

Baskets are priced anywhere from $10 to $300, with most costing between $35 and $50. Factors that enter into pricing are the products in the basket, the time the basket takes to assemble, and the uniqueness and artistic quality of the design. Most businesses give quantity discounts for corporate customers or other large orders.

▣ Potential Earnings

You can assemble about eight simply designed baskets per hour, while more complex baskets take fifteen minutes or more apiece. Simple designs need not be the least expensive ones. If you sell twenty-five baskets a week, fifty weeks a year at an average of $40 a basket, you will produce $50,000 in gross sales. However, immediately before holidays, a one-person business with some temporary help from family or neighbors can produce $2,000 a day. One order of 100 baskets can produce $3,000 to $4,000. The cost of the basket and its components should be about 40 to 50 percent of what you charge. Mary Ann Jacobs counsels, "Keep prices fair. A 50 percent markup is sufficient, plus a little extra for packaging."

OVERHEAD: low (20 percent or less).

⚡ *Best Home Businesses* **Estimate of Market Potential**

Total number of gift basket makers in the United States, including home-based businesses: 16,749. We considered not including gift baskets in this edition because of the relatively large number of firms making gift baskets and the difficulties some people we spoke with have had in making their businesses a success, but we kept it in because people who are clever in creating unique niches, designs, and marketing activities can produce an adequate income doing what can be enjoyable and creative work.

▣ Best Ways to Get Business

- Call on corporate and organizational buyers, show your portfolio, and leave sample baskets for decision makers.
- Obtain publicity in local and national publications about your unique baskets.
- Network and develop personal contacts in organizations, such as trade and business associations and church groups, and periodically provide a gift basket for a door prize at their meetings.
- Talk about and display your baskets at home parties and open houses,

and then take orders (as they do at Tupperware parties), and give a gift basket to the hostess.

- Give your flyers or brochures to reps exhibiting at gift shows, who can place your baskets with retailers. Be careful about placing baskets in retail stores, though, if you have items in your basket that don't stay fresh for long periods of time.
- Leave flyers or brochures with clients when you deliver their orders, and mail flyers or brochures to prospective clients.
- Exhibit at craft fairs and home shows.
- Use direct mail with your own mailing list of people who have contacted you as a result of your publicity and exhibits at shows.
- Donate baskets to nonprofit organizations for their fund-raisers in exchange for an acknowledgment in their printed materials and an announcement from the podium during the event.
- Get an 800 number to use with your publicity and direct mail.

First Steps

1. If you have no experience in design, take a course in floral design or visual arts through a community college or a university extension program.
2. Take a short course in starting a gift basket business at an adult-education program like the Learning Annex.
3. Attend any of the hundreds of craft, gift, and novelty trade shows around the country, looking for product ideas and suppliers to prepare your business.
4. Locate sources of supplies at trade shows and through wholesalers found in the yellow pages. Using local suppliers will reduce or eliminate shipping costs.
5. Talk with people in the gift basket business in the area.
6. Obtain a MasterCard and Visa merchant account because many of your customers want to charge their purchases. (See *Working from Home* for tips on getting a merchant account.)
7. Plan to have people available to come in and help you with assembling baskets for large orders. Assembly of less-complex baskets can be kept out of your home at a reasonable cost by using the services of sheltered workshops employing the handicapped.
8. Order and keep sufficient materials and supplies on hand that you can get quantity discounts for. Make sure the materials you use are easy to store. Do not buy merchandise that will go out of date (like a calendar), spoil, or get stale.

☐ Where to Turn for Information and Help

ORGANIZATIONS

Gift Association of America, 612 W. Broad Street, Bethlehem, PA 18018; (610) 861-9445, fax (610) 861-0948.

Gift Basket Retailers International, 1205 W. Forsyth Street, Jacksonville, FL 32204; (904) 634-1902.

BOOKS

Building a Better Gift Basket Business, Debra Paulk. Festivities Publications, 1205 W. Forsyth Street, Jacksonville, FL 32204. 1993. $59.95.

The Business of Gift Baskets: How to Make a Profit Working from Home, Camille Anderson and Don L. Price, P.O. Box 7000-700, Redondo Beach, CA 90277; (310) 316-0611. 1991.

The How-to's of the Gift Basket Business, Carol Starr, Bags 'n' Baskets, 8045 Antoine, Box 147, Houston, TX 77088. $12.95.

MAGAZINES

Gift Basket Review, 1205 W. Forsyth St., Jacksonville, FL 32204; (800) 729-6338; (904) 634-1902.

■ ■ ■ ■ ■

GROWER OF SPECIALTY FOODS, HERBS, AND FLOWERS

If you enjoy gardening, you may be able to cultivate your hobby into a full-time home-based livelihood without owning the acres of land typical of today's corporate farm or even the traditional family farm. Backyards, basements, or a small parcel of a few acres is all you need to grow herbs, sprouts, mushrooms, edible flowers, and specialty vegetables in urban and suburban areas.

In fact, urban farming is becoming an important part of agriculture in America. Charles Walters, Jr., publisher of *Acres USA* magazine, says, "The only bright future in agriculture is to get a few acres, grow the product, and be near where the people are." Walters advises, "Find yourself a couple of hundred customers and make yourself a living."

Over the past thirty years, Americans have developed a robust appetite for exotic, unusual, and healthy foods. They are looking for colorful ingredients, new flavorings, organically grown produce, and ethnic specialties. As a result, gourmet shops, restaurants, upscale grocery stores, health-food stores, and now even mainstream supermarkets are eager to offer specialty foods to their customers. And the public is seeking out specially grown foods, flowers, and condiments at swap meets, produce stands, farmers' markets, and country shops.

The popularity of farmers' markets has been a particular boon to vest-pocket farmers. In West Los Angeles, for example, farmers' markets have grown from three a week in 1990 to seven in 1994 to ten in 1995. People growing the perfect lettuce or tomato can charge premium prices—often more than supermarkets do—as people line up to buy.

Herbs, potpourris, flowers, fruits, and vegetables, even oat grass to help the digestion of household cats are also in demand at farmers' markets. Other items in demand include:

- Herbs are used in cooking, teas, medicines, condiments (e.g., specialty vinegars and mustards), perfumes, and aromatherapy
- Potpourris are used in gift baskets and sold via many mail-order catalogues and retail outlets
- Some flowers are dried and sold in country shops, gift stores, and catalogues while others are cultivated for their appearance on the epicurean plate or their taste as in "edible" flowers such as carnations, bachelor's buttons, borage, calendula, pansies, and rose petals. (Some bars even use borage and other blooms in mixed drinks!) And of course, some flowers are grown simply for their beauty in arrangements purchased by florists, hotels, restaurants, and many offices.
- Unique fruits are prized and organically grown fruits are cherished by many.
- Healthy vegetables, grown without pesticides, are the mainstay of health-food stores and are fast becoming desired in traditional supermarkets.

Often getting into this business begins with a desire to get closer to nature and return to a simpler life. It's attracting green-minded people like David and Susan Mountain, who have turned their love of mushrooms into a business: growing exotic mushrooms. David and Susan, like dozens of others we've read about, have sought out a lifestyle quite different from one they may have known earlier as corporate executives in major metropolitan areas. People like the Mountains frequently move to a calmer location in Vermont, Oregon, Washington, Montana, Idaho, or in the warmer southern states, where they can have a small parcel on which to pursue their love of nature while earning a living, part-time or full-time.

Sometimes it's the desire to stay in a rural area that attracts people to specialty growing. Robyn and Robert Rohlfing live in Plymouth, Nebraska, for example, where they are successful organic herb producers. They market most of their herbs locally and have had the same clients for nine years. Robyn calls herself an "oddball farmer" and explains that of all the herbs used in the United States for cooking and medicinal purposes, only 10 percent of them are grown in this country.

Even if you don't live in a temperate climate, you can still be in business by growing flowers, herbs, or produce in a greenhouse. Greenhouse nurseries have become the sixth largest agricultural commodity in the U.S. in recent years, as the interest in tropical plants, trees (for woody ornamentals), medicinal herbs, and hydroponically grown vegetables (especially tomatoes) has created a year-round demand. Greenhouse expert Ted Taylor also points to the popularity of "juicers" as another reason to be in the greenhouse business, growing organic fruits and vegetables to feed the juicer craze.

So, whether your love is garlic or ginger, mushrooms or marigolds, tomatoes or baby white potatoes, there's probably a way for you to turn your love of food and flowers into a new career or just some extra cash.

✔ Knowledge and Skills You Need to Have

- You must be willing to learn what you need to do to grow crops of sufficient quality and quantity to make a living. A love of food or for growing things is essential to keep you motivated through the entire learning process. Growing produce, herbs, or flowers is part art, part science, and mistakes are costly. You need to have knowledge of plants, growing patterns, plant disease, insects, fertilizers, and many other fields.

- You must be sensitive to market needs and demands, to what people want to eat, what they find appealing, who's buying what, and when they're buying.

- Good bookkeeping skills are important because you need to know what it costs you to grow and how much profit you are making.

- Tenacity and persistence are required as you contact wholesalers, supermarkets, groceries, restaurants, cataloguers, gift basket stores, herbalists, and other potential customers to sell your goods. Selling produce or flowers is like selling any other product; you must show your customers that your product is of high quality and you must be amenable to their needs.

🐄 Start-up Costs

Land. How much land you need to earn a full-time living depends on what kind of crops you have, the time your crops need for maturity, and crop rotation. If you don't have zoning problems, or if you outgrow your backyard, find out if your city will rent low-cost land. For example, the Department of Water and Power of the city of Los Angeles rents plots of land. Or you can lease land from a friend or neighbor who has a large yard.

Supplies. You will need seed, fertilizers, growing pots, planting boxes, hoses, and other supplies. Expect to invest from $500 to $2,000 at first.

Building a small greenhouse requires $500 to $1,000 for a wood structure or $2,000 to $20,000 for a steel structure depending on size and materials used.

A vehicle to service your accounts.   You should be able to get a used truck for around $4,000 or a used van for $6,000 to $8,000; new delivery vans cost around $14,000 to $16,000.

Setting up your business.   Desk and furniture and a low-cost computer should run around $1,500. Business cards and stationery cost around $100 to $400.

🔼 Advantages

- There are many ways to be in this business, offering you a variety of choices if you like farming. You can specialize in flowers or produce, food items or medicines, or do bottling, pickling, drying, body-care products, aromatic pillows, or just about anything you can think of that uses herbs, flowers, or produce.
- This business provides the freedom to live an alternative lifestyle and still be close to cities.
- It provides the opportunity to experience a connectedness with the earth through growing living things.
- It's a way to express an environmental consciousness while earning one's living.
- This is a business you can start part-time in your backyard or basement.
- You can meet many other people who enjoy what you enjoy through marketing your goods.

🔽 Disadvantages

- Your livelihood is vulnerable to the weather and the seasons. After all, farming is the occupation that gave rise to the saying "feast or famine." If you live in a colder clime, your profits may be too seasonal for a full-time income.
- The popularity of growing particular "in" crops may result in heavy competition. In some cases, large agribusiness is now entering niche markets, pushing out smaller growers.
- Land near cities can be expensive, and it can be difficult to make a profit. Dr. Booker T. Watley, Tuskagee University plant geneticist and agronomist, says that a farm needs to be within forty miles of an urban center with a population of 50,000 or more, reachable on a hard-surface road.
- Growing crops is hard, dirty, physically uncomfortable work.

- Within cities, if your property is not zoned to allow agricultural use, you may have problems with zoning officials.

$ Pricing

A rule of thumb is set the retail price for what you sell at four times the cost of growing it. In addition, Richard Alan Miller, author and leading consultant in this field, advises, "Add value before it leaves the farm." Adding value to your products prior to sale—for example, washing, cutting up, and mixing varieties of lettuce or processing basil for pesto sauce—will multiply the price you can charge.

One aspect of pricing you should be aware of is that many prices for produce, flowers, and herbs are greatly influenced by the market, meaning that you have little control over your price if your costs are higher than expected.

回 Potential Earnings

TYPICAL ANNUAL GROSS REVENUES: $10,000 to $12,000 an acre for flowers, herbs, and spices.

Alternatively, according to Ted Taylor, greenhouse expert, a 30-by-96-foot greenhouse holding 10,000 six-inch pots can bring in $2.50 profit per pot, or about $20,000 in ninety days. Income potential from producing gifts, condiments, or other goods you sell from your home or through a catalogue varies according to market and locale. Grower sales at farmers' markets in West Los Angeles in 1993 ranged from an average of $266 a day in West Hollywood to an average of $954 a day in Santa Monica.

OVERHEAD: moderate (20 to 40 percent).

⚡ *Best Home Businesses* Estimate of Market Potential

The desire for organically grown and trendy foods should continue to drive the demand for home-grown specialty food for years to come.

🡒 Best Ways to Get Business

- Offering a unique product, where you have an edge in the market. As Richard Alan Miller says, "Instead of growing basil, grow Thai basil"
- Selling directly to the public at farmers' markets and swap meets
- Selling directly to local restaurants, groceries, health-food stores, and exporters. Schools, colleges, and universities are also excellent markets. Bring samples of your product with you when you go to sell. It is also suggested that you make a video of your facilities and growing methods.
- Charging people to harvest their own food. If your land is located near a well-traveled roadway, Dr. Booker T. Whatley suggests charging 60 per-

cent of supermarket prices. You need to have an attractive sign that will encourage people to stop.

ⓕ First Steps

1. Check your zoning to be sure your property can be used for growing food.

2. Find an untapped market in your area and begin experimenting with growing a crop in your own garden.

3. Agricultural universities may not provide classes needed for very small farms, but you can learn about farming by taking workshops listed on bulletin boards of food cooperatives and reading about what will grow in your area and the best ways to grow it.

4. Decide whether you're going to grow organically or nonorganically and whether you are going to become a commercial producer selling to food stores or a quality producer selling to upscale restaurants or directly to the public at farmers' markets.

5. Do a feasibility study with a small crop the first year—on two acres of land, if possible.

ⓞ Where to Turn for Information and Help

ORGANIZATIONS

Contact the horticultural and agricultural departments of universities and the state or county agricultural extension offices in your area.

American Herb Association, P.O. Box 1673, Nevada City, CA 95959. Focuses on medicinal herbs.

American Herbal Products Association, P.O. Box 2410, Austin, TX 78768; (512) 320-8555. For those involved in producing products made from or with herbs.

International Herb Growers and Marketers Association, 1202 Allanson Rd., Mundelein, IL 60060; (708) 949-4372. The largest commercial herb association in the country.

National Association for the Specialty Food Trade, 8 W. 40th Street, Fourth Floor, New York, NY 10018; (212) 921-1690 or (800) 255-2502. 1,400 members.

Professional Plant Growers Association, P.O. Box 27517, Lansing, MI 48909; (517) 694-7700.

NEWSLETTERS

The growth of newsletters in this field has been tremendous over the past few years. This is a partial list, and you can learn about others by reading some of the books listed below.

Acres USA, P.O. Box 8800, Metairie, LA 70011; (504) 889-2100.

Cut Flower Quarterly, Publication of the Association of Specialty Cut Flowers Growers, MPO Box 268, Oberlin, OH 44074; (216) 774-2887. For small growers of flowers.

The Field Report, Nature Unlimited International, Inc., 1210 Third St., Columbus, NE 68601; (402) 562-8711.

Growing for Market, Fairplain Publications, P.O. Box 3747, Lawrence, KS 66064; (913) 841-2559. An excellent monthly for small, primarily organic growers of flowers and herbs.

Organic Gardening, Rodale Publishing, 33 East Minor Street, Emmaus, PA 18098; (800) 666-2206; (215) 967-5171.

National Wholesale Herb Market News Report, U.S. Department of Agriculture, available from *Fruit and Vegetable Market News*, 536 South Clark, Room 942, Chicago, IL 60605; (312) 353-0111.

Potpourri Party Line: For Those Who Grow Herbs, Arrange Dried Florals, or Make Potpourri, edited by Dody Lyness. Berry Hill Press, 7336 Berry Hill, Palos Verdes, CA 90274-4404.

BOOKS

From Kitchen to Market, Stephen F. Hall, Dover, NH: Upstart Press, 1992.

Growing Gourmet and Medicinal Mushrooms, by Paul Stamets, Berkeley: Ten Speed Press. 1994; (800) 841-2665.

Herbs for Sale, by Lee Sturdivant, published by San Juan Naturals, P.O. Box 642, Friday Harbor, WA 98250; (206) 378-2648. Excellent resource for business. The author also has written *Flowers for Sale.*

Herbs You Can Master, Carol R. Peterson, Snoqualmie, WA: Mt. Garden Publishing Co., 1994.

How to Make $100,000 Farming 25 Acres, Booker T. Whatley and the Editors of The New Farm, Emmaus, Pa.: Rodale Press, 1987. Rodale publishes a variety of books on farming; write for a catalogue: Rodale Press, 33 East Minor Street, Emmaus, PA 18098; (800) 666-2206; (215) 967-5171.

Knott's Handbook for Vegetable Growers, O. A. Lorentz and D. N. Maynard, New York: John Wiley and Sons, 1988.

Native Plants of Commercial Importance, Richard Alan Miller, Oak, Inc., 2185 S.E. Portola Drive, Grants Pass, OR 97526; (503) 476-5588. Oak, Inc., also offers technical reports and farm plans.

The Potential of Herbs as a Cash Crop, Richard Alan Miller, Berkeley, CA: Ten Speed Press, 1993.

Secrets to a Successful Greenhouse, Ted Taylor, Greenearth Publishing, Box 243, Melbourne, FL 32902; (407) 951-3484.

■ ■ ■ ■ ■

HOME INSPECTOR

If you have a background or interest in construction or a related field, you can put on a white collar and become a home inspector. Home inspection took off as real estate prices skyrocketed making buyers wary of paying princely prices, yet not knowing whether the roof would leak or the furnace would go out the night they moved in (as happened to us with the first home we bought).

In the 1980s, many lending institutions also began to require home inspections as a condition to making mortgage loans, in order to ensure that the property was in good condition. Additionally, laws were passed in California, Florida, and Texas that resulted in a demand for home inspections. The California law, for example, requires that sellers disclose any known problems with their homes before sale. As a result, to protect themselves from lawsuits, some sellers started calling inspectors too. Now, having a home inspected is growing in popularity across the nation for both buyers and sellers. Ninety percent of home inspections are still done for buyers, though.

The role of the home inspector is to take an objective look at a home and help the clients avoid costly surprises. The inspector typically spends two to three hours visually examining all aspects of a home, including the roof, foundation, and attic; insulation; walkways; heating and air conditioning; and plumbing and electrical systems. The inspector then tells the buyers about the condition of the home, pointing out problems, such as signs of water damage, that may not be obvious to an untrained eye.

Following the inspection, the inspector prepares a written report. If defects are found, the buyer may choose either simply to accept the problems or to obtain a larger mortgage to fix the problems, or renegotiate the offer to make the seller correct the problems.

When working for a seller, the information provided by a home inspector helps the homeowners come up with a realistic price for their home based on its actual condition. After living in a home for fifteen years, owners may overlook problems to which they have become accustomed but which lower the value of the home.

Home inspectors have no vested interest in any particular work being done on the house. The professional code of ethics of the American Society of Home Inspectors (ASHI) prevents inspectors from doing the repairs they believe are needed or from offering to do them. If the inspector is still in the construction business, he or she could be seen as drumming up business as a contractor.

Jules Falcone, spokesman for ASHI, says, "This business is growing fast. There has been a 50 percent increase in the number of inspectors in the last five years." According to ASHI, home inspection in 1993 was a $287-million industry, up from $216 million in 1991. Falcone points out that the popularity of home inspection is spreading from urban areas, where the trend began, to small cities and even rural areas, largely because consumers everywhere are becoming increasingly aware of the tremendous value home inspection provides. Even so, the frequency of inspection varies widely with neighborhood and selling price. As few as 3 percent of homes in low-income and/or rural areas might be inspected, as opposed to 95 percent in affluent urban neighborhoods. The national average of homes inspected is between 30 and 40 percent of homes sold.

Although no laws exist that require home inspections per se, real estate disclosure laws and standards have created a climate in which buyers are more frequently opting for inspection. In addition, more careful lending practices by savings and loan associations may result in home inspections becoming as common as appraisals and termite inspections. And the federal government may soon require home inspections as a condition for obtaining FHA and VA mortgage loans. So industry experts predict that home inspection will grow significantly during the 90s when, they say, as many as 90 percent of all homes sold will be inspected.

Inspectors are becoming more efficient and are better able to provide lengthy, customized reports thanks to advances in computer technology. Some inspectors carry laptop computers, which allow them to generate reports on the spot. Sophisticated word-processing software allows the insertion of customized stored descriptions of specific problems and remedies without extra typing.

Membership in the American Society of Home Inspectors affords a great deal of credibility. The association requires each candidate to pass a rigorous written test, and regular members must fulfill continuing-education requirements to maintain membership. Although home inspectors do not need to be licensed, the association regulates the industry meticulously through its stringent membership requirements.

☑ Knowledge and Skills You Need to Have

- You need to have a background in or an understanding of construction to evaluate the structural soundness of a home—including wiring, plumbing, heating, air-conditioning, and roofing and building materials. You should also be familiar with the construction of swimming pools, decks, and spas and the operations of built-in appliances. You need to be able to detect signs of failure, wear, and age as well. Field experience and training are both essential.

- You need to be familiar with the building codes in your state and local community.

- Inspectors need to have an inquisitive mind and enjoy solving puzzles. Although most of the work is routine, you must figure out the causes of cracks, water stains, leaks, and so forth. And you can't have a fear of heights or claustrophobia, because you will need to go up on roofs and in crawl spaces beneath homes.

- You will be working face-to-face with clients and need to have good people skills and verbal abilities to point out maintenance problems and explain how simple maintenance can prevent big problems.

- You must be able to write clear, accurate, legible reports. These reports will be vital documents in real-estate sales, so careful attention to detail and accuracy are essential to prevent lawsuits.

- You must have errors-and-omissions insurance to cover your liability for oversights and mistakes. This will be difficult to obtain until you have passed the ASHI test, but once you have, you will be able to purchase it through the association.

◘ Start-up Costs

	Low	High
Computer or laptop with hard disk	$1,000	$ 3,000
Ink-jet or laser printer	300	1,600
Suite software	250	400
Specialized software and/or forms for home inspectors	400	3,000
Office furniture	400	1,000
Business cards/letterhead	100	600
Association membership	175	200
Tools such as screwdriver, flashlights, ladder, electrical tracer, circuit tester, volt meter, moisture meter, and gas-leak detector	300	800
Errors-and-omissions insurance	2,000	2,000
Total	$4,925	$12,600

In addition, brochures and promotional materials are available from the ASHI (see below).

℡ Advantages

- Inspectors are in demand in today's real estate market, where people want value for their money.
- The income potential is good, and the field is growing.
- The work is varied, and much of it is done outdoors.
- Licensing may be right around the corner, which will put you in on the ground floor of a new profession. Licensing increases demand and stature and limits competition, and usually when licensing is introduced people already practicing in the field are automatically licensed. Texas is already licensing inspectors.

🗔 Disadvantages

- The buying or selling of a house is often an emotional issue, so you can be working with people whose nerves are on edge as they worry about problems and costs.
- Some realtors regard home inspectors as a threat, fearing they'll lose the sale or reduce the commission if a problem is discovered. But with realtors increasingly required to disclose defects, they are beginning to see that inspections are to their benefit.
- How much business you have is tied to the ups and downs of the real estate market.

💲 Pricing

Fees for a home inspection range from $150 to $400, depending on your location. In smaller and rural areas, fees will be at the low end.

🖵 Potential Earnings

TYPICAL ANNUAL GROSS REVENUES: $75,000. Most home inspectors can conduct two and sometimes three inspections a day for an average of 200 to 300 inspections a year. This takes into account that home inspection is a seasonal business with December and January tending to be slow. A busy inspector can conduct 400 or more inspections per year. At an average rate of $250 per inspection, incomes range from $50,000 to $100,000.

OVERHEAD: average (25 percent). Car expenses may come to $20,000 per year.

📈 *Best Home Businesses* Estimate of Market Potential

Total number of home and building inspection firms in the United States, including home-based businesses: 16,019. The growing expectation for homes to be professionally inspected will drive growth for this field.

🗎 Best Ways to Get Business

- Get referrals from realtors, attorneys, and mortgage lenders. Call on these professionals directly or make contacts by networking at business, trade, and professional organizations. Jules Falcone estimates that 60 to 70 percent of a new inspector's business will need to come from real estate agent referrals because the heart of this business is the buyers.
- Give lectures in real estate offices on topics such as how not to let inspection kill your deal. Anytime you can provide high-quality information face-to-face you will be appreciated.

- Exhibit at real estate–related events like real estate board award banquets, fairs, and seminars. Local ASHI chapters sometimes buy booth spaces in which members can participate.

- Get publicity in real estate sections of the newspaper and then use reprints in your promotional and sales materials to establish credibility. Printed advertising doesn't work unless it is targeted to the real estate community.

Franchises

AmeriSpec Home Inspection Service, 1855 West Katella Avenue, Suite 330, Orange, CA 92667; (800) 426-2270. Their training program teaches people how to conduct home inspections, write reports, and get business. A background in related fields like construction, real estate, escrow, and property management is helpful, but not required. The franchise fee is $15,900 to $21,900.

The Building Inspector of America, 669 Main Street, Wakefield, MA 01880; (800) 321-4677. Provides training for doing residential and commercial property inspections. The franchise fee is $8,900 and up.

HouseMaster of America, 421 West Union Avenue, Bound Brook, NJ 08805; (800) 526-3939. Does not require you to know or learn how to do home inspections yourself because they provide the training for inspectors you hire. The franchise fee is $17,000 to $35,000, depending on the size of the territory.

First Steps

If you have no background in construction or real estate, Lawrence Hoyt, president of the ASHI, recommends spending a day with a local inspector to see what his or her day is like. If you like what you see, you can gain the training, credentials, contacts, and experience you need by apprenticing with an established freelance inspector. You can locate inspectors through the yellow pages or through ASHI local chapters.

You can also learn about the field by attending local chapter meetings of the ASHI. ASHI publishes a manual and offers training, educational workshops, and training institutes.

Some community colleges are now offering courses in building inspections with the guidance of the association. Home-study courses are also available for $250. Such courses are advertised in the ASHI Technical Journal. You can also learn the field by affiliating with one of the franchises listed above.

Whichever route you take, it is wise to gain experience doing inspections under someone else before you start to do them on your own. We also suggest talking with people in real estate to find out their opinions of home inspection in your community and to determine if the market is saturated.

☐ Where to Turn for Information and Help

ORGANIZATION

American Society of Home Inspectors, 85 West Algonquin Road, Suite 360, Arlington Heights, IL 60005-4423; (708) 290-1919.

BOOKS

ASHI Training Manual. American Society of Home Inspectors. $99 plus $7 shipping and handling.

The following books are written for consumers, not professionals, but provide insight into the basics of home inspection.

The Complete Book of Home Inspection, Norman Becker, New York: McGraw-Hill, 1980.

How to Buy a House, Condo, or Coop, Michael Thomsett and the Editors of Consumer Reports Books, New York; Consumer Reports Books, 1990.

NEWSLETTERS

ASHI Reporter. For members of the American Society of Home Inspectors. Articles, notices of seminars and conferences, forms, product announcements, new technology. Monthly.

COURSES

Courses on establishing a home-inspection business and/or technical courses are offered by:

HomePro, 2841 Hartland Road, Suite 201, Falls Church, VA 22042; (800) 966-4555; (703) 761-1400.

Home-Tech, 5161 River Road, Bethesda, MD 20816; (800) 638-8292.

Carson Dunlap & Associates, Ltd., 120 Carlton Street, Suite 407, Toronto, Ontario M5A 4K2; (416) 964-9415 or (800) 268-7070.

Robinson & Hanson Home Inspection Trainers, 1433 Leimert Blvd., Oakland, CA 94602; (800) 698-0292.

Inspection Training Associates, 1016 S. Tremont Street, Oceanside, CA 92054; (800) 323-9235.

■ ■ ■ ■ ■

IMAGE CONSULTANT

People have used clothing to communicate who they are and their status throughout the ages, but it was not until the 1970s that a popular consciousness developed that how one looks and presents oneself has a direct effect on career, love life, and self-esteem. John Molloy, in his classic book *Dress for Success*, portrayed wardrobing as a science, and today more and more people subscribe to the idea that you can shape your image through your choice of clothing, hairstyle, and even gestures and speech. In addition, as the corporate world has gotten more competitive and tougher, businesspeople (men and women) everywhere recognize that winning the key contract or job is often a question of "looking good" in the eyes of your customer.

As a result, image consulting has grown from being virtually unknown in the mid-1970s to an industry in the 1990s. In the 1970s, image consultants were hired primarily by wealthy women, but in the 1980s, image consultants' clients grew to include many professionals, corporate executives, and even corporations themselves. The recession of the early 90s cut the number of image consultants by about 50 percent, but the profession is beginning to rebound as image consultants are tapping into other new markets including:

- an "active" aging population concerned with maturing elegantly as well as comfortably
- a growing number of self-employed people who must market themselves effectively to prosper
- people with small clothing budgets looking for employment in the shrinking job market and needing to make the best possible impression
- people changing fields who need advice on a new look and behavior to suit the new environment.

Because image consultants now have to help clients move from field to field, they must stay on top of current developments in the business, fashion, and technical worlds more than ever. The hospitality industry is one that needs constant attention, for example.

Through videotapes, computer-aided imaging, and other audio-visual aids, image consultants help their clients use clothing, makeup, hairstyle, speech, and body stance to create a desired effect. The goal, according to Jacqueline Thompson, who is president of Image Industry Publications and publisher of *Directory of Personal Image Consultants*, is to help people ensure that their visible image matches their inner talents and aspirations.

In addition to helping clients with the components of their image, some consultants audit their clients' closets and then go shopping with them. Some consultants also go through clients' closets showing them how to make the most of what they have and throwing out items that are unworkable. Some consultants actually do their clients' shopping for them, but others simply provide a proposal and let the client do his or her own shopping. Alternatively, clients may select items from a catalogue or television shopping service but ask the consultant for advice before actually ordering. A new specialty, which requires special expertise, is having the consultant shop at a discount store for the client.

Today's clients are both men and women. They may come to the consultant having realized that they are being repeatedly passed over for a desired promotion in favor of more attractive-looking candidates. Or they may simply be people who want to be sure they're presenting themselves in the best possible light. Single or newly divorced men and women also come to image consultants wanting to create a more appealing image.

Sometimes the client's look simply needs updating, according to Brenda York, who has done image consulting since 1976 and whose Academy of Fashion and Image in McLean, Virginia, offers training for image consultants. At other times, the consultant needs to help the client enhance his or her desirable features and play down or camouflage less-appealing ones through choice of color, use of accessories, or type of tailoring.

Other than working with individual clients, the best contracts involve working with an entire organization, assisting all the executives, sales personnel, or customer-service representatives in looking and presenting themselves at their best. Corporate image consultants are concerned with both the company's visual image and its customer and public relations. Some consultants also specialize in preparing corporate representatives for public appearances. Brenda York also says that more and more industries are switching to uniform attire, so some consultants get the job of recommending styles such as blazers and three-piece suits for retail personnel of both sexes.

About 50 percent of the image consultants who belong to the Association of Image Consultants International work with the visual aspects of image such as clothing style and selection. Another 30 percent work primarily with the verbal aspects of image, offering speech coaching and presentation skills training.

Other aspects of this business that are emerging in the 90s, especially in the corporate market, include focusing on nonverbal communication skills, etiquette, aromacology, and cross-cultural communications. Particularly as Americans deal in business with more and more people of other cultures, cross-cultural communications and etiquette will be popular topics for seminars and corporate training. The consultant may work with clients one-on-one, taking them out to social or business events, or may offer in-house training classes.

☑ Knowledge and Skills You Need to Have

- The type of background you need depends on what aspects of the field you will be consulting in: wardrobe, speech, etiquette, etc. Typical backgrounds include experience in fashion, clothing, cosmetics, teaching, broadcasting, speech, acting, or modeling.

- You need to have an extroverted but warm and nurturing personality. A good image consultant can't dictate or impose a verbal or visual persona on another person. You must provide feedback and suggestions in a tactful and caring way. This also means that you need to be a good communicator, intuitively understanding and drawing out your clients' needs and personalities while helping them.

- Creativity and a visual orientation are useful talents, especially if you specialize in fashion or color. Whereas image consultants in the early days of the industry were prone to follow formulas and believed there were sets of rules for how to dress for success, today the profession stresses bringing out an individual's strengths within the boundaries of what our culture expects and values.

- Image consultants need to be skillful at presenting themselves. Essentially you have to be a walking, talking, breathing example of what you teach. You need to have excellent speaking and teaching skills, because this is how you get business.

- You must enjoy and be willing to learn constantly, keeping abreast of fashion and behavioral trends in business so that your skills don't become outdated.

Start-up Costs

Fashion/Visual Specialization

	Low	High
Training	$ 500	$2,500
Reference books on style, color, etc.	100	200
Set of color swatches for advising on use of color	200	200
Business cards/letterhead	100	600
Portfolio of before-and-after photographs	250	500
Media kit with articles by and about you, and testimonial letters	50	100
Price list of services	50	100
Personal wardrobe with two or three complete outfits	1,500	5,000
Polaroid camera	80	200
Organizational dues	250	250
Total	$3,080	$9,650

Verbal/Speaking Specialization

	Low	High
Computer with hard disk	$1,000	$3,000
Ink-jet or laser printer	300	1,600
Suite software	250	400
Business cards/letterhead	100	600
Brochures	100	1,000
Camcorder and monitor	1,000	2,500
Organizational dues	250	250
Total	$3,000	$9,350

Advantages

- People are always interested in and curious about their image, making this an easy topic to talk to people about, the first step for getting business.
- There is plenty of opportunity to use your creativity in providing a valued service to people who appreciate what you do.
- The work can be gratifying. Sometimes even small changes can dramatically improve the lives of your clients, and you'll hear about the sales records, promotions, and new jobs they've attained with your help. Image consultants may also get credit for weddings.
- If you are working with wardrobes, you can often get clothing free or at a discount from retail chains.

Disadvantages

- Because many businesspeople and companies are not yet familiar with the benefits of image consulting, you must educate them before you can sell your service.
- Advertising doesn't work to sell your consulting. You usually have to demonstrate your skills and build a relationship with people before they will hire you. Some people may initially think your work is superficial or insignificant.
- Multilevel organizations selling cosmetics have diluted the profession by casting their sales representatives as image consultants. You need to present yourself as a professional.
- Clients may be easily offended or resistant to your feedback and suggestions.
- If your clients are mostly individuals, you will probably need to sell products or teach seminars in addition to providing private consultations in order to earn a sufficient full-time income.
- This industry is sensitive to the economy because hiring an image consul-

tant is a discretionary purchase. If your clients are people looking for jobs, you may need to accept a delay before they pay you.

💲 Pricing

Image consultants provide their services through private consultation, in group workshops, or in corporate seminars. Fees have come down in recent years, according to Brenda York who trains consultants, and range from $25 to $150 per hour (average $85) for a wardrobe person, and $75 to $300 per hour for a professional speech consultant. In addition, consultants may give full-day workshops and seminars to individuals and companies, with fees ranging from $750 to $2,000 per day, depending on the number of participants, the company, and the nature of the workshop (speech, wardrobe, etc.)

Some consultants receive annual retainers from corporations for regularly working with their executives and sales staffs. A consultant might receive $2,500 per year to work with a certain number of executives or employees each month.

🖳 Potential Earnings

TYPICAL ANNUAL GROSS EARNINGS: For a wardrobe consultant working full-time earnings are $25,000 to $35,000 per year. For a full-time speech, body language, or corporate consultant, earnings are in the $50,000 to $75,000 range (plus expenses).

📈 *Best Home Businesses* Estimate of Market Potential

Total number of image consultants in the United States, including home-based businesses: 3,205. Although subject to the ups and downs of the economy, consciousness about appearance and self-presentation is expected to continue. Influencing this may be the fact that we will soon be presenting our visual as well as our spoken image over telephone wires so inexpensively that it will be considered commonplace to look at someone while you talk with him or her, even when speaking to someone half a world away.

📭 Best Ways to Get Business

- Networking is the number-one way to get business in this field. That means keeping in touch with business-training consultants and other image consultants. It also means making personal contacts by participating in organizations and professional and business associations, particularly in industries or fields in which you have experience. This way, potential clients can get to know you and feel comfortable with you before they hire you.
- Word of mouth is also especially important. You will want to get clients who have lots of contacts and can tell others about how much you

helped them. It can help to do a few complimentary sessions with key individuals to begin with and get some word of mouth going.

▪ Give free speeches and seminars to higher-income groups on image and use these as an opportunity to show off the dramatic results you can achieve; show slides or videotapes of your clients before and after. (Be sure you have obtained their written permission.)

▪ Write articles or get publicity about your successes to attract more clients.

🔖 First Steps

1. Many private training programs designed to teach you how to be an image consultant are listed in the *Directory of Personal Image Consultants*. Their fees range from several hundred to several thousand dollars. Contact the programs that interest you for more information. There are also many books on the various aspects of image consulting, some of which are listed below.

2. Brenda York recommends that image consultants who want to work with individuals begin their business as a sideline. Often clients prefer evening and weekend sessions anyway, and by starting part-time you can gain some experience and build a clientele before leaving your job.

3. If you wish to work within a corporate setting, target a particular industry and concentrate on marketing to that industry. Any industry in which the appearance of the personnel plays an important role is a good candidate—for example, hotels, entertainment facilities, health-care industries, and retail stores. Contact the human-resource directors to discuss your doing a two- to three-hour introductory seminar for their personnel. You can identify human-resource directors through the local chapter directory of the American Society of Training and Development. You can also find human-resources personnel simply by reading want ads in the newspapers. Contact these individuals personally. Direct mail alone will rarely be effective. You might contact public-relations firms about working with their clients for media appearances.

📖 Where to Turn for Information and Help

ORGANIZATIONS

Academy of Fashion and Image, 1903 Kirby Road, McLean, VA 22101; (800) 450-4455; (703) 442-0593. Provides training courses, including a correspondence program, and a resource library offering telephone reference service.

Association of Image Consultants International, 1000 Connecticut Avenue, N.W., #9, Washington, DC 20036; (800) 383-8831.

Image Industry Council International, P.O. Box 422643, San Francisco, CA 94142; (415) 905-5727, fax (415) 759-9229.

Image Industry Publications, 10 Bay Street Landing 7F, Staten Island, NY 10301; (718) 273-3229. Publisher of books in this field, headed by Jacqueline Thompson.

National Speakers' Association, 1500 South Priest Drive, Tempe, AZ 85281; (602) 968-2552. A description of NSA can be found in the Employee Training entry.

BOOKS

The Directory of Image Consultants, compiled by Jacqueline Thompson, Image Industry Publications. Lists 260 image consulting firms in the most recent edition. Published biannually, $94.95.

Do's and Taboos around the World, edited by Roger E. Axtell, New York: Wiley, 1985.

Flatter Your Figure, Jan Larkey, Englewood Cliffs, NJ: Prentice Hall, 1991.

How to Start Your Own Fashion and Image Consulting Business, Brenda York, McLean, VA: Academy of Fashion and Image. $9.95. Audiotape available for $8.95.

Image Impact: The Complete Makeover Guide, edited by Jacqueline Thompson, Image Industry Publications. Written by nineteen of the industry's pioneers.

The Language of Color, Dorothee L. Mella. New York: Warner Books, 1988.

Say It Right: How to Talk in Any Social or Business Situation, Lillian Glass, New York: Putnam, 1991.

That's Not What I Meant! How Conversational Style Makes or Breaks Your Relations with Others, and *You Just Don't Understand,* Deborah Tannen, New York: Ballantine, 1990.

You Are the Message: Secrets of the Master Communicators, Roger Ailes with Jon Kraushar. Homewood, IL: Dow Jones-Irwin, 1988.

NEWSPAPER

Image Networker, P.O. Box 62475, Colorado Springs, CO 80962; (800) 723-1144.

■ ■ ■ ■ ■

INDOOR ENVIRONMENTAL TESTER

The 1980s and early 1990s saw the environmental and health movements converge and turn indoors with the realization that our homes and offices are assaulting us with a variety of pollutants that are making us sick. A number of indoor environmental experts have told us that today everyone is environmentally at risk, and most people are so conditioned to feeling less than optimal that they just don't recognize it. The point is, for example, that even a common product like shoe polish contains benzene, a carcinogen, but most people are unaware of the potentially dangerous pollutants in their lives. To help raise awareness, CHEC, the Children's Health and Environmental Coalition, is uniting hundreds of grassroots groups across the country that are working to counter the harmful impact of environmental contaminants, particularly those that research finds account for recent increases of cancer in children.

Increased awareness of indoor pollution is giving rise to a variety of new businesses through which people can turn their personal commitment to improving the environment into concrete services from which they can earn a living. The most promising of these is testing the indoor environment for unhealthy conditions and working with homeowners, businesses, office-building supervisors, architects, real estate agents, and many others to increase awareness of environmental dangers and to test these environments and fix any problems discovered. Over the past five years, in fact, testing services have gathered much momentum, so that while it used to be upscale homeowners who previously formed the clientele, now major corporations and industries are spending money to make sure their environments are safe. This trend will increase, too, as various government agencies (like OSHA— the Office of Safety, Health Review Commission) and Congress prepare new guidelines to regulate office-building air-quality standards, smoke-free environments, and other hazards.

Environmental testers test for a variety of things:

- indoor air pollution caused by mold spores, dust, bacteria, formaldehyde, and toxic gases, such as carbon monoxide and sulfur dioxide. Such pollution can come from appliances, furnaces, stoves, air-conditioning vents, copy and fax machines, furniture, rugs, paper products, and many other building materials or office-supply materials

- electromagnetic radiation from high-voltage transmission lines, home electrical wiring, meters, appliances, electric blankets, water beds, video display terminals (VDTs), and other office equipment

- lead found in paint, dishware, lead solder, and crystal. Lead can also be tracked in on shoes from the ground (which got there as airborne residue from car exhaust) and deposited onto rugs

- geomagnetic influences such as magnetic grid crossings and underground water under a room

- toxic substances of all kinds in carpet fibers, dyed fabrics, cosmetics, foods, pesticides, and many common cleaning supplies

- asbestos used in insulation

In short, indoor environmental testers may get involved in testing in many areas, and the field is already giving rise to a number of new subcategories of professions.

Certified Bau-biologist. A bau-biologist is a "building biologist" (*bau* is German for building), someone who is trained to look at many aspects of the indoor environment of a building and determine if there are toxic elements present in the building materials, air quality, and furniture.

EMF Testers (Electromagnetic Field testers) who examine bedrooms, offices, and particularly computer areas for low-frequency emissions from the video terminals. Although science has yet clearly to define just what, if any, are the effects of low-frequency electromagnetic fields emitted from VDTs and other electronic equipment, studies from Finland, Sweden, and elsewhere have raised concern by linking such emissions with brain tumors, childhood leukemia, cancer, and miscarriages.

Air Quality Testers, who focus on measuring dust and toxic particulates in the air that might irritate people with asthma, sinus conditions, cancer, leukemia, and other illnesses that are severely aggravated by poor air quality.

Feng Shui Specialists, who derive their expertise from the ancient Chinese art of placement. Such people often design or redesign homes, buildings, and even furniture in rooms to orient them in a certain direction that increases spiritual harmony and personal health.

Radon Testers, who must now be licensed in many states to perform radon tests on houses and buildings. (The EPA will soon require that nearly all houses be tested for radon upon sale.)

Lead Abatement Specialists, who must be licensed to supervise the removal of lead from homes and buildings.

Mary Cordoro is a certified bau-biologist and environmental consultant in Los Angeles whose company A Room of One's Own diagnoses problems associated with sick building syndrome. As Mary says, the corollary to this industry is that one must not only diagnose the problem, but you must also be prepared with solutions for how to solve or abate it. This means that you must become familiar with alternative building materials, furniture suppliers, and other ways of building and solving problems. In the past few years, however, Mary's business has expanded enormously, and she now finds herself working with many architects, real estate agents, and designers who seek her assistance at earlier and earlier stages of home design.

Joe Riley's business, Healthwaves, specializes in testing for electromagnetic problems. Together with his wife, a Ph.D. in neurophysiology, he checks for electrical problems, and although they do not fix the problems themselves, they began earning $1,000 a week right away. Referrals keep his business going week after week.

Audrey Hoodkiss came into the field because of her own environmental illness. She had been an interior designer when she developed a chemical sensitivity. She now works with medical patients who need to redecorate to create a healthier environment. Jim Nagra worked as a taxi driver to support himself while he started what has become a successful business as an environmental-equipment broker. He sells everything over the phone, from environmentally safe shoe polish to pollution-busting vacuum cleaners.

Kathryn Metz is a feng shui practitioner and certified bau-biologist. Her company, The Art of Placement, has had schools, homes, restaurants, health-care facilities, and small businesses for clients. Kathryn examines the room angles, the decorations, the placement of furniture, and many other details and, using a traditional Chinese theory steeped in Taoism and Confucianism, in which she trained for many years, she provides recommendations of how to turn the environment into a healthy zone.

These are just a few of the examples of this emerging environmental business, ripe for creative development. They and other businesses in various stages of being defined could develop into some of the fastest-growing opportunities of the 90s.

☑ Knowledge and Skills You Need to Have

- Environmental testing requires the ability to synthesize vast amounts of information, because new research on environmental and health issues is surfacing weekly. New problems, remedies, and resources, new non-toxic and low-toxic materials, and new shielding mechanisms are becoming known, requiring some understanding of chemistry and toxicology; although you can learn quickly. But you have an ongoing obligation to clients to stay educated; constant reading, networking, and periodic attendance at professional workshops are called for.

- This work demands an intense interest in health and a willingness to be self-taught, because there are few courses in this area. You need to maintain your own constant research to keep abreast of changes in both abatement and remediation solutions. You also need to know a lot about products that are on the market and specialize in one area of inspection.

- Interpersonal skills are required to advise people who are living with extreme difficulty because of serious sensitivities or illnesses. You also need to be able to recognize the emotional needs of hypochondriacs and psychosomatics and not let them become dependent on you.

- Intuition and the ability to be highly sensitive to your own bodily reactions is helpful (however, you don't want to use your own body to sense for problems; use meters).

▓ Start-up Costs

	Low	High
Computer with hard disk and modem	$1,000	$ 3,000
Fax machine	300	900
Printer	300	1,600
Suite software and contact management software	250	400
Telephone equipment	100	200
Errors and omissions insurance*	200	500
Office furniture, especially ergonomic chair	400	1,000
Business cards, letterhead, envelopes	100	600
Professional-quality testing equipment to measure air quality, EMF levels, etc.	5,000	20,000
Total	$7,650	$28,200

* Few insurance companies can cover you for liability because there is no category to put you in as yet as a business. You may need to call yourself an interior designer to get a business liability insurance policy; and you must also write waivers into your contracts that say that you are not responsible for any abatement work that is performed by other contractors after you.

▓ Advantages

- This is a challenging and stimulating field that will certainly grow.
- It provides the environmentally conscious with the opportunity to do meaningful work.
- Helping people feel better and get well can be highly rewarding and fulfilling.

▓ Disadvantages

- Because you work in *sick* buildings, you expose yourself to hazardous pollution.
- The clientele is predominantly people who are environmentally ill and cancer patients, so the work can be emotionally draining. You must guard against absorbing the emotional pain of the people you serve.
- This work is viewed by many as controversial, particularly the electromagnetic aspect. You may feel that you have to justify what you're doing to some people.
- You need to acquire a lot of technical knowledge.

▓ Pricing

Environmental testers sometimes charge by the hour and sometimes by the job, especially for people on fixed incomes. Hourly rates range from $60 to $150, with $75 the most typical. Representative on-the-job rates are $125 to $150 for an electromagnetic check for senior citizens, and $500 for a 2,500-

square-foot home. Rates for evaluating a commercial building can go as high as $5,000.

▣ Potential Earnings

TYPICAL ANNUAL GROSS REVENUES: $75,000 based on billing twenty hours per week, fifty weeks a year, at $75 an hour. An experienced tester can complete electromagnetic checks in two to three hours. Full home checks may take three to ten hours.

OVERHEAD: moderate to high (20 to 40 percent); you need to purchase many pieces of testing equipment.

▣ *Best Home Businesses* Estimate of Market Potential

Increasing understanding of the relationship between harmful substances in our indoor environments and our health will drive this business as more people seek to rid their homes and offices of toxicity.

▣ Best Ways to Get Business

- Developing relationships with doctors and dentists who will refer patients with possible environmentally caused complaints. Some doctors will subcontract with a tester and include the testing service as part of a patient's total health-care program, in which case the tester's findings are reported directly to the doctor, who will relate them to the patient.
- Getting listed in health- and environmental-resource guides.
- Getting referrals from environmental-resource groups and city planning departments.
- Listing in the yellow pages under Environment and Ecological Services and listings related to hazardous-waste disposal.
- Making contacts at environmental conferences, symposiums, and trade shows.
- Speaking and conducting seminars on indoor pollution.
- Writing articles for magazines and newspapers.
- Obtaining publicity about your work.

▣ First Steps

1. Become an expert. This is a fast-changing field. So develop a broad and eclectic understanding of what's going on in building biology (a term popular in Europe), indoor ecology, and suspected health problems.
2. Contact recognized organizations and authorities in the field.

3. Start conducting environmental audits for family and friends, and encourage referrals.

Where to Turn for Information and Help

ORGANIZATION

National Electromagnetic Field Testing Association, 628-B Library Place, Evanston, IL 60201; (708) 475-3696.

BOOKS

Cross Currents: The Promise of Electromedicine, the Perils of Electropollution, Robert O. Becker, Los Angeles: Jeremy P. Tarcher, 1990.

Currents of Death: Power Lines, Computer Terminals, and the Attempt to Cover Up Their Threat to Your Health, Paul Brodeur, New York: Simon and Schuster, 1989.

Ecopreneuring: The Green Guide to Small Business Opportunities from the Environmental Revolution, Steven J. Bennett, New York: John Wiley and Sons, 1991.

Electromagnetic Man, Cyril Smith and Simon Best, New York: St. Martin's Press, 1989.

The EnviroClean Sourcebook of Environmentally Responsible Cleaning Products, available from (800) 466-1425.

The Green PC, Making Choices That Make a Difference, Steve Anzovin, Blue Ridge Summit, PA: Windcrest/McGraw-Hill, 1994.

Interior Design with Feng Shui, Sara Rossbach, New York: Dutton, 1987.

The Naturally House Book: Creating a Healthy, Harmonious and Ecologically Sound Home Environment, David Pearson, New York: Simon and Schuster, 1989.

Nontoxic, Natural, and Earthwise: How to Protect Yourself and Your Family from Harmful Products and Live in Harmony with the Earth, Debra Lynn Dadd, Los Angeles: Jeremy P. Tarcher, 1990.

MAGAZINES AND NEWSLETTERS

Delicate Balance, 1100 Rural Avenue, Voorhees, N.J., 08043; (609) 429-5358.

Environ: A Magazine for Ecologic Living and Health, Wary Canary Press, Box 2204, Fort Collins, CO 80522; (303) 224-0083.

Environmental Business Machines, Catalog & Newsletter, A Publication of GeoSoft, P.O. Box 643, Bellows Falls, VT 05101; (800) 557-6769.

In Business: The Magazine for Environmental Entrepreneuring, JG Press, 419 State Avenue, Second Floor, Emmaus, PA 18049.

Indoor Air Review, IAQ Publications; (301) 913-0115. Monthly.

The Reactor, Box 575, Corte Madera, CA 94925; (415) 924-5141.

VDT News, P.O. Box 1799, Grand Central Station, New York, NY.

TRAINING

Environmental Testing and Technology, P.O. Box 230369, Encinitas, CA 92023; (619) 436-5990. Offers extensive, practical, hands-on training for indoor air-quality testing and electromagnetic-field testing and control. The air-quality course lasts five days and the EMF course, two days. Training is designed to provide practical approaches, and you will be able to use instruments and sampling methods. $2,000 to $3,000 for five-day and $750 for two-day course. Contact Peter Sierck.

Institute for Bau-Biology and Ecology, Box 387, Clearwater, FL 34615; (813) 461-4371. Program begins with a home-study correspondence course, which you take for $1,000, covering construction materials, architecture, and related topics; then once you have completed this, you take classes on location (in Florida) and you obtain certification in about two years.

Safe Environments, Berkeley, CA; (510) 549-9693; contact David Bierman. Offers the same training as Environmental Testing and Training, above.

WORKSHOPS

The Art of Placement. Kathryn Metz gives workshops around the country on feng shui; (310) 208-5282.

A Room of One's Own. Mary Cordaro gives workshops in consulting and bau-biology; (310) 838-2892.

■ ■ ■ ■ ■

INFORMATION BROKER

Information is more than ever the key to business success. But with the quantity of information in the world doubling every seven years or less, many companies are simply drowning in information. One new profession that has emerged as a result of the information explosion is the information broker.

An information broker is like an investigative reporter or market researcher, skilled at tracking down and locating specific information that a business needs to compete and succeed. A company might hire an information broker to do background research about a new product concept, to do a patent search on a product they want to introduce, or to learn as much as possible about a new market. Some companies also use information brokers to track the goings on of competitors. Other clients might include professionals whose work requires that they become what information industry pioneer Sue Rugge calls *instant experts*, clients such as lawyers preparing for trial, advertising agencies developing an ad campaign, marketing and public-relations firms preparing a proposal, or private investigators and management consultants working on a particular project.

Some information professionals do their work through interviewing and library searching, but most learn to tap into the 7000+ computer databases that exist on dozens of on-line services. These databases contain abstracts or the full text of articles from thousands of publications around the world, including newspapers, magazines, newsletters, professional journals, and books, thus making it possible to find just about any news item or research result within seconds rather than days or months. Being on line also affords the broker the opportunity to exchange E-mail with other people around the world who may know something about the topic being researched.

Increasingly, information brokers tend to specialize in the type of information they research. Some may focus on law, finance, or medicine, while others work in researching high technology such as bioengineering or computers. The professional who specializes can become proficient at using a small number of databases, thereby increasing his or her reputation for successful searches at a low cost.

☑ Knowledge and Skills You Need to Have

- To do this business well, you must have a love for information and reading. Your clients are most often seeking details that are not readily available, and so you often need to skim or read volumes of data to find the missing piece.

- Creativity and persistence are required to track down information; you have to think of various possibilities for how to locate the data you need. Then you need the critical ability to distinguish what is important to your client from all the information that's available.

- On-line searching is expensive; you must, therefore, become proficient at using the specific procedures and codes required by many of the databases so that you can perform your searches in the least amount of time at a minimum cost to your client.

- Although information searching is becoming more widely used by companies, you still need to have the ability to sell an intangible service to people who may not be familiar with what you can do for them.

⬛ Start-up Costs

	Low	High
Computer with hard disk and high-speed modem	$1,000	$ 3,000
Fax machine	300	900
Printer	300	1,600
Suite software (mostly word processing)	250	400
Office furniture, especially ergonomic chair	400	1,000
Business cards, letterhead, envelopes	100	600
On-line database access and accounts; training and documentation in their use	1,000	2,500
Organizational dues	250	250
Total	$3,600	$10,250

⬛ Advantages

- Low start-up costs make this business easy to get into quickly.
- This business involves interesting and varied work that results in constant learning.
- It offers an opportunity to be creative and to provide valuable information to clients.
- The field is growing and provides ample opportunity for newcomers who are able to market information effectively.

⬛ Disadvantages

- Obtaining clients can be difficult because many people are as yet unaware of the potential use of your service for their business.
- You may not be able to fulfill client requests on time and within budget.
- You may need to spend a lot of time marketing to establish a client base.
- Learning to use a variety of on-line databases can get to be expensive without proper training.

⬛ Pricing

Information brokers charge by the hour or by the job. Hourly rates range from $25 to $100, although experienced brokers may earn as much as $200 per hour. Pricing by the job involves estimating how many hours the job will take, allowing for unexpected difficulties in finding the information, and understanding the costs involved in on-line searching. Expenses such as charges for on-line databases and printed copies of articles you find are either billed at cost or are marked up by 15 to 20 percent.

⬛ Potential Earnings

TYPICAL ANNUAL GROSS REVENUES: $17,500 to $75,000. The low-end estimate is based on billing 500 hours per year (10 hours per week) at $35. The high end is based on billing 750 hours per year (15 hours per week) at $100 per hour.

OVERHEAD: moderate (between 20 and 40 percent).

Best Home Businesses Estimate of Market Potential

Total number of information broker firms in the United States, including home-based businesses: 4,567. This field is growing rapidly and the continued proliferation of information accompanied by downsizing of corporations will create a swelling demand for years to come.

Best Ways to Get Business

- Networking and personal contacts in companies or organizations such as trade associations, particularly in industries or fields in which you have experience
- Speaking and offering seminars on information at meetings and trade shows
- Writing articles for magazines or newspapers, or starting your own newsletter
- Collaborating with other information brokers to do specialized work and overload
- Getting media publicity about you
- Advertising in trade journals if you are in a speciality field

First Steps

Sue Rugge believes that finding a special niche is the first step in starting this business. She advises, "Specialization is necessary. I think it is essential to penetrate a market. You must have viability. Pick a market that has a trade association with local and annual meetings. Go to the meetings, speak to the group, write articles for their publications. Word of mouth is our most powerful marketing tool, but it takes a lot longer to get it going if you are trying to work in many different markets. When you can cluster your clients in a group that speaks to each other, word of mouth goes faster."

Where to Turn for Information and Help

ORGANIZATIONS

Association of Independent Information Professionals, 245 Fifth Avenue, Suite 2103, New York, NY 10016; voice phone (212) 779-1855, fax (212) 481-3071. Professional association for information brokers; publishes books and a newsletter and offers conferences and workshops.

Information Industry Association, 555 New Jersey Avenue, N.W., Washington, DC 20001; (202) 639-8260.

Information Professionals Institute, 46 Hiller Drive, Oakland, CA 94618; (510) 649-9743, fax (510) 704-8646. Offers a variety of seminars, books, and a complete Resource Kit listing books and periodicals of use to working and aspiring information brokers. For information on their seminars, contact IPI, 3724 F.M. 1960 W, Suite 214, Houston, TX 77068; (713) 537-8344.

Society of Competitive Intelligence Professionals, 1700 Diagonal Road, Suite 520, Alexandria, VA 22314; (703) 739-0696.

COURSES

Some colleges and universities offer courses on information brokering open to outside students. A few are listed below. Check with your local college or university for others.

Emporia State University, Emporia KS; (316) 341-5203
San Jose State University, San Jose, CA; (408) 924-2494
Simmons College, Boston, MA; (617) 521-2798
Southern Connecticut State College, New Haven, CT; (203) 397-4530
University of Buffalo, SUNY, Buffalo, NY; (716) 645-2412
University of Pittsburgh, Pittsburgh, PA (412) 624-5230

You can also contact the Information Brokering Mentoring Program for Beginning Information Brokers, Marketing Base, P.O. Box 720, Sebastopol, CA 95472; (800) 544-5924; (707) 829-9421; fax (707) 823-2713.

BOOKS

The Burwell Directory of Information Brokers, published by Burwell Enterprises; c/o Helen Burwell, Burwell Enterprises, 3724 F.M. 1960 W, Suite 214, Houston, TX 77068; (713) 537-9051. Updated annually.

Directory of Computer-Readable Databases, Gale Publishing. Annual.

Find It Fast: How to Uncover Expert Information on Any Subject, Robert Berkman, New York: HarperCollins, 1994.

The Information Broker's Handbook, Sue Rugge and Alfred Glossbrenner, Windcrest/McGraw Hill, 1995. Available from Sue Rugge, 46 Hiller Drive, Oakland, CA 94618; (510) 649-9743.

Information for Sale: How to Start and Operate Your Own Data Research Service, John Everett and Elizabeth Powell Crowe, Blue Ridge Summit, PA: McGraw-Hill, 1994; (800) 822-8138.

A small selection of database vendors commonly used by professional information brokers include:

CompuServe, 5000 Arlington Centre Boulevard, Columbus, OH 43220; (800) 848-8199. Popular database service, offering E-mail and access to many databases including *Knowledge Index* (KI), a low-cost collection of professional databases from Dialog for use during off-peak hours. (Note: the use of KI for commercial purposes is prohibited.)

DataTimes, 1400 Quail Springs Parkway, Suite 450, Oklahoma City, OK 73134; (800) 642-2525; on-line database for about 200 full-text newspapers.

Dialog Information Services, 3460 Hillview Avenue, Palo Alto, CA 94304; (800) 334-2564. The largest of the database services, offering hundreds of databases.

Dow Jones News/Retrieval, Dow Jones and Company, Box 300, Princeton, NJ 08540; (800) 522-3567 or (609) 520-4000. Primarily financial information.

Mead Data Central, Box 933, Dayton, OH 45401; (800) 227-4908 or (513) 859-1611. Offers Nexis, a full-text database, and Lexis, a legal database service.

Newsnet, 945 Haverford Road, Bryn Mawr, PA 19010; (800) 345-1301 or (610) 527-8030. Full-text retrieval of over 800 printed newsletters. Ellen Keech (610) 527-8030.

MAGAZINES

Database and *CD Rom Professional,* Online, Inc., 11 Tannery Lane, Weston, CT 06883; (800) 248-8466.

Information Today; Link-UP; and *Searcher,* Learned Information, Inc., 143 Old Marlton Pike, Medford, NY 08055.

■ ■ ■ ■ ■

MAILING LIST SERVICE

As much as you may not like receiving junk mail or business announcements, there is a silver lining in the amazing growth of direct mail in this country: It has generated many new business opportunities for the savvy entrepreneur who cashes in on running a mailing list service. A mailing list service is actually one of the easiest businesses to start from home with a computer and can grow into a substantial business. The start-up costs are low, and the learning curve is short too.

Mailing list services perform a variety of tasks, but the essential nature of the business is to use computers to establish and maintain lists of names for mailings, and in many cases to perform those mailings for many kinds of clients following U.S. postal regulations for bulk mail. In particular, the main services of a mailing list firm include:

List maintenance.   You maintain or build computerized mailing lists for businesses that do not have the in-house expertise or personnel to do their own. You may turn over your work to your client or print labels for them on a regular basis, such as biweekly or monthly, or on demand.

Doing mailings.   You handle bulk mailings for retail stores, hotels, and businesses of all kinds that give you lists of names for you to put on labels and mail at the lowest cost.

List creation.   You produce your own mailing lists on your computer and then rent the names. You can also sell monthly updated reports of your lists.

List brokering.   You find lists from associations, clubs, and other groups whose list of names can be valuable to other people. You thus act as a broker between a list seller and a list buyer.

Teaching about mailing lists.   List marketing, supporting, and teaching mailing list software to others

Mailing list services find customers from the many small businesses that want to use direct mail but do not have their own mailing lists, or do not have them computerized. A significant source of income for mailing list services therefore is to create or maintain mailing lists for many kinds of businesses.

You begin by designing the list (which names to include, in what format, along with other facts that might be included in a database of names). For example, a clothing store might have the names of its clients, but with your service, you create a computer database that includes all customers along with their birthdates, color preferences, and even the husband's address so you can remind him to buy his wife a gift. You then keep the list up-to-date, entering in names of new customers and performing other services to keep the list clean (by eliminating duplicates) and current. A mailing list service that knows how to work with database software can arrange, for example, to design a database that allows the store to create a mailing list ten days before Valentine's Day addressed to all husbands whose wives like to wear red.

Many mailing list firms make a large portion of their income from actually doing the mailing for businesses. For example, Katie Allegato of Allegato and Associates in Kissimmee, Florida, helps many of her clients do the mailing. She obtains their mailing lists, cleans them, sorts them, and prints out labels complete with Postnet bar codes that entitles the mailing to the bulk-mail discounts. She also has the labels sorted using special software so that the pieces are eligible for greater discounts if they meet the requirements of "saturation walk sequence," or "carrier route," or "automated walk sequence/delivery point bar code."

This task is actually one of the most complex aspects of running your mailing service. As postage costs have risen and the quantity of mail delivered has skyrocketed to more than 170 billion pieces per year, the U.S. Postal Service has made major efforts to automate and computerize the delivery of all mail, but bulk mail in particular. For this reason, the software that bar codes, sorts, and categorizes mail must follow strict regulations established by the Postal Service. Doing bulk mailings thus consists of the following steps:

1. Your client brings you either a diskette loaded with names or simply a list of names typed up.

2. To achieve the lowest postal rate for a bulk mailing, you need to clean the list of duplicates, and then employ sophisticated software that allows you to compare the names and addresses to lists of exact addresses that are stored on CD-ROM disks to verify them.

3. Once you verify addresses, you then print out mailing labels complete with bar codes showing the delivery point codes (which is an 11-digit number that includes the zip code plus the four extra digits that were added, plus two more digits from the street address).

By following this procedure, you can generally perform a bulk mailing for a client at 5 to 10 cents less than the cost of regular first-class postage. And this small amount adds up, particularly for clients who might mail 10,000 pieces every few weeks. Allegato says, for example, that one of her clients, a hotel resort in the area, might spend $10,000 to $15,000 per year in mailings, but by handling their mailings as bulk, they save $5,000 to $8,000.

Compiling and selling your own mailing lists is another way to make money as a mailing list service. While you can't compete with large mail list companies that sell thousands of names in any one of thousands of categories, you can create lists that are tailored to your city, or your specific area, or the particular needs of your clients. For example, some businesses only want to mail to all owner-occupied homes in a ten-square block. You can buy print directories of your city and key in just that area, creating your own mailing list. (Large mailing houses often don't handle small requests, anyway, so a home-based business is sometimes the only place a small business can go to purchase a list of 200 to 500 names.) Other kinds of lists you can create yourself can be based on other public records, such as new businesses in your city (which you get from public records of new business licenses), new homeowners, sole-practitioner chiropractors, and so on. You can also sell monthly updates on the lists you compile to add value to your monthly reports. Allegato phones new businesses to verify phone numbers and obtains additional information, such as contact names, titles, whether it's a male- or female-owned business, whether it's minority owned, and whether it's a new or relocated business, as well as the size of the business based on the number of employees. These reports can then be issued every month and can be sold on a six- or twelve-month subscription basis.

Finally, some list services broker lists; they may have a client who wants to purchase a certain kind of list and they then find it for them. And of course, handling mailing lists is complex enough that many services tutor or teach it to small businesses that prefer to do their own mailings.

As Allegato concludes, this is a great business that you can do as much or as little of as you like, and at your own leisure. It is also a good business to run if you do desktop publishing, because many stores and businesses need help designing their flyers or brochures in addition to doing the mailings. Allegato has clients who bring her deadly ugly promotional pieces, and with her experience in direct mail, she is able to advise them herself or send them to a desktop publisher she knows.

✅ Knowledge and Skills You Need to Have

- You need to learn about the specific U.S. postal regulations for bulk mailings and how to make mail automation compatible. This includes sorting, stuffing, traying, sacking, as well as using bar codes, carrier route numbers, and rates. The Postal Service offers many booklets to explain their regulations, and you can take workshops from them as well.

- You need to know how to use a computer and several basic database and mailing list programs. As the sophistication of the industry changes, too, you will need to keep up to date with new software technology. For example, you need to know how to use the new CD-ROM products available that contain every U.S. address and allow for address verification. (Many people, for example, write their addresses incorrectly or they are keyboarded incorrectly; so that although 13559 Ocean Boulevard, Venice, CA, may look like a valid address, if it doesn't exist, it can't be delivered. Verifying the address so that every piece is deliverable is required for the greatest bulk mail discounts.)

- You need to be able to type accurately and quickly.

- You need to be responsible about meeting deadlines.

◼ Start-up Costs

	Low	High
Computer with hard disk and CD-ROM drive	$1,000	$3,000
Printer	300	1,600
Suite software	250	400
Database and mailing list software to maintain list of names	250	400
Address verification software	900	900
Bar coding/sorting software	900	900
Permits from post office*	100	300
Office furniture, especially ergonomic chair	400	1,000
Business cards, letterhead, envelopes	100	600
Total	$4,200	$9,100

* You might also lease a postage meter machine (such as a Pitney Bowes model) to use for clients who bring you their bulk mail already folded and stuffed in envelopes with labels and bar codes.

◼ Advantages

- Mailing list services are relatively easy to start and sell.
- Because many businesses would like to do mailings if they knew how, your customer base can be large. This means you do not need to rely on a few important customers for most of your income.
- Your business can be operated on a part-time or full-time basis, or even as an adjunct to another business.

◼ Disadvantages

- The work is routine; there is little challenge to most mailing list services.
- The work requires exceptional attention to detail.
- Postal regulations change and are sometimes complex. You need to be sure you understand what you are doing, or your clients will find another service.
- Unless you take the necessary precautions, you risk developing repetitive-motion injuries as a result of constant keyboarding.

◼ Pricing

For entering names into a mailing list, many services charge from 6 to 7 cents per line of input. Thus, a three-line entry consisting of name, street address, city/state/zip runs 15 to 25 cents per name. Some services charge $1 per name to maintain the list for a year.

For printing out labels, services charge from 3 to 5 cents per label (including the label stock); envelopes run 10 to 12 cents per envelope printed.

Purging a list averages 1 to 2 cents per name on the list, and to use a mailer's bulk mail permit costs an average of 4 to 5 cents per piece. Thus, a client who uses a list service to clean a list, print bar-coded labels, and get bulk-mail rates pays roughly 8 to 12 cents per name plus the actual cost of the postage, which may be as low as 14.5 cents or 19.8 cents as of this writing. A service mailing out 10,000 pieces thus earns $800 to $1,200 for the work.

Potential Earnings

TYPICAL ANNUAL GROSS REVENUES: $40,000 to $100,000 per year based on surveys of home-based mail list services.

OVERHEAD: low (20 percent or less).

Best Home Businesses Estimate of Market Potential

Total number of mailing list services in the United States, including home-based businesses: 9,503. A mailing list business continues to be one of the easiest to start and find customers to serve. An outgrowth of a mailing list service might be faxing information for clients using the *broadcasting* capability of your fax machine or software. Even though laws have been passed to limit the use of "junk fax," electronic transmission of information is growing.

Best Ways to Get Business

- Directly approaching personnel of locally owned stores to ask how they handle their mailing lists. In stores that ask customers to fill out cards, or to sign guest books, ask what they do with the names they get.
- Calling associations, clubs, churches, and hotels in your area to see if any of them are interested in having you maintain their mailing lists or handle their mailings
- Spreading the word through personal contacts to reach small businesses, organizations, churches
- Networking in business organizations, chambers of commerce, and leads clubs. Network also with printers and desktop publishers who might be doing work for businesses about to do mailings.
- Contacting people you know or can readily meet in networking organizations who are involved in direct selling of products with companies such as Avon, Mary Kay Cosmetics, Rexall, and Watkins
- Sending direct mail yourself to businesses in your area
- Advertising in the yellow pages

First steps

1. Learn to use mailing list software and CD-ROM products for verifying addresses and sorting.

2. Attend bulk-mail workshops at your post office. Read their books and ask questions so that you are certain that you understand how to handle bulk mailings.

3. Work on acquiring customers.

🔲 Where to Turn for Information and Help

ORGANIZATIONS

Direct Marketing Association, 11 West 42d Street, New York, NY 10036; (212) 768-7277. Many publications. Annual meeting. Also has Ethical Business Practices, Mailing List Practices, and Fair Information Practices Guidelines.

National Postal Forum, 1350 Beverly Road, Suite 209, McLean, VA 22101; (703) 442-8198. Nonprofit educational forum that sponsors trade shows for the mail industry.

MailCom Conference, P.O. Box 8477, Philadelphia, PA 19101; (607) 746-3450.

U.S. POSTAL SERVICE PUBLICATIONS

Domestic Mail Manual, List ID DOM, File Code 2S, available from Superintendent of Documents.

International Mail Manual, List ID IMM, File Code 2S, available from Superintendent of Documents.

BOOKS

The Complete Direct Mail List Handbook, Ed Burnett, Englewood Cliffs, NJ: Prentice Hall, 1988.

Mailing List Services on Your Home-Based PC, Linda Rohrbough, Blue Ridge Summit, PA: Tab/McGraw Hill, 1994; (800) 822-8158.

Standard Rate and Data Service, 3004 Glenview Rd., Wilmette, IL 60091; (800) 851-7737; the rate guide for mailing list rental for the entire industry.

SOFTWARE

ArcList and *AccuMail,* Group 1 Software, 4200 Parliament Place, Suite 600, Lanham, MD 20706; (800) 368-5806 and (301) 731-2300; *AccuMail* is the leading CD-ROM package for list verification, and *ArcList* is software for list management.

AUDIOTAPES

How to Make Money in the Mailing List Business, Katie Allegato, Here's How, Box 5091, Santa Monica, CA 90409.

■ ■ ■ ■ ■

MAIL-ORDER BUSINESS

The idea of opening your mailbox to find it stuffed with checks intrigues upwards of eight million people a year. Even though a small percentage of these people actually try a mail-order business, and perhaps as few as one person in twenty-five succeeds, the fact that you probably know someone or know about someone who's making money this way makes the idea all the more attractive.

In a mail-order business, instead of selling products face-to-face or by phone, you sell products by placing advertisements, usually classified ads, in publications or by doing advertising using a catalogue or another form of direct mail. You then fill the orders that come in from these ads. While the cost of getting into a mail-order business is rising, someone who is selling products that cannot be found elsewhere or that are otherwise difficult or time-consuming to find can establish a profitable mail-order business from home.

According to Simmons Market Research Bureau, Americans are ordering merchandise by mail or phone more than ever. The percentage of Americans who are shopping by mail or phone has grown from 36.2 percent in 1983 to 52.6 percent in 1993. That's more than one out of every two adults. A Direct Marketing Association study conducted by the WEFA Group, an economic modeling and forecasting firm, found that revenue from catalogue sales at $53.4 billion in 1993 were up 49.6 percent from 1987. Catalogue sales are projected to increase to $69.5 billion in 1997. Consistent with this, the proportional use of third-class mail continues to grow both in quantity and as a proportion of all U.S. mail. It grew from 32.5 percent of all mail in 1983 to 38.4 percent in 1993. All other classes of mail (first, second, and fourth) were less in 1993 than 1983. It's no wonder so many Americans are shopping by mail. Americans today are simply too busy to go shopping. While department stores struggle for survival, Americans can use catalogues to shop anytime and anyplace.

Although the average American household receives about fifty pounds of junk mail each year, a well-done specialty catalogue can stand out from the rest. David Starkman, who with his wife, Susan Pinsky, publishes the *Reel 3-D Enterprises* direct-mail catalogue of 3-D photography products, claims that "often a mail-order catalogue can actually do a better job of providing information about a product than having it stocked in a store where the clerks have little knowledge about your product."

Starkman also finds that selling by mail is more recession proof than selling through retail stores. You don't need to rely on whether someone goes into a store to get your products. You can generate your own business by sending information about your products directly to your customers. Also, you don't need to keep an inventory of products on hand. And by using the database capability of a personal computer, you can track who is buying from you and build a select list of repeat buyers and those who have made recent orders.

All sorts of products are being sold successfully by mail, including books, toys, artwork, makeup, foods, recipes, novelties, instructional materials, and career or financial information. The best mail-order products however, are ones that:

- you own and completely control, preferably manufacture, or at least can obtain from more than one supplier
- are not readily available in local stores
- are unique and attractive, lightweight and easy to mail, requiring no special packaging, sturdy rather than fragile
- can be offered for a substantial markup
- require little inventory
- are consumable or part of a complete line that provides an ample base for repeat orders
- have no breakable mechanical parts to be returned

Herman Holtz, author of *Mail Order Magic*, points out that specialized, brief how-to reports or folios of a few thousand words each are an example of the ideal kind of mail-order product that meets these criteria. Books are also ideal because they don't break and are rarely returned.

✅ Knowledge and Skills You Need to Have

- You have to be able to research the market and find out what's already available. You don't want to try to sell something someone else has done better and cheaper.
- You will need to become skilled at marketing, advertising, and selecting or designing your product.
- Direct mail requires creating a strong ad, direct-mail piece, or catalogue, which involves being able to write, photograph, lay out, and paste up material about your products. If you don't have these skills, you will need to acquire them or hire others to do them for you while you learn what works. It's a fallacy to think, however, that you must have a glossy catalogue of full-color pictures. Attractive, clear, well-designed materials that present a lot of information about your products in an interesting way work best.
- You must be able to wear a lot of hats and be willing to do routine, menial tasks, like filling requests and shipping orders.

▣ Start-up Costs*

	Low	High
Computer with hard disk and modem	$1,000	$ 3,000
Fax machine	300	900
Printer	300	1,600
Copier for incoming orders	300	800
Suite software (word processing, spreadsheet, and database)	250	400
Initial test using direct-mail piece or print classified advertising	300	8,000**
Credit card terminal	125	1,000***
Office furniture, especially ergonomic chair	400	1,000
Answering machine or voice mail (not a service, because you must be able to get the exact message, and no service can answer the detailed questions buyers are likely to have	125	200
Business cards, letterhead, envelopes	100	600
Total	$3,200	$17,500

Other additional items you may wish to get include a shrink-wrap system with a heat seal for packaging your products, for $200 to $500, and a postage meter, which you can rent for $30 a month.

  * Costs of purchasing mailing lists are not included. They vary widely, depending on the list you're renting.

  ** Initial test pieces can run as little as $300 for a small classified ad in a niche market magazine or as much as $8,000 for publishing a catalogue showing your products. The higher figure here is based on producing 25,000 copies of a catalogue using a web press with three spot colors.

  *** Your sales will increase by approximately 50 percent if you have the capability to take charge cards, particularly MasterCard and Visa. To offer these cards, obtain a merchant account from a bank or through membership in a chamber of commerce or business association. The terminal for getting credit card approvals will cost from $125 to $225. However, banks rarely issue merchant accounts to new home-based mail-order businesses, so you may have to go through one of the companies that act as a broker between you and banks. These companies make a hunk of their profit by charging you from $700 to $1,000 for a terminal. For more information on getting a merchant account, see chapter 14 in *Working From Home.* Alternatively, you might look into the company called CheckAmerica, listed in the resources, that lets you take a customer's checking account information. They process a check for you with approval from the customer, and for an extra fee can guarantee the check.

Advantages

- Since there are no fixed hours, a mail-order business can be started on a part-time basis while you are still employed. Many people begin mail-order businesses by working ten or fewer hours a week.
- Unlike retail sales,
  - you don't have the overhead of monthly rent for a store
  - you can specialize in products that wouldn't sell enough to support a shop
  - you have more control over people seeing your product because you can take your product to the customer instead of depending on your customer to come to you
  - direct mail is not dependent on weather
- Unlike a service business that involves selling your time, with a flourishing mail-order business your income doesn't stop because you take time off.

Disadvantages

- To make money, you've got to find the right products and sell them for a price people will pay, with the right promotions, to the right customers—which is a challenge.
- You are tied to the business; filling orders day in and day out can be tiresome. Mail comes in six days a week; you can't turn it off. All you can do is wish for a slow week.
- Since you are doing your business by mail, you may have limited face-to-face contact with people (not a disadvantage for some people).

Pricing

While the general rule of thumb in mail order is to sell products for at least three to four times your in-the-mail cost of the products, you need to find the pricing level for your particular type of products. If your products are unique (which is desirable) and you therefore have nothing to compare them with, try out prices on a preliminary basis with as many people as you can who you think would be buyers of your product. (Two or three is not enough.) Such a trial will help you establish the first prices to test in your ads, direct mail, or catalogue.

Potential Earnings

TYPICAL ANNUAL GROSS REVENUES: Depends entirely on the product line, but the upside potential is greater than for most salaried jobs.

OVERHEAD: high (more than 40 percent) because of advertising costs.

🔧 *Best Home Businesses* Estimate of Market Potential

People are buying more by mail, but mail order is not an easy business to establish. An extremely promising avenue of growth for this industry is sales made over online computer services, such as Compuserve, Prodigy, and the Internet.

🔲 Best Ways to Get Business

- Getting publicity, but this requires that you have unique products. Send press releases with a full-color photograph announcing your products to new-products editors of publications targeted to your customers. From the inquiries and orders you receive you can build your own mailing list.
- Mailing a direct-mail piece or catalogue to your own list; people on your list know you and/or have already bought from you.
- Advertising in magazines targeted to your customers. In this way you can get orders and develop your own list. Small classified ads can be cost-effective.
- You can rent or trade mailing lists. Look for lists that have names of people who are like your customers.

🔧 First Steps

Getting started in the mail-order business is a three-step process:

1. Create or select your products.
2. Develop or rent a mailing list or, alternatively, identify publications in which to advertise.
3. Produce and distribute your catalogue, direct-mail piece, or advertisement.

🔲 Where to Turn for Information and Help

SUPPLIERS

A number of companies will help you get started in the mail-order business if you would like a faster way to get started. They usually import and warehouse merchandise of all kinds (figurines, jewelry, watches, handbags, and so forth) and provide you with catalogues of this merchandise along with circulars, order forms, envelopes, and other sales materials, and with instruction manuals for how you can sell these items through the mail. They will ship the merchandise directly to you or drop-ship it to your customers.

Of course, these items may not meet the criteria identified above, so by selecting the items yourself, you might be able to get better prices and will have more control over the products, from selection to advertising and pricing. The advantage to working with one of those companies is that they supply you with all the materials you need and some guidance as well.

Mail Order Associates, 120 Chestnet Ridge Road, Montvale, NJ 07645; (201) 391-3660.

The Mellinger Company, 6100 Variel, Woodland Hills, CA 91367; (818) 884-4400. Mellinger does not import items and then sell them to you, preferring that you deal with the suppliers directly. The company provides you with the names of foreign suppliers and provides books, manuals, tapes, and seminars to teach you the ins and outs of making your own deals. They do offer a number of items they will sell you to get you started. Since 1968, Mellinger has also sponsored an annual international trade show where overseas suppliers exhibit their goods directly to Mellinger clients. Cost of their program is $225.

Specialty Merchandising Corporation, 9401 De Soto Avenue, Chatsworth, CA 91311; (818) 998-3300. Sells products at prices fairly close to what gift shops pay at major gift marts.

TRADE ASSOCIATIONS

American Marketing Association, 250 South Wacker Drive, Chicago, IL 60606; (312) 648-0536.

Direct Marketing Association, 11 W. 42d Street, New York, NY 10036; (212) 768-7277. Offers courses on direct-mail advertising.

NEWSLETTERS

Mail Order Messenger, Box 17131, Memphis, TN 38187-0131.

Profits, Carson Services, Box 4785, Lincoln, NE 68504; (402) 467-4230.

Target Marketing Magazine, North American Publishing Company, 401 N. Broad Street, Philadelphia, PA 19108.

BOOKS

Building a Mail Order Business: A Complete Manual for Success, William A. Cohen, New York: Wiley, 1991.

The Catalog of Catalogs III: The Complete Mail-Order Directory, Edward Palder, Rockville, Md.: Woodbine House, 1993. An extensive listing organized into 650 subject categories of mail-order suppliers of specialized goods.

Direct Marketing Sourcebook, John Kremer.

Direct Marketing: Strategy, Planning, Execution, Edward L. Nash, New York: McGraw-Hill, 1994.

Drop Shipping Marketing Methods, New York: Drop Shipping News, P.O. Box 7838, New York, NY 10150.

The Golden Mailbox: How to Get Rich Direct Marketing Your Product, Ted Nicholas, Chicago: Dearborn, 1993; (800) 322-8621.

How to Create Successful Catalogs, NTC Publishing Group, 4255 West Touhy Avenue, Lincolnwood, IL 60646; (800) 323-4900.

How to Start & Operate a Mail-Order Business, Julian L. Simon, New York: McGraw-Hill, 1993.

SOFTWARE

Mail-order software organizes and automates order-entry, inventory-tracking, and accounting aspects of running a mail-order business. Two of these specialized programs are:

Easy Order, The Micro Tyme Network, 1422 Pine Hill Drive, Garland, TX 75043; (214) 840-9313.

The Mail Order Wizard, the Haven Corporation, 1227 Dodge Street, Evanston, IL 60202; (800) 782-8278.

CHECK SERVICES

Check services enable you to accept orders for products or services as well as receive payments by phone, fax, or through your modem. You simply obtain a checking or savings account number from your customer and transmit the information to a processing center by fax or modem. You or your bank receives a check by mail. This service goes by various names, such as:

VoiceCheck from CheckAmerica, Inc., 258 E. Altamonte Drive, Altamonte Springs, FL 32701; (800) 539-2666.

Check by Phone service is offered by a number of companies including the National Association of Credit Card Merchants ([407] 737-8700).

■ ■ ■ ■ ■

MANAGEMENT CONSULTANT

Professional consulting is among the fastest-growing segments of our information society, with an estimated 20 to 25 percent increase over the balance of a decade. There are some half million consultants of all kinds in the U.S., split among hundreds of specialties ranging from automation and affirmative action to wage and salary administration and warehouse arrangement, from packaging and purchasing to telecommunications and traffic. The Institute of Management Consulting breaks its membership into over 260 different specialties. Most numerous, however, are management consultants, the subject of this entry. *Best Home Businesses* also separately covers marketing consultants, computer consultants, image consultants, specialty consultants, security consultants, wedding consultants, and public-relations specialists.

According to Bill Mooney of Mooney and Associates, this entry is better titled "Consulting to Management," because management consultants are a class of individuals who perform a wide range of tasks for companies and executives. In fact, as Mooney suggests, the first thing that one must do in understanding management consulting is to define it. As Mooney then indicates, "Consulting is the business of solving problems for people in organizations."

American companies tend to rely on the use of management consultants (and other kinds of consultants) more than other countries in the world. According to Mooney, the three principal reasons for the use of consultants in the 90s are:

1. More and more companies need to solve problems to be in compliance with dozens of government agencies (federal, state, city, or county) or quasi-governmental agencies like the Air Quality Management Department.

2. Companies constantly need to introduce and integrate new technologies from either the hard side (e.g., those based on the physical and mathematical sciences) or the soft side (e.g., human-resource concepts and technologies developing out of the humanities and psychology).

3. Because of the tightening economy and the increase in global competition, problems must be solved in an efficient, cost-effective manner, which means engaging outside consultants to save on the costs of hiring the expertise in-house. Outside consultants also provide a company with a wider breadth of experience and a wider variety of contacts than its in-house employees have. In fact, as corporations scale back personnel (as they have been rampantly doing for the past decade), consultants are increasingly being paid to implement projects as well as provide guidance and expertise.

Paul Franklin, a consulting trainer in Portland, Oregon, and publisher of *The Professional Consultant*, adds that change itself has become a driving force behind the increasing use of consultants. Companies now may either use a consultant to help plan new strategies and then do the work inside, or use their internal managers to strategize and implement a new business plan, but use a consultant to validate the work.

We might add to these reasons that consulting provides a lifestyle that people want. People at the level of skills needed by consultants want more control over their work. They want greater variety, more challenge, more respect. They want to be their own boss without a significant capital investment—and consulting fills this bill. Management consulting is thus an excellent home-based business if you can fulfill the qualifications listed below and are able to develop a reputation for helping companies large or small become more successful and profitable.

☑ Knowledge and Skills You Need to Have

- As internationally known consultant Howard Shenson (who died in 1993) said, "Consultants are the high priests of the information revolution. They possess the knowledge that drives our economic system." Knowledge is therefore first on the list of prerequisites for management consulting. Mooney refines this definition into three categories: technical know-how; expertise; and experience. Millions of consultants have technical know-how, but that is not sufficient to succeed. Thousands of academics have knowledge but not the experience of solving problems. Your clients will always ask you who else you have helped to solve problems like theirs. As Bill Mooney points out, it is best to be seen as an authority; and if you can't do that, you should be an expert; and if you can't do that, you should be a specialist rather than a generalist.

- You need to be research-and-development oriented. This means you have to know how to use questions to get significant information and be able to do "information inquiry" market research. Beyond that, you must also know how to analyze the answers you get and apply them to the benefit of both your business and your clients.

- You have to use strategic planning to get a competitive edge. This means you must be able to identify needs and directions that your clients may not have even thought about yet. You must have the ability to see future trends and directions for the industries you are working in.

- Consultants need to have people skills in order to understand clients' needs and problems and to communicate what they understand.

- You need excellent communication skills, written and oral, as you will be dealing with the CEOs, senior executives, and managers of companies. You will likely write many reports and speak in front of groups of executives.

- You have to be willing to take risks. As Shenson's research showed, many if not all successful consultants ranked high in entrepreneurial spirit. So develop yourself as an entrepreneur.

- As Bill Mooney points out, you also need a continuous improvement program of your own. You have to learn how to analyze your own problem-solving record, to identify what you can specialize in, to evaluate the market for your type of work, and to position yourself against the competition. You must also have a program to continually update your skills, knowledge, technique, and specialty as well as keep aware of the latest developments in the industry you work in and the consulting industry in general.

⬢ Start-up Costs

	Low	High
Computer with hard disk and modem (or notebook computer)	$1,000	$ 4,000
Fax machine	300	900
Laser printer	300	1,600
Color ink-jet printer	350	600
Suite software (word processing, spreadsheet, and database) and contact management software	250	400
Specialized software: contact manager, presentation software, project management software	250	1,000
Copier	300	800
On-line services	200	500
Errors and omissions insurance	200	500
Office furniture, especially ergonomic chair	400	1,000
Business cards, letterhead, envelopes	100	600
Organizational dues to a consultants' organization	250	250
Organizational dues to organizations in the field in which you work	250	500
Reference books and continuing education	400	1,000
Total	$4,550	$13,650

⬢ Advantages

- You receive maximum pay for what you know and can do.
- The work offers variety and challenge. You can work with many different companies and be involved in a wide assortment of problems and solutions.
- It can be satisfying for you to see your ideas and strategies implemented and to get positive feedback when they are working.
- Consulting stimulates your creativity. Most consultants are problem solvers. They have a different way of looking at situations than the client and can therefore respond with innovative solutions.

⬢ Disadvantages

- The failure rate is high, according to Jim Kennedy of Kennedy Publications, a management publishing company. Not everyone has the counseling skills that must supplement technical expertise. And it can take a long time to close a deal.
- The work can be lonely and solitary.
- The result of your work may not be known until far into the future when the company succeeds or fails.
- Consultants want to sell their knowledge and advice; clients want to buy benefits. Until you can demonstrate to the client that he or she is going to

see tangible results as a result of your work, you won't be successful in marketing. This is the consultant's Catch 22. As Bill Mooney points out: you need to clone your successes.

$ Pricing

Consultants can charge by the hour, by the day, or by the job. According to the most recent reliable study of professional fees (conducted in 1991 by Howard Shenson), the national average in 1991 for all types of consulting was $1,102 per day. In major markets the average was $1,218 per day; in small markets, $900 per day. The median daily fee for the 10 percent of professionals reporting the highest billing rate was $1,994 per day; for the bottom 10 percent, $486 per day. The average daily charge for large clients was $1,173 per day; for small clients, $891 per day. Unfortunately, no adequate formal survey has been taken since this one. You can probably add 10 to 20 percent to these fees to correlate fees to the mid-1990s.

回 Potential Earnings

TYPICAL ANNUAL GROSS REVENUES: $110,000 based on billing 100 days a year at the national average rate of $1,102 per day.

Mooney points out that consultants who bill less than 100 days per year are those who have cash-flow problems, whereas the successful consultants are those who bill between 100 and 150 days per year. Paul Franklin adds that the bulk of consultants make $30,000 to $60,000 per year, but those who develop their businesses and think in terms of success earn $150,000 to $300,000.

OVERHEAD: moderate (20 to 40 percent).

ⓩ *Best Home Businesses* **Estimate of Market Potential**

Total number of management consultants in the United States, including home-based businesses: 62,345; however, **Business Week** stated this number to be 80,000 in a cover story on consulting in its July 25, 1994, issue. The outlook for management consulting is bright. The more change there is for corporations—in their structure, size, operations, and markets—the greater the demand for consultants for both their expertise and their labor.

🖻 Best Ways to Get Business

- Contacting former clients and colleagues to get referrals is the number-one method of getting business for management consultants, according to Mooney.
- The second-best technique is to perform what Mooney calls "informa-

tional inquiries." This is done by calling companies to ask some general questions about a business or management problem you are studying or for which you would like to write an article. Such inquires give you an opportunity to get to know a company and to begin building a relationship with their key people. It may be that one of your questions rings true with someone at the company, and they then hire you to find the answers for them.

■ Speaking and writing are also essential to getting business. Both of these help build authority and expertise in your field. Giving seminars, workshops, and talks or writing articles helps to establish for your audience what kinds of problems you have solved so they will know what kinds of problems you can solve. You should also write letters to the editors of newspapers, create articles for newsletters, and develop a concept for a business book that a trade publisher might want to publish.

■ Create audiotapes, videotapes, and other educational/informational tools that your prospective clients might want to buy to get to know you.

■ Be proactive in identifying potential new clients. A story Mooney related to us exemplifies this principle: There once was a consultant who was a marketing specialist. He sent out 200 résumés cold and got zero responses. After reflection, he decided to try this tactic. He took ten companies and developed a proposal that outlined what he could do that would add value to their organization. He sent out his proposals and got two responses, out of which he got one contract offer, which turned into a major moneymaker for him.

■ Become active and participate in many professional organizations, including management-consulting organizations in your area to trade and business associations in the fields in which you work.

■ Develop an informational brochure featuring the key information your client needs to know about your specialty. Advertise this free brochure in classified ads or mention in the articles that you write that you will send one to anyone who requests it.

First Steps

■ You need first to "position" yourself as a consultant. Ask yourself: (1) what kinds of problems you can solve, (2) what kinds of companies need those problems solved, and (3) what kinds of problems do you have experience solving. Use these answers to develop a sense of your technical know-how, expertise, and experience. From there, you can develop a short list of fields or functions in which you can specialize. You can't be all things to all people, as Mooney says. He calls this step a SWOT analysis: discover your own strengths, weaknesses, opportunities, and threats.

- Find some companies you would like to work with. Invest the time to learn about them. Follow these steps to select companies:
  - Identify a niche for your market.
  - Research the companies you can work with.
  - Figure out their needs. Think creatively about how you can help them.
  - Be proactive. Present a proposal to the companies identifying exactly what you can do.
- Make a commitment to be successful. If you are successful in other areas of life, you can be successful in consulting if you make the commitment. The majority of consultants live on the bottom strata of consulting; imagine yourself as being on the top and believe in your own abilities to succeed.
- Make a list of everyone in your area whom you know personally who would be a good prospective client or who is in a position to refer clients to you. Don't stop until you have at least twenty people. Send a letter to each of these people saying that you've gone into business for yourself as a consultant and want to take him or her to lunch. Let the person know in the letter that you would like to ask several questions about his or her most pressing issues. Then call to set up a time. Most will accept the invitation for lunch. Talk about what you do; you should always be able to pick up two or three clients this way.

▢ Where to Turn for Information and Help

ORGANIZATIONS

Depending on your level of experience and location, you should try to join both organizations for consultants and trade organizations in the field in which you work. Two management-consulting organizations you may wish to contact are:

American Association of Professional Consultants, National Bureau of Professional Consultants, 3577 Fourth Avenue, San Diego, CA 92103; (800) 543-1114; (619) 297-2207. Association for newcomers in consulting with less than five years experience. Membership costs $100 and includes a newsletter, resources, annual conference, and networking. Also allows you to take the American Management Association's self-study course that leads to a certificate in business management and consultancy, comparable to an MBA (takes about 18 months to do). To join the AAPC, write a letter on your letterhead.

Institute of Management Consultants, 521 Fifth Avenue, 35th Floor, New York, NY 10175-3589; (800) 221-2557; (212) 697-8262. Membership of more than 2,000 consulting firms, including sole practitioners. Offers a certification program for consultants with more than five years experience.

Kennedy Publications, Templeton Road, Fitzwilliam, NH 03447; (800) 531-0007. Although this is not an organization, Kennedy Publications is one of the primary publishers of consultant information, including a newsletter (*Consultant News*), a directory that describes over 1,500 consulting firms in North America (*Directory of Management Consultants*), and a useful catalogue of 100 titles and special reports on marketing, client-consultant relationships, inspiration, and practice improvement (*Catalog of Management Consulting Books*).

National Consultant Referral, Inc. (NCR), 8445 Camino Santa Fe, #207, San Diego, CA 92121; (800) 221-3104. An association for consultants seeking freelance contract work. NCR is an expert services broker which matches clients seeking consultants with consultants seeking clients. Consultants must pay 20 percent of their fee to NCR.

NEWSLETTERS

Management Consultant International (404) 636-6610. Published monthly.

Marketing Conferences and Seminars, by LEARN in Manhattan, Kansas. Newsletter for training people.

The Professional Consultant, edited by Paul Franklin. See National Training Center entry below.

BOOKS

Building a Consulting Practice, Robert O. Metzger, Ph.D., Newbury Park, CA: Sage Publications, 1994.

Complete Guide to Consulting Success, Howard Shenson and Ted Nicolas, Dearborn Trade, 520 N. Dearborn St., Chicago, IL 60610-4354; (800) 621-9621.

Consultant and Consulting Organization Directory, Gale Research, 645 Griswold St., Detroit, MI 48226; (313) 961-2242. This directory accepts free listings and is available at reference libraries.

Contract and Fee Setting Guide for Consultants and Professionals, Howard Shenson, New York: John Wiley, 1990.

How to Succeed as an Independent Consultant, Herman Holtz, New York: Wiley, 1988.

Million Dollar Consulting, Alan Weiss, Ph.D., New York: McGraw-Hill, 1994.

Shenson on Consulting, Howard L. Shenson, New York: Wiley, 1990.

MAGAZINES

You should read at least six if not a dozen magazines in many different fields to increase your awareness of business, government, and the management fields in which you work. Also recommended are *Home Office Computing, Fortune, Inc.,* and *Business Week.*

National Training Center, 123 N.W. Second Avenue, Suite 405, Portland, OR 97209; (800) 223-5085. Directed by Paul Franklin. Publishes the newsletter *The Professional Consultant*, as well as audiotapes and books, and provides training and coaching.

Seminar: How to Build & Maintain a Profitable Consulting Practice, 1-day seminar offered around the country by the Center for Consulting and Professional Practices, a division of William Mooney Associates, 19401 South Vermont Avenue, Suite K100, P.O. Box 6159, Torrance, CA 90504; (213) 321-9342. Bill also provides one-on-one coaching to help independent consultants attract more and better clients.

■ ■ ■ ■ ■

MARKETING CONSULTANT

After management consultants, marketing consultants form the next largest number of professional consultants in the country. And there's a good reason for their abundance, because no business can stay in business without good marketing. The problem is, many businesses don't have the in-house expertise to cover all their marketing needs, or they simply do not have the staff to do it all themselves.

Marketing is actually a catch-all phrase for a large assortment of activities that businesses undertake to get customers. Marketing actually includes the following categories, each of which has many variations as well:

- *Advertising:* classified ads, display ads, broadcast advertising, bulletin boards, direct response advertising, yellow-page advertising, and many more forms.

- *Direct mail:* catalogues, brochures, flyers, sales letters, introductory offers, and many other forms of direct mail that require knowledge of mailing lists and effective copywriting.

- *Promotions:* sampling, price incentives, giveaways, stock displays, newsletters, circulars, seminars, trade shows, and other kinds of promotion.

- *Publicity:* new-product launches, corporate press kits, sample articles, volunteer activities, charitable contributions, and many other activities that can be done to generate publicity for the company.

- *Sales:* discounts, guarantees, return policies, warranties, two-for-one pricing, special offers, and many other concepts of how to sell.

Most company managers cannot spend much of their time analyzing and implementing the plethora of marketing possibilities, and this means that marketing consulting is in demand in nearly every industry. Small companies in particular that cannot afford a marketing department are likely to hire a marketing consultant from time to time to help with (a) the strategy behind a marketing campaign, (b) the implementation of that campaign, or (c) an analysis of its effectiveness.

The realm of marketing consultants is thus extremely wide and open to either generalists in all fields or to specialists in particular niches. (In general, it is better to specialize, we believe, and most consultants agree.) Helen Berman, for example, is a marketing consultant who focuses strictly on improving the effectiveness of sales departments in media and magazines. Her clients hire her to come in for a few days to help their salespeople improve their skills and close more deals. She is usually hired for several days at a time to analyze the situation at the company, then to develop a new strategy and get the salespeople to implement it. Helen sees her role as a natural outcome of today's competitive business environment. As she says, "Selling is a profession, but nobody goes to school to learn selling; I teach these skills. I am essentially selling marketing tools that teach these sales-people how to sell to people who run companies."

In contrast, take Ross Simmons, whose company Florida Events, Inc., in North Palm Beach has been a home-based business since 1980. Ross special-izes in helping shopping centers to set up special promotions that bring business to all the stores. Whether it's a strip mall or enclosed mall, Ross meets with the store owners or mall management and, depending on their budget, helps to determine a schedule of special events that will bring in bodies. He has done every type of show imaginable targeted at families, seniors, singles, and even specific ethnic groups. Ross does what he calls "teaching businesses how to market themselves beyond the 'so-what' factor, the sense on the part of a consumer to think that Store X is not so special because there's Store Y right around the corner." He works with malls and individual stores to come up with unique marketing plans that draw special attention to them.

Linda Jagoda, a Phoenix marketing consultant who serves a wide variety of clients, tells her clients, "Marketing saves you when times are the toughest." She makes the point that a company's marketing consultant can be just as important as its CPA.

So, if you have an inclination to help a company achieve its goals and you believe that you have the experience to deliver what you promise—sales—then marketing consulting might be a lucrative avenue for you to pursue.

☑ Knowledge and Skills You Need to Have

- Expertise in all forms of marketing or a specialization in one major area, such as direct mail, advertising, sales, PR, and other areas
- Good management sense; you must be prepared to work with high-level

executives who are seeking solutions to real problems for their company. Your work will directly influence the bottom line.

- Good communication skills and self-confidence about your work. You need to be articulate, friendly, extroverted, and energetic.

- You must be almost a psychologist so you can understand the business you are working in, what their goals are, what kind of help they need, and the best way to help them. Often what the owners or on-staff marketing people tell you is what they think you want to hear or what they need to say to protect their own jobs. You must be able to roll up your sleeves and figure out how to solve problems as if it were your own company.

◼ Start-up Costs

	Low	High
Computer with hard disk and modem, or laptop computer	$1,000	$3,000
Fax machine	300	900
Laser printer	300	1,600
Suite software	250	400
Other software (desktop publishing in case you design brochures or flyers for your clients)	100	500
Office furniture, especially ergonomic chair	400	1,000
Business cards, letterhead, envelopes	100	600
Reference materials/seminars/workshops	500	1,000
Organizational dues	250	250
Total	$3,200	$9,250

◼ Advantages

- It can be gratifying to experience a company expanding and succeeding because of your ideas.

- The profession is generally lucrative, particularly if you have a specific expertise and a reputation within a certain industry. You can earn well over $100,000 per year.

- Each marketing assignment is different; you get to work on a wide variety of cases with many different companies. Your job is seldom dull.

- It's easy to sell your services; most companies recognize that they need help with marketing from time to time.

◼ Disadvantages

- As an outsider, it can take time to figure out the politics of the companies you work with, and what is really happening to explain why they brought you in.

- Your impact on the bottom line is highly visible, and all eyes stay on you.

You are held accountable for the success or failure of the entire company, even when market forces beyond your control or a bad product cause its demise.

- You have to keep up your own marketing efforts at all times because once you work with a client, it could be months before you go back.

- You must know what you are talking about at all times. There is no room for equivocation in this business. Clients expect that you will deliver on what you promise.

- As with all consulting, cash flow can be a problem. You need to set up clear contracts with milestones indicating when you will be paid.

$ Pricing

As with all consultants, pricing can be by the hour, day, or month, or contract. Most contracts are by the day or involve a monthly retainer. Hourly fees range from $50 to $150, and daily fees range from $500 to $1,200 and more, depending on the level of expertise you have, your reputation, and your success rate in the industry in which you work. For example, a novice consultant in direct marketing might be able to command only $50 per hour, but an expert in sales or promotions might be able to get $2,000 to $4,000 for a two-day workshop to train others how to handle a campaign.

Many consultants give a discount for longer assignments such as a month (in which case they offer a monthly retainer that entitles the client to X hours of their time for a fixed fee that must be paid each month for three, six, or twelve months).

🖵 Potential Earnings

TYPICAL ANNUAL GROSS REVENUES: $50,000 to $150,000 per year, depending on the level of expertise and kinds of clients you take on, as well as the number of days you work.

OVERHEAD: low (20 percent or less).

📈 *Best Home Businesses* Estimate of Market Potential

Marketing is an essential activity for virtually all businesses and increasingly for nonprofit and government organizations. The continuing growth of small businesses and the increasingly competitive conditions of practicing a profession (law, medicine, et al.) provide thousands upon thousands of potential clients for marketing consultants who can help them get what they most want—business.

🖢 Best Ways to Get Business

Like most consultants, getting business depends largely on referrals and word of mouth. To augment this, you can:

- get as much publicity as you can generate by writing articles and speaking in front of business groups. Ross Simmons sends letters regularly to editors and others in the hope of getting them printed, and he has now become an expert in marketing who appears on many local business talk shows and in the local newspapers.

- If you have some speaking experience, join the National Speakers' Association to increase your networking.

- Go to your local chamber of commerce to see if new businesses have joined who might be potential clients. Look also among license filings for new businesses (although these young companies may not be able to afford you).

First Steps

1. Determine which marketing areas you know best based on your experience, and select one or two that you consider yourself to be an expert in. Be sure to read up and learn as much as you can about this area.

2. Start small with a few clients on projects that have a finite beginning and ending, so that you have some specific results to point to when trying to get more clients.

3. If necessary, handle some jobs on a voluntary basis to get experience working in an area that you need to learn about: direct mail, exhibits, brochures, or whatever.

4. Join an association of marketing people to make connections; you may be able to get a subcontract assignment from a colleague.

Where to Turn for Information and Help

ORGANIZATIONS

American Marketing Association, 250 South Wacker Drive, Chicago, IL 60606; (312) 648-0536.

Direct Marketing Association, 11 W. 42d Street, New York, NY 10036; (212) 768-7277.

National Speakers' Association, 1500 South Priest Drive, Tempe, AZ 85281; (602) 968-2552. A description of NSA can be found in the Employee Training entry.

International Association of Business Communicators, 1 Hallidie Plaza, Suite 600, San Francisco, CA 94102; (415) 433-3400.

Promotion Marketing Association of America, Inc., 257 Park Avenue South, New York, NY 10010; (212) 420-1100. Professional association for companies and consultants involved in promotional marketing.

Public Relations Society of America, 33 Irving Place, New York, NY 10003; (212) 995-2230.

BOOKS

Building a Consulting Practice, Robert O. Metzger, Ph.D., Newbury Park, CA: Sage Publications, 1994.

Databased Marketing, Herman Holtz, New York: Wiley, 1993.

Guerilla Marketing, Jay Levinson, Boston: Houghton Mifflin, 1993.

How to Get Clients, Jeff Slutsky, New York: Warner Books, 1992.

Market Mapping, Sunny Baker and Kim Baker, New York: McGraw-Hill, 1993.

Million Dollar Consulting, Alan Weiss, Ph.D., New York: McGraw-Hill, 1994.

Power Marketing for Small Business, Jody Horner, Grant Pass, OR: The Oasis Press, 1993.

NEWSLETTERS

Management Consultant International, Lafferty Publications/USA, 2970 Clairmont Road N.E., #800, Atlanta, GA 30329; (404) 636-6610.

Marketing Conferences and Seminars, Learning Resources Network Inc., 1554 Hayes Drive, Manhattan, KS 66502; (913) 539-5376.

The Professional Consultant, edited by Paul Franklin. See National Training Center in the Management Consultant entry above. *Note:* See also the resources (organizations, books, newsletters, etc.) listed under the entries for Management Consultant and Specialty Consultant.

■ ■ ■ ■ ■

MANUFACTURER'S AGENT

The drive by companies across the country to cut costs is reaching deep into the heart of how manufacturing companies sell their goods. Whereas in the good ol' days, a plastics or chemical or automotive company might have a national sales force of twenty salesmen, today even large manufacturers are seeking out independent agents to represent them and sell their products. Small manufacturers have always relied on independent agents, but today their importance is increasing even more as well. The irony about this is that many experienced salespeople tell us that being a manufacturer's agent or manufacturer's representative is actually the graduate level of selling, offering potentially higher earnings and freedom from the company politics of being an employee.

Agents or independent reps take on many kinds of products, from chemicals and adhesives, to gift items and sporting equipment, to electrical equipment and tubing, to valves and heavy machinery. To be successful as a manufacturer's rep, Lionel Diaz, senior vice president of the Manufacturer's Agents National Association (MANA—the largest association of independent agents) says that there are really only three qualifications to be in this business:

1. You have to have products to sell. He recommends that you have from eight to ten lines to represent because the average cost of a sales call is $300 to $400 (travel time, phone calls, gas, etc.). By having more than one product to sell to customers, you can amortize your costs over more lines. (You generally cannot take on, however, competing products in the same line. Few manufacturers find that beneficial.)

2. You need a customer base to sell to. Actually, says Diaz, this is perhaps the most important of the three qualifications, because you can easily get lines, but finding somebody to buy from you is much harder. He also points out that, many times, your customers can help you get new lines.

3. Finally, Diaz feels that a new agent needs sufficient capital to keep going for about a year, because it can often take a long time to build up a business sufficient to support yourself and/or a family.

The logical next question that a new agent usually asks is how do you find products to sell? Part of the answer, says Diaz, is to work in area you know. It helps to have a background in the products you are selling, because it's clearly easier to understand them and explain their virtues than to sell something you know nothing about. More and more companies are turning to agents who have background in their technology, or who have used their product. Other than such expertise or experience, Diaz believes that having a dedication to sales and an entrepreneurial spirit are critical in convincing a manufacturer to take you on as an independent rep. (Another hint is: The back of MANA's magazine, *Agency Sales*, contains hundreds of want ads from companies seeking agents/reps.)

Agents may sell from manufacturer to other manufacturers who use raw materials in a finished product, or finished products to wholesalers or retailers, or both. Each line you carry is different. Some agents even hire subagents to help them sell, creating a full-service agency. Agents get paid on a commission basis, which varies greatly from line to line and depends also on many factors (see below). However, agents must keep track of all their expenses, not only in order to deduct them from income for tax purposes, but also to be able to assess if a line is making them a profit. You might spend from a few thousand to $10,000 in business expenses before that line begins to turn a profit.

Overall, however, the life of the independent agent can be gratifying and financially remunerative. Although the sad portrait of Willy Loman from *Death of a Salesman* may stay with us for years to come, the reality is that independent agenting is a future sales trend that is likely to change the world of sales. Diaz points out, in fact, that whereas fifteen years ago, MANA had only 1,500 members, today they are 8,000 strong and growing quickly.

✅ Knowledge and Skills You Need to Have

- According to Diaz, it helps considerably to have some sales experience or, barring that, an expertise in a field that you can work in, such as electronics, adhesives, foods, plastics, machinery, or whatever.

- Sales is a people-oriented business, so you also need charm, wit, self-confidence, and a good appearance. Much of your success depends on how you present yourself and your ability to develop a relationship with your clients.

- You need to have a modicum of knowledge about sales commission structures so that you can cut a good deal for yourself. This means you should study the industry and know how much other salespeople in your line of work are getting (or could get).

- You need to be able to multitax your brain, as you will be handling many ideas, clients, products, schedules, and future goals all at once.

- Some amount of agency sales are now occurring in import and export, and therefore it helps to have knowledge of import/export opportunities.

🖱 Start-up Costs

	Low	High
Computer with hard disk and modem or laptop computer to use on the road	$1,000	$3,000
Fax machine	300	900
Printer	300	1,600
Suite software	250	400
Two-line telephone equipment for home	100	200
Cellular phone for travel	400	1,000
Office furniture, especially ergonomic chair	400	1,000
Business cards, letterhead, envelopes	100	600
Reference books of manufacturers/maps/etc.	100	300
Total	$2,950	$9,000

📊 Advantages

- Sales can be an extremely high-income-producing business.

- Many salespeople can meet a lot of people and make many friends in the process.

- You have a lot of flexibility in choosing your products and determining your own lifestyle.

⏏ Disadvantages

- Perhaps the major problem with sales is your cash flow; it can be months before you get a check from your manufacturers.
- Salespeople often must travel a great deal for long periods of time, depending on your client base and your territory.
- Sales is a competitive business; you must be aggressive in some instances and take the lumps with the sugar.
- Some large retailers are refusing to deal with reps, insisting on dealing directly with the supplier company.

$ Pricing

As we said above, reps are paid on a commission basis. However, there is a tremendous diversity of commissions, depending on many factors, such as:

- type of product line—commissions on high technology are vastly different from commissions on toys or jewelry
- number of product lines you carry for a manufacturer
- level of difficulty in selling a product (if you are selling against a major competitor, your commission will likely be higher than if you have little competition)
- the size of your territory and expenses in selling such as mileage you have to drive to meet your customers (distance between customers)
- the amount of sales; many commissions operate on a sliding scale, with lower commissions paid for the first orders, then greater percentages paid as the quantity builds up

In general, one can say that commissions range from 3 to 15 percent. The most recent MANA survey in 1992, for example, indicated that chemicals (industrial and maintenance) paid between 7.5 and 15 percent commissions, while paper products paid 5.5 to 12.5 percent. In short, it all depends! You have to do some research in your field.

▣ Potential Earnings

TYPICAL ANNUAL GROSS REVENUES: Gross revenues for reps in their first to third year of sales averaged $124,000. This is gross income, however, and one must subtract considerable expenses such as office, telephone, auto insurance, gas, airfare, and so on.

OVERHEAD: moderate (20 to 40 percent).

⚒ *Best Home Businesses* Estimate of Market Potential

Corporate paring of in-house personnel and what will probably be thousands of new start-up businesses resulting from the downsizing of the defense industry, plus new technologies derived from fields like genetic engineering will spur the continued growth of opportunities for independent manufacturers' agents.

Best Ways to Get Business

- Get *Thomas' Registry of Manufacturers* and scour it for companies that make what you think you can sell.

- Use your library or a CD-ROM product like *Marketplace Business* to research potential markets for your product. Look in telephone books, directories, and other print and on-line publications. Visit your local chamber of commerce to locate possible clients.

- As Lionel Diaz put it, you simply have to "stick your head down and run." Essentially, this means that hard work and lots of shoe leather are needed to be successful in this business. Getting clients involves a whole range of activities, from cold-calling to networking to making presentations to more cold-calling.

- Other than that, you must be driven to succeed, and you need to have a good product. No amount of fire in your belly will compensate for a bad product.

First Steps

1. Develop a desire to be a salesperson. Write down your sales goals and objectives over the next three years.

2. Find some products you might be interested in repping. Talk to other people and potential customers before agreeing to take them on.

3. If you are new to the sales business, you will need to write a résumé and letter to manufacturers explaining why you want to sell their product and how you intend to do it. When you agree to take on a product line, be sure to sign a contract with the manufacturer.

4. Take some classes in presentation skills, communication, and image to develop your polish.

5. Consider joining MANA and/or an association in your particular area (automotive, hardware, jewelry, etc.). MANA is a horizontal organization, consisting of agents from all fields. Vertical organizations consist of agents all within the same field.

6. Add product lines within a reasonable timetable to achieve your maximum limit.

7. See the entry on export agent also.

🔲 Where to Turn for Information and Help

ORGANIZATIONS

International Union of Commercial Agents and Brokers, P.O. Box 19352, 1000GJ, Amsterdam, Holland. Has up-to-date information on contracts and the laws of the land for many countries for exporting.

Manufacturers' Agents National Association, P.O. Box 3467, Laguna Hills, CA 92654-3467; (714) 859-4040. MANA is the national association for independent sales agents. MANA publishes the leading magazine in the field, *Agency Sales*. Membership in MANA entitles you to their magazine, a membership directory, information on tax strategies, insurance programs, contract guidelines, seminars, a national conference, and a quarterly newsletter. They also have a workshop for new agencies.

DIRECTORIES

Thomas' Register of Manufacturers, Thomas Publishing Company, 5 Penn Plaza, 9th Floor, New York, NY 10119; (800) 222-7900, ext. 200. Available both in print in libraries and as an on-line database on CompuServe and Dialog. Provides the names and addresses of manufacturers and can be used as a prospect list.

BOOKS

A book specifically addressing this field is:

Making $70,000+ a Year as Self-Employed Manufacturer's Representative, Leigh and Sureleigh Silliphant, Berkeley: Ten Speed Press, 1988.

In addition, there are many books on selling, sales presentations, and negotiation techniques. A few of the classics include:

The Art & Skill of Successful Negotiation, John Ilich, Grand Rapids, MI: Bengal Press, 1983.

The Greatest Salesman in the World, Og Mandino, Cutchoguek NY: Buccaneer Books, 1993.

Professional Sales Representation, Frank Lebell, Tallahasee, FL: Herman Promotions, 1981.

Think & Grow Rich, Napoleon Hill, New York: Fawcett, 1983.

You Can Negotiate Anything, Herb Cohen, New York: Bantam, 1983.

MAGAZINES

Agency Sales, MANA, P.O. Box 3467, Laguna Hills, CA 92654-3467; (714) 859-4040.

Target Marketing Magazine, 401 North Broad Street, Philadelphia, PA 91908; (215) 238-5300.

SOFTWARE

Marketplace Business, MarketPlace Information Corporation, 3 University Office Park, Waltham, MA 02154; (617) 672-9200.

Reps for Windows, CBC Software, 540 N.E. Northgate Way, Suite C539, Seattle, WA 98125; (206) 448-3301

AUDIOTAPES/VIDEOS

Nightingale-Conant, 7300 North Lehigh Avenue, Niles, IL 60714; (800) 323-5552. Publishes many excellent audio programs to develop sales and leadership skills.

■ ■ ■ ■ ■

MEDICAL BILLING SERVICE

Home-based medical billing services have become one of the fastest-growing businesses of the decade and may continue to offer good opportunities for some people if your area is not yet saturated.

Medical billing services work directly with doctors, chiropractors, dentists, and other providers of medical care to process their insurance claims to Medicare, Medicaid, and private insurance companies.

Medical billing grew quickly in recent years because of two changes in the processing of health-insurance claims. First, as of 1990, a federal law went into effect requiring doctors to submit claims for Medicare reimbursements on behalf of their Medicare patients rather than having the patients file the claims themselves. Because the majority of medical claims are for people over sixty-five, this meant that many doctors were faced with filing hundreds of claims per week Second, with the volume of Medicare claims rising rapidly due to an aging American population, Medicare and many private insurance companies decided that claims had to be submitted electronically to save time and money over the traditional method of paper claims through the mail. The creation of new PC-based medical billing software greatly facilitated this electronic process, as claims could be keyboarded right on the computer and sent over the phone lines directly to Medicare or intermediary clearinghouses for processing by private insurance companies.

Many doctors' offices could not keep up with these two developments and hired outside billing services to handle their electronic claims processing. Some billing services also handle other aspects of the claims process for doctors, such as invoicing and collecting the 20 percent copayment that most insurance companies require the patient to pay, keeping track of past due and uncollectible accounts, and taking phone calls from patients about their bills.

✔ Knowledge and Skills You Need to Have

Medical billing requires that you have a full understanding of the regulations for making health-insurance claims. You must keep up, in particular, with Medicare and Medicaid rules and billing procedures, which frequently change.

Medical billers must be familiar with the two diagnostic and procedure coding systems used by doctors on the claim forms to show Medicare and private insurance companies what services are being billed and why.

You must learn to use a computer, modem, and specialized software employed in processing claims electronically.

Medical billers must feel comfortable marketing to and working with health-care providers and their office staff. You need to be convincing and persuasive about how you can manage their claims without errors or glitches. If you handle all of a doctor's billing and patient accounts, you must be especially organized and trustworthy, because the doctor is entrusting his financial security to you.

⬛ Start-up Costs

	Low	High
Computer with hard disk and modem	$1,000	$ 3,000
Fax machine	300	900
Printer	300	1,600
Suite software (mostly word processing)	250	400
Medical billing software	1,000	6,000
Office furniture, especially ergonomic chair	400	1,000
Brochures	100	1,000
Business cards, letterhead, envelopes	100	600
Total	$3,450	$14,500

⬆ Advantages

- The work can be challenging and interesting because of the complex nature of health insurance and Medicare rules.
- Once your business is established, processing claims electronically takes little time and can be done at your convenience, day or night.
- A successful medical billing service can be quite profitable.
- Depending on what kind of health insurance reform legislation is passed, this business may be changed and in the unlikely event of a single-payer system being adopted, go out of existence.

ⓟ Disadvantages

- Some cities may be saturated with medical billing companies, so checking out your market is critical before you go into business. One way to do this is to talk with your own doctors and to call other doctors' offices.
- There is a fair amount to learn if you have no experience in health insurance or medical claims.
- Selling your services can be difficult; getting past the front-office staff to the doctor or office manager takes persistence and good communication skills.
- If you handle patient accounts, collecting money from reluctant patients can be emotionally draining.
- Unless you take the necessary precautions, you risk developing repetitive-motion injuries as a result of keyboarding thousands of claims.

💲 Pricing

Medical billing services often charge from $1.50 to $4.00 per claim processed, depending on competition and location. A service with six clients might process an average of 400 claims per doctor per month, yielding from $3,600 to $9,600.

Some medical billing services charge by the hour. Hourly fees range from $15 to $50, with the higher amounts for those services that do full-practice management for doctors.

A few billing services charge a percentage of claims collected, although this method usually pertains to successfully processing old claims that were once denied.

🖳 Potential Earnings

TYPICAL ANNUAL GROSS REVENUES: $20,000 to $100,000, depending on the number of the clients you are able to obtain and the number of claims processed for each client. A minimum of four to six doctors or practices is required to be reasonably profitable.

OVERHEAD: low (less than 20 percent).

🉐 *Best Home Businesses* Estimate of Market Potential

In some communities, doctors are not aware of medical billing services. In other areas, however, the market is saturated with billing services. This field may shrink or grow, however, depending on the nature of health reform.

▶ Best Ways to Get Business

- Your own doctor and contacts or referrals from health-care providers you may know.

- Direct-mail brochures and letters appealing to doctors who are having problems with billing, collections, and frequently changing office staff. Follow up all direct mail with a personal phone call and appointment to present your services.

- Cold-calling by phone or in person to doctors' offices; because doctors are usually extremely busy, your goal is to get an appointment for a time when you can make a twenty-minute presentation.

- Talk with the marketing directors at local hospitals about participating in one of the monthly meetings they hold for staff doctors. After these meetings hospitals will often have a mini-trade show so doctors can learn about new products and services.

- Hospitals earnestly market doctors, encouraging them to join their staffs. You can offer the hospital to include in its promotions a discount on your services for new doctors who affiliate with the hospital.

- Contact the local medical society about offering a discount to its members.

First Steps

If you do not have experience in the medical field, begin by taking one of the many community-college or adult-education courses available in medical billing and coding procedures. You can also attend various Medicare-sponsored classes about electronic claims processing for Medicare claims; contact the Medicare office in your area for information about these classes. Before purchasing a medical billing software package or business opportunity, be sure to shop around to compare the features and prices.

Where to Turn for Information and Help

ORGANIZATIONS

International Billing Association, 4040 West 70th Street, Minneapolis, MN 55435; Professional trade organization for third-party billing companies already in existence. Does not provide information on starting up.

National Association of Claims Assistance Professionals (NACAP), 4724 Florence Avenue, Downers Grove, IL 60515; (708) 963-3500. Contact Norma Border, Director of Member Services. An association for people in the medical billing and claims assistance fields. Offers a newsletter and certification exam.

BOOKS

Directory of Medical Management Software, AQC Resources, 1757 W. San Carlos St., Suite 111, San Jose, CA 95128; (800) 995-8702.

Health Service Businesses on Your Home-Based PC, Rick Benzel, Blue Ridge Summit, PA: Windcrest/McGraw Hill, 1993; (310) 391-8024.

NEWSLETTERS

AQC Resource Newsletter: Medical Claims Processing, 1757 W. San Carlos St., Suite 111, San Jose, CA 95128; (800) 995-8702 or (408) 295-4102. Newsletter for the billing industry. $59 per year.

ProClaimer Analyst, Strategic Decisions Plus, Inc., P.O. Box 2108, Silverthorne, CO 80498; (303) 262-9290.

COMPUTER BULLETIN BOARDS

InfoAlliance, 6701 Seybold, Suite 131, Madison, WI 53719; (608) 277-2990. Offers E-mail and forums for people in the billing industry. Contact Chad Meisinger.

Medical Billing and Transcription Section of the Working From Home Forum on CompuServe Information Service. (GO WORK once on CompuServe.)

MANUALS AND COURSES

Institute of Consulting Careers, Inc., 222 S.E. 16th Street, Portland, OR 97214; (503) 240-0931.

■ ■ ■ ■ ■

MEDICAL CLAIMS ASSISTANCE PROFESSIONAL

Medical claims assistance professionals, often called CAPs, are the other side of the coin relative to medical billing services. Whereas billing services work with doctors, CAPs are hired by patients to help them handle a variety of claims tasks.

First, CAPs file claims for people whose doctors do not file private insurance claims for them. (Doctors must file Medicare claims for patients but are not required to file private insurance company claims.) This is a great relief for many people who simply do not want to file their own claims as well as those who may be too ill or too befuddled by the process to do it themselves.

After the claims have been filed and processed, CAPs may also check the "explanation of benefits notice" to verify that the insurer or Medicare has paid the correct amount. Errors in payment are frequently made, but a good CAP knows how to spot incorrect amounts or mistakes that can cost the patient money. The CAP also monitors the copayment that the patient makes to determine that the doctor does not charge a larger amount than the insurer has established as the allowable fee.

Finally, if an insurance claim is denied, CAPs investigate the reason and try to get the denial overturned. Many claims are denied because of simple mistakes such as improper coding by the doctor's office, duplicated charges, or late filing. Some claims are denied based on a policy restriction, but a good CAP can negotiate either with the insurance company to pay the claim or with the doctor to reduce the charges.

Claims assistance professionals are coming into prominence quickly as the career expands. The main reason for the growth in the profession is the great need: literally millions of consumers are recognizing that they desperately need help when it comes to understanding our complex systems of Medicare and private health insurance. As one CAP put it, there are many powerful groups to protect the interests of the insurance companies, the hospitals, and doctors, but the average person with insurance has nobody to help him or her. Lori Donnelly, who operates a successful claims assistance business in Pennsylvania, points out that this is a new business and many consumers don't even know about it, so there is a wide-open client base for many new businesses.

☑ Knowledge and Skills You Need to Have

- You need an excellent knowledge of the health-insurance industry: how it works, how claims are processed and why they may be denied, and what steps a person can take to appeal a rejected claim.

- You must be able to read and understand health-insurance policies and know what services they cover and at what rate. You also need to keep up with Medicare regulations and its changing coverages and payments.

- Good communication and negotiation skills are essential. You may find yourself disputing a denied claim with an insurance company on one side and, on the other, trying to get a doctor to lower a fee. You must be able to represent your clients and get them the maximum benefit possible.

- You must be patient, helpful, and empathic. Many of your clients will be seniors or families in crisis who need someone to listen thoughtfully to their medical and financial problems.

- You need superb organizational skills, because you may have as many as 300 clients, each with many insurance claims at different stages of processing.

♟ Start-up Costs

	Low	High
Computer with hard disk	$1,000	$3,000
Fax machine	300	900
Copier	300	800
Printer	300	1,600
Suite software (mostly word processing)	250	400
Office furniture, especially ergonomic chair	400	1,000
Brochures	100	1,000
Business cards, letterhead, envelopes	100	600
Total	$2,750	$9,300

⬆ Advantages

- This is a "feel-good profession" because you are helping people maximize their health-insurance benefits and avoid costly mistakes made by doctors and insurance companies.

- The work is interesting, and each case is different. You can meet many kinds of people as your clients.

- Your clients appreciate and respect you. They view you as a professional and will often seek your advice on many insurance matters. CAPs are similar to tax preparers and financial consultants.

- The health-insurance claims business is gigantic, with a large client base of over 35 million Americans on Medicare and over 220 million Americans with private health insurance.

⬇ Disadvantages

- There is a fair amount to learn if you have no experience in health insurance or medical claims.

- Some cases can be complicated with many doctors, clinics, labs, and hospital bills that you must unravel and put in sequence in order to negotiate with an insurance company over payments and benefits.

- You need many clients (several hundred) to build your business. It may take six months or more to develop a large client list.

- Selling your service can be difficult. Because the profession is new, you will have to spend time and money to educate potential clients about your service and benefits before they sign on with you.

- Depending on what kind of health-insurance reform legislation is passed, this business may be changed and, in the unlikely event of a single-payer system being adopted, go out of existence.

💲 Pricing

CAPs usually charge according to one of three methods:

- Many charge a fixed monthly or annual fee per person or family to process and review all new medical claims they have. Typical fees range from $200 to $400 per person for a year, with a sliding discount for couples and families.

- Other CAPs charge by the hour, ranging from $20 to $75 per hour, depending on the locale and the complexity of the case.

- Some CAPs charge 5 to 10 percent of all benefits paid by an insurance company. This method is usually used when you work on claims that have already been denied and you are able to get a reimbursement for your client.

In addition, most CAPs charge a sign-up or registration fee of $35 to $75 to cover the cost of registering a person and obtaining all his or her insurance information.

▣ Potential Earnings

TYPICAL ANNUAL GROSS REVENUES: $20,000 to $60,000, based on having 100 to 300 clients each paying $200 per year for services.

OVERHEAD: low (20 percent or less).

⁇ *Best Home Businesses* Estimate of Market Potential

Medical claims processing shows strong demand. People need help with complicated medical claims.

▣ The Best Ways to Get Business

- Notify family, friends, and other contacts you have to get a few initial clients. Referrals from satisfied customers and word of mouth will follow from there.
- Giving speeches or presentations at senior centers and assisted-living facilities
- Networking in professional organizations and making personal contacts. Bankers, lawyers, and accountants are often a source of referrals since they may have clients in need of your services.
- Getting to know hospital discharge planners who may be able to refer patients to you
- Selected display advertising in community newspapers, local magazines for seniors, and assisted-living center newsletters

▣ First Steps

If you have little background in health insurance or medical claims, take a community-college course or purchase a manual that deals with setting up this business. Focus on learning all the basic regulations about Medicare and private insurance. Begin filing claims for family and friends, and review the explanation of benefits they receive to learn how to spot errors and process appeals on denied claims. An additional path to this business is to work with an established claims professional who needs clerical assistance in exchange for learning the business.

▣ Where to Turn for Information and Help

ORGANIZATIONS

National Association of Claims Assistance Professionals (NACAP), 4724 Florence Avenue, Downers Grove, IL 60515; (708) 963-3500.

Contact Norma Border, Director of Member Services. An association for people in medical claims assistance and medical billing. NACAP offers a newsletter, manuals, and a certification exam.

BOOKS

Beginning Medical Terminology, Phyllis Cronbaugh, Strategic Decisions Plus, Inc., P.O. Box 2108, Silverthorne, CO 80498; (303) 262-9290.

Health Service Businesses on Your Home-Based PC, Rick Benzel. Blue Ridge Summit, PA: Windcrest/McGraw Hill, 1993; (310) 391-8024.

MANUALS AND COURSES

Institute of Consulting Careers, Inc., 222 SE 16th Ave., Portland, OR 97214; (503) 240-0931.

SOFTWARE

Med$ure, Time Solutions, 45 Kellers Farm Road, Easton, CT 06612; (203) 459-0303.

■ ■ ■ ■ ■

MEDICAL TRANSCRIPTION SERVICE

Medical transcriptionists turn recorded dictation by physicians and other health-care professionals into reports, manuscripts, consultations, and patient-care documents. Having a medical transcript produced quickly is vital to health-care providers' cash flow because many insurance companies are requiring transcribed reports before they will pay doctors or hospitals. Transcribed copy also supplies health-care providers with the necessary documentation for review of a patient's history and care and provides legal evidence of patient care and data for research and statistical purposes. Patient-care documents are also used to render continuing patient care.

Increasingly hospitals and doctors in private practice are contracting out their medical transcription work. In part, this is because there is a shortage of qualified transcriptionists. According to the American Association for Medical Transcription (AAMT), this job is in demand throughout the country, and in some communities the demand is critical. Still another factor is computer technology. As Pat Forbis, associate executive director of AAMT, observes, "The technology that took us out of our homes is back into our homes. Today if a transcriptionist has a modem and the proper interfaces, he or she can access hospital digital dictation equipment using the phone lines."

In addition, research shows that home-based transcriptionists may be more productive than transcriptionists working in hospitals and offices. A study by the University of Wisconsin Hospital and Clinics found that the statistics "consistently showed that what would take six to eight hours to produce in the office would take three to four hours to do at home."

Independent transcriptionists tend either to take overload work from hospitals or to work with doctors in private practice. Transcriptionists doing work for hospitals must know about all specialties of medical practice, while a transcriptionist working for physicians may concentrate on a limited number of medical specialties, such as orthopedics, neurology, or surgery. Transcriptionists can also seek work from agencies, which may treat them either as subcontractors or as employees. Some of these agencies will let you work from home.

Vicki Fite, founder of Southwest Medical Transcription, says, "Marketing this business is easy when you have a high-quality product. Doctors are quite particular, and rightly so, about the material transcribed. The one thing that can really hurt you in this field is if you put out an inferior product. If you make a bad mistake you can count on losing about five accounts from that one source."

Services that can increase your competitiveness include offering pickup and delivery, seven-day-a-week service, same-day service, and a phone-in dictation system. Home-based medical transcriptionists can gain a competitive edge by offering remote printing or downloading into medical facilities' computer systems. This is a plus because turnaround time of transcription is a primary concern to health-care providers. So if a transcriptionist is able to provide a less-than-twenty-four-hour turnaround and not compromise quality, it is an advantage. Additionally, twenty-four-hour or second-and-third-shift coverage is a plus.

☑ Knowledge and Skills You Need to Have

- As a medical transcriptionist, you need to have the discipline to sit in front of a computer and concentrate throughout the day, with earphones linking you to transcribing equipment.

- You need excellent listening skills and good eye, hand, and auditory coordination. You also need to be able to understand diverse accents and dialects.

- You must be able to keyboard efficiently and accurately using word-processing, dictation, and transcription equipment.

- In addition to having keyboard speed, you must be able to transcribe quickly, because the faster you transcribe, the more you earn.

- You need to understand medical diagnostic procedures and terminology and spell them accurately (anatomy and physiology, clinical medicine, surgery, diagnostic tests, radiology, pathology, pharmacology, and whatever medical specialties you work with).

- A love of the English language and the language of medicine is helpful because often you must become a *word detective*, interpreting how terms are being used.

■ Start-up Costs

	Low	High
Computer	$1,000	$3,000
Printer (may not be necessary if you are using a modem)	300	1,600
Separate phone line for modem or fax (annual cost)	120	250
Transcriber or appropriate transcribing unit with conversion capability to different sizes of tapes	200	800
Word-processing software compatible with your client base	100	250
Additional specialized software (medical spelling correction, abbreviation expanders, macro builders, and output counters)	200	400
Office furniture, especially an ergonomic chair and a bookcase	400	1,000
Business cards, letterhead, envelopes	100	600
Reference books (medical-transcription style guide, medical dictionary, drug reference, multiple word books to address various medical specialties)	250	800
Total	$2,670	$8,700

■ Advantages

- This is a rapidly expanding field, with more work than there are trained transcriptionists.
- The medical field can be interesting.
- The work is steady and recession resistant.
- One can be an employee of a hospital and still be home based. Career opportunities include teaching and consulting.

■ Disadvantages

- As many as one to two years of education may be required if you have little or no experience.
- You must be highly self-disciplined and focused while you work. The work demands total involvement, both physically and mentally. Every distraction creates a slowdown in productivity and possibly even quality.
- The demand for increasingly fast turnaround times creates time pressures and at least occasionally the need to work nights and weekends.
- Not everyone has an aptitude for science or language, or is temperamentally suited to being plugged into a pair of headphones hour after hour, day after day.

- Unless you take necessary precautions, you risk developing repetitive-motion injuries as a result of keyboarding.

💲 Pricing

AAMT suggests that transcriptionists charge by the character, but some charge by the line or by the page, and with the adoption of computers, others are now charging by the byte. However you charge, it is important to define what is meant by *word, line,* or *page,* because definitions vary from transcriptionist to transcriptionist and client to client.

Charges range from 10 cents to 20 cents per line (remember that what constitutes a *line* varies among transcriptionists) or $5 to $6 a page. Sometimes transcriptionists charge $15 to $30 an hour for doctors who are difficult to understand, particularly those with heavy accents. Turnaround time and technology requirements also influence pricing; you can charge more for second- and third-shift, twenty-four-hour, or weekend coverage.

🖳 Potential Earnings

TYPICAL ANNUAL GROSS REVENUES: $30,000 to $60,000, based on billing 2,000 hours a year (40 hours a week) for an experienced transcriptionist.

OVERHEAD: low (20 percent or less).

📈 *Best Home Businesses* Estimate of Market Potential

Many parts of the country feel a shortage of medical transcriptionists. Even if doctors convert to using voice-recognition technology for dictating reports, transcriptionists will be needed to edit the doctors' dictation that appears on a computer monitor.

📰 Best Ways to Get Business

- Directly soliciting work from doctors, hospitals, and attorneys with medical disability cases (can include malpractice cases).
- Responding to classified ads for medical transcriptionists, proposing to do the work at home.
- Advertising in the publications of the medical societies to which doctors belong in your community.
- Taking overload or referral business from other transcriptionists.

👣 First Steps

If you already know this field, you might begin by contacting the facilities where transcribing is done, such as hospital medical records departments, chief information officers, radiology offices, pathology offices, and emergency rooms. Additionally, transcription is done in clinics, in private physicians' offices, counseling centers, and in government offices such as Worker's Compensation, occupational rehabilitation, and medical examiners.

If you don't have experience in the medical field, see if your local colleges or vocational schools offer courses. AAMT has developed a list of competencies, skills, abilities, and performance standards that should be achieved. (See listing that follows.) Students are encouraged to evaluate educational programs based on the length of the program, whether actual physician voices and dictation are included on practice tapes, and what types of reports and how wide a variety of specialties, voices, and accents are covered. Some community colleges offer relevant courses.

▯ Where to Turn for Information and Help

ORGANIZATIONS

American Association For Medical Transcription (AAMT), Box 576187, 3460 Oakdale Road, Suite M, Modesto, CA 95357; (209) 551-0883 or (800) 982-2182. The association publishes a bimonthly journal, holds educational meetings and conferences, produces educational materials and videos, and sponsors local chapters and state and regional associations. The association also offers a voluntary certification program. Successfully passing the examination for certification entitles one to the credential of certified medical transcriptionist (CMT). Complimentary packets are available upon request.

BOOKS

Health-Based Businesses on Your Home-Based PC, Rick Benzel, Blue Ridge Summit, PA: Windcrest/McGraw-Hill, 1993; (310) 391-8024.

The Independent Medical Transcriptionist, Donna Avila and Mary Glaccum, Rayve Productions, Inc., Box 726M, Windsor, CA 95492; (800) 852-4890.

The Medical Transcriptionist: Independent Contractor or Employee, Harvey Shulman and Craig Etler, AAMT. See address above.

Perfect Transcripts for WordPerfect, Stenograph Corporation, 1500 Bishop Court, Mt. Prospect, IL 60056; (800) 323-4247; (708) 803-1400.

NEWSLETTERS AND JOURNALS

BIS Source, published semiannually by the Business Issues Section of AAMT. Call the above toll-free number for information about BIS membership.

JAAMT, published bimonthly by AAMT. Call the above toll-free number for subscription information.

MT Monthly, published by Computer Systems Management, 1633 N.E. Rosewood Drive, Gladstone, MO 64118; (816) 468-4403 or fax (816) 468-5572 for subscriptions and information.

HOME-STUDY COURSES

At-Home Professions, 2001 Lowe Street, Ft. Collins, CO 80525; (800) 359-3455. Call for information about cost and amount of time it may take you to complete their course. This course won an award for its instructional design.

California College for Health Sciences, 222 West 24th Street, National City, CA 91950; (800) 221-7374, ext. 367. Offers an interactive home-study course in medical transcription as part of an accredited Associate's Degree program.

Health Professions Institute, P.O. Box 801, Modesto, CA 95353; (209) 551-2112. Call for information about cost and amount of time it may take you to complete their course.

■ ■ ■ ■ ■

MEETING PLANNER

If you enjoy arranging and designing formal events and have excellent organizational and negotiation skills, you may find a career in professional meeting planning to suit your talents. Meeting planners work most often with corporations, associations, and nonprofit groups to plan conferences, sales meetings, conventions, trade shows, fund-raising events, special banquets, hospitality events, shareholder meetings, and other professionally oriented affairs. (The career of *event planner* is related but usually refers to people who plan weddings or one-time parties for personal or business functions.)

In the past recessionary years, meeting planners were considered a dispensable luxury for businesses, but in today's high-pressure climate, many companies are beginning to realize that they cannot spare a single body in-house to handle all the details of a meeting. Savvy companies also know that a successful meeting can go a long way to improve customer relations or to motivate their own employees. Instead of exhibiting at trade shows, some companies are using their budgets for unique meetings and events for customers and prospects. As a result, they are willing to hire trained, creative, and professional meeting planners who know where to find high-quality goods and reliable services.

Meeting planners must know about many related fields, from hotellerie to catering to travel. For example, planners may be asked to negotiate the best rate for a conference room at a hotel, or to buy catering services for 250 people, or to find a great deal at a golf resort where the company can have its annual retreat. Planners may also need to book speakers, buy flowers and gifts, set up special promotions, arrange for cars and limos, find entertainers, set up tours and activities for visiting guests, or any of a multitude of other things that have to do with a meeting.

Because the demands on a meeting planner can make it a high stress job, today's planners make intelligent use of computers, faxes, and the telephone to accomplish their job without mistakes. In fact, the most effective meeting planners develop and maintain a large database of vendors and suppliers whom they can trust for flowers, food, entertainment, and other needs. They will also list hundreds of contacts they've made in the hotel and travel industries from whom they can get good rates for hotels and airlines. They may also use project-management software to keep track of the myriad arrangements behind the scenes of an event, thereby avoiding slipups and mistakes.

According to Robin Gross, a home-based planner and director of the West Coast office for MariMac Corporation, one specialty area for meeting planners today is developing incentive programs and contests for company executives and salespeople. Such programs have become a popular way for businesses to boost sales, enhance productivity, or improve safety records. In keeping with the trend for companies to downsize staff, they often contract out with specialists to provide the format and techniques for these contests, and this provides an ideal area of specialization for meeting planners with expertise in sales promotions or office or plant management. The winners of many of these contests or promotions earn a trip or cruise to an exotic location, so the meeting planner must be able to make arrangements and book all the necessary tickets.

☑ Knowledge and Skills You Need to Have

- You must have excellent organizational skills and an eye for detail.
- You also need a sound business sense, because to get some contracts, you will need to calculate a budget for the client and then stick to it.
- You must have excellent presentation and communication skills. You will often work with high-level executives planning a conference or convention.
- You must be good at negotiating prices and schedules with vendors (printers, hotels, airlines, florists) and maintain the budget you were given.
- You must be responsible when it comes to handling money and paying bills, as clients often give you access to an account with which you pay printers and hotels.
- You need knowledge of the travel industry almost at the level of a travel agent if you intend to accept jobs for off-site conventions, conferences, retreats, and sales meetings. You may also need to book airline tickets, hotels, amusements, and daily events.

- You should have troubleshooter skills to solve problems, as few meetings proceed without a hitch.
- Creativity is valuable in this business. Companies are looking for new and exciting promotions and conferences beyond the realm of the ordinary. You must be able to come up with exciting and offbeat ideas that you can implement at a reasonable cost.

■ Start-up Costs

	Low	High
Computer with hard disk and modem	$1,000	$3,000
Fax machine	300	900
Printer	300	1,600
Suite software (word processing, spreadsheet, and database) and contact management software	250	400
Two-line telephone equipment	100	200
Errors and omissions insurance	200	500
Office furniture, especially ergonomic chair	400	1,000
Business cards, letterhead, envelopes	100	600
Reference books and dictionaries	100	300
Total	$2,750	$8,500

■ Advantages

- Meeting planning is an enjoyable profession overall.
- It can be exciting to organize and make an event come off well that pleases a lot of people.
- You may get to travel and stay at exclusive resorts and great hotels for sales meetings and conventions.
- You can meet interesting people and make valuable contacts in the hotel and travel industries.
- Meeting planners often have flexibility in picking the kinds of jobs they want to work on.

■ Disadvantages

- The work can be stressful. You often have to put in long days and work hard when the meeting occurs.
- The job is extremely detail oriented: forgetting one little task can put a damper on an entire event or make a client angry.
- If you book entertainment, you may be considered an agent and need an agent's license, so check the regulations in your state.
- The job is subject to economic downturns; when the economy is bad, companies may have fewer meetings or they may spend less on those meetings they do have.

$ Pricing

Meeting planners may charge either by the hour, by the day, or by the project. The average hourly fee is $40 to $60 per hour; daily fees run $400 to $500 per day. Planners handling large events such as conventions or sales conferences may try to charge 15 to 20 percent of the overall projected budget for the entire project.

▣ Potential Earnings

TYPICAL ANNUAL GROSS REVENUES: $25,000 to $100,000 per year.

OVERHEAD: low (20 percent or less).

⁇ *Best Home Businesses* Estimate of Market Potential

Human beings show no signs of eliminating meetings. In fact, a survey by *Day-Timers* found workers spend up to one-quarter of each day in meetings. At the same time, the work week is lengthening, contributing to overworked workers expecting that meetings will be worth their time. These factors, together with the reality that meeting planning is the kind of function that often gets outsourced by corporations, suggest steady growth in the demand for meeting planners.

▣ Best Ways to Get Business

1. Network among caterers and travel agents so you can hear about potential conferences and conventions that may be taking place.
2. Contact your city's convention and visitors' bureau to learn about various meetings and events going on in your community. Then call the appropriate organizations or companies involved to find out if they can use your assistance.
3. Volunteer to plan a charity or civic event as a way to demonstrate your capabilities, make key contacts, and get referrals, but be careful about giving away too much time and free advice.
4. Go to networking groups and business meetings; get business cards from every meeting.

⊞ First steps

Getting started in this business is easiest if you a have a public-relations or communications background, or have worked for a corporation in this capacity. But even if you don't have this kind of experience, you can learn about the business by working with a meeting planner in your area or by calling caterers, convention centers, and other businesses involved with meetings to see if you can help out with a few meetings on a trial basis. In addition, you should contact Meeting Professionals International, listed below, for their start-up kit and other information they offer about the profession.

✛ Related Businesses

Exposition Manager. The growth of expositions and trade shows of all kinds around the country has led to many new opportunities for people interested in either sponsoring and running expositions or managing them for other exposition companies. Trade shows run the gamut from small springtime flower and patio expositions to gigantic computer or electronic shows that bring in 150,000 people in three days. Although most exposition organizers are not home based, there are a few companies focused on smaller shows that are operated by home-based owners. In addition, many exposition companies hire floor managers to help run the shows, and these people most often work from their home. For more information on becoming involved in expositions and trade shows, contact the International Association for Exposition Management listed below.

◻ Where to Turn for Information and Help

ORGANIZATIONS

Meeting Professionals International, 1950 Stemmons Freeway, Dallas, TX 75207; (214) 712-7700. Has about 12,000 members, of which 1,000 are home based. Offers a membership kit with information for people interested in the career.

International Association for Exposition Management, P.O. Box 802425, Dallas, TX 75380; (214) 458-8002, fax (214) 458-8119.

Professional Convention Management Association, 100 Vestavia Office Park, Suite 220, Birmingham, AL 35216; (205) 823-7262. A professional association for people who manage conventions and meetings. The association also publishes a textbook, *Professional Meetings and Management.*

NEWSLETTERS

Meetings & Expositions, published by the American Society of Association Executives, 1575 Eye St., N.W., Washington, DC 20005-1168; (202) 626-2789. A monthly publication for association managers and others involved in planning meetings.

BOOKS

Affairs of the Heart: How to Start and Operate a Successful Special Event Planning Service, Nancy DeProspo Gluck, P.O. Box 250, Lanoka Harbor, NJ 08734; (908) 237-0957. Includes form and contracts for event planning (mostly oriented to wedding planning but also contains information on event planning).

MAGAZINES

There are several magazines in this field, including *Meeting News, Successful Meetings* (Bill Communications, Inc.; [212] 592-6263), *Incentive Travel Magazine, Travel and Leisure, Traveler,* and others that are of value to meeting planners.

■ ■ ■ ■ ■

MULTIMEDIA PRODUCTION

If you have an interest in education, training, communications, or a creative bent to develop a product that needs to be published, you definitely want to explore the hot new field of multimedia. Growing out of the advent of CD-ROM hardware and software, digitized sound boards, high-speed video cards, and linkages between PCs, photography, and video cameras, today's multimedia service stands at the forefront of the newest wave in computer product development.

Essentially, a multimedia service can do any or all of four businesses:

- You can develop and sell your own multimedia concept on a CD-ROM disk, handling your own distribution just as any other CD-ROM or software publisher does.
- You can develop your own multimedia product but use another publisher to market it for you, just as if you were an author and got a book publisher to publish your book in exchange for a royalty.
- You can become a large-scale publisher and buy ideas from other people who have developed multimedia products.
- You can become a multimedia consultant based on your technical or creative expertise and sell your services to businesses, educational institutions, and other clients who need to produce multimedia for their employees or members.

Whichever path you choose, the field is growing quickly, and it is now estimated that there are several hundred multimedia products on the market that will mushroom to tens of thousands within years. As of this writing, commercial multimedia products range from many encyclopedia/reference CD-ROMS to courses on how to play a guitar or golf, to adventure games and children's stories, to complete Beethoven or Tchaikovsky symphonies with analysis and explanation of their history and music theory. Many of the best-known film directors are also buying multimedia companies or offering to take part in producing a title, because if successful, a multimedia product can sell millions of dollars worth of disks in a short time.

In addition, companies and businesses everywhere are beginning to use multimedia as the method of choice for employee instruction and training. Whereas a decade ago, CAI (computer assisted instruction) was limited to text, today's multimedia training package can include video footage, music, animation, and photos, increasing the effectiveness of the training. Computer-based training is currently a $1 billion industry, and it is expected to increase multifold within a few years as more and more companies move to use multimedia in their training to cut down on the costs of sending employees to training centers and hiring instructors.

The driving force in multimedia is the hardware. Today, faster speeds for CD-ROM drives and video cards, as well as greater compression of video and audio tracks, make multimedia more powerful. A developer can now take many diverse pieces of information such as video clips, sound bites, photos, text, artwork, and animation—and combine them all into one presentation that runs from a CD-ROM disk to provide hours of interactive entertainment or information. At the same time, new developments in software are making it easier for novices to put together a multimedia presentation by using simple authoring systems that use a flowchart-like timeline to tell the computer when to insert the animation or video clip, for how long it should run, and which music to overlay in the background.

Multimedia has a wide range of applications. It can be used by businesses in sales training, conferences, conventions, and product demonstrations; it can be used in education to teach and help children learn at their own rate; it can be used for family recreation and fun in the form of games, stories, and reference materials; it can be used to provide cultural and geographic information in an interactive format for tourists in hotels, kiosks, and airports; and it can be harnessed to provide sophisticated workshops or tutorials to professionals of all kinds such as doctors, lawyers, and teachers.

To be in this business, you must enjoy creating new ideas and putting together information in an artistic and entertaining way. It has been said that multimedia is a solution in search of a problem, but at the pace multimedia disks are selling today, it seems to have found its problem: people love information delivered in a fun, attractive, interactive package.

✔ Knowledge and Skills You Need to Have

- It helps to know about one of these fields in advance to reduce your learning curve: media production, video, audio, video postproduction, camera work, lighting, microphones.

- If you are interested in producing your own multimedia presentations, an ability to understand the various components of multimedia technology is useful. You should also be willing to stay continuously up to date and abreast of new developments that affect the hardware and software aspects of production, as well as the market changes.

■ If you want to be on the creating end of multimedia—producing training materials, education products, or entertainment—you need to have a good visual and graphic-design sense, plus creativity.

■ Multimedia technology and markets change quickly. It helps to be future oriented and to have a certain amount of moxie to visualize how the product might be used in years to come.

■ A certain amount of savvy about how to use materials is critical. As Dan Wodaski, author of *Multimedia Madness*, points out, virtually everything is owned by someone else and so you will need to obtain permissions to reuse materials in your product. But this can work to your advantage because you can bargain with a photographer, for example, to use his or her photos for free in your product if you insert a credit line.

⬛ Start-up Costs

	Low	High
Computer (high level) with a half gigabyte or larger hard disk and at least 8 meg of RAM	$1,000	$ 3,000
Other computer equipment (internal and external) and software*	7,000	17,000
Printer	300	1,600
Office furniture, especially ergonomic chair	400	1,000
Business cards, letterhead, envelopes	100	600
Total	$8,800	$23,200

* The total price of a professionally equipped multimedia workstation ranges currently from $8,000 to $20,000. Other than your computer, you need a seventeen-inch or larger monitor, a fast SCUSI hard drive, a scanner, a video capture card, sound card, a MIDI synthesizer (optional), a video overlay card if you are doing kiosk work (this card allows you to play video in a window off a laser disk), a microphone and good-quality speakers, sound-editing software, image-editing software, a MIDI sequencer, and possibly a CD ROM recorder to produce CD ROM disks. You also need multimedia authoring software such as **Authorware Professional, Icon-Author,** and Macromedia's **Director or Q/Media.**

⬛ Advantages

■ You are on the cutting edge of new computer products; the field is exciting and fun, and few people are currently involved.

■ As more and more companies understand the use of multimedia for training, the field will become increasingly lucrative, adding to and in part replacing a large portion of the $47-billion training industry.

- As computer technology changes, you will continue to be in the forefront of new ideas and ways of thinking and doing things.

⏸ Disadvantages

- The learning curve is six months to a year if you don't have a background in this area.
- Because multimedia is a new field, you may have difficulty finding people who need it, and the people who need it could have trouble finding you. So although your job opportunities are good, it's hard to make matches that pay off.
- There is still a lot of ignorance or uncertainty about just what a multimedia show can do for a business, which makes marketing your service difficult at times.

💲 Pricing

The pricing for a multimedia service varies tremendously. Technicians may earn from $25 to $35 per hour; but high-level consultants, programmers, designers, and concept people can earn $80 to $100 per hour. (If you create your own commercial product, you are not apt to be taking in any money until you get your product to market and begin selling copies.)

🖥 Potential Earnings

TYPICAL ANNUAL GROSS REVENUES: $35,000 based on billing 1,000 hours (20 hours per week at $35) to $80,000 based on billing 1,000 hours at $80. If you create a product that sells 100,000 copies and you earn $3 to $15 royalty per copy, you can obviously do quite well.

OVERHEAD: moderate (20 to 40 percent); purchasing and upgrading equipment drives the costs of this business.

📈 *Best Home Businesses* Estimate of Market Potential

One of *the* best home businesses for the 90s. Multimedia is a hot spot in the economy with sales of CD-ROM drives about doubling each year. As interactivity and the information superhighway take shape, the demand for programming will grow.

⏭ Best Ways to Get Business

If you are going to be your own publisher, you need to create a product and begin distributing it through dealers, wholesalers, and so on. This also means that you may need to associate with animators, photographers, sound experts, designers, and video producers to help you produce your idea. But the field is wide open for new developers to produce children's stories, games/

adventure disks, simulations, and many kinds of products that are even unimagined at this time.

If you are going to work with or for other publishers, you will need to create a portfolio of your own work. You should work up a sample product that shows potential clients what you can do for them. You might focus on corporations that need to do presentations or training. You can show your work to businesses like wallpaper stores, real estate offices, and others who might be able to use multimedia in their stores for product explanations and demos.

First Steps

1. Attend workshops and read magazines about multimedia.
2. Study the equipment you need and make purchases to build your studio.
3. Create some sample product as your multimedia résumé.

Where to Turn for Information and Help

ORGANIZATIONS

Association for Multi-media International, Inc., 10008 North Dale Mabry Highway #113, Tampa, FL 33618; (813) 960-1692; fax (813) 962-7911. Has local chapters and sponsors an international competition for single images and business graphics.

CompuServe Information Service, 5000 Arlington Centre Boulevard, Columbus, OH 43220; (800) 848-8199. Many forums focus on specific hardware platforms or software applications for multimedia, such as the Multimedia Forum (go to IICS, International Interactive Computer Society in section 17 on CompuServe on Multimedia). Also Microsoft has a Multimedia Jumpstart CD ROM file you can request over the Internet.

International Interactive Communications Society, twenty-six chapters, 5,000 members, 14657 S.W. Teal Blvd., Suite 119, Beaverton, OR 97007; (503) 579-4427. The professional association in interactive multimedia.

BOOKS

Absolute Beginner's Guide to Multimedia, Ron Wodaski, Indianapolis: Sams Publishing, 1994.

Designing Interactive Multimedia, Arch Luther, New York: Bantam, 1992.

Multimedia Madness, Ron Wodaski, Indianapolis: Sams Publishing, 1993.

Operating a Desktop Video Service on Your Home-Based PC, Harvey Summers, Blue Ridge Summit, PA: Tab/McGraw-Hill, 1994; (800) 822-8158.

Technology Edge: Guide to CD-ROM, Dana J. Parker, Boston: Boyd & Frasier, 1993.

MAGAZINES

Because multimedia is a rapidly growing field, many new magazines are coming into existence, sometimes absorbing older titles. To find out both what magazines appeal to you as well as to keep you abreast of the field, scout your local magazine dealer to find which ones you like best. Some current titles to look for are **CD-ROM World, CD-ROM Professional, Desktop Video World, Multimedia World, NowMedia, PC Graphics & Video,** and **Wired.**
  Some publications of particular note are:

Medio (800) 788-3866, which is one of the growing number of magazines produced in a CD-ROM format.

Morph's Outpost on the Digital Frontier, P.O. Box 578, Orinda, CA 94563; (510) 238-4545, which is a technical trade publication.

CD-ROM

The Guided Tour of Multimedia, produced by Graphix Zone, 914 S. Hoover Street, Los Angeles, CA 90006; (800) 942-4000.

How to Start Your Own Homebased Multimedia Publishing Business, Interactive Learning Technologiez [sic], 3817 Wildfire Lane, Burtonsville, MD 20866; (301) 989-9713.

NowMedia, produced by *Millimeter* Magazine, 826 Broadway, New York, NY 10003, (212) 477-4700, fax (212) 228-5859, is a CD-ROM about CD-ROM production. It also contains nine directories.

Professor Multimedia, Individual Software, 5870 Stoneridge Drive #1, Pleasonton, CA 94588; (510) 734-6767. An instructional CD-ROM that uses multiple media to explain multimedia.

TRAINING

There are many workshops and seminars around the country teaching multimedia techniques. Contact **Graphix Zone** at (800) 55-GRAFX (in California, call [714] 953-7013),

First Light Video Productions, 8536 Venice Blvd., Los Angeles, CA 90034, has a thirty-two-page catalogue filled with videotape-based training courses about video production and some CD-ROM-based courses on working in multimedia, including *How to Create Multimedia,* by Jasmin Multimedia; (800) 777-1576.

■ ■ ■ ■ ■

NEWSLETTER PUBLISHER

Chances are that you find several newsletters in your mail each week. Some are ones that you subscribe to, whereas others are sent to you by organizations to which you belong or companies wanting your business. They are part of the 1.5 million newsletters published in North America, according to the estimate of the Newsletter Publishers Association—an increase of 10 percent over the last ten years. Sometimes the distinction between newsletters, magazines, and newspapers gets blurry, but a newsletter is usually considered to be a publication that is one to eight pages in length, with a format no larger than 8½ by 11, that is not available on newsstands.

In the United States alone, there are more than 20,000 subscription, membership, and free newsletters, bulletins, and similar serial publications—and more are appearing every year. That represents a real opportunity for a home-based publisher.

There are three primary ways you can make money publishing newsletters:

■ *You can publish your own special-interest newsletter.* In this case you earn your income from subscriptions and/or advertising. You need to select an identifiable group of people who are motivated to pay for information you can provide that they could not easily obtain elsewhere. For instance, you might offer news items for sufferers of rare diseases and their families; describe business developments in another nation or group of nations; track an emerging field or technology; or discuss financial transactions of an industry. Some newsletters focus on subfields within a particular industry. In 1994, for example, there are 192 travel newsletters being published in North America. They focus on topics ranging from specific destinations to mode of travel (air, train, or sea), type of traveler (gays, nonsmokers, single men, etc.), bargains, and luxury tour packages.

Another possibility is to write about an everyday item. For example, Seena Sharp of Sharp Information Research discovered a few years back that there was no publication at all for the earring industry, because jewelry publications do not cover this market.

Potential markets for newsletters that we found while researching this edition of this book are newsletters serving business network organizers, business plan writers, computer repair and maintenance service operators, desktop videographers, errand service operators, expert brokers, export agents, in-home health providers, mailing list service operators, professional practice consultants, calendar service operators, duplicating services, home tutors, leak detection services, plant caregivers, proposal and grant writers, referral services, restoration services, and several of the specialties in the travel group of businesses. Whether these are viable as newsletters we can't predict, but the possibility is there.

For a newsletter to be profitable, annual subscriptions should cost no less than $50 a year. Depending on the sophistication, uniqueness, and availability of information, newsletters may carry subscription prices of $500 or more. Additional sources of income include renting your list of subscribers as a mailing list, using the newsletter to sell products that you either produce or buy from others, and mentioning in the newsletter that you are available for speaking and consulting engagements.

Newsletters are not necessarily mailed anymore but may be sent by fax or published on-line, accessible by computer. Be aware, however, that once you put your newsletter on-line, you may lose control of your copyright and have more trouble getting paid. One way to avoid those problems is to make a particular article available on-line, with a teaser: "For more information, contact . . ."

For print newsletters, if you are already equipped with a computer, high-resolution laser printer, desktop-publishing and design or clip-art software, your start-up costs can be as low as several hundred dollars, which includes sending free sample issues along with a reply card on which subscribers can write their charge-card number for ordering. A more direct but expensive approach is to mail out 5,000 to 20,000 copies of your first issue along with your order form and reply envelope.

- ■ *You can produce (publish) newsletters for other people.* Companies, churches, clubs, charities, accountants, and real-estate agents are all potential clients for a newsletter business. Whether designed to communicate with employees or members or to promote products to past, present, and potential customers, newsletters are more apt to get people's attention than most forms of direct mail. In this case your client usually pays you a flat fee or an hourly rate to develop his or her newsletter, on a periodic basis, such as monthly or quarterly.

Standard rates for writing in-house company newsletters range from $20 to $60 per hour or from $200 to $500 for two to four pages to $500 to $1,000 for four to eight pages. Rates for writing for retail stores range from $175 to $300 for a four-page publication. Small associations pay from $15 to $25 per hour for writing projects; large groups pay up to $85 per hour.

If you have the necessary computer hardware and software and, of course, the skill to use them, you can offer complete production services. Your tasks would include layout, pasteup, and preparation for printing, in addition to writing and editing the material. You might also handle contracting with a printer and maintaining the mailing list for the distribution of the newsletter. Providing photographs for the newsletter is also a good way of adding to your revenue. Each of these services should be priced separately, even when you charge the client a flat fee per issue.

- **You can write a standard monthly newsletter usable by the same type of client.** The newsletter appears to be that of a particular client, such as a dentist or an environmental consultant, because the first page is customized to have a message from the client plus any other custom touches he or she may wish to add. Professionals and small companies who don't have the time, staff, or budget to produce their own newsletters but for whom newsletters are a good marketing tool are candidates for using a newsletter service.

Alexander Auerbach, who, with his partner Rick Weiner, publishes *Out of the Blue*, a monthly newsletter for former IBM employees, used publicity to launch his newsletter.

They got coverage in several major newspapers, which published *Out of the Blue*'s 800 number, and hundreds of calls came in.

Auerbach says the thing to keep in mind is that you're not in the newsletter business; you're in the information business. You have to ask yourself what you know that other people will find newsworthy and timely. In order for a newsletter to succeed, you have to find a niche, and there must be a demand for the information. That was the winning combination for Nancy Mills when she launched **Travelin' Woman,** a know-before-you-go newsletter for women travelers. Debuting in March 1994 on a $400 budget, **Travelin' Woman,** attracted 500 subscribers in six months from the roughly 55 million women who travel each year. Because **TW** was the first newsletter for these knowledge-thirsty consumers, it was written about in 80 national and international publications, generating more than 1,000 inquiries. So a rule of thumb for creating a newsletter success is to "find a niche and scratch it."

✅ Knowledge and Skills You Need to Have

- You need to be an excellent writer, with an ability to compose succinct, informative items that meet the needs of your target audience. Newsletter subscribers don't want to wade through lengthy articles to find the information they're seeking.

- You must have a clear sense of the types of articles that will interest your audience and satisfy them that they are receiving something of value.

- You need some talent for design in order to create a newsletter that is visually appealing. It helps if you are familiar with typefaces, layout, graphics, and the printing industry generally.

⬛ Start-up Costs

	Low	High
Computer with hard disk and modem	$1,000	$ 3,000
Ink-jet or laser printer	300	1,600
Word processing, page layout, graphics, database, and mailing list software	1,000	2,000
Photo-imaging software	500	1,000
Desktop scanner	1,000	2,000
Photocopier	300	800
Postage meter	50	500
Envelope-stuffing machine	200	500
Fax	300	900
Answering machine	100	200
Total	$4,750	$12,500

⬛ Advantages

- With today's fax and modem technology, most newsletter publishers can live anywhere—in a large metropolis, small town, or rural area.

- Although it can be difficult to get subscribers, once you establish a loyal following it is relatively easy to make profits through renewals.

- Newsletter publishing can lead naturally to spin-off products and services such as special reports, seminars, audiotapes, books, and even starting a mail-order catalogue company, as David Starkman and his partner, Susan Pinsky, did (see entry for Mail-Order Business).

- Because you rarely have direct contact with your subscribers (unless you're doing public-relations newsletters for local business/professional clients), you seldom have to get dressed up to work in your home office.

⬛ Disadvantages

- Building up circulation, and profits, can take awhile.

- You must do a great deal of careful planning before ever writing an article. If you don't adequately research your market to find out whether your idea is original enough, interesting enough, and capable of generating stories for years to come—as well as determining whether there are enough potential subscribers to make your venture successful—the newsletter could fail.

⬛ Pricing

Discussed in the descriptions about the various ways to be in the newsletter business.

🖳 Potential Earnings

TYPICAL ANNUAL GROSS REVENUES: $60,000, based on 1,000 subscribers at $60 a year. Earnings may be increased by renting your mailing list, selling other products to your subscribers, or accepting advertising. However, getting up to 1,000 subscribers is likely to take a significant amount of marketing.

OVERHEAD: moderate (20 to 40 percent). Overhead can be less if you are producing newsletters for others and not bearing a heavy marketing cost.

📉 *Best Home Businesses* Estimate of Market Potential

The outlook for newsletter publishing is good as careers become more specialized, new industries emerge, people's interests diversify, new problems are identified, and more laws and regulations come into existence.

🔼 Best Ways to Get Business

- Sell subscriptions through direct mail to lists that you rent or trade.
- Run small classified inquiry ads as a low-cost way of gauging interest and generating names. Then send a direct-mail package to those who respond. You save a lot by mailing only to people who have expressed interest in your newsletter.
- Send a sample issue with an invoice to subscribe. Be sure to label the newsletter SAMPLE COPY in bold lettering.
- Offer a trial subscription to prospective subscribers with an invoice sent separately right after mailing their second-to-last issue, instructing those who do not wish to subscribe to return the invoice marked "cancel." For those who do not pay immediately or cancel, send follow-up reminder invoices.

Tip: If you base a subscription on the number of issues someone will receive rather than a period of time, should you decide to increase your frequency of publication (i.e., from quarterly to monthly), you can rebill subscribers sooner.

🔧 First Steps

1. Select a subject for your newsletter, learn about your potential subscribers, research competition as well as other efforts to serve your market. If you are not already an expert in the subject of your newsletter, read and learn everything you can to become an expert.
2. Define a focus and a format for your newsletter.
3. Develop samples and test your concepts out with people who are like your prospective subscribers.
3. Develop a marketing plan and begin testing it.

🔲 Where to Turn for Information and Help

ORGANIZATIONS

Desktop Publishing Forum, CompuServe Information Service, 5000 Arlington Centre Blvd., Columbus, OH 43220; (800) 848-8199. Once online, enter "GO DTPFORUM."

The Newsletter Publishers Association, 1401 Wilson Boulevard, Suite 207, Arlington, VA 22209; (800) 356-9302; (703) 527-2333, fax (703) 841-0629. Publications include *A Newsletter Launch Checklist* (free of charge); *Success in Newsletter Publishing* ($39.50 plus $3.50 for shipping and handling); and *How to Launch a Newsletter* ($11.50 plus $2 for shipping and handling). Also sells an audiotape, *Raising Capital for the Newsletter Venture* ($13).

BOOKS

Circulation for Fun and Profit, John M. Chilson, Circulation Solutions, 10590 Kipling Way, Westminster, CO 80021; (303) 469-3179.

The Newsletter Handbook, Wesley Dorsheimer, New York: Hippocrene Books, 1993.

Home Based Newsletter Publishing, William J. Bond, New York: McGraw-Hill, 1992.

How to Do Leaflets, Newsletters and Newspapers, Nancy Brigham, Cincinnati, OH: North Light Books, 1991.

Producing a First-Class Newsletter, Barbara A. Fanson, North Vancouver, BC: International Self-Counsel Press Ltd., 1994.

Publishing Newsletters, Howard Penn Hudson, New York: Scribners, 1988.

DIRECTORIES

To determine what newsletters already exist in your chosen field, check any of the following directories, which are available in most libraries. These directories range in price from $140 to almost $500.

Hudson's Subscription Newsletter Directory, edited by Joan W. Artz, H & M Pubs., 1994.

Newsletters in Print, John Krol, Detroit: Gale Research Company, 1994.

Newsletter Yearbook Directory, Coral Springs, FL: B. Klein Publications, 1993.

Oxbridge Directory of Newsletters 1994, New York: Oxbridge Communications, 1994.

Ulrich's International Periodicals Directory 1994–95, New York: R. R. Bowker, 1994.

See also the *Newsletters* volume of *Standard Rate and Data Service.*

Fulfillit, JSK Programming Services, Inc., 60 Surrey Lane, East Falmouth, MA 02536-9909; (800) 950-1577. Software that keeps track of subscribers; prints labels, invoices, and renewal notices; and produces management reports.

✚ Related Business

Directory Publisher   Chances are you use a directory of some kind every day. It may be a telephone directory or a professional or trade directory related to your work. Directories are invaluable sources of information that people gladly pay for. If you identify a need for which there is no organized and easy-to-use source of information, you have taken the first step along the way to being able to publish a directory that may list people, sources of information, services, objects or things, sometimes their prices, and even perhaps some type of rating.

About half of the directories published charge the people, products, or companies for being listed. These directories are apt to be distributed without cost to assure their distribution. To do well at directory publishing, you have to love detail and be willing to investigate and explore cracks and crevices, sometimes literally as well as figuratively, for information.

To get an idea of the many directories already in existence, take a look at *Directories in Print*, published by Gale Research. It can usually be found at the reference desk of libraries. A how-to book on this topic, *Directory Publishing: A Practical Guide*, by Russell A. Perkins, is published by Morgan-Rand, 200 Samsome Street, Philadelphia, PA 19103 (215) 938-5511. The same company produces a newsletter called the *Morgan Report on Directory Publishing*. An organization with a number of small directory publishers as members is the *Publishers Marketing Association*, 2401 Pacific Coast Highway, Suite 102, Hermosa Beach, CA 90254; Jan Nathan, 372-2732; fax (310) 374-3342.

■ ■ ■ ■ ■

PRIVATE INVESTIGATOR

Most private detectives on television are shown with downtown offices. So it may come as a surprise to learn that a large number of private investigators work from their homes. Added to that is the fact that the field of private investigation is changing and growing. Hallmark Systems, a company that studies the private security industry, projects that the number of private investigators will grow by 2 percent a year through the year 2000.

In the past, private investigators have been kept busy working for attorneys on criminal and civil cases, tracking down white-collar crime for corporations, locating missing persons, and doing insurance investigations. However, today's private investigators are specializing in many types of investigation. For example, some private investigators are using computer technology to search public records and consumer information to assist with business deals, corporate fraud investigations, preemployment screening, and even premarital checks. Although increasingly stringent privacy laws are restricting access to some of these public records, particularly driver's license information, the use of computers and other new modes of communication is thus changing the nature of private investigators—allowing more people to become home based.

Private investigators are required to be licensed in most states, with Alabama, Colorado, Idaho, Kansas, Mississippi, Missouri, Oregon, South Dakota, and Wyoming being exceptions at the time of this writing. (But be sure to check with your state to be certain no changes have occurred. For example, some municipalities in nonlicensing states require private investigators to register with the city or the police department.) In those states that have licensing, the requirements vary and usually involve some sort of experience in investigative work, which may even be met by working in a collection agency.

Contrary to the TV image created by characters like Rockford, Spencer, and Mike Hammer, being a private investigator is not necessarily a dangerous business. Most private investigators don't carry a gun, and according to Bob Taylor, an investigator from East Brunswick, New Jersey, who has been in the business for twenty-five years, weapons are unnecessary. Most work these days consists of background checking on individuals that companies or private citizens are thinking of becoming involved with, including prospective employees, deal makers, and marriage mates.

In fact, you can create a profitable business providing only one or a few of these specialized services. For example, you can build a business doing background screening and reference checking of prospective employees, business partners, or tenants; verifying credit; or doing skip tracing—that is, finding difficult-to-locate people. In many states, however, providing a specialized service does not relieve you of becoming licensed as a private investigator.

☑ Knowledge and Skills You Need to Have

- From one to three years' experience in some type of investigative work, such as law enforcement, claims adjusting, collections, or even investigative journalism, is required by most states for licensing. Some states will do a background check on you when you apply to take their test.

- People skills are important, including the ability to read people, develop rapport, manage conversations, and persuade people to give you information. As Bob Taylor says, "You have to be more of a communicator than a Joe Friday."

- You have to be able to write an investigative report and take a statement. One PI indicates that experience taking statements for an insurance company is similar to the kind of experience you need on this job.

- Creativity and intuition are necessary for gathering information that is sometimes difficult to find. You also need tenacity and persistence to get the information you seek. On-the-job training is critical in this area.

⬛ Start-up Costs*

	Low	High
Computer with hard disk and modem	$1,000	$3,000
Ink-jet or laser printer	300	1,600
Fax	300	900
Pocket organizer to keep track of expenses	20	100
Suite software	250	400
Office furniture	400	1,000
Business cards/letterhead	100	600
Tape recorder for interviewing	50	200
Total	$2,420	$7,800

* You might also wish to have an 800 telephone number to encourage clients to call you, because many people are hesitant to call a private investigator.

⬛ Advantages

- Private investigators enjoy prestige and a glamorous image.

- Private investigators enjoy the challenge of fitting together bits of information for a variety of cases.

- It can feel good to capture someone who is cheating others out of money, or to locate someone who was being sought by loved ones.

⬛ Disadvantages

- It can take at least two years to establish a large-enough clientele to operate full time.

- Your hours are typically long, and you're often required to work weekends and evenings.

- Private investigators have difficulty making firm time commitments because of the unpredictable demands of some cases. If you're on a stakeout, for example, you need to stay with the person under surveillance until you get the information needed.

- As society becomes more sensitive to invasions of privacy, some channels for PI work using public records may be closed off.

⑤ Pricing

Hourly fees for private investigators range from $25 to $125, with $40 to $70 typical in metropolitan areas.

🖭 Potential Earnings

TYPICAL ANNUAL GROSS REVENUES: $50,000, based on billing 1,000 hours a year at $50 an hour. Private investigators also bill separately for many expenses associated with investigations, such as parking, film, tolls, and so on, as these expenses can mount up over the course of a year.

OVERHEAD: moderate (20 to 40 percent).

📈 *Best Home Businesses* Estimate of Market Potential

Total number of private detective firms in the United States, including home-based businesses: 36,094. Concerns about personal and financial security and a continually mobile society are anticipated to keep the demand for private investigators growing.

🖻 Best Ways to Get Business

- Directly soliciting trial lawyers and their office managers, insurance companies, and corporate personnel departments.
- Yellow-pages advertising if seeking private clients for collections and marital work (which accounts for only 25 percent of private investigators' work today).
- Direct mail, such as introductory letters and newsletters, followed up by phone calls.
- Speaking at meetings.
- Presenting seminars on specialized topics such as debugging.

⑤ First Steps

- If you do not have the experience to qualify for a license, the best way to get into this field is to apprentice with a private investigator.
- Obtain a license where needed. Some states that require a license will provide a list of recommended books to use in studying for the exam.

◻ Where to Turn for Information and Help

ORGANIZATIONS

American Society for Industrial Security, 1655 N. Fort Meyer Drive, Suite 1200, Arlington, VA 22209; (703) 522-5800. Annual convention and trade show, including seminars. All aspects of investigation.

Association of Certified Fraud Examiners, 716 West Ave., Austin, TX 78701; (800) 245-3321. Geared toward fraud and corporate security.

National Association of Investigative Specialists, Box 33244, Austin, TX 78764; (512) 928-8190. Publishes and distributes many books and manuals.

National Association of Legal Investigators, 2801 Fleur Drive, Des Moines, IA 50321.

BOOKS

Competitor Intelligence: How to Get It; How to Use It, Leonard M. Fuld, New York: John Wiley and Sons, 1985.

Handbook on Corporate Fraud, Jack Bologna, Boston: Butterworth-Heinemann, 1992.

Requirements to Become a P.I. in the 50 States and Elsewhere, Joseph J. Culligan, Research Investig., 1994. Culligan is also the author of *You, Too, Can Find Anybody: A Reference Manual* and *When in Doubt, Check Him Out: A Woman's Survival Guide for the 90's,* from the same publisher.

Techniques of Legal Investigations, Anthony M. Golec, Springfield, IL: Charles C. Thomas, 1985. $53.25.

The following are all published by BRB Publications, 4653 S. Lakeshore #3, Tempe, AZ 85282; (800) 929-3764. Also 1200 Lincoln #306, Denver, CO 80203.

Asset/Lien Searching. Directory of U.S. jurisdictions holding real property, lien, and corporate records.

County Court Records. Directory of local courts and how-to information on obtaining court and other county-level records.

Federal Courts—U.S. District & Bankruptcy. Locations of courts and federal records centers. This book also explains court records systems.

Local Court & County Record Retrievers. Profiles of retrieval services.

LOCUS—The Ultimate Locator. Matches zip codes with places.

The 1994 MVR Book. Regulations and descriptions of each state's motor vehicle records system.

The Sourcebook of Public Record Providers, Michael Sankey, Business Research Bureau Inc., 700 Fee Fee Road, Maryland Heights, MO 63043; (314) 569-1700; 1992. State Public Records. Profiles 400 companies providing database and retrieval services.

Another publisher of books in this area is Thomas Publications, Box 33244, Austin, TX 78764; (512) 928-8190.

MAGAZINES AND NEWSLETTERS

P.I. Magazine, 755 Bronx, Toledo, OH 43609.

TRAINING PROGRAMS

Institute of Consulting Careers, Inc., 222 S.E. 16th Street, Portland, OR 97214; (503) 240-0931. Offers a complete program in private-investigation techniques.

■ ■ ■ ■ ■

PROFESSIONAL ORGANIZER

The professional organizer has emerged as the knight in shining armor of the information age. Our lives today are oversaturated with an ever-increasing flow of information. Our mailboxes are stuffed with mail, and most people have more belongings than previous generations, as evidenced by the fact that older homes never have enough storage space. Yet most people feel they have less time than ever to manage and organize all the added *stuff* in their lives. The professional organizer steps into our homes and offices to help us take control and put our lives in operating order.

Professional organizers help us organize everything from paper files to computer files, from desktops to filing cabinets, from bookshelves to closets and kitchens. As organizer Harriet Schechter puts it, "As an organizer, instead of editing words, I edit other people's time and space."

Although this profession is just a few years old, it has doubled every year since 1985; the National Association of Professional Organizers currently has about 650 members. Practitioners generally specialize in one of five principal categories:

- **Space planning**—setting up and laying out a home or office so people can get the maximum and most efficient use of the space they have, taking into consideration such things as lighting, traffic patterns, noise, and comfort needs.

- **Time management**—assisting clients to set goals, develop action steps, define priorities, and schedule and delegate tasks and activities.

- **Paper management**—helping people know how to respond to and what to do with incoming materials and setting up filing and retrieval systems so they can find things when they need them. Increasingly, organizers also help people manage electronic information.

- **Clutter control**—restoring a sense of order and preventing the further accumulation of clutter.

- **Closet/storage design**—designing and organizing closet and storage space.

Some organizers work only in residential settings; others work exclusively in offices, serving organizations such as banks, hospitals, schools, professional practices, and other business enterprises. Some organizers develop a particular specialty like packing and moving, or paying bills and putting finances in order.

Schechter, whose company, The Miracle Worker Organizing Service, says an organizer's clients are not necessarily disorganized people. "Often they are quite the opposite," she says, "but are overwhelmed with too many projects and a reluctance to delegate." The point is, everyone who feels he or she could benefit from being more organized is a potential customer. But first that person must decide if he or she wants the service, and then must be willing to pay for it. At this time only a small percentage of those who need the service are willing to pay. It's not uncommon for a potential client to wait three years before deciding to call for help.

For Schechter this business is almost like a calling. "Good organizers have an overwhelming need to bring order to the world," she says. "They get satisfaction from helping people organize their lives."

Susan Silver, Los Angeles organizer and author of *Organized to Be the Best! New Timesaving Ways to Simplify and Improve How You Work*, finds that "this is a very creative business. It provides many creative outlets to express your abilities. As an organizer, you can be an author, seminar leader, trainer, or hands-on consultant."

Silver believes that metropolitan areas provide the best opportunities for organizers because these areas have a larger market filled with people who are overloaded with paper and information and who have hectic lifestyles. Oddly enough, an organizing business can actually do quite well during a recession, when companies are looking for ways to stretch every dollar. Silver explains, "In tough times we have to find better ways to do more with less." So with creative marketing, this service can be positioned as a cost saver—a way to trim off fat and compensate for downsizing. (A related business, in fact, is an Expense Reduction Service; see Bill Auditing.)

☑ Knowledge and Skills You Need to Have

There is no specific training or background required to be an organizer. The following skills are important, however, in order to do it successfully.

- You need to be organized yourself and an expert in this field without being a perfectionist. People expect that you truly have answers to their problems, not just intuitive ideas of how to make something work a little bit better. You should have a knowledge of various systems, products, furniture, supplies, and accessories for organizing a home or office. Dee Behrman, who specializes in working with medical, dental, and legal offices, believes that "a broad-based product knowledge is essential so you can offer your clients a range of options and customize a system for their particular needs." In working with four medical offices, for example, she found that each one wanted to use a different type of chart.

■ You need to be analytical, punctual, and able to deliver on your commitments. You must be able to understand your clients' needs and develop clear plans for how to make order out of their chaos. You must feel challenged instead of stressed by disorder.

■ You must be compassionate toward, not judgmental of, your clients. As Harriet Schechter says, "You must have a poker face when you see people's disorder. Some people are insane over a small pile of papers; others seem unperturbed by huge mountains of stuff." Flexibility is, therefore, an important trait. You must work with each person's individual needs and quirks; you cannot have a cookie-cutter mentality that imposes one regimen on all.

■ Although many organizers are not computer literate yet, a sound knowledge of computer hardware and software to streamline an office will quickly become a must for any organizer to remain competitive. For example, if you are familiar with the software programs *Ascend*, *Approach*, or *InfoSelect*, you might be able to teach your clients to adopt such products to improve their use of the computer.

■ You must be willing to admit you don't have all the answers and to keep your mind open to new ideas and new ways of doing things.

🐾 Start-up Costs

	Low	High
Computer with hard disk and modem	$1,000	$3,000
Ink-jet or laser printer	300	1,600
Suite software	250	400
Time-management software	50	275
Form-design software		200
Office furniture	400	1,000
Business cards, letterhead, envelopes	100	600
Brochure or press kit	100	1,000
Organizational dues	250	250
Total	$2,450	$8,325

📑 Advantages

■ This is still a new field—new enough that competition may not be a significant problem.

■ The need for professional organizers will grow as the amount of information we must process continues to grow and our lives keep on getting more complex. Many businesses and individuals will appreciate the value of what you can do.

■ Your clients can see dramatic results of your work quickly.

- It is satisfying to feel that you are helping people create order out of their chaos.

- There is ample opportunity to use your creativity.

- There are many different facets of what you can do as an organizer, so you need not get bored doing the same thing over and over again.

- This is an evolving business, so if you like to grow, working as a professional organizer matches the need.

⊡ Disadvantages

- Because this is a new field, many people don't know what an organizer is. Some confuse it with *union organizer* or *community organizer.* So you often must educate clients before you can sell your service.

- Some clients are not at all well organized (that's why they need you), so sometimes you're working with people who reschedule a lot, can't find their checkbooks, forget their appointments, and so forth.

- This work demands a lot of time and energy to get under way, and it may take as much as a year or two before you'll be able to make a full-time income.

- You won't have much repeat business unless you have clients who hire you on a retainer or you are an on-site consultant to a larger company, so you will continually have to look for new clients.

- Professional organizers tend to burn out after a few years of constant contact with clutter.

⑤ Pricing

Organizers can charge in one of three ways:

Fixed fee. Fixed fees are charged for specific jobs like organizing a work space or setting up a filing system. For example, Jeffrey Mayer of Chicago charges $1,000 to organize an executive's desk. An organizer might also charge a fixed fee to do an introductory training program, a needs assessment, a workshop, and a follow-up session. For example, Susan Silver sells such packages to corporations. Fees for such programs will vary with their length and the level of personnel with whom you are working. You can charge more to train executives than you can to train secretaries.

Hourly rate. Fees range from $25 to $150, depending on your location, experience, and expertise. Residential and garage organizers will tend to be at the lower end of the scale; corporate organizers charge more.

Retainer. Organizers contract to work with a company for a certain period of time each month. Retainers may range from several hundred to several thousand dollars a month.

▣ Potential Earnings

TYPICAL ANNUAL GROSS REVENUES: $20,000 to $40,000, based on billing 400 to 800 hours a year (eight to sixteen hours per week) at $50 an hour. Beginners will seldom be able to bill more than a few hours a week.

OVERHEAD: low (20 percent or less).

▨ *Best Home Businesses* Estimate of Market Potential

Total number of professional organizers in the United States, including home-based businesses: 5,087. The role of professional organizers will become increasingly accepted by businesses of all sizes as the amount and variety of sources of information continue to grow.

▧ Best Ways to Get Business

- Teach workshops and classes for community-college and adult-education programs, and speak before community and business organizations.
- Network in organizations, such as trade and business associations, as well as with professionals who work in industries related to this field, like business consultants, interior designers, and architects, who can refer clients to you.
- Personal contacts with people you meet
- Yellow-pages advertising under Organizing Services or Personal Services
- Publicity through news releases and writing articles
- Listing in the directory of the National Association of Professional Organizers
- Writing a newsletter, with organizing tips, for past and potential clients
- Developing cross-referrals with other types of professional organizers

▦ Franchises

Priority Management Systems, 500 108th Avenue N.E., Suite 1740, Bellevue, WA 98004; (800) 221-9031. Sets you up in business as a trainer for middle- and upper-level managers on topics such as priority setting, project planning, and time management. Management experience is required. In business since 1984. The minimum fee is $29,500.

Closet organizers design and install storage systems that make the most of every square inch of space and keep a full closet neat and tidy. You can design and build such systems yourself, or you can become a distributor for a closet organizing company such as:

Closet Classics, 3311 Laminations Drive, Holland, MI 49424; (616) 399-3311.

First Steps

- Read books on organizing, time management, and efficient office systems. Develop a specialty or focus for the type of organizing you will do and which industries you want to work with.
- To practice your craft, volunteer to work for friends, charity, or nonprofit organizations that will give you letters of recommendation.
- Begin speaking and offering workshops on your specialty and start networking, because these will be your primary ways to get business.

Where to Turn for Information and Help

ORGANIZATIONS

National Association of Professional Organizers, 15 North Mill Street, Nyack, NY 10960; (914) 353-9270. Newsletter, conferences, and local chapters.

BOOKS

How to Be Organized in Spite of Yourself, Sunny Schlenger and Roberta Roesch, New York: Signet, 1990.

How to Get Organized When You Don't Have the Time, Stephanie Culp, Cincinnati: Writer's Digest, 1986. Also available: *How to Conquer Clutter,* by Stephanie Culp.

More Time for Sex: The Organizing Guide for Busy Couples, Harriet Schechter, New York: Dutton, 1995.

Organized to be the Best! New Timesaving Ways to Simplify and Improve How You Work, Susan Silver, Los Angeles: Adams-Hall Publishing, 1991; (800) 888-4452.

Winning the Fight Between You and Your Desk, Jeffrey J. Mayer, New York: HarperCollins, 1993.

MANUALS

Harriet Schechter's How to Become a Professional Organizer Resource Packet, 3368 Governor Drive, Suite F-199, San Diego, CA 92122. For information, send a self-addressed, stamped, business-size (number 10) envelope.

NAPO Resource Registry, National Association of Professional Organizers, 1604 N. Country Club Road, Tucson, AZ 85716. Send check payable to NAPO. $15.

The Get Organized! News, P.O. Box 144, Gotha, FL 34734; (407) 292-0911.

Messies Anonymous Newsletter, 5025 Southwest 114th Avenue, Miami, FL 33165; (305) 271-8404.

NAPO News, National Association of Professional Organizers, 1604 N. Country Club Road, Tucson, AZ 85716; (914) 353-9270.

■ ■ ■ ■ ■

PROFESSIONAL PRACTICE CONSULTANT

Being a businessperson and a practicing professional are quite different roles, each with its own set of required skills. An increasing number of dentists, doctors, chiropractors, osteopaths, podiatrists, psychotherapists, lawyers, CPAs, and other professionals are recognizing this difference and are thereby turning to specialized consultants for advice, or even to have them actually manage the business side of their professional practices. In the medical field, in particular, changes in health care and insurance are causing doctors to take a greater interest in controlling costs and maximizing profits.

Full-service private practice consultants handle virtually any aspect of running a professional's practice. They may deal with payroll; hire, train, and fire personnel; handle collections; do billing; manage the facility (if the client owns a building); oversee investments and pension plans; or select computer hardware and software. They may also help with patient scheduling. There are consultants who serve as efficiency experts and work to increase their clients' productivity and profitability. Others may offer advice about taxes or government regulations.

Some practice consultants are generalists, working with a variety of professions, although about 75 percent of the clients for this business are physicians, dentists, and professionals in the medical field. Other consultants are highly specialized—working, for example, only with anesthesiologists or dentists. Their clients include solo practitioners as well as group practices, and sometimes even hospital administrators may use their services. Although a consultant may run the entire business for a client, most are not stationed in the office but, rather, working from home. They visit offices periodically to conduct business and see their clients.

The demand for professional practice consultants has exploded in the past decade, with only a small percentage of the 600,000 or so doctors in private practice being served. There is plenty of opportunity for the practice consultant because the practices of medicine, law, and accounting have become more sophisticated and more competitive. Professionals—and doctors in particular—need to spend more time keeping up with their field. At the same time they are feeling greater pressure to market and administer their practice as a business. In fact, some consultants specialize in showing professionals how to improve their marketing, although 75 percent of their work is still in practice management.

Connecticut-based consultant Scott Brown, whose company is called Focus Management, works with a wide assortment of professionals, including attorneys, dentists, psychiatrists, CPAs, orthodontists, and graphic designers. His main function, he says, is to improve each practice's marketing by identifying a message the practitioner can present to patients or clients that will help bring in new referrals. After collecting data on the business, Brown helps his clients establish long-range goals to improve profitability. He then designs a marketing, training, and management plan tailored to the needs of each business, and implements the plan. Most of his consulting jobs last from six to twelve months, and clients generally see results in that time.

Brown says that the essence of his business isn't marketing, training, or management, but helping his clients reframe how they look at themselves and their practice. Much of what he encounters is "attitude problems—for instance, they haven't set goals, or are looking at the down side of the business, or haven't made enough contacts."

Success, ironically, has created some problems for Brown, who occasionally feels overwhelmed managing many different businesses—and having to switch gears between clients whose practices are so different. But he takes a philosophical view. "You have to love what you're doing, and take the ups and downs as they come," he says. "It's just a matter of trying to find the right balance."

☑ Knowledge and Skills You Need to Have

- You must be able to "manage" a practice, which means you need to have either experience or education in office management in the medical, insurance, legal, or accounting field. Successful consultants have primarily come from two backgrounds. Some began as staff in a professional's office and learned the business from the ground up. Others are CPAs or MBAs who saw the need and decided to specialize in this field.

- In addition to being competent in handling professional business practices, you must have confidence and high self-esteem in order to communicate that you know your stuff when talking with the professionals, office staff, and government agencies you will be dealing with. You should also have good people skills, since forming an appropriate relationship with your clients and their staffs is critical. You are a combination consultant, marketer, therapist, problem solver, and motivator.

- You need to be able to manage your time effectively in order to balance running your own business with running the businesses of multiple clients.
- You need common sense and an organized mind to deal effectively with client or patient-care issues and office systems.

▪ Start-up Costs

	Low	High
Computer with hard disk and modem	$1,000	$ 3,000
Ink-jet or laser printer	300	1,600
Copier	300	800
Suite software	250	400
Additional spreadsheet and accounting software	150	400
Fax	300	900
Malpractice insurance	500	1,000
Telephone headset (you spend a lot of time on the telephone going over facts, figures, schedules)	40	70
Office furniture, especially an ergonomic chair	400	1,000
Business cards, letterhead, envelopes	100	600
Brochure	100	1,000
Organizational dues	250	250
Total	$3,690	$11,020

▪ Advantages

- This business is largely recession resistant because doctors need help running their practice as a business even more acutely in tough times.
- This is an excellent opportunity to use any management skills you may have developed during your career.
- You are working among one of the most highly educated sectors of our society, with interesting and ambitious people.
- The work involves handling a variety of problems, which means you must always learn to deal with new things. There's no boredom in this business. You can learn as much as you care to.
- Practice-management consultants may have clients throughout the country, which is a plus if you love to travel.
- The business is easy to set up from home. All you need is a phone and some office equipment. Your clients will not usually come to your office.
- Professional practice consulting offers high income potential.

▪ Disadvantages

- It can take months to obtain your first client, creating a lag time before you make money. You might also experience peaks and valleys in your own cash flow if you do not bill consistently.

- Often you will be working on someone else's schedule because your clients will want to see you at their convenience.
- The work can be stressful because many unexpected demands arise. There is a great deal at stake in managing someone else's business. Risks are high and consequences can be significant. Your clients can see quickly if you are having an impact on their bottom line.
- As a personal service, you are limited in your earnings by how much time you can bill, unless you hire employees.

$ Pricing

Private practice consultants charge in two ways:

By the hour. Rates range from $60 to $300.

On retainers. Rates range from a few hundred dollars (which purchases several hours) to thousands of dollars a month. You might give your clients a choice of an hourly rate, a monthly rate, or a six-month retainer. If they prefer a retainer, give them a discount.

Potential Earnings

In 1992 (the most recent year for data), surveys show that doctors earned $177,500 on the average. Practice-management consultants can equal the earnings of their affluent clients. Some consultants bill up to sixty hours a week.

TYPICAL ANNUAL GROSS REVENUES: $90,000 to $187,500 or more, based on thirty billable hours a week at $60 to $125 per hour. Income also depends on the number of practices you are managing at any given time.

OVERHEAD: moderate (20 to 40 percent).

Best Home Businesses Estimate of Market Potential

Operating a professional practice in the 90s is increasingly competitive, demanding a sophisticated management and business approach that is often unfamiliar and unappealing. This feeds the market for professional practice consulting.

Best Ways to Get Business

- Have contacts in the medical or consulting field prior to starting the business. Network with those contacts to get a few clients and build new contacts through professional and civic associations.
- Position yourself to get referrals from your first few clients. This is one of the most important and effective techniques.

- Send targeted mailings to certain types of professionals, and follow through with face-to-face meetings and telephone calls. Be prepared with a high-quality, persuasive prospecting presentation that demonstrates what you can do for the client.

- Offer workshops on practice-management issues to professional medical or legal organizations in your area. You might speak on maximizing profits or a topic that captures immediate attention.

- Write columns with tips and guidance about practice management for business and professional journals.

- Serve on fund-raising committees in organizations that have doctors as members.

Franchises

Professional Management Group, Box 1130, Battle Creek, MI 49016; (800) 888-1932. Provides bread-and-butter business services for professionals. They seek people who have some accounting, business, or financial background, and who are familiar with some aspects of the health-care field. They offer preceptor (observer) and mentor (apprentice) arrangements, new-consultant workshops, and continuing education. The fee is approximately $25,000, and the franchise provides geographical exclusivity.

First Steps

- Take educational programs on professional-management topics from institutes and professional associations.

- Work for an established firm that does professional practice consulting—in effect, apprenticing.

Where to Turn for Information and Help

ORGANIZATIONS

Society of Medical-Dental Management Consultants, 6215 Larson Street, Kansas City, MO 64133; (800) 826-2264.

BOOKS

Encyclopedia of Practice and Financial Management, Lawrence Farber, Oradell, NJ: Medical Economic Books, 1985.

Managing Your Medical Practice, Charles R. Wold, New York: Matthew Bender. Loose-leaf, updated annually. $100.

Medical Practice Management, Horace Cotton. Oradell, NJ: Medical Economic Books, 1985.

Medical Practice Management Desk Book, Charles H. Walsh and Morton Walker, Englewood Cliffs, NJ: Prentice Hall, 1982.

Practice Management for Physicians, Donald L. Donohugh. Orlando, FL: W. B. Saunders, 1986.

■ ■ ■ ■ ■

PUBLIC-RELATIONS SPECIALIST

Public-relations specialists help establish a high profile for their clients. This is important because, in today's information age, visibility is power. They obtain publicity for their clients in magazines and newspapers, and on radio and television. They produce written materials such as press kits, press releases, news releases, annual reports, speeches, and brochures that call attention to their clients.

There are several reasons we have included this business on our list of best businesses for the 1990s. The Public Relations Society of America estimates that there are 155,000 public-relations specialists in the U.S., including those who work from home. And the Bureau of Labor Statistics projects a 40 percent increase in the number of public-relations specialists through the year 2000. Indeed, the demand for public relations is growing.

PR, as it is often called, is considered a cost-effective way for businesses, nonprofit organizations, and even government agencies to market their services to the public. In fact, Daniel J. Edelman, founder of Edelman Public Relations Worldwide, says PR is actually more efficient than advertising under four circumstances:

- when introducing a revolutionary, breakthrough product
- for small companies with little budget for advertising
- when TV is not an option, as with some product that can't be advertised or does not fit well with television
- when public opinion is negative and has to be turned around quickly.

Also, corporations and organizations of all sizes are cutting back on their in-house PR staff. As a result, more and more companies are contracting out their public-relations work.

Finally, with today's personal computers, faxes, modems, and other modern technology, a PR specialist working independently at home can produce the same quality of work once reserved for large, high-budget agencies. Information available from on-line databases, coupled with the capabilities of desktop publishing and electronic communications, enables the PR specialist to create and send written materials and artwork to and from virtually anywhere instantaneously.

Clients for a home-based PR agency might include businesses, nonprofit organizations, public agencies, and individuals, particularly book authors and professionals who are seeking to use PR to market their services (as is suggested for many businesses throughout this book). In fact, many lawyers, consultants, doctors, and other professionals eagerly seek publicity, and they are willing to pay for a PR specialist to help them get a television or radio appearance or a story in a print medium.

Some PR professionals find a particular niche by specializing by field (such as high technology, medicine, environmental products) or by type of work (such as annual reports, employee communications, newsletters, copywriting, or media or investor relations). Some work only with certain types of clients such as authors, restaurants, environmentally conscious companies, and so forth.

Judie Framan began working out of her home in southern California some eight years ago, after serving as a corporate communications manager for many years. Some of her contacts from her corporate jobs became clients, and little by little her business grew and became successful. Framan points out that companies hire freelancers in part because most have developed a special expertise and have lots of useful contacts. For instance, in the twenty-plus years she has been in the communications business, she has established relationships with a number of trade journals covering many different industries. Knowing the types of stories those editors are looking for helps her match her clients' needs with the needs of editors.

The skilled public-relations practitioner, Framan emphasizes, must be persistent and follow up on every lead. "Don't take 'yes' for an answer," she reminds others, because even after you've gotten a commitment from an editor, you can't relax. "The amount of follow-up you have to do in public relations is unbelievable," she says. "Editors are extremely busy, and even after you've convinced someone to run your story, you need to make sure the story doesn't die." A tactful phone call can make all the difference.

☑ Knowledge and Skills You Need to Have

- PR specialists need strong communication skills. You have to be able to write well to attract attention and interest with the materials you prepare for your clients.

- You must have good telephone skills. At the same time, you need to be both diplomatic and persuasive.

- You must have a good memory for names because much of your day is spent contacting reporters, producers, and editors by phone. You need to have or be able to gain knowledge of the media that your clients want to reach and establish relationships with the editors and producers who will make publicity decisions. You need to know the deadlines they operate under; their focus or theme; the type of guests, features, or articles they like to run; and so forth, so you will know how to talk to them about your clients.

■ You must be creative and colorful to provide clients with a new angle that will capture the interest of their market and the media. You must follow current trends, news, interests, needs, and likes and dislikes by keeping up with the latest in sports, entertainment, business, and world events.

■ Freelance PR specialists must be able to come up with stimulating ideas on their own because they don't have other staff with whom they can discuss ideas or brainstorm concepts and angles for getting publicity.

■ You need to be able to organize abstract ideas or technical jargon into tangible, meaningful material for publications, speeches, newsletters, ad copy, and so forth.

■ A PR specialist must have a lot of energy. PR projects are referred to as campaigns. There are deadlines, and there is little down time to regroup and recharge emotionally and physically.

■ You need to be able to handle rejection without taking it personally.

Start-up Costs

	Low	High
Computer with hard disk and modem	$1,000	$3,000
Ink-jet or laser printer	300	1,600
Fax machine	300	900
Suite software	250	400
Desktop publishing software	100	500
Telephone headset (can increase phone productivity by one-third)	40	70
Office furniture, especially an ergonomic chair	400	1,000
Business cards, letterhead, envelopes	100	600
Brochure or press kit	100	1,000
Organizational dues	250	250
Two phone lines for business, with call-forwarding and conferencing features	(part of overhead)	
Total	$2,840	$9,320

You may be able to barter for many of these costs and thereby reduce start-up expenses.

Advantages

■ This business can be exciting and vastly stimulating. It provides enjoyable and interesting experiences, and you get to meet interesting people.

■ You are not limited to doing any particular thing at any given time. Throughout the day you can move from one kind of activity to another.

■ You have an opportunity to be creative, amusing, playful, and trendy.

■ Public relations is perceived as prestigious.

⏸ Disadvantages

- Public relations is a competitive field. Many people who were unable to find a job in a corporation after college start out doing public relations on their own, working from home. Through internships at school, they have had some experience and will work at cut-rate prices, which may bring down the price others can charge. It is also always hard to convince clients that your services are worth as much as they are, because PR results are partially intangible.

- You must prove your value over and over again with your clients. You're only as good as the PR you got on your last job. There is always the pressure of how many stories you can place and what response your news releases generate.

- The work can be stressful because of deadlines, time pressures, and the fact that often you do not control the end result for your client, which may lie in the hands of editors and producers who have their own priorities, whims, and preferences.

- PR is sensitive to the economy. Some businesses pull back on PR expenses if times are tough even though such times are ideal for doing more PR.

- This business has a slow start-up. You can expect two years of taking out less than you're putting in.

- Prospecting never ends. You always need to have business lined up after your current projects come to a close. The average client relationship lasts only nine months.

💲 Pricing

Fees for PR services range from $200 to $1,500 per day. The national average for experienced public-relations consultants is $850 per day. PR professionals serving large corporations average $1,000 per day, while those working for smaller companies average $600 per day. The highest rates for PR professionals are for those who provide consulting services; they may charge as much as $200 per hour. Rates also vary by region of the country.

🖵 Potential Earnings

The median annual earnings for sole practitioners after business expenses and before income taxes range from $40,000 to $60,000. Billing twenty hours a week should be a minimum goal; thirty billable hours is realistic.

TYPICAL ANNUAL GROSS REVENUES: $35,000 to $75,000 for independent public-relations specialists.

OVERHEAD: low (20 percent or less).

⚡ *Best Home Businesses* Estimate of Market Potential

Total number of public-relations firms in the United States, including home-based businesses: 26,582. The outlook for continual outsourcing of public-relations functions by all sizes of organizations is positive.

▣ Best Ways to Get Business

- Networking and personal contacts in organizations, such as trade and business associations, particularly in industries or fields in which you have experience. This can serve two purposes: to identify companies that may want your services, and to identify associations that may want you to do PR for them too.
- Speeches before business or community groups promoting the benefits of public relations
- Volunteer work for nonprofit organizations
- Telemarketing, particularly if you can barter with a professional to do it for you
- Publishing a newsletter for former and prospective clients
- Identifying potential PR opportunities for companies by reading the electronic news services and then contacting the companies by phone to let them know of the leads you've developed.

⛓ First Steps

Many colleges and universities have certificate programs in public relations that can provide you with an understanding of the field and a credential without your having to earn a four-year degree. Another way to get experience is to work part-time assisting an established freelancer, doing it for free if necessary.

▢ Where to Turn for Information and Help

ORGANIZATIONS

International Association of Business Communicators, 1 Halladie Plaza, Suite 600, San Francisco, CA 94102; (415) 433-3400. Professional association for public relations, marketing, and writers working in corporate communications.

PR and Marketing Forum, CompuServe Information Service. CompuServe, 5000 Arlington Centre Boulevard, P.O. Box 20212, Columbus, OH 43220; (800) 848-8990 and (614) 457-8650;

Public Relations Society of America, 33 Irving Place, New York, NY 10003; (212) 995-2230.

BOOKS

There are many basic textbooks in public relations that you can find in college bookstores.

DIRECTORIES

Bacon's Information, Inc., Bacon's Information, Inc., 332 South Michigan Avenue, Suite 1020, Chicago, IL 60604.

Business Periodicals Index, H. W. Wilson Company, 950 University Avenue, Bronx, NY 10452. Annual.

Gale Directory of Publications and Broadcast Media, Gale Research, Book Tower, Detroit, MI 48226. Annual.

Gebbie Press All-in-One Directory, Gebbie Press, Box 1000, New Paltz, NY 12561. Annual.

O'Dwyer's Directory of Public Relations Firms, 271 Madison Avenue, New York, NY 10016.

MAGAZINES AND NEWSLETTERS

PR Reporter, Box 600, Exeter, NH 03833. Weekly newsletter of PR, public affairs, and communications.

Public Relations Journal, 33 Irving Place, New York, NY 10003; (212) 995-2230.

Public Relations News, 1201 Seven Locks Road, Potomac, MD 20854; (800) 777-5006.

SOFTWARE

MediaManager PR Productivity Software, MediaMap, 215 First Street, Cambridge, MA 01242; (617) 374-9300. Integrates a media database, list-management capabilities, contact management, an editorial calendars database, task and project management, and a briefing book module for creating custom, in-depth press kits for product tours and interviews. Available in Macintosh, DOS, and Windows versions. $795.

■ ■ ■ ■ ■

REAL ESTATE APPRAISER

Real estate appraisers estimate the value of residential and commercial property. People need to have real estate appraised prior to the sale of property, when getting insurance, in the event of a loss, at the time of bankruptcy, pending a merger or acquisition, for investment decisions, during a divorce, and at many other times in the course of owning their home or building.

The real estate appraisal industry underwent a fundamental transformation in 1992 when Title XI of the Financial Institutions Reform, Recovery, and Enforcement Act (FIRREA) became effective, requiring that states establish minimum licensing and certification standards for real estate appraisal work involving many federally related transactions. FIRREA was written to counteract the inflated values that some appraisers had placed on properties in the 1980s. These inflated appraisals were significant factors in the failure of so many savings and loan institutions and the consequent bailout costing federal taxpayers hundreds of billions of dollars.

The implications of FIRREA were clear, though: because many buyers purchase homes through federally insured mortgages, it effectively required all appraisers, experienced or new, to obtain a license or certification to practice their trade. The new law was in sharp contrast to the past, when appraisers generally learned the rules of appraisal through apprenticeship and experience. The good news, though, is that the career of appraisal is still thriving, and as old-time appraisers retire, the doors open for new ones to come in. According to the Appraisal Institute, the largest association of professional appraisers, the opportunities for appraisers are now excellent. As they say, "With the increasing complexity of real estate investment, the need for appraisal services has grown. The increased application of environmental and other land-use regulations by local and federal governments continually provides new opportunities for appraisers."

Real estate appraisers use their knowledge of building structure, construction, finance, demographic statistics, and business trends to analyze and evaluate the value of a property. In addition to viewing the property, appraisers may also do original and secondary research, including examining public records, survey drawings, blueprints, and government regulations. Appraisers then produce a written report that documents their analyses and presents their conclusions. Banks, mortgage companies, buyers, sellers, tax collectors, lawyers—in short, all the parties to a transaction—count on the appraisal to help them close the sale or come to an agreement on a better settlement price for the property. Banks and buyers, of course, don't want to approve a mortgage for a property that is worth only half of its sale price, and sellers and their lawyers or real estate agents, of course, want to maintain the prices as high as they can.

Because of FIRREA, the requirements to become an appraiser vary slightly by state but are roughly comparable. These include:

- 75 hours of course work for licensing which allows you to appraise complex residential properties under $250,000 and noncomplex one-to-four-unit properties under $1 million
- 105 hours of course work for residential certification for residential properties with a value in excess of $1 million
- 165 hours of course work for general certification which allows you to appraise residential and commercial properties at any value.

In addition, both the license and certification also require 2,000 hours of appraisal experience and the successful completion of an exam. As you can see, there is still quite a heavy reliance on experience. Appraisers must, therefore, find another appraiser to work for as an apprentice during a period of about two years before they are eligible for licensing or certification.

But appraising can be lucrative. Greg Edwards, an appraiser in Santa Monica, California, has been working in this field for thirteen years. Through his contacts and networking, he is an approved appraiser for several banks and thus finds that he is often called upon for appraisals most days of the week for at least one if not two assignments. Greg comments, however, that the appraisal business is now becoming more and more computerized; in the old days, he would go to city hall to look up records on past sales of homes, whereas he now checks records using an on-line service so that his numbers are no more than twenty-four hours old. In addition to homes and buildings, some appraisers appraise shopping centers, industrial sites, farms, peat bogs, mines, pond bottoms, as well as collections of jewelry, art, and other valuables.

☑ Knowledge and Skills You Need to Have

- You will need to obtain a license or certification for your state. This requires course work time and experience, as indicated above.

- You need sound judgment, a good visual sense, and the ability to synthesize a lot of data about a piece of property.

- Appraisers must have a knowledge of architecture, construction, and building materials, but also of finance, mortgage equity, present value calculations, and other economic factors.

- Because appraisers write reports, you need to have a command of English and the ability to write well. You also need to know how to take photos, as most appraisals require photos of the property from outside as well as inside.

- It helps to be good at networking and getting your name around, as knowing lawyers, bankers, mortgage officers, insurance agents, and others who use appraisers can make the difference between getting business or not.

▣ Start-up Costs

	Low	High
Computer with hard disk and modem	$1,000	$ 3,000
Fax machine	300	900
Printer	300	1,600
Suite software	250	400
Software for appraisals	900	1,500
On-line services	200	500
Course work for exams	1,000	2,000
License or certification	1,000	1,000

	Low	High
Errors and omissions insurance	600	1,200
Office furniture, especially ergonomic chair	400	1,000
Organizational dues	250	250
Business cards, letterhead, envelopes	100	600
Camera—35 mm	150	300
Total	$6,450	$14,250

▶ Advantages

- This is not a desk job; you're outside much of the time instead of sitting down. An appraisal takes about four hours for a single-family home; you do need to spend about one hour, however, writing your report.

- Computers and modems mean you spend even less time in offices.

- Overhead and risk are low in comparison to other businesses in the real estate field.

- Your clients (banks, lawyers, etc.) become regular customers if they like your work.

▶ Disadvantages

- Your hours can be erratic and unscheduled until the last minute. Job requirements may necessitate that you attend evening meetings or do your work at the property owners' convenience.

- Appraisers are being sued and held legally responsible for losses of savings and loans and banks. You need to have errors and omissions insurance.

- The new licensing/certification process is time-consuming. It may be difficult to find an appraiser to work for in your area.

$ Pricing

The typical appraisal fee on a residence is $275 to $300.

▣ Potential Earnings

TYPICAL ANNUAL GROSS REVENUES: $75,000 for residential appraising, based on completing six appraisals per week at $250 each. Commercial appraisers, who must have more qualifications, can earn over $100,000 per year.

OVERHEAD: low (20 percent or less).

▨ *Best Home Businesses* Estimate of Market Potential

Total number of real estate appraisal firms in the United States, including home-based businesses: 36,611. Demand for appraisers is lessening as information becomes available in computer databases, often reducing their role to confirming data.

▣ Best Ways to Get Business

- Personal contacts with mortgage companies and banks to get on their list of approved appraisers.
- Networking in organizations such as mortgage bankers' associations and mortgage brokers' associations.
- Create some samples of your work to show to banks and mortgage companies.

⬢ First Steps

The first step is to start working on your license. Course work entails 75 to 165 hours of classroom time as indicated above. You can take the courses from one of the associations below—some of which hold their seminars around the country, or at local real estate schools.

◻ Where to Turn for Information and Help

ORGANIZATIONS

The Appraisal Institute, 875 North Michigan Avenue, Chicago, IL 60611-1980; (312) 335-4100. With 33,000 members, the largest appraisal organization composed of both residential and commercial appraisers. Offers self-study courses, seminars at various locations around the country, books, and exam prep materials.

Appraisers Association of America, 386 Park Avenue South, Suite 2000, New York, NY 10016; (212) 889-5404. This association is for appraisers of personal property other than real estate. Offers courses through New York University.

National Association of Independent Fee Appraisers, 75-1 Murdoch Avenue, St. Louis, MO 63119; (314) 781-6688.

National Association of Real Estate Appraisers, 8383 East Evans Road, Scottsdale, AZ 85260; (602) 948-8000. Mostly residential appraisers.

BOOKS

Appraising Residences and Income Properties, Henry S. Harrison, New Haven, CT: H2 Company, 1989.

Fundamentals of Real Estate Appraisal, William L. Ventolo, Jr., and Martha R. Williams, Chicago: Dearborn, 1993.

APPRAISAL SOFTWARE

a la mode, 1015 Water Wood Pkwy., Building F, Edmond, OK 73034; (800) 252-6633 and (405) 359-3346, fax (405) 359-8612. Produces software for real estate appraisers covering most aspects of an appraiser's desk work.

Dataquick Information Systems, 9171 Towne Centre Drive #600, San Diego CA 92122, (619) 455-6900, offers a "desktop appraisal" service. This service, known as VERI-FACTS, offers quick retrieval of property profiles and residential sales comparables, enabling the user to make a preliminary analysis of home equity.

■■■■■

RÉSUMÉ-WRITING SERVICE

Recent studies show that Americans change jobs on the average of seven times over the course of their working lives. And with an increasing number of companies being downsized, merged, or acquired, there are now even more applicants competing for fewer jobs. This means that thousands of students and workers need résumés that will help give them an edge in today's tough job market. Without a doubt, résumés are a de facto requirement for nearly all job seekers.

The result of our job-seeking society is that there is a tremendous, and constant, demand for professional résumé writers who specialize in helping people develop and create a competitive résumé that will get results. Résumé writers no longer simply type up someone's credentials in an attractive form. The résumé writer begins by interviewing clients about their background, skills, accomplishments, strengths, and weaknesses and how and to whom they want to present themselves. The writer must then creatively organize this information into a concise and appealing format that highlights the clients' most noteworthy accomplishments and skills. Clients are customarily given a limited number of copies of their completed résumé, usually twenty-five to fifty, as part of the basic price, although they can purchase more for an additional charge.

Many résumé services provide additional assistance for extra fees, such as writing cover letters; designing the letterhead so that the cover letter, résumé, and accompanying documents can be presented as a matched set; doing mass mailings of the letter, résumé, and other materials to prospective employers. Some services even provide additional "career" consulting, helping candidates get a better handle on what jobs may be good for them based on their background and qualifications. Other services may get involved in writing telephone scripts for job seekers to use in making calls, or even in providing mock job interviews to help the client perfect his or her presentation skills.

Résumé services serve two primary groups of clients:

- college and university students
- people already in the business and professional community, including those leaving the military.

The first group includes seniors who are about to graduate, sophomores and juniors seeking internships, and older students returning to the workforce after having gone back to school. The second category includes business and professional clients who are seeking an opportunity to advance their careers and the growing ranks of those who have been victims of mergers, purges, or downsizings. Another source of business is physically handicapped people, referred to you by your state department of rehabilitation, who are in need of résumés.

Steve Burt, who runs a résumé service in Gainesville, Florida, exemplifies a successful full-service résumé developer in business for eleven years. Half or more of his clients are university students whose level of writing skills are seldom adequate to put together a competitive résumé. He says, "My clients usually come to me with nothing in hand or perhaps an old résumé. Sometimes they don't know what type of work they want to pursue, and I may find something in their background that suggests a direction for their job search. He advises that "to succeed in this business you've got to separate yourself from others and offer a high-quality service."

✓ Knowledge and Skills You Need to Have

You do not need to have a background in personnel or employment counseling to help a client develop an effective résumé. You can become an expert on résumés by reading the vast amount of material written on this subject, a representative list of which appears at the end of this section. You do need the following skills and abilities:

- Extremely strong copywriting skills and the ability to organize information logically and concisely are an absolute necessity. You also need a good command of the English language, including punctuation, spelling, and grammar.
- The ability to interview people is vital. You need to be able to make them feel comfortable and draw out key information about their skills and experience.
- At the same time, you need to be able to think like the personnel directors who will read the résumés and be able to anticipate the questions they will ask so you can cover them in the résumés you prepare.
- You should have some talent for design and layout in order to put together a visually attractive résumé.
- You must live within twenty minutes of a college or university or of business establishments so your clientele can conveniently meet with you. Preferably you will live near both a college or university and a business district.

■ Most importantly, you must enjoy this type of work. You need to be able to show a personal interest in every client's résumé and believe everyone has some valuable skills and experience that can be highlighted to get him or her a job.

◙ Start-up Costs

	Low	High
Computer with hard disk and modem	$1,000	$ 3,000
Laser printer	300	1,600
Suite software	250	400
Copy machine	700	1,000
Supplies (high-quality résumé paper)		
Office furniture, especially an ergonomic chair	400	1,000
Business cards, letterhead, envelopes	100	600
Brochure or price list	100	1,000
Because you're seeing people in your home, your office needs to convey a professional image. It's best to have a separate entrance to your office. And if you don't already have them, you'll need:		
Two identical comfortable chairs	600	1,000
End tables or coffee table	100	500
Appropriate artwork	50	500
Total	$3,600	$10,700

▣ Advantages

■ You get the satisfaction of knowing you're helping others succeed. As Steve Burt says, "It's great to hear people call with a job and tell you that they got it because of the résumé you wrote."

■ You are in the mainstream of the job market and are always learning a great deal about where employment trends are going. This makes you a valuable resource in your community.

■ You meet people with a variety of interesting backgrounds.

■ Résumé writing can be an add-on service to other businesses like word processing, desktop publishing, career counseling, manual writing, business-plan writing, or a specialized temporary service.

▣ Disadvantages

■ People sometimes confuse your business with a simple typing service and expect to be charged accordingly. You have to make it clear that you are a professional writer and need to charge for your knowledge and creativity.

■ The work can be seasonal (particularly among the student market). This means that you are often extremely busy before graduation times, career expos, and graduation.

■ People may call you at any time of the day or night.

■ It can sometimes be disadvantageous to be home based because you may miss out on walk-in traffic and some people may not want to come to your home. You therefore need to turn being home based into an asset, such as the fact that you give very personalized service.

💲 Pricing

Frank Fox of the Professional Association of Résumé Writers (PARW) says résumé writers should be billing out at $50 to $85 an hour. Following are typical prices for developing and writing résumés:

■ One-page student résumés: $50 to $100, with an average price of $85.

■ One-page résumé for middle managers: $50 to $125, with an average of $65.

■ Two-page résumé for engineers: $50 to $200, with an average of $150.

■ Two-page executive résumé: $100 to $300, with an average of $200; full curriculum vitae can command prices of over $300.

🖩 Potential Earnings

TYPICAL ANNUAL GROSS REVENUES: $40,000, based on preparing twelve résumés a week, fifty weeks a year, at $75 per résumé. According to Frank Fox, a résumé writer billing 75 percent of his or her time could earn at least $50,000 per year, and the income potential in this business can be as great as $70,000 to $90,000 per year with add-on services, such as cover letters, consultations, copies, and so on.

A typical résumé takes 1.5 to 2 hours to complete. This includes interviewing, writing, and meeting with the client to turn over the completed résumé and collect the fee. Keep in mind, however, that the résumé business is seasonal, with the busiest months being January, February, March, and May and the least-busy months being July, November, and December. During busy times, Steve Burt has booked as many as twenty-three appointments a day!

Frank Fox also points out that the résumé business soars during periods of recession and high unemployment. During off-seasons, résumé writers may offer workshops. And although some also provide word-processing services, Steve Burt believes that it is important to distinguish yourself from a secretarial service. To distinguish himself from less-professional résumé services, Burt has joined the Better Business Bureau and has also become certified by the Professional Association of Résumé Writers.

OVERHEAD: moderate (20 to 40%).

⚡ *Best Home Businesses* Estimate of Market Potential

Total number of résumé-writing firms in the United States, including home-based businesses: 12,248. Downsizing of corporations and government agencies is predicted to last through the nineties, providing a continuing demand for the service of résumé writers.

⬡ Best Ways to Get Business

The most successful methods for getting business, according to the results of the Professional Association of Résumé Writers 1990 membership study are:

- Yellow-pages advertising
- Classified ads under "Employment, Professional" section in college or university newspapers and in newspapers read by businesspeople and professionals
- Networking in professional, trade, and civic organizations and referral groups. In particular, consider joining and getting certified by the Professional Association of Résumé Writers. Besides networking opportunities, PARW now offers a rigorous certification testing process that can help establish your professional credibility.
- Direct mail of the following to graduating students, attendees at job fairs, and so forth:
  - postcards and letters describing your service
  - pamphlets mailed to seniors (by renting a mailing list from a college or university) right before school starts in September and January.
- Keep a database of your clients for one year and, prior to the end of the year, send out a mailer to clients suggesting they may want to update their résumé or have you write a new cover letter.
- Referrals from print shops, radio spots, and job fairs
- Giving workshops, seminars, and speeches on how to write a résumé

Other methods that can work include:

- Offering to pay a cash referral fee to existing clients who refer new clients to you
- Developing reciprocal referral arrangements from employment agencies that don't offer a résumé-writing service. These agencies like their clients to have good-quality résumés. You may also be able to get referrals from desktop publishing or word-processing firms that set type for résumés but don't handle the professional writing of them.
- Placing notices on bulletin boards at colleges, print shops, large companies, and so forth.

🔧 First Steps

If your writing skills need polishing, take a writing course. Concentrate on developing your vocabulary; it's your ammunition. Your toughest client to get is the first one. You have to be prepared to answer the questions *What makes you think you could write my résumé?* and *Why are you better?* Develop samples so people can see what an excellent job you do. Do several résumés for free to show sample styles for various careers.

🗂 Where to Turn for Information and Help

ORGANIZATION

Professional Association of Resume Writers (PARW), 3637 Fourth Street North, Suite 330, St. Petersburg, FL 33704; (800) 822-7279. This organization with about 700 members provides a newsletter, professional membership identification, including name and logo to use in advertising layouts, and a toll-free consultant line. Has also established professional standards and offers a Certified Professional Résumé Writer credential to individuals who pass a rigorous test.

BOOKS

There are now 380 résumé-writing books in print that you can find in bookstores and libraries to familiarize yourself with the many approaches and styles. Compare examples in these books; some may actually be poorly done. (Is it surprising that résumé writers produce so many books about writing?) Here are some books recommended by experienced résumé writers.

High Impact Resumes and Letters: How to Communicate Your Qualifications to Employers, Ronald L. Krannich and William J. Banis, Manassas, VA: Impact, 1988.

How to Comply with Federal Employee Laws, Sheldon I. London, London Publications, 1991. Available from Professional Association of Resume Writers

The Overnight Resume, Donald Asher, Berkeley: Ten Speed Press, 1990.

Perfect Resume, Steve Jackson, New York: Doubleday, 1981.

Power Resumes, Ron Tepper, New York: John Wiley and Sons, 1989.

Resumes That Get Jobs, Jean Reed, New York: Arco, 1990.

The following books describe the business of résumé writing:

Start Your Own Resume Writing Business, Pfeiffer Staff, San Diego: Pfeiffer & Co., 1994.

The Resume Pro: The Professional's Guide, Yana Parker, Berkeley: Ten Speed Press, 1992.

Resume Writing for Profit, Mark Connelly, Cassell Communications, Inc., 1993.

The Upstart Guide to Owning and Managing a Resume Service, Dan Ramsey, Dover, NH: Upstart Press, 1994.

■ ■ ■ ■ ■

SCOPIST

Court reporters record exactly what people say during a legal deposition (a hearing before trial to gather evidence and obtain information from the litigating parties and witnesses) and in courtrooms. The court reporter of yesteryear worked with a stenotype machine that produced narrow paper notes, such as what most of us have seen in *Perry Mason* episodes. Today, modern court reporters work with computer-based writing machines that record their stenographic notes onto floppy disks. When the court reporter goes home, however, these notes must be translated from their raw phonetic form, in which entire syllables or words are recorded using only a few keys, into words and sentences to produce a transcript that lawyers and judges can read.

The problem is that even sophisticated computer-assisted transcription (CAT) software can translate a court reporter's notes only to a modest extent, leaving the transcript with punctuation errors, misspellings of proper names, and occasional wrong word choices (such as *to, too,* and *two*). This means that the court reporter must spend a few hours cleaning up and formatting the transcript, a tiresome task if you've already spent five to eight hours in a deposition or courtroom.

Enter the scopist, also called a "notereader" because he or she reads the court reporter's notes. Scopists are a kind of assistant to court reporters, taking responsibility for transforming transcripts into proper written English. Scopists reread the CAT versions of each document, edit and punctuate the material, double-check the spelling of technical terminology, medical words, and people's names, and proofread the document. If the scopist cannot understand a computer-translated portion of the text, he or she must also know how to read the raw stenotyped notes that are contained on the court reporter's disk.

Freelance scopists are usually hired directly by self-employed court reporters or by agencies that supply freelance court reporters. Whereas the court reporter must go to the deposition or courtroom, scopists can usually work from home unless they need to go into the agency to have access to the same software used by the court reporter they are working with.

As CAT software becomes more proficient at automatic translation of court reporters' notes, the nature of scoping may change. For the moment, however, freelance scoping can provide a good living, especially in larger cities in the Northeast, Midwest, and on the West Coast.

✅ Knowledge and Skills You Need to Have

- Scopists must be able to understand and read stenotype, because you may need to go into the raw notes of documents to check the originals when the automatic translation fails or is insufficient.

- Quick, accurate keyboarding skills are essential. The faster you transcribe, the more you earn.

- You must be good at spelling, grammar, and punctuation, and have an excellent command of vocabulary along with familiarity with medical and technical terminology from a variety of fields. (Many legal proceedings focus on accidents, malpractice, or lawsuits involving products or patents.)

- You need to feel comfortable working on a computer and using a modem. Many court reporters send their files to their scopists by modem to save time.

🐂 Start-up Costs

	Low	High
Training	$1,800	$ 2,500
Computer with hard disk and modem	1,000	3,000
Fax machine	300	900
Printer	300	1,600
Suite software (mostly word processing)	250	400
CAT software*	900	4,000
References	100	300
Office furniture, especially ergonomic chair	400	1,000
Brochures	100	1,000
Business cards, letterhead, envelopes	100	600
Total	$5,450	$15,300

* There are about twenty brands of computer-assisted transcription software that are not compatible with one another, so a scopist must work with court reporters who use the same software. The choice of software seems to be regionalized with court reporters on the East Coast favoring one program, while those on the West Coast lean toward another.

📑 Advantages

- The training is not as rigorous as that needed to become a court reporter. You only have to know how to read stenotype notes, not how to type on a stenotype machine.

- The hours are flexible. You have the freedom to select your own time and work from your home.

- People in this field report that they enjoy the work, reading many kinds of cases and testimony reflecting the drama of people's lives.

▶ Disadvantages

- Scoping requires substantial preparation. Learning shorthand theory and reading stenotype can take six months or more.
- Scopists work behind the scenes. They do not go to depositions or trials, and so they miss out on the actual drama of legal battles.
- Scopist work can be high-pressure, with short turnaround times to scope a document and prepare the final transcript.
- The pay is not as good as court reporting.
- Getting work can be a Catch 22 situation: you need to gain a reputation and prove yourself with a court reporter before getting work.
- The job can cause eyestrain and repetitive-motion injuries from long hours of keyboarding if preventive precautions are not taken.

💲 Pricing

Most scopists work by the page. An average fee is 70 to 80 cents per page, and the range is from 60 cents to a dollar per page. On a good day, a scopist can scope about 150 pages. Fast typists can do more. Many scopists also charge extra for expedited jobs.

▣ Potential Earnings

TYPICAL ANNUAL GROSS REVENUES: $20,000 to $37,500, based on scoping four to five days per week, fifty weeks per year, and earning $120 to $150 per day.

OVERHEAD: low (20 percent or less).

🗹 *Best Home Businesses* Estimate of Market Potential

The market for scopists appears to be steadily growing as the U.S. becomes increasingly litigious. The technology court reporters use has changed, but their need for assistance has not.

▣ Best Ways to Get Business

Directly contacting court reporters and court reporting agencies in your area. You can locate court reporters through the yellow pages, from a list available through your state's court reporters' association, or from membership in the National Court Reporters Association (see listing below). You can also join CompuServe's Court Reporters Forum (see listing below).

ⓗ First Steps

1. Check the community in which you live to determine the market for new scopists. Call a court reporter to discuss your interest and obtain specific advice.

2. Attend an accredited notereader/scopist program. Call the National Court Reporters Association for information on schools offering scopist programs.

◻ Where to Turn for Information and Help

ORGANIZATIONS

National Court Reporters Association, 8224 Old Courthouse Road, Vienna, VA 22182; (800) 272-6272 or (703) 556-6272, fax (703) 556-6291. An association for both court reporters and scopists. Offers a monthly magazine, holds an annual conference, and sponsors continuing-education training seminars and employment-referral service. There are also court reporter associations in most states. Contact NCRA for an association in your area and referrals to court reporter schools.

CompuServe Court Reporters' Forum. Founded in 1992, the Forum now has over 1,400 members, including a special section for scopists. Scopists find work through contacts made on this forum. Obtain a CompuServe starter kit at a retail store or call CompuServe at (800) 872-4768 for information on how to join.

COURSES

At-Home Professions, 2001 Lowe St., Ft. Collins, CO 80525; (800) 359-3455. Their course teaches reading stenotype but not how to use a specific court reporter software package.

Legal Service Institute, 1436 Bugle Lane, Clearwater, FL 34624; (813) 531-2637 or (215) 755-2437.

In addition, scopists may attend many of the 400 court reporter training programs offered throughout the U.S. Although the court reporting program takes two years or more, scopists can finish in much less time. A few schools have specific short programs for scopists:

The Court Reporting Institute, Philadelphia, PA; (215) 854-1853. Eight months in the evening (three nights per week).

The Denver Academy of Court Reporting, Denver, CO; (303) 427-5292.

Wisconsin Indianhead Technical College, New Richmond, WI; (715) 246-6561, ext. 4347. A.A. degree as scopist/notereader.

BOOKS

Legal & Paralegal Businesses on Your Home-Based PC, Kathryn Sheehy Hussey and Rick Benzel, Blue Ridge Summit, PA: Windcrest/McGraw Hill, 1994; (310) 391-8024.

■ ■ ■ ■ ■

SECURITY CONSULTANT

One way of doing something about the sense of being bombarded and threatened by crime is making a career in the security field. The private security field is growing because security considerations are increasingly a routine part of everything from building design to organizational policy. Indications are that security concerns will be with us well into the future.

According to Steve Keller, security consultant and former executive director of the International Association of Private Security Consultants, there are three subfields in the security area:

Certified Site Consultant. This type of security consultant evaluates the physical design of buildings and spaces on site. He or she goes to the location, checks out the needs, and writes a report on what is needed, be it live security via guards or electronic security via cameras and electric lights, or a combination of methods. As a certified consultant, this person may recommend but not sell equipment, such as alarms or video monitoring systems.

Systems Designer. This type of consultant does work at the design phase of consulting, drawing up the plans for new and established sites using computer software to diagram and evaluate the security needs. The designer may also develop new electronic tools to be used at a location.

Academic/Expert Witness. This type of security consultant may teach security to law-enforcement officials and others, as well as serve as an expert witness in legal proceedings in which the security of a location has been broken (fires, thefts, break-ins, etc.).

Security consultants may or may not be private investigators. In any case, these fields may overlap. For example, security consultants may conduct background investigations on personnel and preemployment screenings for their clients—services that private investigators also provide.

Steve Keller is certified as a security consultant, and he focuses primarily on museums and historical sites. Because of his special expertise, Keller finds himself traveling around the globe to work with many of the world's most prestigious museums that are his clients. His knowledge of the many security measures to preserve artwork and sculpture from fire, theft, and vandalism have made him well known. But Keller points out that specialization is a major key to success in this field. The more you specialize and develop a knowledge base in one area, the greater the chances of building your business through word of mouth and referrals, because similar security measures are needed by similar types of businesses or sites.

Unlike private investigators, security consultants are not licensed. Professional recognition in the field is achieved by passing a rigorous examination given by one of the two associations listed below.

☑ Knowledge and Skills You Need to Have

- Several universities now grant degrees in security administration; however, experience in crime prevention through working in a police department, military-police unit, or doing survey work for a private security service will provide the necessary knowledge and experience.
- You need the ability to analyze situations and sites. Because many of your jobs may require you to write a full security report, you should also be able to write acceptable, error-free English.
- You need to know how to draft and read blueprints. If you do design, you should also be able to use a computer and architectural drawing software.
- You must know how to use electronic equipment like closed-circuit TVs.

🐷 Start-up Costs

	Low	High
Computer with hard disk and modem	$1,000	$3,000
Fax machine	300	900
Printer	300	1,600
Suite software (word processing, spreadsheet, and database)	250	400
Errors and omissions insurance*	700	2,000
Office furniture, especially ergonomic chair	400	1,000
Brochure	100	1,000
Business cards, letterhead, envelopes	100	600
Camera	100	200
Tools	100	300
Total	$3,350	$11,000

* Errors and omissions insurance is a necessity in this business.

⬆ Advantages

- Security consultants command professional respect and provide valued services.
- New technologies introduced into security work make the field challenging and interesting.

⬇ Disadvantages

- It takes at least two years to establish a clientele.
- To succeed as a security consultant, you've got to be good at it.
- People summon you only when they have a problem.

💲 Pricing

Security consultants can command from $75 to $150 per hour.

🖳 Potential Earnings

TYPICAL ANNUAL GROSS REVENUES: $75,000, based on billing 1,000 hours a year at $75 per hour.

OVERHEAD: moderate (20 percent or less).

📈 *Best Home Businesses* Estimate of Market Potential

Total number of security consulting firms in the United States, including home-based businesses: 4,934. As stated earlier, security is a growing field. Not only are companies and individuals increasingly concerned about security, but the increasing amount and complexity of security technology is driving the need for more specialized expertise.

▶ Best Ways to Get Business

Other than specializing and finding a niche market as advised by Keller, the following are the best ways to get clients:

- Getting articles you've written published
- Getting publicity about your work
- Direct mail to a limited targeted group, followed up by phone calls
- Yellow-pages advertising
- Networking and personal contacts in organizations, such as trade associations and professional associations for the type of clientele you are seeking (industrial, law firms, educational, historic sites, etc.)
- Getting listed in bar-association directories of expert witnesses

🗒 First Steps

- If you do not have enough experience to qualify you as a security consultant, the best way to obtain the necessary knowledge and experience is to take a job in which you conduct surveys of new-client premises for a private security service.
- Become certified by the International Association of Private Security Consultants.

⬜ Where to Turn for Information and Help

ORGANIZATIONS

American Society for Industrial Security, 1655 North Fort Myer, Suite 1200, Arlington, VA 22209; (703) 522-5800. Offers certification.

International Association of Professional Security Consultants, 7910 Woodmont Avenue, Suite 1430, Bethesda, MD 20814-3105; (301) 913-0030. This association is for private consultants but requires one year experience to join. They do offer some training materials, though, and an annual conference. Offers certification.

BOOKS

Security Consulting, Charles A. Sennewald, Boston: Butterworths, 1989. The classic text in the field.

MAGAZINES

Security Magazine, Box 5080, Des Plaines, IL 60018.

Security Management, American Society for Industrial Security (see above).

Security, Technology, and Design, published by Steve Lasky, Park Ridge, IL; (708) 692-5940.

TRAINING VIDEOS

Horizon Institute, Inc., produces a number of training videos in the security consulting area, including *How to Be a Successful Security Consultant,* P.O. Box 5757, Deltona, FL 32728; (904) 789-3225.

■ ■ ■ ■ ■

SPECIALTY CONSULTANT

In the profile of Management Consulting that appears earlier in the book, we point out that there are an estimated 500,000 consultants of all kinds in the country. The largest categories of consulting are management, marketing, and computer consulting, but there are still hundreds and perhaps even thousands of other areas of consulting and specialized individual consultants who focus on very particular areas of business, science, education, technology, and dozens of other professions. (This book covers several of these specialties separately—image consultant, professional practice consultant, wedding consultant, and security consultant.)

Specialty consultants include:

■ "hard side" professionals such as technical people in mathematics, mechanical engineering, chemical engineering, physical sciences, space sciences, medical areas, television and radio electronics, and the many other mathematical/scientific fields

■ "soft side" professionals such as people in human resources, health administration, education, law, government, and business.

As we mentioned in the Management Consulting entry, a critical factor fueling the drive to consulting is that companies can no longer afford to maintain permanently on staff the kinds of expertise they need only from time to time. A company that formerly had on staff both a mechanical engineer and an electrical engineer might have only one (or neither) on staff today and would hire out for the expertise on a piecemeal basis. As Paul Franklin, director of the National Training Center and editor of *The Professional Consultant* newsletter, points out, a new era has also dawned in the workforce: more and more people are intentionally seeking the kind of lifestyle and career of consulting. In the past, says Franklin, many people would try consulting, but if a job opened up, they would take it. Now, once they become freelance consultants, they more often stick with it and make it their primary occupation. One proof of this, for instance, is the tremendous growth in consultant associations and special-interest groups.

Specialty consultants frequently enter the business after losing a long-standing job in which they became experts in a particular field or masters of an entire domain for one company. They begin by continuing to work for that company on a part-time or contract basis but then often realize that there are other companies that can also use their expertise and experience. In fact, we frequently found that specialty consultants eventually learn to broaden their business by combining their different skills and interests along with their expertise and experience. Some get into projects at a very early stage, helping the company formulate their plans and then overseeing the implementation.

Gary and Susie Kenny, of SF&K Writing & Design, for example, are specialty consultants who focus on work patterns and computers. Susie, who has a background in financial banking, and Gary, who is a writer, now work with banks and financial institutions that are renovating or upgrading their business procedures to computerize and streamline their information-handling ability. Gary and Susie work directly with the bank to evaluate and plot the work flow, and then they work with the computer programmers and designers to implement a system that fits the bank's requirements. They specialize even further in planning workflow procedures using document-imaging systems.

A few other specialty consultants we have met also realize that they can make money by selling any supplies or equipment they are recommending. Jack Layton, a radio broadcasting veteran for many years, for example, left his company after a downsizing and realized that there were over 2,000 radio stations that could use his technical background. He decided to do consulting in broadcasting and two-way radio communications. He has now also branched out into selling the kinds of equipment that stations need if they are updating their studios.

The range of specialty consultants is vast, and we have met many of them, from graphological to architectural to environmental to geochemical to toxic waste to parenting experts . . . and the list goes on. *John Naisbitt's Trend Report* projects three fast-growing areas including consulting on environmental compliance, diversity in the workplace, and retirement planning. Whatever your background, however, there is probably a consultancy career open to you, as long as you can find enough clients to whom you can sell your knowledge or for whom you can parlay that knowledge into other related work.

☑ Knowledge and Skills You Need to Have

Many of the same knowledge and skills described under Management Consulting apply to this entry. In addition to those, we would add the following:

- Specialty consulting is just that: you must have a real specialty with some substantive experience and expertise to sell. Without a true specialty and experience in it, you won't get sufficient recognition to draw in clients. However, newly passed laws and regulations at the federal, state, and sometimes local level create demand for people who are able quickly to learn more than anyone else. Newly introduced technology can afford such a window as well. A well-known name in desktop video was a cook when he heard about a new technology that interested him.

▣ Start-up Costs

	Low	High
Computer with hard disk and modem (or laptop computer)	$1,000	$4,000
Fax machine	300	900
Laser printer	300	1,600
Color ink-jet printer	350	600
Suite software (word processing, spreadsheet, and database) and contact management software	250	400
Specialized software: contact manager, presentation software	250	500
Copier	300	800
On-line services	200	500
Errors and omissions insurance	200	500
Office furniture, especially ergonomic chair	400	1,000
Business cards, letterhead, envelopes	100	600
Organizational dues to a consultants' organization	250	250
Organizational dues to organizations in the field in which you have your specialty	250	500
Reference books and continuing education	400	1,000
Total	$4,550	$13,150

⬙ Advantages

- Because of your special knowledge, you may be accorded a lot of respect and attention.

- You will likely have little competition. In some fields, there may be only two or three people who do what you do, or a few hundred at the most. That means, whenever a business needs your type of knowledge, the chances are good that you will be called to bid on the project.
- Consulting is a perfect home-based business. You can work with clients anywhere, while maintaining a low-expense home office.

⚏ Disadvantages

- The failure rate is high, according to Jim Kennedy of Kennedy Publications, a management publishing company. Not everyone has the personality or counseling skills that must supplement their technical expertise to be successful.
- By nature, consultants are independent types who get bored with the work and need to move on to a new project and a new challenge. Consultants must, therefore, learn to stick to a project until they finish it.
- Your specialty may be too small, so the number of companies that need your services may not be sufficient to support a full-time livelihood or they are spread out over the continent or the world and you may not be able effectively to market to create the critical mass necessary to sustain a specialty practice. You may need to branch out into other areas, but in so doing you may lose the distinction and advantage of being a specialist.
- Depending on your specialization, you may have clients all over the country or world who require you to travel frequently or for long periods of time.
- Some contracts can obsess you to death; you need to learn to separate work from family time.

⑤ Pricing

Much of this kind of consulting is done on an hourly or daily basis. Specialists command the highest prices, whatever the market will bear: from $50 to $250 per hour in general. You can easily test the waters by quoting the highest price you can imagine and seeing if your client blinks. If so, simply back down and negotiate a lower fee, which may be best done by customizing the work order to have some reasonable relationship to what you stated your original fee to be. Expect former employers, who may have reduced their workforce to the point where they can no longer do their primary work, to pay you a premium—a multiple of your prior salary plus fringe benefits.

▣ Potential Earnings

TYPICAL ANNUAL GROSS REVENUES: $30,000 to $120,000 per year, based on billing fifteen to thirty hours per week for forty weeks at $50 to $100 per hour. (Your hourly rate makes a big difference, as you can see, so start as high as you can.)

OVERHEAD: low (20 percent or less).

⟟ *Best Home Businesses* **Estimate of Market Potential:**

The same factors that propel the demand for management consulting apply to specialty consulting fields. The continuing reality of shrinking organizations and outsourcing of work and functions will benefit those who have the ability to provide their advice and assistance on an independent basis.

⬛ Best Ways to Get Business

- Consultants tend to be point-in-time marketers: they pick up the phone and call five former clients to see if anyone has any work for them; when the answer is no, they let it go. Instead, says Paul Franklin, you need to define your target market and learn how to keep your name in front of the people who have work to give out. These people are inundated with offers from consultants. We call this "top of the mind marketing"; if you want these people to remember your name, you must be at the top of their minds whenever they have work to give out. That means frequent phone calls to say hello, sending faxes or articles of interest to them, and other techniques—often the more creative the better—to keep you on the "top of their minds."

- Build a relationship with your clients. It's not simply like hiring a guru; you are not selling only your expertise, you are selling yourself as a problem solver. And once they are convinced you have a track record, they will check if you have the breadth and depth to handle the job. More and more consulting is coming to mean implementing, not just advising.

- Nurture repeat and referral business consistently and continually; it is estimated that it costs a consultant five times more to get a new client than to get a contract with an old client.

See also the advice of Bill Mooney in the Management Consultant section.

⬚ First Steps

Paul Franklin suggests the following steps:

1. Frame a vision of what you want your business to be like in three years. Write down your business plan in as much detail as you can. The forty-

seven questions and the structure for answering them in our book *Making Money with Your Computer at Home* can help you with this task.

2. Build a marketing plan for your first year. Identify what you will do to market your business. Recognize that you now have zero clients, so 100 percent of your time goes to marketing.

3. Figure out a way to differentiate yourself from your competition, either by defining a specialty very tightly or by creative pricing or contracting.

🖸 Where to Turn for Information and Help

ORGANIZATION

American Association of Professional Consultants, National Bureau of Professional Consultants, 3577 Fourth Ave., San Diego, CA 92103; (619) 297-2207. Association for the newcomer in consulting with less than five years experience. Membership costs $100 and includes a newsletter, resources, annual conference, and networking. Also allows you to take the American Management Association's self-study course that leads to a certificate in business management and consultancy, comparable to an MBA (takes about eighteen months to do). To join the AAPC, write a letter on your letterhead.

NEWSLETTER

Marketing Conferences and Seminars, by LEARN in Manhattan, Kansas. Newsletter for training people.

BOOKS

Building a Consulting Practice, Robert O. Metzger, Ph.D., Sage Publications, 1994.

Contract and Fee Setting Guide for Consultants and Professionals, Howard Shenson, New York: John Wiley, 1990.

Million Dollar Consulting, Alan Weiss, Ph.D., New York: McGraw-Hill, 1994.

MAGAZINES

Read any and all magazines in your field of specialization. Keep up to date with the names, companies, and technologies of your industry. Also read business publications, particularly what your clients and prospective clients read, such as *Business Week, Forbes, Fortune, Inc.,* and the *Wall Street Journal.* Each of these publications is read by more than 50 percent of senior corporate executives. Only the *Wall Street Journal* is read by a majority of small-business owners, according to a study of affluent Americans by Payment Systems, Inc. The business section of the local newspaper is read by 92 percent of executives and 84 percent of business owners.

■ ■ ■ ■ ■

TAX PREPARATION SERVICE

Although many people don't realize it, there's actually no license required at the federal level and in most states to do tax preparation. Pretty much anyone can hang out a shingle and claim to be able to help other consumers file their taxes. You don't need to be a CPA or a lawyer or even have a bachelor's degree in accounting. In fact, many CPAs, lawyers, or accounting people know very little about filing taxes because they specialize in other financial areas. Federal and state tax laws are a specialty in and of themselves.

Now we are *not* suggesting that you take this to heart and become an untrained tax preparer. One way to start this career is to go to a school such as those run by H&R Block to learn tax preparation. If you prove to be adept, you may be offered a position with the company providing the training, which gives you, in effect, a paid apprenticeship. However, the relatively limited knowledge you can acquire about the extremely complex tax systems of the federal government and most states may limit your ability to be self-employed and you may be circumscribed to working for a tax preparation company for only certain kinds of clients (mostly individuals).

A more lucrative alternative if you enjoy the puzzle of dealing with taxes is to become a licensed tax preparer known as an "enrolled agent." This category of tax preparer is still somewhat unknown, but the enrolled-agent (EA) designation is the only one specifically granted by the federal government to people who pass an exam and demonstrate proficiency in handling tax matters. (The Enrolled Agent status began in 1884.) An EA is entitled to appear before the IRS at hearings to represent their clients. EAs may prepare taxes for individuals, corporations, partnerships, estates, trusts, and any entities with tax-reporting requirements.

There are no academic requirements to become an EA; you must pass, however, a rigorous two-day examination given by the IRS each year, and following your acceptance as an EA, you must complete seventy-two hours of continuing-education courses every three years. Only about 30 percent of the applicants taking the IRS exam pass each year, because the examination is quite rigorous. Although there are about 375,000 CPAs in the country, there are only about 35,000 EAs. If you have worked for the IRS for five years, you don't need to take the test.

Gary Lundgren of Lundgren Tax Consulting in Minneapolis worked for a state tax agency and now focuses on clients who are in trouble with the agency and facing collection procedures. Gary helps clients who are about to lose their bank accounts or even their homes or businesses. He files appeals and even appears before the IRS for his clients, aiming to reduce their tax liability (and often winning large concessions). As Gary acknowledges, it helps to specialize in a particular area of taxes because it is hard to know it all, and specialization allows you to charge more.

Whatever your personal feelings are about taxes, they are an inescapable aspect of life, like birth and death, as the saying goes. So if you enjoy numbers and finance, tax preparation may be just the career for you.

☑ Knowledge and Skills

- You need to have a good mind for figures and a feel for the process of calculating taxes. This helps you be more efficient in your work and recognize when something is not right.
- You need to be able to read quickly and understand the implications of tax cases.
- You need to have an interest in your clients' situations, being empathetic while remaining professional so as not to put yourself at risk for a client who falsifies information. You should have high moral and ethical standards.
- You should be willing to work and study hard to pass a rigorous standard exam and to maintain your professional knowledge. Tax law keeps changing, so you must recognize that this career requires constant learning.

🐖 Start-up Costs

	Low	High
Computer with hard disk and modem	$1,000	$ 3,000
Fax machine	300	900
Printer	300	1,600
Copy machine (high quality because you need to make many copies of forms and returns)	500	1,500
Suite software	250	400
Special tax preparation software that prints tax forms and sends electronic filings	200	1,200
Reference materials (books, tax guides, CD-ROM publications of tax codes and interpretations updated each year)	500	3,000
Errors and omissions insurance	200	1,200
Office furniture, especially ergonomic chair	400	1,000
Brochures	100	1,000
Business cards, letterhead, envelopes	100	600
Total	$3,850	$15,400

🔼 Advantages

- Tax preparation is a good business and is going to get better because, according to new guidelines, the government and the IRS are becoming more aggressive in seeking people who do not file or who take advantage of the system. The IRS will also be requiring more Americans to file their taxes electronically (by 1995); this means that more tax returns will be done by professionals who will have the approved software for electronic filing.

- The tax business can be very lucrative; tax specialists can charge $100 per hour.

- Understanding taxes can make you, contrary to popular opinion, popular at parties. Everyone will want to know if you can help them.

Disadvantages

- Taxes are extremely convoluted and confusing. The last major tax reform was in 1986, and since then there have already been 5,000 changes passed by Congress. It is nearly impossible to keep up with the field. You need to devote about one day per week simply to reading new tax laws or their interpretation by other people.

- Most tax preparation is seasonal. You need to plan your cash flow well.

- Doing taxes can become repetitive and dull, although every company or situation is different.

- You are at some level of risk if you have an unscrupulous client who blames you for errors based on misstatement of facts. At the same time, your confidentiality is equally important; the IRS will penalize you and cause you to be criminally prosecuted for disclosing confidential information to third parties who don't have a right to know information about your client.

- You need lots of storage space because IRS regulations require you to keep copies of your clients' tax returns (for three years).

Pricing

Most standard tax preparation is done at a rate per tax form filled out, ranging from $80 to $100 for a simple 1040 return. Complex tax returns are often handled at an hourly rate, such as $25 to $150 per hour depending on the nature of the work, and whether or not your client expects you to dig through a shoebox or has made your job easier by coming in with an organized file of tax information.

Potential Earnings

AVERAGE ANNUAL GROSS REVENUES: $75,000 to $140,000. The average tax preparer can handle up to 700 returns per year, at an average of $200 per return, hence $140,000 as a maximum capacity for a one-person shop.

? *Best Home Businesses* **Estimate of Market Potential:**

One seemingly immutable reality of our tax system is that it grows increasingly complex and demanding. The more complex the system, the more help people and businesses need in filing their taxes. People who help others with taxes should do well despite the ready availability of tax preparation software.

Best Ways to Get Business

- Word of mouth and referrals are the two best methods for tax preparers. Taxes are a personal matter, so people tend to use someone whom a friend has recommended as trustworthy and competent.

- Networking among CPAs and attorneys is also useful. They can refer clients to you.

- Advertising in local publications can bring in some clientele, particularly if you have a specialty that you can advertise: partnerships, collections/ audits, etc.

- Do a short mailing list to people or new businesses that have moved into your area; you can buy it from a list broker at a reasonable cost.

First Steps

1. If you have no tax background, you might begin by taking a course from a tax company such as H&R Block. This will allow you to test the waters and find out if you enjoy this kind of work. Once you pass their courses, you can work for a tax company and then consider taking the EA exam.

2. If you have some experience in taxation, you can prepare for the EA exam by studying last year's test, which is available from Commerce Clearinghouse (see information below). There are also some companies such as Thomas's that provide training for the exam.

Where to Turn for Information and Help

ORGANIZATION

National Association of Enrolled Agents (NAEA), 200 Orchard Ridge Drive, Suite 302, Gaithersburg, MD 20878; (301) 212-9608, fax (301) 990-1611. NAEA is the principal association for enrolled agents, with 8,000 members from among the 29,000 enrolled agents in the country. They also have local chapters. For those interested in the career, they offer a home-study course ($110) that takes roughly three months to prepare for the IRS exam. Once you become an enrolled agent, NAEA offers marketing and PR materials you can use in your business and a National Tax Practice Institute to teach EAs how to specialize in representation before the IRS, which increases your ability to take on difficult audit cases.

Federated Tax Service, 2021 W. Montrose Ave., Chicago, IL 60618; (800) 621-5199.

National Association of Enrolled Agents (NAEA), 200 Orchard Ridge Drive, Suite 302, Gaithersburg, MD 20878; (301) 212-9608, fax (301) 990-1611. Has a home-study course for exam candidates that takes about three months to do. They also have a National Tax Practice Institute for four days each year in which you can get specialized training in representing clients before the IRS.

National Association of Tax Practitioners, 720 Association Drive, Appleton, WI 54914; (800) 558-3402 ([800] 242-3430 in Wisconsin), offers a training seminar.

Thomas Tax Seminars, 4833 Skycrest Way, Santa Rosa, CA 95405; (800) 638-3763, offers a home-study course that takes between 65 to 100 hours to complete.

NEWSLETTERS

Tax Hotline, P.O. Box 38477, Boulder, CO 80322; (800) 288-1051. A monthly newsletter for anyone interested in taxes. $59 per year.

Tax Wise Money, Agora Inc., 824 East Baltimore Street, Baltimore MD 21202; (800) 433-1528. $39 per year.

BOOKS

Commerce Clearing House (800-TELL-CCH) is one of the largest American publishers of guides and professional materials in book form and on CD-ROM for tax preparers. The following publications are useful:

U.S. Master Tax Guide (also available on floppy disk)
IRS publications
Internal Revenue Manual
state tax reports
Federal Tax Weekly (a newsletter)
CCH SmartTax (CD-ROM product with Federal Tax Service and IRS-related publications and information)
Research Institute of America, 90 Fifth Avenue, Second Floor, New York, NY 10011; (800) 431-9025; (212) 645-4800, fax (212) 337-4280, is another highly respected publisher of tax information.

Another book recommended by practitioners is:

How to Practice IRS: A Procedural Manual for Practitioners, Robert Schriebman, Commerce Clearing House; (800) TELL-CCH; 1992.

SOFTWARE

There are many software programs available for professionally preparing taxes, ranging from $99 to $4,000. Among these are:

1040 Professional Tax Consultant, Stallion Software, Inc., P.O. Box 1505, Sugar Land, TX 77487-1505; (713) 242-0288.

1040 Professional Tax Preparation Package, Dunphy Systems, Inc., 6740 Huntley Rd., Suite 103, Columbus, OH 43229; (614) 431-0846, fax (614) 431-0776.

ProSystem fx for Windows, CCH Computax Inc., 800 West 6th St., Suite 1100, Los Angeles, CA 90017; (800) 45-PROFX and (213) 624-9571, fax (213) 955-2144.

TaxShop 1040, TenKey Publishing, Inc., 5422 Carrier Drive, Orlando, FL 32819; (800) 639-1040 and (407) 351-0966, fax (407) 351-3525.

Ultratax/1040, Creative Solutions, Inc., 7322 Newman Blvd., Dexter, MI 48130; (800) 968-8900 and (313) 426-5860, fax (313) 426-5946.

■ ■ ■ ■ ■

TECHNICAL WRITER

If you have an interest in things technical and the ability to write clearly and logically you can earn up to $800 a day in the continuously growing field of technical writing and editing. In fact, the need for technical writers is so strong that the Bureau of Labor Statistics projects a 34 percent increase in the number of professionals between now and the year 2000. By some estimates, there are already more than 100,000 technical writers in the United States and up to 25 percent of those are home based.

Technical writers may work on a wide range of projects. In fact, whenever any new product involving technology is introduced, information in the form of brochures, manuals, reference cards, instructional materials, reviews, and media releases needs to be developed for a variety of audiences: the buyers of the product; the users (who may be different from the buyers); the people who install the product and those who repair it; and, of course, the people who sell and promote it. Each of these audiences creates a need for a different type of information.

In a nutshell, technical writing has four distinct markets:

1. Writing articles for trade and popular magazines to explain concepts or products to tradespeople or consumers
2. Writing publicity materials, such as press releases and feature articles, for manufacturing and service companies that need editorial coverage in business and consumer publications

3. Writing and editing technical books and instructional materials, including computer hardware and software documentation

4. Writing technical information about new products and processes in the form of user manuals, instruction booklets, and policy and procedure manuals.

All these areas are lucrative and open to the person who knows a field well and can present information in the format required.

Harriet Serenkin, a technical writer based in New York City, primarily writes computer documentation for corporations and manuals for popular word-processing programs like *WordPerfect* and *Word for Windows*. Having majored in math, she worked at the American Institute of Physics, where she got on-the-job training in technical copyediting, and had experience as a science editor at a publishing house. The charm of freelancing appealed to her, though, so she eventually decided to go out on her own.

Serenkin gets most of her business through networking, particularly with colleagues in professional associations such as the Editorial Freelancers' Association, the Society for Technical Communication, and the New York PC Users Group. "I am constantly marketing," she says. "I always have business cards with me and give them out generously." She strongly believes in becoming active in trade groups—joining committees, attending meetings, getting to know others in the field. She also occasionally does some things for free, just to get publicity—such as writing a "tips and tricks" column for her PC Users Group newsletter. Through her column, she has gotten paying writing jobs.

☑ Knowledge and Skills You Need to Have

- Technical writers must have good writing skills and knowledge of a few specific scientific areas such as engineering, chemistry, computers, electronics, or medicine.

- You need to have the ability to understand and translate technical information into terms that are clear and understandable to nontechnical readers.

- You must be able to learn about new high-technology products in order to understand what must be communicated and at the same time have an appreciation for the needs of people who may have little knowledge, experience, or patience with technology.

- You must have an organized mind so that the manuals you write and edit flow logically. You should also be able to think visually to help determine when an illustration can help your writing.

☕ Start-up Costs

	Low	High
Computer with hard disk and modem	$1,000	$3,000
Ink-jet or laser printer	300	1,600
Suite software	250	400
Office furniture, especially an ergonomic chair	400	1,000
Business cards, letterhead, envelopes	100	600
Total	$2,050	$6,600

🖳 Advantages

- You can set your own hours and work whenever you want to in your home-office.
- An increasingly technological world provides a favorable market for this type of work.
- Making technically difficult things understandable to people can be very rewarding.
- The work is varied enough so that you don't get bored.

🖵 Disadvantages

- Technical writing is hard work because you are dealing with information that is often difficult to explain, and if you don't have a background in what you're writing about, it can take time to learn about it before writing.
- Sometimes the pressures of working under tight deadlines can be stressful.
- If someone is interested in doing more creative and imaginative forms of writing, technical writing can seem restrictive.
- You seldom know where your next job will come from. But this uncertainty can be a challenge; some people may find it exciting.

💲 Pricing

A 1993 (the most recent) survey by the Society for Technical Communication found the following rates charged by self-employed technical writers:

- under $20 per hour—6%
- $20 to $29—22%
- $30 to $39—40%
- $40 to $49—18%
- $50 to $60—7%
- over $60—4%

In addition, the 1994 edition of *Writer's Market* reports that technical writing fees range from $35 to $75 per hour, or $35 per manuscript page, depending on the degree of complexity and type of audience.

Writing articles for trade magazines can pay $400 to $500 per article. Technical writing on instructional design projects pays from $250 to $800 per day.

▣ Potential Earnings

TYPICAL ANNUAL GROSS REVENUES: $30,000 to $75,000, based on billing 1,000 hours per year (twenty hours per week) at $30 an hour at the low end or 1,250 hours per year (twenty-five hours a week) at $60 per hour at the high end.

Technical editing (not writing) averages $38 per hour, and an editor can expect to edit three to eight pages an hour. Technical editing is slow work because it takes time to figure out what the writer meant.

OVERHEAD: low (under 20 percent).

⚡ *Best Home Businesses* Estimate of Market Potential:

The increasing pace of introducing electronic products feeds the demand for technical writers People who can turn complex data into understandable instructions and information should do well. This service is not limited to print. Technical writing can take the form of on-line help, computer-based training, and CD-ROM self-help materials. Technical writers may extend their services to include desktop-publishing what they write.

▣ Best Ways to Get Business

- Networking and personal contacts in trade associations and computer user groups, and at trade shows where prospective clients exhibit
- Assignments from previous employers
- Responding to classified ads for technical writers in newspapers
- Placing ads in the trade publications read by your prospective clients in the fields in which you work
- Finding work through agencies that place temporary technical personnel, including technical writers
- Joining a writers' organization and using its job-referral service
- Directly soliciting work from the companies you want to write for, stressing the advantages of using freelance writers for peak workload situations. Michael Greer got 40 percent of his business this way.
- Becoming part of a trade publication's cadre of regular freelance contributors.

⚡ First Steps

- If your current employer has a need for technical writing, offer to take on assignments to build your portfolio and develop experience. You may make your former employer your first client when you go out on your own.

- Use the methods described in *Best Ways to Get Business* to break into the field.

🗋 Where to Turn for Information and Help

ORGANIZATIONS

The following organizations are composed of either purchasers of technical writing or people in the field of technical writing.

American Society of Engineering Education, 1818 N Street, N.W., Suite 600, Washington, DC 20036; (202) 331-3500.

American Society for Training and Development, 1640 King Street, P.O. Box 1443, Alexandria, VA 22313-2043; (703) 683-8100, fax (703) 683-8103. Publishes a journal and a catalogue of resources. Its special-interest groups are of particular interest to technical writers.

Editorial Freelancers' Association, 71 West 23rd Street, Suite 1504, New York, NY 10010; (212) 929-5400 (open 2–6 P.M., M–F), fax (212) 929-5439.

Institute for Electrical and Electronics Engineers, 345 East 47th Street, New York, NY 10017; (800) 678-4333; (212) 705-7900.

International Association of Business Communicators, 1 Hallidie Plaza, Suite 600, San Francisco, CA 94102; (415) 433-3400.

National Society for Performance and Instruction, 1300 L Street, N.W., Suite 1250, Washington, DC 20005; (202) 408-7969.

National Writers' Association, 1450 South Havana, Suite 424, Aurora, CO 80012; (303) 751-7844. Benefits include newsletters, research reports, consultation, marketing, agent referral, etc. Membership $50 (general) or $60 (professional; credits required).

Society for Technical Communication, 901 North Stuart Street, Suite 304, Arlington, VA 22203; (703) 522-4114. The society has local chapters, some of which have an employment referral service or résumé bank.

Writers' Guild of America West, 8955 Beverly Boulevard, West Hollywood, CA 90048; (310) 550-1000. **Writers' Guild of America East,** 555 West 57th Street, New York, NY 10019; (212) 245-6180. Publishes the *Directory of Informational Program Writers*.

BOOKS

Designing, Writing and Producing Computer Documentation, Lynn Denton and Jody Kelly, New York: McGraw-Hill, 1993.

ID Project Management: Tools & Techniques for Instructional Designers & Developers, Michael Greer, Englewood Cliffs, NJ: Educational Technical Publication, 1992; (800) 952-BOOK.

Instructional Design: Principles and Applications, Leslie J. Briggs et al., Englewood Cliffs, NJ: Educational Technology Publications, 1991.

Literary Marketplace with Names and Numbers. New York: R. R. Bowker Company. Published annually.

Principles of Instructional Design, Robert M. Gagne et al., HarperCollins Publishers, 1992.

The Technical Writer's Freelance Guide, Peter Kent, New York: Sterling, 1992.

Writer's Market: Where and How to Sell What You Write. Cincinnati, Ohio: Writer's Digest Books. Published annually.

MAGAZINES AND NEWSLETTERS

Sources of information about what various publications are doing and who is coming out with what new products:

Adweek, Network A/S/M Communications, 1515 Broadway, New York, NY 10036; (800) 722-6658; (212) 536-5336.

American Journalism Review, 8701 Adelphi Road, Adelphi, MD 20783; (800) 827-0771; (301) 431-4771.

COURSES

United States Department of Agriculture Graduate School offers reasonably priced courses in English and writing skills. Write for a catalogue: Graduate School, USDA, South Agriculture Building, 14th Street and Independence Avenue, S.W., Washington, DC 20250. Or call to speak with a course counselor at (202) 447-2187.

See corporate training for the Society of Applied Learning Technology.

✚ Related Business

Manual Developer (Safety and Employee). Companies of all sizes need comprehensive, informative, and legally passable documents for their employee manuals. Nearly every company that employs more than ten or fifteen people must have available standard and consistent information that spells out for employees the policies and procedures for performance reviews and promotions, termination, sexual harassment, vacation and benefit terms, regulations on safety and substance abuse, dress codes, employee development, and many other issues. But although large companies have an in-house personnel department, many smaller ones cannot afford a full-time permanent position in the human-resources area. As a result, companies can either purchase off-the-shelf employee manuals or hire an outside writer to help them tailor one to their needs.

This is a good sideline business particularly for a technical writer who understands government regulations on safety and hazardous materials. As OSHA and other government agencies increase the number of regulations that companies must follow, we expect that this business will increase..

Several software products on the market that can help you produce the manuals in an efficient manner include the *Employee Handbook Toolkit*, from Palo Alto Software (144 East 14th Avenue, Eugene, OR 97401; (800) 229-7526 or (503) 683-6162), which contains templates for forty-five standard issues in personnel, safety, compliance, and other areas of interest; and *SafetyPlanBuilder* and *EmployeeManualMaker*, both from Jian Tools for Sales, Inc. (1975 El Camino Real, Suite 301, Mountain View, CA 94040-2218; [415] 254-5600.) A book is *Business Environmental Handbook*, by Martin D. Westerman, Grants Pass, OR: PSI Research, 1994.

■ ■ ■ ■ ■

TEMPORARY-HELP AGENCY

When you think of a temporary-help service, you probably think of the traditional temp agency that provides secretarial, administrative, and clerical personnel. These services are the third-fastest-growing sectors of our economy, with an annual growth rate of over 10 percent a year. It would be difficult for a home-based business to compete head-to-head with traditional temp services, which are staffed with many employees who test, train, and place hundreds of temporary personnel in a single day.

Home-based businesses can, however, compete successfully as *specialized* temporary services. Specialized temporary services are the fastest-growing part of the temporary-help agency. In some fields they are referred to as *registries*. No doubt their growth is in response to the frustration employers experience when they call a regular temporary help agency but cannot get workers with a specialized skill. A specialized temporary service is able to send them just the type of specialist they need and save them the cost and time of looking for someone, training new personnel, and paying employee benefits.

A temporary agency can specialize in providing any type of personnel, including:

- attorneys
- association executives
- assemblers
- bookkeepers
- convention help
- court reporters
- data-processing personnel
- escrow personnel
- hospital social workers
- insurance workers

- legal secretaries
- librarians
- marketing specialists
- medical records personnel
- medical secretaries
- nurses
- paralegals
- pharmacists
- printing pressmen
- short-order cooks

You need not limit yourself to this list of known specialty services if another field you know of uses temporary workers in your market.

A specialized temporary service works like any other temp agency. The specialty service first recruits its pool of specialists. Then when clients need them, the specialists are put on the service's payroll. The service pays all the taxes and benefits and then bills the client companies that have used the temporary help at a rate that covers costs and profits. With the use of a personal computer, specialized temporary services can be operated from home and outperform the traditional larger services, because whereas the latter compete primarily on price, specialized temporary services can compete on the quality of the specialized personnel they are able to send out.

For several years, Judith A. Wunderlich operated the Wunderlich Graphic Agency from her home in the suburbs of Chicago. She specialized in finding freelance workers in the graphic-arts field, such as photographers, copy editors, proofreaders, designers of all types, desktop publishers, typesetters, copywriters, keyliners, and illustrators. She built a successful business, earning $50,000 in her first year while being a full-time mother and working fewer than thirty hours a week. So successful was she, in fact, that she expanded her business and now runs a full (permanent) placement agency *outside* her home, along with a printing and graphics studio.

Wunderlich says that home-based temp agencies remain viable, even though some people are slow to accept the idea. She points out that the companies with whom she placed people never knew she was home based, because she worked with them exclusively over the phone. "The biggest problem for a home-based temp agency is when you have employees," she says. Most localities have zoning restrictions that restrict the number of employees a home-based business can have. Some even prohibit employees who are not members of your immediate family.

You should also check with your state labor department to find out if there are any state licensing requirements for home-based temp agencies. Wunderlich says there are none in Illinois and thinks the majority of states don't license temp agencies, but it is a good idea to investigate first so as to avoid problems later on.

One way to locate specialists for your agency is to run classified ads. Once a specialist contacts you, you should put him or her into a computer database. As with most services, many of these specialists are self-employed individuals who want temp work to tide them over while they start their own businesses. They do not want to be permanent employees.

When a company requests a particular type of specialist, you can simply turn to your database to locate a person whose qualifications meet the employer's needs. Wunderlich points out, however, that you should be careful to include each specialist's complete employment history in your database so that you never send anyone to a company from which he or she has been laid off.

☑ Knowledge and Skills You Need to Have

- You need to have a knowledge of and contacts in the field you're specializing in, so stick to what you know. Nurses, for example, operate the best temporary nurses' registries.

- You need to know how to use a computer and database software.

- You should know something about the routines and forms a temporary service uses, such as time sheets and contracts.

- You need to be organized and adept at record keeping because you will have to keep track of which specialists you have sent out, for how much time, and at what price. This is a task you can accomplish more easily with special software.

🐂 Start-up Costs

	Low	High
Computer with hard disk and modem	$1,000	$ 3,000
Ink-jet or laser printer	300	1,600
Fax	300	900
Suite software, payroll, scheduling, and accounting with a payroll module (unless you use an outside payroll service)*	900	2,100
Telephone headset	40	70
Office furniture, especially an ergonomic chair	400	1,000
Business cards, letterhead, envelopes	100	600
Brochure	100	1,000
Organizational dues	250	250
Forms, time cards, and contracts	n/a	50
Attorney's fee for consultation on employment laws, taxation, and potential liability	150	500
Liability insurance to protect you from lawsuits arising from acts of your employees	600	600
Working capital	5,000	20,000
Total	$8,840	$30,770

* Specialized software for temp services that has a database with payroll and accounting capabilities costs $10,000, but it is not necessary for a small service.

Advantages

- Most of your work is done on the phone, so this is a home business that truly allows you to do most of your work *at* home.

- This business provides high earnings relative to the time and energy involved.

- There are no materials and no inventory. The business can almost run itself.

- You're not doing the work; the temps are. Therefore, your income is not limited by the number of hours you work.

- There's a strong need for this service.

- It can be a fifty-two-week-a-year business because even holidays and vacation times can be busy.

- Temporary-help services do better than most businesses during recessions.

Disadvantages

- Cash flow is the challenge of this business because you must pay the specialists at least every other week, but there is a delay between the time you must pay them and when you will be paid. Therefore you need to make certain not to rely too heavily on only one client. Some services offer a 2 percent discount for payment within a specified number of days.

- Unless you are willing to grow very slowly, you need to have a nest egg of about $20,000 to cover operating expenses. This may mean taking out a loan.

- You need to keep up with the changing tax, workers'-compensation, and employment laws. These changes affect your responsibilities to the specialists you employ.

- You have a potential liability for employee misconduct; therefore, you need insurance to cover yourself. It may be wise to incorporate as well, although incorporation increases your cost of doing business and involves additional red tape.

- You may need to bond employees, depending on the type of temps you provide.

Pricing

You mark up the going salary for specialists by 40 to 50 percent, depending upon availability and skill level. The more skilled the specialist, the higher the pay rate. To stay in touch with the going rates for full-time employees in your field, keep current with trade publications and the latest information published by the Bureau of Labor Statistics.

▣ Potential Earnings

TYPICAL ANNUAL GROSS REVENUES: Income will vary depending on the value of the specialists you are placing and how many specialists you place each week. Based on ten people working fifteen hours a week at $21 an hour fifty-two weeks a year, and after deducting payroll costs and the employer share of payroll taxes, you will have $69,628, from which you will deduct your other business costs.

OVERHEAD: modest (20 to 40 percent).

▥ *Best Home Businesses* Estimate of Market Potential:

Total number of temporary employment firms in the United States, including home-based businesses: 23,337. As we write this, the economy is in recovery; jobs are being created. For every job that is being created in the "permanent" workforce, ten temporary jobs are created. Manpower, Inc., is the nation's largest private employer—employing more people than General Motors. In the nineties, finding a niche in the temporary-help field is one of *the* best home businesses.

▥ Best Ways to Get Business

- Sending out direct mail in the form of a letter, postcard, or brochure (depending on what your competition is doing). This works well because there is such a need for this service that customers will save mailers for years.
- Networking in business and trade associations in your field.
- Publishing a newsletter for past, current, and potential clients.
- Publicity about your special business.

▤ First Steps

Ideally, you would start in a field you know well. If you've worked in the medical field, for example, you could select a medical specialty. Or if you've worked in a bank, you could set up a bank-related service. If, however, you aren't in a field that lends itself to a temporary service, you can bring in experts to help you learn the ins and outs of the field.

For example, Linda Morse and Dorothea Green had no experience in the escrow field when they started Escrow Overload. To make up for their lack of knowledge, they hired escrow experts to help them develop tests and criteria for interviewing specialists for their database. Again when they expanded into Lender's Overload, they had never been loan officers, so they brought in loan processors to help them choose good personnel. Morse also suggests that going to one national convention of the National Association of Temporary Services will provide quite an education.

Mary Lou Ridgeway, finding herself out of a job after many years in the insurance industry, began placing people she knew in temporary positions. She found that insurance firms didn't think they could get skilled temps and welcomed the opportunity to let her help them; in the process she created a specialty for herself that has made her happier and more successful than she had ever been in an office job.

You can begin building your database of specialists by taking out classified ads in trade and professional publications in your specialty. There is little cost involved in building your database prior to opening your business. Another way of attracting personnel as you grow is to give referral bonuses to temps of yours who refer others to you. Once you have a strong pool of specialists, send out a direct-mail piece to employers who would have frequent needs for them.

☐ Where to Turn for Information and Help

ORGANIZATION

National Association of Temporary Services, 119 South Saint Asaph Street, Alexandria, VA 22312; (703) 549-6287. Your employees are eligible to join a group insurance plan through this organization, which also publishes the *National Association of Temporary Services Research Reference Kit,* a helpful guide to writing business plans for obtaining loans.

MANUAL

The Temporary Help Manual, National Association of Secretarial Services, 3637 Fourth Street North, Suite 330, St. Petersburg, FL 33704; (800) 237-1462 or (813) 823-3546. Although written for secretarial services, this manual outlines how to get started as an independent in the temporary-help field.

■ ■ ■ ■ ■

TRANSCRIPT-DIGESTING SERVICE

Providing that you have the ability to write clearly, this is a business that takes a minimal amount of time to learn, costs little to start, and has the potential for earning good money. As a transcript digester, also called a deposition digester, you become part of the legal field, summarizing statements taken under oath from parties involved in legal proceedings.

Lawyers do not like to be surprised in the courtroom when someone takes the stand. In fact, a legal maxim is to "never ask a question you don't know the answer to." Discovering what people are going to say before they appear at a trial plays an important role in the American legal system. So prior to a trial, lawyers take testimony in what is called a deposition. Depositions are recorded by a court reporter, and then the entire testimony is transcribed into a document that lawyers study carefully before the trial. As you can imagine, the transcripts are quite long, so to save time for the lawyers (many lawyers now charge up to $400 per hour), transcript digesters rewrite wordy, rambling, repetitive testimony using concise, well-organized, readable sentences. A good digester can condense the number of words in a transcript by 80 percent or more without cutting out relevant points.

Digesters also digest trial transcripts during the course of a trial. An attorney may need an expedited transcript of a previous day's proceedings to prepare for cross-examination. In lengthy trials, which can last for months, digests of prior testimony are essential. Digests are also used in making appeals.

Sometimes digests are prepared by trained paralegals. In fact, digesting transcripts is part of paralegal training, but a digest can also be done by someone who has the ability to analyze and write succinctly. As digester Mary Barnes points out, "Good writing skills are more important in this business than legal knowledge. The writing needs to flow so the transcripts don't have to be read two or three times.

Today more and more law firms are using outside services. In the five years since Barnes and her husband started their home-based digesting company, their business has expanded beyond the two of them to twenty part-time employees.

A digester's clients range from the solo practitioner to firms with 100 or more lawyers. Each firm has its own reasons for using independent digesters. The lawyer in solo practice may be buried in motions by a large firm and need outside help. The large law firms realize the economic advantage of using outside services who would bill at $90 an hour instead of a licensed attorney.

☑ Knowledge and Skills You Need to Have

- As a deposition digester, you must be familiar and comfortable with legal terminology and procedures so you can read and understand what is said in transcripts and condense it without changing the meaning.

- You must be able to read and type quickly. The faster you read and type, the higher your earnings.

- You must also be able to synthesize and write concisely. The digester's role is not to decide whether testimony is relevant, but to know how to condense it skillfully.

- Prior expertise in a field can be helpful in understanding whatever terminology might be involved in a trial. For example, a construction background would be useful in cases dealing with construction defects. In other cases, a general understanding of the principles of accounting, finance, or science might come in handy.

- You must prepare your digests on a computer using word-processing software, because you will be rewriting every paragraph two or three times in order to reduce the number of words. You should also know how to use a modem to transmit your completed digests.

■ Start-up Costs

	Low	High
Computer with hard disk	$1,000	$3,000
Printer	300	1,600
Word-processing software	250	400
Desk and ergonomic chair	400	1,000
Business cards, letterhead, envelopes	100	400
Brochure	100	1,000
Total	$2,150	$7,400

■ Advantages

- Transcript digesting pays better than such similar businesses as word processing and notereader/scopist.

- You can learn what you need to know to do this business in as little as three weeks, although you will continue to hone your skills as you work.

- The work is interesting and challenging. You learn useful information that you won't come across anywhere else.

■ Disadvantages

- The work is isolating. You are at your computer many hours each day.

- Because you are at the keyboard so long, you can suffer from computer-related disabilities. It's important to use an ergonomic chair, a keyboard pillow with wrist rests, and a glare screen. Also, you should get up frequently and walk around.

- This is a fairly new business. In many geographic areas, attorneys will not be familiar with outside digesting services, and you will have to persuade them that a skilled writer and nonattorney can do the work. The best way to do this is to assure them that you don't leave anything out, or select testimony you think is relevant. You understand everything but rewrite it in a concise form.

$ Pricing

Novice transcriptionists receive 80 cents per page. Experienced digesters get $2.50 to $4 per page. You'll earn substantially less when working through an agency, and agencies expect a digester to produce at least ten pages per hour. Ten to twenty pages per hour is typical for digesters in an eight-hour day.

Potential Earnings

TYPICAL ANNUAL GROSS REVENUES: $38,000 to $100,000.

OVERHEAD: low (20 percent or less).

Best Home Businesses Estimate of Market Potential:

The United States has 5 percent of the world's population and 66 percent of the world's lawyers, providing lots of clients for transcriptionists. Transcriptionists are part of a trend over the last several decades to use subprofessionals in order to control the cost of legal services. This trend will continue.

Best Ways to Get Business

- Making personal contacts with people in law firms
- Offering to digest one fifty-to-one-hundred-page deposition for free
- Looking for classified ads from law firms seeking digesters
- Using display ads in legal publications as a long-term investment to build your name recognition
- Directly soliciting law firms by phone and making an appointment to talk with them about your services. You can use a salesperson to set up appointments for you, but this person must know the business.
- Listing with agencies that will refer work to you

First Steps

If you have no experience, paralegal programs usually have courses in deposition digesting and writing skills. Or you can teach yourself using the tutorial listed below. Once you have mastered the skill, to gain experience you might consider working for an agency at first, before marketing yourself directly to law firms. You can locate deposition-digesting agencies in your community through ads in local legal publications.

⬜ Where to Turn for Information and Help

TUTORIALS/TRAINING COURSES

Hillside Digesting Services' Transcript Digesting Manual, P.O. Box 2888, Fallbrook, CA 92088; (800) 660-3376. A complete training course with exercises and samples; requires an IBM-compatible computer and word-processing software.

The Working From Home Forum on CompuServe offers files covering the basics of digesting transcripts, a sample deposition, and sample summaries in various formats. This material is available in Library 5.

BOOK

Legal & Paralegal Businesses on Your Home-Based PC, Kathryn Sheehy Hussey and Rick Benzel, Blue Ridge Summit, PA: Windcrest/McGraw-Hill, 1994; (310) 391-8024.

■ ■ ■ ■ ■

WEDDING CONSULTANT

Marriage has taken on a new importance in the 90s, and today's weddings are getting more expensive. Brides and grooms are older; often they both have careers. It's more likely that they are paying for their own wedding than that their parents are covering the bill. Many of today's brides and grooms are children of divorce or are returning to the altar for a second or third marriage; they want their marriages to last.

It's not that today's couples aren't cost-conscious, but they are creating a fantasy and they want it to be perfect. Gaining popularity are fully costumed theme weddings based on medieval and Renaissance times. A big wedding makes a psychological statement. It says, "We're taking this marriage seriously." It's almost as if the bigger and fancier the wedding, the more of a commitment it represents and therefore the greater the chances the marriage will last. Gerard Monaghan, president of the Association of Bridal Consultants, says, "Some brides have been designing their wedding since they were two and a half years old." The result is that weddings have become big business.

Brides and grooms and their families spend $33 billion a year to create the wedding day of their dreams. The informal family wedding of the past few decades has been replaced by the elaborate, formal wedding. In fact, today's weddings are more like productions, with the average wedding costing from $7,000 to $8,000, and some going as high as $200,000. (The typical planned wedding costs between $12,000 and $15,000.) Today's weddings usually involve a formal wedding gown and veil for the bride, a tuxedo for the groom, several bridesmaids and groomsmen, ushers, floral arrangements, invitations, special napkins, cake and table decorations, beverages, music, seating for 100 to 200 people, a photographer, a videotaping service, a wedding makeup artist, a catered reception or sit-down meal, and of course a dream honeymoon.

Producing this one-day event is a considerable task, and one for which most couples are not well prepared. Growing up in the more informal decades of blue jeans and beer, most couples today have little or no experience with how to create an elegant, formal occasion. And because the bride and her mother probably both work, they seldom have the time to organize such an event.

That's where the wedding consultant comes in. Also called *bridal consultants, wedding planners,* and *wedding coordinators,* wedding consultants play the role for the bride and groom that a contractor plays in building a dream home or a director plays in the making of a movie. The wedding consultant works with the bride and groom and their families to help the couple articulate what they want, establish a wedding budget, and create their dreams within it. The wedding is an event that needs to be planned and produced. The consultant coordinates the production of the wedding, from finding and renting the facilities to negotiating contracts and overseeing the many elements and personnel involved, such as florists, photographers, videographers, caterers, travel agents, musicians, and disc jockeys.

The wedding-consulting business has grown tremendously over the past several years. "Ten years ago there was no list of wedding consultants," says Gerard Monaghan. "Now there are approaching 10,000 wedding consultants listed in the yellow pages coast to coast." Of that number, about 50 percent are home based. Although Monaghan acknowledges that the number of weddings has dropped somewhat as a result of the baby boomers' passing the peak marrying age, he expects a new surge in weddings beginning in 1995 as the children of the boomers come of age. Thus, Monaghan predicts, the wedding-consulting business will grow substantially, and rapidly, over the next ten years—which means this is a particularly good time to get into the business. Also, he believes the amount spent on each wedding will continue to rise. Because wedding consultants typically work with weddings costing a minimum of $10,000, the upward drift of wedding spending should keep consultants busy for many years.

☑ Knowledge and Skills You Need to Have

- Wedding consultants need to be gregarious, enjoy pressure, and be able to keep their wits about them when all about them is in turmoil. They must be able to take the unexpected in stride and calm the nerves of those around them.

- This is a people business, so communication skills are a must. The wedding consultant must be an expert at helping all those involved handle the tensions and emotions of situations in which feelings about every little detail run deep. For example, Monaghan points out that "one of the unspoken functions of the wedding consultant is to serve as a buffer between brides and mothers." Therefore, knowledge of human behavior and psychology is helpful.

- Wedding consultants must be creative negotiators. They must develop solutions and negotiate prices with suppliers so that a wedding costing $10,000 seems like a wedding costing thousands more, thus justifying their fee.

- Wedding consultants need to be effective arbitrators to help the bride and groom reach decisions harmoniously on such things as the guest list, music, and facility—so that a wedding does, indeed, take place.

- Wedding consultants must keep up with and be knowledgeable about fashion, food, music, and wedding styles.

- Wedding consultants must have basic business and financial-management skills and organizational ability, not only to run their own business but also to oversee the wedding budget.

- A good wedding consultant is both creative and practical—creative enough to talk about the nuances of wedding gowns or make a VFW hall look like a palace, but practical enough to make sure everything gets ordered and delivered on time.

- You need contacts with high-quality, reliable wedding services: photographers, printers, florists, hotels, bakeries, makeup artists, jewelers, caterers, travel agents, musicians, and disc jockeys.

▰ Start-up Costs

	Low	High
Computer with hard disk and modem	$1,000	$ 3,000
Ink-jet or laser printer	300	1,600
Suite software	250	400
Office furniture, especially an ergonomic chair	400	1,000
Wardrobe*	500	5,000
Business cards, letterhead, envelopes	100	600
Brochure	100	1,000
Organizational dues	250	250
Total	$2,900	$12,850

* Wedding consulting is a glamour business, so you need to have a wardrobe, makeup, and hairstyling in accord with the image of your clientele. You need three types of outfits: (1) business suits for meetings with suppliers; (2) more casual yet attractive clothing for meeting with the bride and bridal party; (3) more formal attire appropriate for attending the wedding.

🔌 Advantages

- This is a glamorous, exciting, challenging business, and the work calls upon you to be creative.
- You are dealing with clients at one of the happiest times in their lives, so your work is fun.
- There is great satisfaction in creating a dream event that may live for a lifetime in a couple's memory and serve as an anchor for their marriage.
- You can branch out to plan other types of events, particularly in smaller communities, where there may not be enough weddings for a full-time business.

📉 Disadvantages

- The business can be very competitive and your profit margins small.
- The work is on weekends and at night, but this fact could be considered an advantage. Because it takes awhile to become self-supporting in this business, you can start on a part-time basis while you work at another job during the week.
- The work is seasonal. May, June, and July are very busy, but the winter months are slow, and although you're planning during the slow months, you can attend only so many weddings during the busy months.
- You are coordinating many elements over which you have no control.
- Because weddings are planned six months to a year in advance, it may be at least that long before you receive a fee. Payment arrangements should be spelled out in a letter of agreement signed by the consultant and the couple.

💲 Pricing

Wedding consultants may charge a flat fee, a per diem rate, or an hourly rate for their services. Flat fees may be from 10 to 15 percent of the wedding budget; because the average wedding involving a consultant costs $15,000, a typical fee may run from $1,500 to about $2,000. Per diem rates range from $300 to $600. Hourly rates range from $50 to $75. Consultants may also derive income, with the consent of their clients, by obtaining referral commissions from wedding suppliers.

🖥 Potential Earnings

TYPICAL ANNUAL GROSS REVENUES: $37,500, based on twenty-five weddings a year at $1,500 per wedding. There are approximately forty *marrying weeks* during the year, according to Gerard Monaghan. A full-time consultant can service fifty weddings a year.

OVERHEAD: low (20 percent or less).

🗲 *Best Home Businesses* **Estimate of Market Potential:**

Total number of wedding consulting firms in the United States, including home-based businesses: 7,861. As the cost of weddings continues to rise and working women (both mothers and brides) are unavailable to plan weddings, hiring an expert to manage them and help keep costs down seems like a winning solution to increasing numbers of people.

▣ **Best Ways to Get Business**

- Calling on, networking with, and cross-referencing to others providing wedding services: photographers, printers, florists, hotel and banquet-hall managers, bakeries, makeup artists, jewelers, caterers, travel agents, musicians, and disc jockeys
- Exhibiting at bridal shows (although purchasing a booth is expensive)
- Advertising in specialty wedding publications or guides
- Building visibility by advertising regularly in wedding supplements to local newspapers
- Listing in the yellow pages
- Getting repeat business by doing parties and other events like anniversaries for your clients, their family, and their friends
- Using direct mail to recipients of wedding planning guides, and sending out newsletters to prospective and past clients
- Offering free consultation for couples, advising them of what will be involved in planning their wedding. Use this time to establish a trusting relationship and to gather information for a written proposal you can submit to them after the meeting.

⬚ **First Steps**

- To gain some experience before you begin working on your own, work for free on a couple of weddings with an established consultant. The Association of Bridal Consultants (listed below) will provide names and addresses of members in your area.
- Establish a network of suppliers on whom you can rely. Attend bridal shows to get to know the trends.
- Organize weddings for friends and relatives for free, to build a portfolio of your work. Be sure to get pictures from the photographer.

⬚ **Where to Turn for Information and Help**

ORGANIZATIONS

Association of Bridal Consultants, 200 Chestnutland Road, New Milford, CT 06776; (203) 355-0464, fax (203) 354-1404. Has 1,300 members.

Membership is composed of all types of professionals working in the wedding industry. Bimonthly newsletter, professional development program, nationwide and regional co-op advertising, bridal and media referrals.

Books

Complete Wedding Planner, Edith Gilbert, Hollywood, FL: Fell Publishers, 1989.

Planning a Wedding to Remember, Beverly Clark, Los Angeles: Wilshire Books, 1989.

Weddings, Emily Post, New York: Simon and Schuster, 1975.

Magazines

Bride's, Conde-Nast, 140 E. 45th Street, New York, NY 10017; (800) 456-6162; (212) 880-8800.

Modern Bride, Cahners Publishing/American Baby, 519 Eighth Avenue, New York, NY 10018; (800) 777-5786; (212) 645-9700.

Vows, 1911 11th Street, Suite 209, Boulder, CO 80302; (303) 444-8333. The only trade publication in this field. (Members of the Association of Bridal Consultants can subscribe for two years for $25; normal subscription rate is $25 for one year.)

Training Course

The Institute of Consulting Careers, Inc., 222 S.E. 16th Street, Portland, OR 97214; (503) 240-0931, offers a program in learning the field of wedding consulting.

■ ■ ■ ■ ■

WEDDING MAKEUP ARTIST

Doing makeup for brides and bridal parties is an exciting and glamorous business. A wedding makeup artist provides on-location makeup services for brides and their attendants to make sure they look naturally beautiful for the ceremony, the photo sessions, and the video camera, which is used for taping the majority of today's weddings.

In recent years the wedding industry has undergone some changes that have led to the popularity of wedding makeup artists. The 1980s witnessed a rebirth of the large and lavish formal wedding and the birth of a wedding industry that includes wedding consultants, videographers, disc jockeys, makeup artists, and, of course, caterers and photographers. Most of these businesses are usually operated from home.

Every bride wants to look her most beautiful on that special day. And particularly in this increasingly media- and image-conscious era, wedding makeup artists are in demand even for modest weddings. But for today's bride, looking great has become an increasingly complex matter. Makeup that might look natural and vibrant in person can look washed out on film or video. Extra makeup to make their features stand out for video, however, can make the bride and her bridal party look too made-up in person. That's where the wedding makeup artist comes in. He or she is a specialist who understands how to make the bride and bridal party find the right balance to meet all the makeup demands of the wedding day.

The wedding makeup artist works with all kinds of clients, from young brides who are getting married for the first time to older brides who are remarrying. Two sessions are required in working with the bride. The first session, before the wedding, provides a time to find out about the plans for the wedding (the color scheme, number of people involved, and so forth) and to show the bride the various possibilities. Stephanie Belasco of Makeup Artistry in Westfield, New Jersey, calls this session the "dry run." It usually lasts an hour to an hour and a half. Then on the day of the wedding, the makeup artist arrives at the wedding site very early, before the photos are taken, does the makeup for the entire bridal party, and puts on the bride's headpiece. At this point, the makeup artist may either leave or stay on hand to touch up the makeup at various times during the festivities.

After the wedding, of course, you want the bride to continue as your client. So you can offer products and special makeup sessions as a way to stay in touch with your clients.

Although Stephanie Belasco doesn't sell products, her clients remain loyal for many years after the wedding. Belasco prides herself on spending "a lot of time, energy, love, and care" on her clients. She makes a point of listening to them and offering moral support. "I tell them it's their day, they're supposed to be relaxing and pampering themselves," she says. When she applies the makeup, she gives her clients a chance to watch what she does and practice so that they can achieve the same look in years to come without assistance. "I offer more than just a one-day service," she explains.

Belasco landed in this line of work quite by accident. Originally trained as a teacher, she entered the job market at a time when teaching jobs were scarce. She took a position in retailing, and then was offered a job selling cosmetics. While working as a freelancer for major cosmetic companies in 1983, Belasco was approached to do a wedding for a prominent family. She took the job, did the makeup for ten people in the wedding party, and found she liked it.

Having a flair for makeup and color is important, says Belasco, but in this field you also have to like people. And you must be reliable, because so many people are depending on you.

Some of her clients compare her to Joan Rivers because of the sense of humor she displays while she's working. Humor is just one way Belasco tries to put her clients at ease. "We all have the same feelings, the same insecurities," she says.

A member of the Association of Bridal Consultants, Belasco gets most of her business through referrals from past clients and from the association and through advertising in bridal magazines. She also networks with other professionals, especially photographers. At one point, she considered installing a toll-free phone number but then realized she might get calls from places around the country she couldn't possibly service.

☑ Knowledge and Skills You Need to Have

- In some states you need to obtain a license as a cosmetician or cosmetologist in order to be a makeup artist. Cosmetologists are also called estheticians.

- You need to know makeup techniques for the camera, which demands specialized highlighting if the makeup is to look natural under various lighting conditions.

- Makeup artists must have good interpersonal communication skills and be sensitive to the bride and her needs. You need to be empathetic and able to handle the range of emotions and ego issues that may arise for a bride under the pressure of her wedding.

- You need to have a basic knowledge of fashion and makeup trends.

- You should have some flair for color analysis and know which colors blend together to produce a desired effect.

🐷 Start-up Costs

In addition to having a car or other means of transportation to get to and from wedding sites, you will have the following expenses in starting this business:

	Low	High
Makeup equipment and supplies	$500	$1,000
Portfolio of photographs of your work*		1,000
Director's chair	100	100
Business cards, letterhead, envelopes, price lists	100	600
Legal fees to develop a contract for use in bookings**		250
Total	$700	$2,950

　* Sometimes you can do makeup for photographers in exchange for getting free samples of photos for your portfolio.

** Even if you develop the contract yourself, use a standard contract from a form book or software package, or borrow a contract from another artist, it's still a good idea to have an attorney review the contract.

📑 Advantages

- Wedding makeup artists are well paid for their time. The pay is better than what a studio makeup artist receives.

- Normally you are working around happy people at a very exciting and positive time in their lives.
- Your work begets more work. Doing a good job for your clients can be one of your best means of marketing, because they will refer their friends to you.
- Because weddings are usually on weekends, this business is easy to start on a part-time basis while you are still employed.

⒓ Disadvantages

- There is no built-in repeat business. You must be clever at creating ways for your clients to continue seeing you for their makeup needs after the wedding or you will have to be constantly recruiting new clients.
- Although a wedding is a positive celebration, it can also be stressful, because there are many people involved, and expectations are high for everything to be perfect. Also, people can become temperamental and emotional under such circumstances.
- Being a bridal makeup artist *types* you. Your portfolio has bridal pictures and not much of anything else, which could limit you should you also want to do work for ad agencies, films, or television.
- The majority of your work is on weekends.

⑤ Pricing

Makeup fees range from $75 to $150 for the bride, and from $25 to $100 for each additional member of the wedding party. In general, wedding makeup artists can charge more in large cities than in smaller locales. Additional fees can be charged for traveling to the site and for staying throughout the ceremony for touch-ups.

🔲 Potential Earnings

TYPICAL ANNUAL GROSS REVENUES: $22,000 to $52,000, based on doing 175 weddings a year for a bride and two members of the wedding party. Weddings are almost always on a Saturday or Sunday, and you can work a maximum of two to three weddings a day.

OVERHEAD: moderate (20 to 40 percent).

📈 *Best Home Businesses* Estimate of Market Potential:

How well wedding makeup artists do seems to depend on the ups and downs of the economy. In tough times, professionally applied wedding makeup is an expense that often gets cut.

▶ Best Ways to Get Business

- Exhibiting at bridal trade shows, showing your photographs, and doing makeovers in your booth.
- Advertising in local bridal magazines, with coupons included.
- Paying a fee to wedding consultants for their referrals.
- Holding a mixer for people in the wedding business—consultants, photographers, caterers, florists, and so forth.
- Getting publicity about your service in the print media, and on radio or TV. Because this is a glamour business that lends itself to photos and demonstrations, it's ideal for the media.
- Networking in organizations and at events for women, and in business organizations where other professionals involved in wedding services gather.

First Steps

Begin by finding out if your state requires that you get a cosmetician's or cosmetologist's license in order to become a makeup artist. If so, obtain the training you need for such a license from a cosmetology or beauty school. The cost of this schooling can range from $150 to $1,000; some schools have scholarships available. The training to be a cosmetician can be completed on a full-time basis in nine weeks. Becoming a cosmetologist requires more training because you are also trained to work with hair.

Learning special techniques for camera makeup and working with different skin tones in different types of lighting requires creativity and experience. The best way to get this experience is by working with another makeup artist as an assistant. Because weddings are on weekends, you can gain this experience while you are still employed. You can also practice on willing friends and relatives until you perfect your technique.

Once you are getting good results, develop a portfolio of photos showing off your work and then start promoting yourself as a bridal specialist, using the avenues for attracting business described above.

Where to Turn for Information and Help

ORGANIZATIONS

Association of Bridal Consultants, 200 Chestnutland Road, New Milford, CT 06776; (203) 355-0464, fax (203) 354-1404.

National Association of Aestheticians, 4447 McKinney Avenue, Dallas, TX 75205; (214) 526-0760.

BOOKS

Diane Von Furstenberg's Book of Beauty, Diane Von Furstenberg, New York: Simon and Schuster, 1976.

How to Be a Photogenic Bride, Sally Van Swearingen and Valerie Smith, 16250 Ventura Boulevard, Suite 215, Encino, CA 91436.

Instant Beauty, Pablo, New York: Simon and Schuster, 1978.

MAGAZINES

Bride's, Conde-Nast, 140 E. 45th Street, New York, NY 10017; (800) 456-6162; (212) 880-8800.

Modern Bride, 519 Eighth Avenue, New York, NY 10018; (800) 777-5786; (212) 645-9700.

Vogue, Conde-Nast, 350 Madison Avenue, New York, NY 10017; (800) 234-1520; (212) 880-8800.

■ ■ ■ ■ ■

WORD-PROCESSING AND OFFICE-SUPPORT SERVICE

Word-processing and office-support businesses provide typing and secretarial services to companies that need to rely on outside agencies to do these tasks. Despite the pervasiveness of personal computers, the demand for off-site secretarial services has been increasing steadily, according to Frank Fox, executive director of the National Association of Secretarial Services. In fact, says Fox, the changes in technology over the past few years have increased, not decreased, the demand for outside services in this field with people who can offer additional talents like skilled word processing, desktop publishing, presentation design, and even database management work.

There are four major markets for freelance secretarial services, according to Fox:

- Brand-new businesses that have no support staff and cannot afford to have one
- Small businesses (including other home-based enterprises) where the proprietor has little time to do his or her own clerical work or to learn new software
- Larger businesses that have cut back on full-time employees and are trying to save money by hiring out their secretarial, desktop publishing, bookkeeping, and other administrative services
- Traveling executives or "road warriors" who need office support of all kinds while they are on the road

Cheryl Myers, who operates a word-processing service in suburban Chicago, says that "the demand for outside services is coming from small- to medium-sized companies that do not wish to invest the time or dollars in in-house systems and personnel. Using an outside service and paying only for the work produced is extremely cost-effective. Also, more and more companies are cutting their administrative costs by allowing their reps to work out of their homes; these sales reps need secretarial services and the cost is covered on their expense accounts."

Myers has had to learn new skills other than word processing since she went out on her own ten years ago. She does a lot more work in the areas of desktop publishing and flowcharting than before; she even uses a scanner to read clients' text and graphics into the computer and is becoming more familiar with the Windows environment, rather than just DOS. She tries to stay up on many different software packages but acknowledges that it's difficult because of the sheer number of programs available.

Myers advises people who want to start an office-support business to treat it as a serious business—which means, among other things, that you get a business phone line and you invest in the proper equipment, including a fax machine. A problem for people providing office support on a part-time basis and who seek to serve customers who expect someone to be available during regular business hours is having their phone adequately covered. "People are so sick of voice mail and answering machines," Myers remarks, "that when I answer the phone, they are happy just to have reached a real human being." A possible solution for this is to have your business calls forwarded to a home-bound person, such as someone who is retired or disabled and who can handle your calls intelligently. Such an individual, using distinctive ringing, might work with several clients and thus answer each person's phone with a greeting in that business's name.

"Another mistake novices frequently make is to undercharge," Myers says. "When people undercharge, says Nancy Malvin, publisher of *Keyboard Connection*, the business is not able to support itself." And if the business cannot support itself, it obviously cannot support you.

Joining a professional group such as the National Association of Secretarial Services, an on-line special-interest group such as the Word Processing Section on the Working From Home Forum on CompuServe, or a comparable local organization can be helpful both in determining how to set pricing and in networking for clients.

Competition in this field can be fierce, but tailoring your business to particular markets is a way to carve out a niche for yourself. Examples of word-processing specialties include academia, law, medicine, résumé writing, small businesses, scriptwriting, and doing work for political candidates and local governmental bodies. Some specialties, such as transcribing legal and medical materials, pay better than others serving academic and student markets. The key to success in this business is the quality of your work and your ability to meet your clients' deadlines. You also have to keep up with new technologies, such as scanners, telecommunications, and multimedia. To be additionally competitive, you may want to offer pickup and delivery.

☑ Knowledge and Skills You Need to Have

- You must have fast and accurate typing skills. You should be able to type at least sixty-five words a minute, and the faster you type, the more you can earn. It even helps to be able to do transcription using a transcriber for faster service.
- This business calls for a customer-oriented service attitude. You need to have the desire and ability to pay attention to your clients' needs in detail.
- The key to success is keeping up, at least in a general way, with developments in computer technology and software.

◼ Start-up Costs

	Low	High
Computer with hard disk and modem	$1,000	$ 3,000
Laser printer	600	2,500
Suite software	250	400
Other specialized software (desktop publishing, presentations, contact management)	300	500
Transcribing machine (optional)	250	800
Scanner (optional)	100	800
Fax	300	900
Office furniture, especially an ergonomic chair	400	1,000
Copy machine	400	1,200
Business cards, letterhead, envelopes	100	600
Direct mail advertising	500	2,500
Organizational dues	250	250
Total	$4,450	$14,450

◼ Advantages

- You can earn additional income by providing other secretarial services such as editing, copywriting, mailing-list management, and desktop publishing. If you keep up with software and hardware technology, you can increase your rates substantially.
- Once you have a satisfied client for your word processing, it is easy to sell that client your other services because they probably need those services too.
- Offering a specialty service or services that are considered "office support" commands more respect than simply being a typing service as in the past.

⬒ Disadvantages

- The field is growing increasingly competitive.
- To a great extent, your income is limited by your speed and the number of hours in a day.
- You may often be working under the pressure of tight deadlines. In fact, some word-processing services specialize in "rush" work and derive a third of their income from premium charges.
- Unless you take necessary precautions, you risk developing repetitive-motion injuries as a result of constant keyboarding.

⬒ Pricing

For word processing, many services charge by the hour, $15 to $30, with higher charges related to the complexity of the material. Some services charge by the page, $2 to $5 for double spacing and $4 to $6 for single spacing, or by character count, such as $1 per 1,000 characters. Although the low figures above reflect what some people are charging, they are probably too low to make money. Another alternative that may be more palatable to customers and profitable to you is to charge by the job, using standards for estimating established by the National Association of Secretarial Services.

You should charge extra for handwritten or difficult-to-read materials, highly edited originals, or materials that include statistical charts, tables, and complex documents because it takes you longer to type them. Charge by the page if, because of interruptions, such as from young children, you would not be able to keep track of your time accurately. Even then, Nancy Malvin points out, you can use a stopwatch or software that performs the same function. You may be able to charge higher rates for certain other types of jobs, such as desktop publishing, résumés, and database management—as high as $50 per hour. You can also charge extra for multiple originals, copies, and other services.

⬒ Potential Earnings

TYPICAL ANNUAL GROSS REVENUES: $30,000 to $45,000, based on a sole practitioner billing thirty hours a week at $20 to $30 an hour for fifty weeks a year.

OVERHEAD: moderate (20 to 40 percent, because yellow-pages advertising under multiple headings can be expensive and also because you may need to upgrade your equipment periodically and to buy additional software packages).

⬒ *Best Home Businesses* Estimate of Market Potential:

Total number of word-processing services in the United States, including home-based businesses: 17,903. As people increasingly have computers in their homes and businesses, success in word processing and office support becomes more dependent on specializing in doing things that customers cannot do on their own or find it inconvenient or difficult to do.

▶ Best Ways to Get Business

- Yellow-pages advertising under Secretarial Services, Typing, Résumés, and Word Processing headings. Eighty-two percent of those responding to a membership survey of the National Association of Secretarial Services in 1990 (the most recent year for which figures are available) ranked yellow-pages advertising as an important part of their marketing efforts. Surveying the audience at the organization's 1994 convention, we found yellow-pages advertising was the most frequent way members get business and, for some, the way they get most of their business.

- Contacting other word-processing services for their overload or work in which you specialize

- Networking in business and professional organizations, such as chambers of commerce

- Responding to help-wanted ads for secretaries to induce the company to send the work out to you

- Advertising focused within a five-to-ten-mile radius (no more than a twenty-minute drive) of your home. Best places to advertise are in university newsletters and church, club, chamber of commerce, and other business bulletins.

- For attracting graduate student business, notices or flyers with tear-off phone numbers on bulletin boards at colleges and universities and in facilities used by students, such as laundromats

- Direct mail in the form of postcards or four-by-six cards with lists of services to new businesses in your area. Names and addresses of potential businesses can be found in city business journals. Follow up mailings with phone calls.

- Offering discounts on future work to customers who refer new customers

- Doing business and cultivating relationships with local merchants who are in a position to refer customers, such as local office-supply stores and printers.

- Approaching hotels about offering your services to their business guests

▶ First Steps

- If you are a slow typist, you can use a software program like *Mavis Beacon Teaches Typing* to help you increase your typing speed within just a few weeks.

- To get this business started, specialize in serving a particular field or industry, such as law or medicine.
- Consider contacting successful established word-processing services about doing overload work for them or even apprenticing to learn about the business.

☐ Where to Turn for Information and Help

ORGANIZATION

National Association of Secretarial Services, 3637 4th Street North, Suite 330, St. Petersburg, FL 33704; (800) 237-1462 or (813) 823-3546. Publishes a monthly newsletter and a variety of manuals on topics like pricing, sales and promotion, and the how-tos of expanding into other related services.

BOOKS

How to Open and Operate a Home-Based Secretarial Services Business, Jan Melnik, Old Saybrook, MA: Globe Pequot Press, 1994.

Word Processing Profits at Home, Peggy Glenn, Huntington Beach, CA: Aames-Allen Publishing, 1993.

MANUALS AND KITS

Starting a Successful Secretarial Service and *Secretarial Service Pricing Manual,* both by Frank Fox, National Association of Secretarial Services, 3637 4th Street North, Suite 330, St. Petersburg, FL 33704; (800) 237-1462 or (813) 823-3546.

Resource Package on Word Processing/Desk Publishing, Nina Feldman, 6407 Irwin Court, Oakland, CA 94609.

NEWSLETTERS

Keyboard Connection, P.O. Box 338, Glen Carbon, IL 62034; (618) 667-4666.

S.O.S. Quarterly, 1431 Willow Broke Cove #4, St. Louis, MO 63146; (314) 567-3636.

The Word Advantage, 432 Higganum Road, P.O. Box 718, Durham, CT 06422; (203) 349-0256.

AUDIOTAPES

How To Succeed Providing Word Processing and Secretarial Services From Your Home, Nancy Malvin, P.O. Box 338, Glen Carbon, IL 62034; (618) 667-4666.

PART II
■■■■■■■■■■■■■■■■■■■■■■■■■■■■■■■■

The Rest of the Best

■■■■■

CALENDAR SERVICE

A calendar service is a new concept that combines the needs of businesses, nonprofit associations, and the public to know what is going on in a given community over the course of a few months or even for as long as a year. The foremost spokesperson and "inventor" of the most successful calender service we know of is Susan Patricia Pawlowski, founder of PRESSXPRESS (pronounced *Press Express*) in Boston.

Pawlowski's calendar service is done largely by fax, although clients first receive a "master copy" 100-page booklet listing all the goings on around town for the next year. Then each week, she faxes subscribers an eight-page update that lists the happenings of that week plus any new events that have been announced. The listings include concerts, sports events, theater openings, trade shows, expositions, award dinners, charity functions . . . anything the public is invited to and would want to attend. She also includes the names of any hosts or celebrities who might be appearing at the events. Pawlowski claims that her goal is to make PRESSXPRESS into "Boston's most complete event resource by fax."

The profit in this business, as Pawlowski discovered, lies in the fact that there is a huge business-oriented market for event information, much larger than the home-based consumer market. In other words, her clients are not so much well-to-do suburbanites with fax machines at home who want to know where to go dancing or which concert to attend, but rather media people who need to cover these events, as well as businesses such as hotels, florists, caterers, and many other service companies who want to know what events are happening in town so they can plan their marketing and sales campaigns. Many charities and nonprofit associations also want to get Pawlowski's information so that they don't end up planning their yearly ball on the same night as the opening of the ballet or some other happening that would reduce their attendance. As she points out, every PR person, event planner, meeting planner, and sales manager wants the information and has no problem paying the $150 per year fee to subscribe.

To start a service like Pawlowski's, you need to know how to collect information and write it up in an intelligent, informative manner. It also helps to know how to use software such as a database program because there are literally tens of thousands of events going on in a community like Boston over the course of a year, so computerizing the information is a necessity. In addition, Pawlowski points out that you should be a people person and have excellent communication skills, because you will be speaking with executives, public-relations people, producers, and many high-level business-people to both solicit their announcements and sell them your service. You will also need to attend many events, as she says, because everyone wants you to come to their function.

We've heard of other calendar services in a few resort communities that cater to tourists and hotels, although these were phone-in services that cost more to operate. Faxing the information is a more-economical way to run a calendar service, and as fax machines proliferate in business and even among the public at large in their homes, we expect this business to grow.

For more information about franchising a PRESSXPRESS in your city, contact Susan Pawlowski at (617) 471-7233 or fax her at (617) 471-7611.

■ ■ ■ ■ ■

COMPUTER BULLETIN BOARD SERVICE

Operating a computer bulletin board service can be a fun and moneymaking enterprise for someone who has a good technical knowledge of hardware and software, and a niche market to serve. However, experts estimate that one in 22 BBs is profitable and about 15 percent break even. Nevertheless, it is now estimated that there are over 57,000 public bulletin boards in the United States and perhaps as many as 200,000 to 400,000 private computer bulletin boards worldwide where millions of people share ideas, exchange files, and simply schmooze via E-mail with professional colleagues, friends, or strangers.

Although the largest bulletin boards are found on national on-line services such as CompuServe or America Online, thousands of boards are home-based operations that originate to serve a special interest or single geographic locale. Some boards stay small with only a few dozen subscribers, whereas others grow to include hundreds of users who pay from $10 a month to $200 a year for use of the board. The most savvy bulletin boards are even now arranging to offer connections to the Internet, formerly a Unix-only environment sponsored by the government but now open.

Scott Wares, for example, started a local bulletin board for fun out of his home in Bakersfield, California, charging $7 a month for people to play games, exchange files, and communicate via E-mail. From that base of knowledge, he and his friend Chad Lessinger, who owned a medical billing company, went on to found a new bulletin board service called InfoAlliance for people involved in medical-claims services. Their board now serves over four hundred private individuals as well as vendors of medical-billing software who use the board to exchange tips on medical billing, software, and other professional matters.

Setting up a bulletin board is fairly easy and can cost only $3,000 to $5,000 if you start small. You will need a separate PC with a hard drive and enough modems and phone lines installed in your home for people to call into. (High-speed modems are recommended.) Scott Wares indicates that with two phone lines, he was able to handle about sixty calls a day, but with four phone lines he would have been able to handle about one hundred fifty calls a day without having users get a busy signal. In addition to your PC and phone lines, you also need a specialized bulletin board software program such as *TBBS* (eSoft), *Wildcat* (Mustang Software), *Major BBS* (Galacticom, Inc.), or *PCBoard* (Clark Development) that allows your callers to communicate with the board. Some software also keeps track of the time people spend on-line for billing purposes.

To let people know about a local BBS, post notice of your existence on the boards of other local BBSs. Consider using printed flyers if you have a place to post them where the type of users who will be interested in your BBS will see them. Word of mouth, of course, is an important way to market your BBS to them. Publicity can also be used to let people know about your board. On a national basis, the popular and massive **Computer Shopper** tabloid publishes some free listings each month. To get listed you can call the BBS Press Service at (913) 478-3088 (300, 1200, or 2400 bps, 8-N-1).

To the extent your budget allows, you may advertise your BBS in local newspapers and computer tabloids and magazines, or computer magazines such as *Boardwatch* (listed below), trade journals, or in the media that your intended audience reads. Another way to develop a BBS is to offer to run one for a private association or organization, because many groups are finding that giving their membership access to a bulletin board increases participation. Also in *Boardwatch*, you will find a list of publishers of lists of BBSs. You can then contact those to have your BBS listed.

Some BBS systems charge a monthly flat fee for unlimited use such as $25 per month, whereas others charge from 1 to 10 cents per minute of log-on time. You may also need to obtain credit-card capability for people to charge their payments or send out invoices each month to users.

In starting a BBS, it helps to be available on-line for at least some time each day as users may want to communicate directly with you if you are the system operator (usually abbreviated to "sysop"). You should also be aware of various laws governing computer privacy and the illegal use of software, in the event that your subscribers exchange programs over your bulletin board. A recent criminal case in Massachusetts is attempting to hold the founder of a private bulletin board liable for damages because subscribers to his board were exchanging commercially available software without permission.

Possibly the most exciting opportunities are beginning to emerge on the Internet, where anyone from anywhere can broadcast or publish to this network of networks. One way some BBSs are attracting local subscribers is by providing a gateway to the Internet for their members. Now is a good time to explore these possibilities.

▢ Where to Turn for Information and Help

ORGANIZATIONS/BULLETIN BOARDS

FDA Electronic Bulletin Board, 5600 Fishers Lane, Room 15B-42, Rockville, MD 20855; (800) 222-0185; (301) 443-3285.

IBMBBS Forum on CompuServe Information Service, 5000 Arlington Centre Blvd., P.O. Box 20212, Columbus, OH 43220; (800) 848-8990.

MAGAZINES

Boardwatch Magazine, 5970 South Vivian Street, Littleton, CO 80127; (800) 933-6038 or (303) 973-6038, or (303) 973-4222—bulletin board phone number. Founded by Jack Rickard, this is the premiere magazine in the field, containing articles of interest to BBS operators, information on the Internet and other on-line services, an extensive list of boards, product reviews, and announcements of new services. Published monthly. $36 per year.

Wired, 544 Second Street, San Francisco, CA 94107; (415) 904-0660, fax (415) 904-0660. On-line: WIRED.COM. *Wired* explores the "digital revolution" and places it in contexts beyond the 0's and 1's of a technical publication.

BOOKS

Creating Successful Bulletin Board Systems, Alan D. Bryant, Reading, MA: Addison Wesley, 1994. Includes a two-line version of TBBS software by eSoft.

Doing Business on the Internet, Mary J. Cronin, New York: Van Nostrand Reinhold, 1994.

How to Successfully Run a BBS for Profit, S. Carol Allen, InfoLink, 56089 Twentynine Palms Highway, Suite 254-FG31, Yucca Valley, CA 92284; (800) 776-3818.

Whole Earth Online Almanac, Don Rittner, New York: Brady, 1993. A topical listing of electronic forums, libraries, and BBSs.

The Whole Internet, Ed Krol, Sebastopol, Calif.: O'Reilly & Associates, 1992.

SOFTWARE

Major BBS, Galacticomm, Inc., 4101 SW 47th Avenue, Suite 101, Fort Lauderdale, FL 33314; (800) 328-1128; (305) 583-5990, fax (305) 583-7846.

PCBoard, Clark Development Co., Inc., P.O. Box 571365, 3950 South 700 East, Suite. 303, Murray, UT 84157; (800) 356-1686 or (801) 261-1686, fax (801) 261-8987.

TBBS (The Bread Board System), eSoft, Inc., 15200 East Girard Avenue, Suite 3000, Aurora, CO 80014; (303) 699-6565, fax (303) 699-6872.

Wildcat!, Mustang Software, Inc., P.O. Box 2264, Bakersfield, CA 93303; (800) 999-9619 or (805) 873-2500, fax (805) 873-2599.

■ ■ ■ ■ ■

DISC JOCKEY SERVICE

If you love music and have a personality that inspires people to have a good time and party, you can earn your living as one of 21,555 freelance or mobile disc jockeys (DJs). Mobile DJs provide professional sound at conferences, parties, weddings, and special events in homes, clubs, churches, hotels, public halls, schools, and companies for far less than the cost of live musicians. They occasionally work for nightclubs, too, although their mainstay is freelancing for people at private occasions.

As a DJ, you select and supply the music and the equipment to play it on. You usually also need to provide some patter to entertain the audience and encourage everyone to dance. Essential equipment includes two high-quality compact-disc players, a cassette deck (to play tapes handed to you by people in the audience and as a backup for the CD players), and if you intend to use records, a professional turntable. You will also need a mixing console, a power amplifier, speakers with clear output, and a cordless microphone for your banter with the audience. You can also add strobe lights and other special effects to enhance your presentation. (With all the equipment, you will also need a van or station wagon to transport it safely, plus a dolly or rolling cart.) The setup for basic equipment runs about $3,500 to $5,000, but you can also find it used for under $1,000.

The most crucial part of your equipment is your disc collection. If you already own a sizable collection of dancing CDs, you can often start out by purchasing a few hundred more new releases to complement what you have. With the cost of CDs, many DJs now scout used CD stores for good values in dance music. In all, you will need to spend $1,000 to $2,000. More useful than buying one popular disc at a time, though, is to subscribe to one of the companies that produces CDs specifically for DJs; each month, you are mailed a number of discs that contain a mix of popular dance songs in whichever style you need: country/western, rap, rock and roll, heavy metal, or whatever (call *Promo Only* at (407) 331-3600 or *RPM* at (800) 521-2537). Such companies produce discs especially for mobile DJs, preselecting the most popularly chosen numbers by audiences so that you don't waste your money buying an entire CD to get one or two hot songs.

In addition, there are several new techniques of running a DJ party that are changing the nature of the business that you need to take into account. First, over the past five years, *karoake* has become a popular fad among many kinds of crowds. In karoake, a guest comes onstage and sings the lyrics to a song while the exact music plays in the background. Lest the words be forgotten, the crooner watches them appear on a computer screen so that he or she can pretend to be the original singer. This new art form has not meant much in the way of new equipment, because the CD player is already built in to your system. All you need are the special CDG discs (compact disc with graphics) that contain the lyrics with the music background and a monitor connected to the CD player to show the lyrics. Karoake is a crowd pleaser, says Jeff Greene, owner of Party Time DJs, because "it serves the function of allowing the guests to become the entertainment and be the center of attention. Instead of having a DJ be the entertainment, the audience is the show. Guests themselves become stars." Greene admits that many people are shy and too reluctant to participate, but he adds wryly that "once you get the crowd singing, you can't stop 'em."

He also points out that owning the karoake equipment is a good sideline business for a DJ because many nightclubs don't own the equipment themselves, and so they hire a mobile DJ for the one or two nights of the week when they feature it.

A second technique of running your DJ business is to offer many more choices than straight DJ work. Greene says that his company offers clients a full range of options: there's your basic spin man at the bottom; then it moves on up to a style of DJ who basically plays full host to the party, complete with games and prizes like Blues' Brothers sunglasses, maracas, and inflatable instruments. His company has also expanded into doing videos of the event for an extra charge.

As you can see, being a simple DJ is not what it used to be in the old days of plastic platters. These days, DJs can charge from $50 on up to $150 per hour. Greene is even able to charge as much as $300 per hour for his top-level DJs. (He now has a dozen employees and three regional offices, all of which grew from his home-based business within five years.) Many DJs also accept jobs at nightclubs which don't pay as well, but if you get your name in their advertising, it's good exposure for your business. Be sure that they let you hand out business cards or flyers, too.

Two caveats to be aware of: First, the work is often seasonal, with especially heavy bookings during the Christmas holidays, spring prom season, May and June (weddings), and early fall (parties). There are lots of events in between, but you will have to develop your reputation in order to get the word-of-mouth referrals you will need. Second, you must be sure that the music you play appeals to your clientele. That means in some areas of the country that you need to have country/western, or Caribbean, or mariachi, or polkas. Greene warns to watch out for trendy music (the kind that appeals to the fourteen-to-eighteen age group), lest you invest in a few popular CDs and, the next week, they are dead.

For more information on learning the DJ business, read the following magazines: *DJ Times* (800) 937-7678; (516) 767-2500 and *Mobile Beat*, which is for the mobile DJ (800) 836-9355.

■ ■ ■ ■ ■

DUPLICATING SERVICE

A spare bedroom, attic, garage, or basement can be a suitable office for an audio, video, or disk-duplicating service. Such a service makes copies of audiotapes and videotapes or computer diskettes for a variety of private individuals and businesses. Although home-based duplicators may not be able to obtain the biggest professional customers ordering tens of thousands of copies, your clients may include the kinds of jobs not wanted by large duplicating services, including:

- Businesses wanting small numbers of employees or customers to receive taped or digital information
- Local software developers seeking low-cost duplication
- Hardware manufacturers that include software and manuals with their equipment
- Motivational speakers and professionals wanting to sell tapes of their speeches and seminars
- Associations and organizations that sell copies of their workshops and meeting sessions
- Musicians wanting to produce their own recordings for sale or as dubs for auditions
- Individuals who want to have old beta-format tapes converted to VHS or eight millimeter
- People who want copies of their home movies transferred from film to videotape or from one format on videotape to another

For videotape and audiotape duplication, you can start with only one type of duplication-and-conversion machine and grow to multiple machines for larger orders and for converting from multiple formats. Some jobs may also ask you to add titles, voice-overs, and graphics to videotapes. You should invest in the best professional equipment you can afford, preferably the kind that can be upgraded with ease. Approximately $1,000 to $1,500 should cover your initial equipment costs and a stock of tapes. Buying used equipment can reduce your start-up costs. An alternative is to rent first, even though it is more costly than buying, because renting allows you to become familiar with a particular type of equipment before you purchase it and gives you time to determine what direction your business will take.

You can charge by the hour for tape duplication or by the tape. We found pricing for duplicating audiotapes varies all the way from 75 cents to $3 each. Videotapes are charged at an hourly rate ranging from $5 to $20. One way to maximize your earnings is to contract with large taping facilities for jobs too large to do on your own equipment. In this way you can bid on big jobs, earning money essentially as a broker.

Tape duplicators might consider expanding their business into providing other services such as taping conferences and speaking events on-site or recording audiotapes for clients in your home studio; however, zoning may prevent you from having people record in your home studio. Other events that you can tape include training sessions, seminars, intracompany video memos, and so forth. You might also consider a service that transfers 35-millimeter slides to videotape, makes 35-millimeter slides from videotape, or makes films for overhead projectors from 35-millimeter slides, videotape, or computer screens. Some people in this field install sophisticated recording studios in their homes and thus are able to serve local musicians. However, before investing thousands of dollars in modifying your home, check to see if a recording studio is permitted within your zoning classification.

For disk duplication, you can start small, even with an old XT-style computer, although you need a floppy-disk drive that accommodates both double-density and high-density disks. You can find specialized software that formats, verifies, and copies disks automatically, without manual intervention. High-end equipment is available that can duplicate 130 diskettes per hour. Instead of hand-feeding the disks as you would with a computer, you pop them in a stacker and the machine runs itself. Such a device costs about $5,000. You might also add adjunct services, as Kjell Petterson of Raleigh, North Carolina, does, such as attaching labels, shrink-wrapping diskettes with manuals, adding stickers, and so on. You can charge more for each add-on service you provide, but be aware that this is a labor-intensive business. Pricing varies with the service you provide, but typically runs between 10 and 25 cents per diskette up to several dollars per diskette with labeling and shrink-wrapping. Petterson says the best way to attract business in duplicating disks is to get on your state's list of vendors and make bids for contracts.

In addition to a general working knowledge of audio, video, or computer equipment, knowledge of electronic technology is extremely useful, particularly if you don't have access to a technician. You should also count on needing a certain amount of storage space for your supplies (tapes or disks, packaging, labels, etc.). Most important is having knowledge of the potential market and how to find a niche for your business. For example, diskette duplicators can find clients among computer-games and software publishers as well as businesses that want to provide one-shot demo disks as marketing devices. As Petterson says, this can be an excellent business to conduct from home, because you can provide fast turnaround for your customers, while you work according to your own schedule.

There is one great caveat for any duplicating service: Duplicating materials that are protected by copyright is illegal. Doing so innocently can still result in a stiff fine and open you up to lawsuits. Selling illegally copied tapes can get you a hefty jail sentence as well. Therefore, you must be certain that the customer either owns the material outright or has bought, leased, or been granted the rights to whatever is to be duplicated.

Resources for disk duplicators include software such as *EZ-Disc Copy Pro,* EZX Publishing, P.O. Box 58177, Webster, TX 77598; (800) 800-2468 and (713) 280-9900. *EZ-DisKlone Plus for DOS* and *WinDisKlone for Windows* are also available from EZX Publishing.

■ ■ ■ ■ ■

FITNESS TRAINER

How would you like to have all the time you want to exercise and work out—and get paid for it, too? You can, because the more Americans do work that binds them to desks and telephones, the more they become involved in exercise and fitness. Of course, a regular stream of scientific evidence continues to pour in that being physically fit increases mental and physical health, keeps us looking more attractive, and may even extend our lives—an increasing concern for the now-graying baby-boomer population. This has made fitness a big business. Although you cannot operate a gym at home, you can establish a successful business as a personal trainer.

Personal trainers design workout routines for individuals or small groups and guide clients through their workouts two or three times a week, either at the clients' homes or at a gym. Some trainers also teach classes like yoga or aerobics, either in their own homes or at facilities they rent. Others specialize in fitness training for children or pregnant women. Richard Salas in Los Angeles, for example, prides himself on being the only gymnastics teacher for adults.

Depending on their reputation and locale, personal trainers charge from $35 to $125 per session. Therefore, billing twenty hours a week (which can mean working with as few as seven clients) at $75 per hour for fifty weeks per year can produce an income of $75,000 a year. Start-up costs are low, because you don't need to purchase any workout equipment yourself. In fact, some trainers sell equipment to their clients. You will, of course, need to look physically fit yourself, and it helps in getting business to be able to talk about as well as demonstrate what you do before groups of people at meetings. Some of the work is physical; you may need to work out alongside your clients at times and also to demonstrate proper form. Gymnastics teachers need to watch their students closely so they can guide them to using effective techniques, which is physically demanding work.

If you use a gym to work out in with your clients, you will need to maintain a membership. You also have to have business cards, a letterhead, and well-done flyers or simple brochures. You must have a sound knowledge of fitness principles, exercise, and workout routines. In addition, you must know how to prevent and deal with injuries. Most successful personal trainers have evolved their own method of training. A solid understanding of nutrition is also helpful. The more background and experience you have, the more credible you will be. In fact, Laura Brooks, of Energy Unlimited in Los Angeles, thinks that younger people are at a disadvantage because they're seen as less experienced.

Certification is a disputed issue in this field. Some outfits offer certification for a fee, but because some credentials (not all) are based on a fee and a test rather than on solid training and experience, their value may be dubious. Check these organizations carefully. Clients want and deserve trainers with solid experience.

The best routes to building a client base are through your personal contacts, referrals from current clients, giving seminars and presentations on fitness, exhibiting at health shows, and doing demonstrations. You might also network with chiropractors and orthopedic surgeons who have patients to refer. Having photos of people you have worked with to show the before-and-after effects of training is effective. Publicity is also valuable.

One of the most challenging aspects of this business is keeping your clients motivated to continue working out. Although it may go unstated, this is a large part of why they hire you. So, in addition to knowing how to design effective workout routines, you must be able to encourage, inspire, and motivate your clients to continue with you, even when they don't see immediate results.

There is a high level of client attrition. You may lose even loyal, long-term clients at any time, so you have to market constantly. In addition, you need to provide lots of personal attention and special handling, particularly if you bring in assistants who are unknown quantities to clients you've established a rapport with. This is an extremely personal business. Because people bare their souls through their physical problems, your trust and empathy are key.

Helena Rose Adams, a Pilates method teacher in Los Angeles (the Pilates method is similar to yoga, but it is done with special equipment consisting of cords and pulleys), says that one of the main advantages of being a fitness instructor is the satisfaction that comes from seeing people improve. A disadvantage is that people cancel at the last minute.

Fitness trainers have national associations. They are two:

Aerobic and Fitness Association of America, 15250 Ventura Boulevard, Suite 200, Sherman Oaks, CA 91403; (818) 905-0040.

American Fitness Association, P.O. Box 401, Durango, CO 81301; (303) 247-4109.

Kinderdance International (Box 510881, Melbourne Beach, FL 32951; [800] 666-1595) offers a franchise for teaching dance and motor-development skills to pre-school-age children.

A book that begins with a wonderful quote from Winston Churchill ("Those whose work and play are one are Fortune's favorite children") is *For Fun and Profit: Self-Employment Opportunities in Recreation, Sports and Travel,* by Crawford Lindsey (Live Oak Publications, Box 2193, Boulder, CO 80306).

■ ■ ■ ■ ■

HAULING SERVICE

Getting rid of things is not a new problem, but it can be a major one. Every time you move, you discover things that don't work, don't fit, or that you simply don't want. And not only when you move. What do you do with the old refrigerator or range when you buy a new one? Or that ratty-looking sofa that your mother insisted you take? Or the debris from the last remodeling project you finally got finished? Or the broken chair? Or the rusted fender in the garage? Or the old fence, the garden debris, the old shed that finally fell down? Unless you have a truck, you have to call someone to haul this stuff away, because most garbage services won't touch it.

That leaves a wide-open opportunity for a hauling service. And what you get paid by the hour or the load is not all the income you can earn. One person's junk is another person's treasure. People get rid of old things like oil paintings, antiques, and rare books; new things like presents they don't want and leftover construction materials; and reusable things of all sorts. You can keep, donate to charities, or sell items of value. The possibilities for selling things is almost limitless—through the classified ads, at flea markets or garage sales, or to anyone who can use what you've got. And because you've got a truck, you can deliver, too.

All you need is a pickup truck or van, preferably one that's equipped with a hydraulic lift gate, along with tarps, blankets, rope, and some toting equipment such as a hand truck and a four-wheel dolly. Of course, you can have more than one truck or van, but if you do, your zoning laws may require you to keep the vehicles in a commercial area, so check with your city. Some hauling services may also arrange for roll-off dumpsters to leave at a site, but storing these may also be subject to your zoning laws.

Your other primary need is to identify places to which to take disposable materials that you haul away. You must make preliminary inquiries with companies that accept these materials. Scrap-metal companies may or may not take old appliances. Dumps may not accept certain types of furniture. Secondhand shops may not want old mattresses or appliances that don't work. You will find that most of these places will pay you for the materials they accept. If you also charge the consumer or business for hauling away the waste, you will be able to keep your rates competitive enough to make it worth your while on both ends.

Some states require a special license to move other people's stuff, so check this out, as well as dumping regulations in your area. Unless you are close to a state line and your business will take you across that line, you will not be bound by Interstate Commerce Commission regulations. In addition, if you are hauling debris, be sure that no hazardous materials such as paint are included. Dumps will not accept hazardous materials, and if they see you dumping them, you will face either a warning or the termination of your account or both. If you discover hazardous materials in the load, remove them and have a specially licensed firm cart away the material for you.

To promote your business, leave stacks of business cards and well-done flyers or simple brochures with realtors, contractors, apartment rental services, condominium management offices, appliance stores, furniture stores, garden-supply stores and nurseries, and senior-citizen clubs. Because consumers usually start out by calling scrap-metal companies, secondhand stores, and interstate movers (for whom their job may be too small), you should be sure these businesses are aware of you. Keep in touch with them regularly so that they will refer clients to you. Going to auctions can also be a good source of business. Let the auction personnel know you're there, and by having a sign painted on your truck or using a removable magnetic sign, people will notice you. Often other moving jobs or other kinds of handy work will develop from a satisfied customer. Classified or small display ads in your local paper and yellow-pages ads are important ways of getting business. We met someone once who claimed he got all the business he needed from the yellow pages because of the name of his company—Grunt N'Dump.

For further information, refer to *How to Earn $15 to $50 an Hour and More with a Pickup Truck or Van,* by Don Lilly, Chesterfield, MO: Darian Books, 1994; (314) 391-3323; $12.95. Also available from Don Lilly is a plan to build an inexpensive liner for your pickup truck, *Pick Up Truck Dump Box Plan,* $10.00, and *The Flea Market Handbook,* by Robert Miner, which explains how to sell the items you are paid to haul away.

Related Businesses: Tree Service, Furniture Renovation, Moving Service, Lawn Aeration (contact Don Lilly at above address for a copy of *Lawn Aeration: Turn Hard Soil into Cold Cash,* by Robin Pedrotti, $19.95.)

■ ■ ■ ■ ■

HOME TUTORING

The alarming decline in the academic skills of children all across America, and the increasing concern among parents and teachers, are causing a resurgence in the profession of professional tutoring. The unfortunate truth is that children of all ages need help in all subject areas, and parents are willing to pay for it. In some cases, a child has a gap or deficiency in a subject area that needs work, such as math or reading skills; in other cases, the child needs to learn proper study skills to become more successful in all subject areas that he or she will be taking in junior or senior high or college. Some parents even have their kindergartners tutored to build their attention spans and develop social skills so that they will be prepared for first grade.

The beauty of a tutoring business is that you can put as much time into it as you want to while working from home. Many tutors work just in the afternoons or early evenings, but some may also take clients in the morning before school begins.

One tutor we met, Lucy Scribner in Salt Lake City, Utah, developed a successful business by beginning to work with children of the same age as her own kids. This allowed her to be familiar with the textbooks that were being used, with the teaching styles of the children's teachers, and with the goals of the school, because her own children were there too. In fact, one of her marketing techniques was to work within her own local public school, where she could get cluster groups of children, thereby charging from three to ten students at a time for a group lesson. This benefited both the parents (who liked having a discounted rate for tutoring) and Scribner (who could make more money per hour than by tutoring just one student at a time).

Scribner points out that tutoring other children actually makes a lot of sense. Many children will simply not learn from their parents, and when they need help, parents recognize that the only way to ensure their child's success is to hire a third party to do the tutoring. As she says, this "natural state of contention" between children and their parents makes the market for tutors large.

To be a tutor, Scribner feels that the most important qualifications are not academic degrees or teaching experience, but simply the enjoyment of working with children and the ability to stay at least one step in front of them in their school lessons. She also believes that helping a child improve his or her self-esteem is a major component of tutoring, as many children will improve simply by feeling better about themselves. Scribner has, therefore, developed her own interactive way of teaching children and providing positive reinforcement.

Marketing your tutoring service is not hard if you start with your own local school where your children attend, or simply by working with one or two students who might be the children of friends or neighbors. Once you are successful with those children, and the parents see results, word of mouth will build your business in leaps and bounds as the parents become your best advertising. Some tutors also post flyers in their schools, supermarkets, and other public places. It also helps to have a distinguishing aspect to your business to differentiate yourself from other tutors: a special teaching method, the use of certain kinds of toys or games in teaching math, a focus on self-esteem building, or whatever.

The fees for tutoring are currently $10 to $20 per hour in many locations. Some tutors offer group rates or multisession rates such as ten lessons for $150. If you tutor three to five students per day for four days a week, you can thus earn $240 to $400 per week during the school year. You can also offer study-skills seminars by procuring a room at a church or at the school, plus you can offer summertime tutoring and remedial classes. All in all a tutoring business can bring in from $15,000 to $30,000 per year, for mostly part-time work.

If you are interested in starting a tutoring business, you can contact Lucy Scribner, who has developed a training course that includes a business guide, with audio and video tapes on working with children: *The Complete Guide to Starting and Operating a Home Tutoring Business,* Lucy Scribner, Personal Motivation Academy, 5719 Parkplace West, Salt Lake City, UT 84121; (801)278-4324. You should also read the Core Knowledge series of books *Everything Your First [Second, Third, etc.] Grader Should Know,* E. D. Hirsch Core Knowledge Series (Dell Publishing), and the newsletter called *The Right to Read Report* from the National Right To Read Foundation, 3220 North Street, N.W., Suite 174, Washington, DC 20007; (800) 468-8911.

■ ■ ■ ■ ■

IN-HOME HEALTH CARE

With the aging of the American population and the skyrocketing costs of hospitalization of any kind, more and more people are released within days from hospitals so that they can recuperate at home. As a result, there is an astonishing growth of "in-home health care," with an estimated seven million Americans receiving some type of medical care at home in 1994 and more than 14,000 home health-care agencies, up from 1,100 such agencies three decades ago. The good news is that continued growth in this industry is predicted to run about 12 percent per year, meaning that if you have an interest in health care and helping other people, an in-home health-care business might be good for you.

The economics of in-home care make sense. Many routine medical treatments can be done at home for much less overhead than at a hospital, and most daily-care (unskilled) attending can be provided by any reasonably trained person or family member.

As a business, the term "in-home health care" means two types of arrangements:

- You take people in your home and take care of their daily needs and minor medical treatment.
- You go to someone's home or arrange for other people to go to someone's home (like a referral service) to take care of people at their own residence.

Here's an overview of each:

In Your Home

A new way of controlling rising medical costs is to place patients in the homes of caretakers instead of in hospitals. Mentor, a Boston-based health-care company, has taken the lead with this new approach. Mentor contracts with independent home-care providers, whom they call medical technicians or mentors, to care for people under the supervision of health professionals. Over nine out of ten patients are people between the ages of six and eighteen who either are too ill for outpatient treatment or require custodial care, but are not necessarily so ill as to require hospitalization. The types of problems such patients have include emotional problems, developmental disabilities, head injuries, and substance-abuse problems.

Mentors take only one patient into their homes at a time. The care provider helps prepare patients for a successful transition back to their own homes as soon as possible. In the case of an emotionally disturbed patient, the mentor provides praise and other rewards for positive behavior and controls, as necessary, out-of-control behaviors by the patient.

No particular background is needed to become a mentor, although mentors must have no criminal record. Mentor provides all necessary training. The company looks for compassionate, caring individuals who have good communications skills and an interest in helping people. Life experience with care-giving is helpful, as is having a knowledge of substance abuse. All types of people are doing this work—singles, empty nesters, parents with children. What is required to get started as a mentor is a spare bedroom, because that's where the patient lives, and a car for taking the patient to outpatient medical facilities.

Mentors are self-employed independent contractors and can expect to earn somewhere in the range of $50 to $60 for each day a patient is in their home, which is comparable to the pay of a mental-health technician on a hospital staff.

This is a burgeoning field. As of this writing, Mentor provides service in thirteen states (Mass., R.I., N.H., Pa., N.J., Md., N.C., S.C., Ga., Tex., Ill., Ohio, and Wis). It is the only company of its kind, but with the cost of inpatient care skyrocketing, we predict that more and more companies will leap in to take up the slack.

For more information, call Mentor Clinical Care at (800) 388-5150.

In the Person's Home

Another alternative that some people are developing with great success is a business that finds reliable, qualified people to send as aides to homebound patients. The aides perform any number of services for the client, from cleaning and cooking, to running errands or taking the person to doctor's appointments. In some cases, the aide is simply companionship for the patient, making sure that the person doesn't fall or forget to take a medication.

To avoid being an employment agency or nursing registry, which require licensing, this business is more like a specialized referral service dealing with homemakers and companions for people who need home-care assistance. The patient pays you a referral fee only and then pays the aide directly. There are two requirements to making this business successful: You must find reliable, honest, and diligent aides, and you must find clients who need them. Like an executive search service or even a nanny agency, this kind of referral service can be hectic to operate, because you must work both sides of the fence at once.

Typical fees for your referral service are two- to four-weeks' salary for the aide, about $400 to $800. To show good faith, many services promise that if the aide does not work out for any reason within the first month, they will replace the person with a new candidate at no charge.

To learn more about this profession, contact the National Association for Home Care, at the **Institute of Consulting Careers, Inc.,** 222 SE 16th Street, Portland, OR 97214; (503) 240-0931. The association offers a program in operating an in-home health-care service.

A related business that seems to be on the rise is what we're calling an Elderly Relative Service, in which you provide visitation, transportation, errand services, household maintenance, and a wide array of other services for elderly clients whose families are not available to provide these kinds of help personally. Your fee can be paid by the clients, their families, or their estates.

■ ■ ■ ■ ■

INTERIOR DESIGNER/DECORATOR

Americans are redecorating and/or remodeling their homes at an unprecedented rate in the 90s. A survey for *Home* magazine at the beginning of the decade indicated that 46 percent of Americans planned to redecorate or remodel in the next five years, compared with 35 percent who did so in the previous five years. The high price of buying a home causes people to improve what they had rather than move up the housing ladder as their parents did.

This means lots of work for interior designers because, according to a Lou Harris survey, almost one out of every seven Americans gets help from a professional home decorator. These numbers translate into five million clients for professional designers in the residential market alone. And, according to Joe Pryweller, senior editor at the American Society of Interior Designers, about half of all designers work primarily with business and industrial clients (contract work), in addition to those who work with residential clients.

What does it take to be an interior designer? It takes someone with a sense of color and balance or proportion, a positive attitude toward change (a designer needs to keep up with fashion trends and at the same time be responsive to what the client desires), and the ability to communicate through graphic presentations.

Designers are now able to use computers in working with clients. With computer-aided design software, such as *Autocad* or *Archicad*, it's possible to devise and present design solutions to clients with three-dimensional realism.

Designers charge for their services in several ways. Some charge a flat fee for design work. Others charge by the hour, at rates ranging from $35 to $125. Still others add a service charge of approximately 20 percent to items they buy for clients, such as furniture, fabric, and floor coverings. Still others charge their clients the retail price of items they are able to purchase wholesale, keeping the difference as their fee. Thus, the client gets the designer's service at a price no greater than he or she would have paid for the products at retail. To avoid misunderstandings, it's important to formalize a client relationship with a contract or a letter of agreement.

Decorating Den is one franchise available in the decorating field. A franchisee drives a van loaded with samples to a customer's home or office and allows busy customers to order directly from him or her. The profit of the Decorating Den franchisee comes from selling items at retail that you buy at wholesale. Decorating Den can be contacted at 7910 Woodmont Avenue, Suite 200, Bethesda, MD 20814; (800) 931-2255; (301) 652-6393.

The largest professional association in this field is the American Society of Interior Designers (608 Massachusetts Avenue, N.E., Washington, DC 20002; (202) 546-3480). Its membership includes interior designers who have completed a degree program or have many years of experience, as well as designers who are working toward their degree. Some people practice decorating without a degree, but in order to become certified, interior designers are required to have a working knowledge of building and fire-safety codes. They also need to know about space planning. The society has several classes of members, including professionals who have obtained a four-year college degree in interior design and/or have acquired sufficient years of experience to pass a three-day examination to become certified as interior designers. Sixteen states, plus the District of Columbia and Puerto Rico, now require licensing of interior designers.

Magazines read by professionals in the field include *Interior Design* (249 West 17th Street, New York, NY 10001), *Interiors* (1515 Broadway, New York, NY 10036), *Interiors and Sources* (450 Skokie Boulevard, Suite 507, North-brook, IL 60062), and *Contract Design* magazine (1515 Broadway, 24th Floor, New York, NY 10036), which specializes in office design.

■ ■ ■ ■ ■

LEAK-DETECTION SERVICE

Imagine being able to offer a service that can save a building owner from replacing a $100,000 roof by fixing a $50 piece of pipe, or that can save a gas station $250,000 with a $4,000 repair! That is exactly what the field of leak detection can do.

Leak detectors locate leaks in just about any kind of system that uses pipes and distribution transition lines: from plumbing and sewer pipes in homes, to piping lines at gas stations and fire sprinkler systems in skyscrapers, to swim-ming pools and public water reservoirs. Leak detectors are even hired to find leaks in pneumatic tubes at bank drive-in tellers.

To detect leaks, inspectors may use inert gases, radio signals, ultrasonic listening devices, thermographs to detect moisture, and nuclear instruments. Few leak-detection companies have all types of equipment needed to detect all varieties of leaks, so most specialize in one area or another. For example, Elsie and Ted McConnel have built a thriving home-based business detecting roof leaks using a nuclear instrument called a Datamax, which they saw exhibited at a trade show they attended because they were managing an apartment building. These newest leak-detection devices are nondestructive and use special instrumentation to detect hydrogen contained in moisture. The reading from the instrument is then put into a computer, which produces a roof graph showing the condition of the roof. Clients then use the graph in a process that leads to a precise repair.

Leak detection has become a significant industry for a variety of reasons. First, there is an ever-increasing array of sophisticated new equipment that can be used to find leaks of all kinds. Second, the cost of construction and new building-code requirements in many parts of the country have made inspec-tions for leaks a necessary step prior to any roof repair. In fact, in areas where buildings are susceptible to moisture damage, inspections are often part of a regular building maintenance program on an annual or biannual basis. Third, with the price of water skyrocketing in many parts of the country, home developers and local governments take immediate action when they believe they may be losing thousands of gallons of costly water from swimming pools, fountains, or water-storage facilities. Finally, leak detection has benefited from the variety of natural disasters that have hit the country, such as the 1994 Los Angeles earthquake that made the phones ring off the hook in leak-detection companies in many areas. For all these reasons, many leak detectors can keep busy sixty to seventy hours per week.

No specific experience is required to go into this business, but good hearing and a mechanical aptitude are helpful when it comes to using the necessary equipment. You also should enjoy marketing yourself, as the best methods for getting business are contacting those people who install piping systems: plumbers, pool experts, water purveyors, and servicepeople who work with concealed piping.

Prices for residential leak inspections range from $175 to $275 and usually take only a few hours to accomplish. The price for leak detection at industrial sites can run into the thousands. Leak detectors may also handle the repair work or subcontract it out, adding substantially to their profit. Total income from leak detection can therefore be quite good, with businesses typically showing earnings of over $50,000 a year; earnings of more than $100,000 are not unusual.

A franchise is available in this field from American Leak Detection. This company provides an eight-week training course and a vast assortment of equipment for $45,000. Nearly all of their 200 franchisees operate from their homes. For further information, contact American Leak Detection, at 888 Research Drive, Suite 100, Palm Springs, CA 92262; or call (800) 755-6697 or (619) 320-9991.

■ ■ ■ ■ ■

MEDIATOR

In recent years, *mediation* and *arbitration*, two forms of *Alternative Dispute Resolution*, or *ADR*, have become widespread methods of settling conflicts as a result of an increasingly clogged court system and rising attorneys' fees and other legal costs. According to the American Arbitration Association, mediation filings alone were up 26 percent in 1992 from the previous year. Many states now require most civil cases to go first to mediation or arbitration, and only if the parties can't reach an agreement does the matter go on to the courts. For instance, in 1994, the Minnesota Supreme Court adopted rules requiring ADR in virtually all kinds of civil litigation (divorce and child-custody disputes are exempted, as they are in most parts of the country). At least forty-six of the fifty states now have some type of official ADR program.

Unlike an arbitrator, a mediator does not decide the merits of a particular case or rule in favor of one of the parties. Rather, the mediator helps people on opposite sides find common ground, make compromises, and settle their claims. Arbitrators and mediators are sometimes referred to as *neutrals*.

Certain types of disputes lend themselves to mediation, whereas in other types of disputes mediation would not be appropriate. Mediation works best where the parties have roughly equal bargaining power. Where power is unequal, traditional litigation may be more suitable, because litigation offers added protection to the weaker party. Mediation is commonly used in construction, homeowners', insurance, labor, real estate, and transportation cases, among others.

Mediation is actually a business you conduct *from* home. Even if you use your home office for business calls or administrative work, you certainly would not want the mediation to take place in your home. Rather, you must conduct mediations in a formal, neutral, and controlled setting such as a conference room.

Mediators must receive some training, but at present there are no uniform nationwide standards for training or credentialing mediators. Only about a dozen states actually require mediators to be licensed; but in only one of those states, Florida, are mediators required to be attorneys. However, in order to become impaneled as an American Arbitration Association mediator, you must meet certain specific requirements. The AAA and other groups will probably hammer out some national standards by the end of the decade.

Retired judges and lawyers constitute the majority of mediators, but a legal background isn't necessary. In fact, one mediator we spoke with emphasized that it is more important to have "a background as a human being." If you have significant experience or expertise in a particular field or industry, such as construction, human resources, real estate, or labor relations, you may want to specialize in that area. Mediators should also be good consensus builders, have calm and calming personalities, be creative at solving problems, and act in a professional and dignified manner. And, of course, mediators also must be completely unbiased and come to the process free of conflicts of interest.

Mediators usually charge by the hour or by the day. The fees normally are split by the disputing parties. Hourly rates vary from about $50 to $250, depending on the person's educational and occupational background (retired judges and lawyers tend to be at the higher end of the scale), his or her mediation training, and his or her area(s) of specialization. Another factor in what a mediator can charge is supply and demand. In some parts of the country, the abundance of mediators has depressed rates.

One disadvantage of this type of work is that you are frequently dealing with people who are angry, and you have to be very careful not to get caught in the crossfire. On the other hand, it feels good to help people reach a constructive solution to their problems.

Jim Stott of Stott, Monsma & Associates in Westlake Village, California, says it's possible to make a living as a mediator, but not by sitting and waiting for the phone to ring. Financially successful mediators probably spend 80 percent of their time doing marketing, and only 20 percent conducting mediations.

Stott stresses the importance of networking with people we call gatekeepers—attorneys, accountants, and mental-health professionals who are involved in mediation—and doing other kinds of marketing. When he started doing mediation, Stott says, he worked the "rubber chicken circuit—the Rotary, Kiwanis, and so on," giving speeches about conflict resolution. To generate business, he does conflict prevention training, writes articles on the subject, and does pro bono work, particularly for churches.

People who want to go into this field should find a particular niche.

For further information, contact a community mediation center in your area and ask about volunteering. Or call The American Arbitration Association, 140 West 51st Street, New York, NY 10020; (212) 484-4000. The AAA provides training and certification for mediators, sponsors conferences, and publishes *Dispute Resolution Times*, a quarterly newsletter, and *Dispute Resolution Journal*, also quarterly ($55 annual subscription). One recent book that offers an overview of the ADR process is *ADR in America*, by Robert Coulson, New York: American Arbitration Association, 1993 ($19.95). It may be ordered directly from the Publications Department of The American Arbitration Association, 140 West 51st Street, New York, NY 10020-1203; (212) 484-4011 or fax (212) 541-4841.

■ ■ ■ ■ ■

MYSTERY SHOPPING

Mystery shoppers, also called *silent shoppers* and *anonymous evaluators*, have actually been around for years, but as management gurus like Tom Peters preach the gospel of being close to one's customers, the emphasis on customer service has given this work new life. While businesses get customer input from feedback cards and toll-free telephone numbers, these techniques do not reveal many problems that can cost customers. Research indicates that nine out of ten dissatisfied customers will stop patronizing a firm without registering a complaint; they will, however, speak negatively to between nine and twelve other people about their dissatisfaction.

Thus a growing number of businesses and organizations are making use of mystery shoppers. The *mystery* about mystery shoppers is also what makes them effective—their identity as an evaluator is not known to the establishment's employees. The mystery shopper poses as a regular customer, then reports to their client about how he or she was treated and about other matters of business concern to the client.

Some market research firms and private investigators do this work, but it can be carved out as a niche on its own. It's been estimated that only one in ten potential businesses, government, and nonprofit organizations that would benefit from mystery shopping use it. So there's a large potential market for this service. One limitation, however, is that some states may define mystery shopping as undercover surveillance, which means that if the state also requires private detectives to be licensed, mystery shopping without a PI license may be illegal in those states. For example, Michigan is known for the stringent enforcement of its private investigator licensing law and there mystery shoppers are required by the state to be licensed private detectives.

Mystery shoppers are used to:

■ Check the quality of customer service. Besides businesses such as department stores, car dealers, and shopping malls, some of the other clients using mystery shoppers include charitable organizations and governmental organizations such as airport authorities who lease departments to restaurants, car-rental agencies, and gift shops. The hospitality industry is a big user of mystery shoppers: Hotels want to know how guests are treated. Restaurants want to know if their facilities are kept clean, how quickly customers are served, and about the quality of the food served.

■ Discover if employees are taking money from the till, stealing merchandise and supplies, or short-changing customers. Employees account for two of every three dollars of loss from shoplifting and other theft. So businesses where the owners are not physically on the premises want to make sure they are not being victimized by their own employees. Bartenders, for example, are watched to see if they give free drinks to friends. Mystery shoppers go to the movies and count the number of ticket buyers to match the total against those reported by the theater manager.

■ Monitor the effect of employee-training programs. Mystery shoppers are sent in, for example, before and after customer service, safety, and security training. Bank employees once played a more passive role, now they are expected to actively suggest other services to customers based on the situation presented or hints dropped about their needs. Shopper reports can let the bank know if the training to help tellers and officers assume this new role is working.

■ Learn if mutual fund sales representatives are telling the truth to their investor customers. The Federal Deposit Insurance Corporation uses mystery shoppers to monitor companies it regulates. If serious regulation of the life insurance industry ever occurs, mystery shopping will most likely be widely used.

■ Determine how billing is done by cellular phone companies. Mystery shoppers let cellular phone companies know if their billing practices are accurate.

■ Find out how collection departments and agencies are treating people who don't pay their bills. Companies want to know if those collecting money for them are effective without violating laws regulating collection practices.

- Check out the performance of competitors. Clients want to know how the service rendered by their competitors stacks up with their own.
- Check security measures. For example, a mystery shopper may sneak into a movie theater without buying a ticket to determine if the theater staff notices and how they react. A mystery shopper whose looks can pass for those of a juvenile might try to buy an alcoholic beverage drink or sneak into an R-rated movie theater.

Customers for a mystery shopping service are most apt to be local establishments whose owners are not on the premises or who own a number of stores in a community. Customers may also be international corporations seeking information about how their local installations are being operated.

A professional mystery shopper needs to be a good observer without being noticed and have a good memory to later recall details. A shopper needs to look like anyone. His or her appearance and personality should not stand out or be memorable. They need to be good enough actors that they appear to be nothing more than ordinary customers so they can return to stores without being spotted as shoppers. Opportunities also exist for people with expertise in the food business and other fields where one needs to be able to recognize theft and unsafe operations.

An advantage of using mystery shoppers is that it generally costs less than buying electronic surveillance systems or keeping constant watch on employees under one kind of suspicion or another.

Mystery shoppers charge retail establishments between $20 to $40 per shop, depending on how many stores there are to be shopped in a chain and how frequently an establishment is shopped. Checking a restaurant or hotel may take several visits, each lasting several hours. In this case, charges may be in the $100 range per site. Persons licensed as private investigators are apt to charge more—up to $80 to shop for a single establishment. The type of report desired—written or oral—will also affect the charge. Some mystery shoppers accept payment in the form of the client's own product or service.

■ ■ ■ ■ ■

PET-SITTING

Americans are nuts about their pets. Pets are apparently more popular than children, at least based on the sheer number of U.S. households that include pets—43 percent, versus 38 percent with children. Furthermore, American homes have almost as many pets as people. Three out of ten households have at least one dog, and just over two in ten households have one or more cats. As popular as dogs and cats are (52 million to 58 million dogs and 49 million to 60 million cats), fish are even more numerous (78 million), but there are only an estimated 13,265 pet-sitting firms in the United States to care for them.

Because pet owners work and travel just like other people, pet-sitting services are gaining customers. Pet-sitters feed and care for pets, homes, and plants. They may also bring in the mail, take trash to the curb for pickup, and do other home-care things for the owner, too. And if the pet is sick, they may need to take the animal to a vet or give medications.

Sheldon Belinkoff, who along with his wife, Janet, operates both a pet-sitting service with over twenty sitters and a pet transportation service, advises, "To really make money at pet-sitting, you must be around seven days a week and be prepared to give up your time. It's a seven-day-a-week business." Carole Tomas of the National Association of Professional Pet Sitters, adds that pet-sitting is "a serious business that no one should enter lightly. It requires knowledge of animal health and behavior, skills in dealing with emergencies and problems, the ability to deal with the public, and the ability to profitably run a business and successfully manage employees or independent contractors. You have to be dedicated, hardworking, and capable of dealing with many kinds of problems."

If pet-sitting appeals to you, there are four ways you can approach it:

■ Some sitters make daily stops at a customer's home to feed and visit with pets as well as water the plants
■ Other sitters actually live in the home while the residents are away
■ Still other sitters open their homes to clients' pets
■ Another approach is to operate your pet-sitting business as an agency or referral service matching sitters to clients.

Whether you choose to do the pet-sitting yourself or develop an agency, your primary market will be working singles, two-career couples, and people who travel regularly or for extended periods of time, such as businesspeople or well-to-do retired people. New residents to a community, who do not yet have family or community ties, are also good candidates for your marketing materials.

The income potential of a pet-sitting business depends on whether you do the sitting or act as an agent. A full-time visiting sitter charges $10 on average per daily visit (although this price varies by area, with major cities sometimes being closer to $12 and smaller cities and suburbs only $7). Unless your travel area is very small, you will be able to cover eight to twelve clients per day (based on half-hour visits plus travel time). On the average, you would earn about $120 per day, minus your travel expenses. At this level of activity, you should net between $450 and $550 per week, or about $2,100 a month. Many sitters also earn additional income by doing other chores for a fee and selling pet products. Some also offer in-home grooming services and dog obedience classes.

If you choose to act as an agency, you have several alternative ways to charge. You may take a commission of 30 to 40 percent for each visit by a staffer or independent contractor. Although this is a large share, it allows an agency to offer bonding and liability insurance to these people.

Classified ads in local newspapers and a yellow-pages listing play an important part in getting business. You can also develop referral relationships with travel agents, cleaning services, pet groomers, veterinarians, pet-food stores, the local humane society—anyone pet owners would call or talk to about finding someone to look after their Spot or Midnight. You should provide them with a stack of attractive business cards that people will keep and attractive flyers to give to their customers. Travel agents might even include your flyer or card with tickets they send out. Posting notices on bulletin boards may produce clients, too.

For more information on the business, contact the National Association of Professional Pet Sitters (NAPPS), 1200 G Street, N.W., Suite 760, Washington DC 20005; (202) 393-3317, fax (202) 393-0336. NAPPS offers group liability and bonding insurance, products you can sell, newsletters, books on running a small business, marketing kits, standard forms and contracts, and a Mentor program that matches a novice sitter with a "seasoned pro." They will also have a certification program that can help your credibility.

A noted book in this business is *Pet Sitting for Profit,* by Patti Moran. Write to her at New Beginnings, Box 540, High Bridge Road, Pinnacle, NC 27043. Another book in this field is *Sit & Grow Rich: Petsitting and Housesitting for Profit,* by Patricia A. Doyle, Upstart Press, 1994; (800) 245-2665.

Franchises are also available at fees ranging from $2,000 to $8,500. These include: Pets Are Inn (12 South Sixth Street, Suite 950, Minneapolis, MN 55402; [800] 248-PETS); Critter Care (1825 Darren Drive, Baton Rouge, LA 70816; [504] 766-4151); and Pet Nanny of America (1000 Long Boulevard, #9, Lansing, MI 48911; [517] 694-4400).

■ ■ ■ ■ ■

PLANT CAREGIVER

If you love plants and flowers and feel you have an affinity for making them prosper and grow, becoming a plant caregiver might be the career for you. Plant caregivers do a wide range of tasks for residential and commercial clients: they water and fertilize plants on a weekly basis, weed and prune as needed, design and lay out plant arrangements, diagnose diseases and care for sick plants, and many other tasks to ensure that a client's plant environment is healthy and colorful.

Getting into this business requires a love of plants and knowledge of how they thrive. It helps of course to have familiarity with many kinds of plants so that you can recommend and select arrangements for your clients, varying the plant colors and textures to create a harmonious, pleasing environment.

Plant Parenthood in Santa Monica, California, is an example of a successful venture in this field. The company began when its owner, Jeanne Jones, who had a background in botany, realized that taking care of plants was an appealing way for her to make a living. Her first contract originated from friends who owned a company located in an office building, and they arranged for her to come in and care for the plants in several offices. Jeanne then expanded her business using ads in the yellow pages, but now word of mouth and referrals mostly drive the growth of her business. Jeanne also has a few affiliations with nurseries, which recommend her to customers who ask the nursery if they know anyone who can help take care of their plants. Jeanne's clients include residential and commercial facilities. Although Jeanne does not do this, other avenues to get business include teaming up with architects, interior designers, indoor environmental testers, and even maintenance and cleaning services.

Plant caregivers charge between $15 to $25 per hour, although the best way to charge is to get a retainer contract for several months at time based on weekly visits. Jeanne goes into a new client's location to assess the needs and bases her rate on how many hours she feels she needs to spend there. She agrees that if you have three to four large clients per day at an average of $75 per visit, you can easily earn $225 to $300 a day. Of course, one advantage of the business is that you can work as many days as you like.

Plant-caregiving services thrive best in warmer areas where people tend to have plants blooming year-round, but the business can work well in any locale. It also helps to focus your clientele in one area, to reduce the amount of time you spend driving from customer to customer. The one problem with the business is that taking care of plants is viewed as a luxury, so some clients cancel their contracts in a recessionary climate or if their own business can't afford to keep you.

■ ■ ■ ■ ■

PROPOSAL AND GRANT WRITER

There are literally thousands of "requests for proposals" (RFPs) put out each year by the federal government, state governments, cities, counties, and special districts in every field and endeavor, from developing or building military equipment, to installing high-technology equipment in offices here or overseas, to furnishing desks and chairs in a government office building. In fact, just about any company that wants to do business with the government (at the federal, state, and city level) must write a lengthy, detailed bid or proposal to get the contract. These proposals are often technical, laying out the exact method of accomplishing the goal, with schematics, timetables, management methods, budgets, and company profiles.

The problem with this process of RFPs is that many companies do not have the skill to write them, thus creating a large market for specialized technical or proposal writers who can help firms write up and publish high-quality documents to win bids. Such writing professionals know the rules and regulations governing the creation and formatting of formal proposals, and they can produce them much more intelligently and knowledgeably than the company might have. In some cases, the proposal writers also learn about the RFPs before the companies do, and they therefore also help to bring business to a company by notifying them of the release of the bid request.

Proposal writers are sometimes generalists with a broad knowledge of diverse fields, but many are specialists in a single area with a background in agriculture, communications, engineering, business, medicine, or another advanced industry. Some writers have enough specific experience in a field that they even advise their clients on how to improve upon the original idea or product that is the subject of the proposal. Nevertheless, as Steve Wilson, a proposal writer in Lansing, Michigan, says, "Any writer with good skills can do this work, whatever your background. Like lawyers, it doesn't matter who your client is; if you can write logically and can understand the technology enough to explain it, you can do it."

Other than their writing ability and specific experience in a field, proposal and grant writers must also have excellent communications and presentation skills because they are frequently interacting with high-level managers and executives of companies. They must also be willing to travel (a nice perk, according to Wilson), because some proposals require the writer to go on location to view the site or equipment. (Wilson has been to Kuwait and Southeast Asia several times.)

Proposal writers should also be well versed in using spreadsheet, database, and desktop-publishing software, because their job often includes producing the final documents along with financial projections, budgets, bidding information, graphs, charts, and tables—all of which must be handsomely laid out and printed. Even if they don't do the actual desktop publishing, they must know how to get the documents published and printed.

The best way to get business is to be proactive. Wilson reads the *Commerce Business Daily* at the library almost every day, searching for proposals that he has an interest in. When he sees a proposal that he might develop, he does some preliminary research and will then call a few companies that might be interested in bidding on it; in this way, he has already perhaps helped a given company become aware of the RFP and is, therefore, more likely to get the work. Other than such research, nearly all proposal writers agree that word of mouth is the next-best marketing method, if you have a successful track record. Some writers will also do advertising or direct mail to companies that might be interested in government or foundation funding.

Making a living as a proposal and grant writer may require a few years of experience as you learn the ropes and develop contacts. Some proposals take one or two days to write, but many can take months to research and create. A successful writer in a specialty area such as energy or business can charge from $2,000 to $10,000 per proposal, depending on length, and may have annual earnings from $50,000 to $150,000.

Other jobs for proposal writers include writing grant proposals for the thousands of grants available each year from over 35,000 private foundations and corporations that provide money to individuals and nonprofit associations for myriad civic, educational, and social-welfare programs. Writers may also work on proposals for companies seeking seed money from the Small Business Administration through their Innovative Research (SBIR) program.

Another service for companies once they have gotten a contract is to assist them with federal contract compliance. Smaller companies are not staffed to meet the onerous paperwork requirements of holding a government contract, particularly a federal contract. From this need have arisen consultants who provide this service on a contractual basis. To do this requires significant experience in administering federal contracts.

Resources for the proposal-writing business include:

• **Catalogue of Federal Domestic Assistance** is available in print, on disk, and online. For ordering information, call (202) 708-5126 or write GSA, Federal Assistance Program Catalog Staff, Reporter's Building, 300 Seventh Street SW, Washington, DC 20407.

• *Commerce Business Daily,* available in libraries and on CompuServe.

• *Doing Business with the U.S. Government: How to Sell Your Goods & Services to the 200 Billion Dollar Federal Market,* Herman Holtz, Prima Pub., 3875 Atherton Road, Rocklin, CA 95765; (916) 632-4400; 1993.

• *Government Assistance Almanac,* by J. Robert Dumouchel, Detroit: Omnigraphics, Inc., is a better-indexed version of the **Catalogue of Federal Domestic Assistance.**

• **Lesko's Info-Power II,** Detroit: Gale, 1993, by the ever-colorful Matthew Lesko, is a valuable work with four and a half pounds and 1,600 pages of information and telephone numbers for both the federal and state governments.

• **Silver Associates, Inc.,** 1647 Buck Hill Drive, Huntington Valley, PA 19006, (215) 947-4817, teaches seminars on proposal writing.

• You also need copies of the *U.S. Government Style Manual* and *The Chicago Manual of Style.*

■ ■ ■ ■ ■

REFERRAL SERVICE

Have you ever had something break and not known whom to call to fix it? Sure, the yellow pages have listings, but how can you know who's good and who's a rip-off? Most city people don't know, and who has time to do research? That's where a referral service can help. You've probably seen ads on television for services offering referrals to doctors or dentists. This idea can be applied to almost any area of need and interest: appliance repair, art events, auto repair, baby-sitters, caterers, child care, contractors and trades-people, hairdressers, house-sitters, landlords, musicians, party locations, pet-sitters, plumbers, printers, real estate agents, restaurants, roommates, shop-ping information, special events, therapists, travel and tourist information, tutors, wedding services, even friendship.

Referral services may be set up to receive their income in one of several ways. Probably the most common is for the service to charge the business or professional a fee, with the service free to the consumers. The business might pay the fee monthly or annually, or pay a commission on each referral. Services that offer roommate matching, friendship matching, or house/pet/baby-sitting often charge both parties equally. An on-line referral service is another possibility, with users paying on a per-use basis or buying an annual subscription good for a certain amount of research time (see Bulletin Board Service). Some referral service owners make close to $100,000 per year, but don't expect that to come quickly. You may make only $3,000 or $4,000 the first year.

The key to a successful referral service is the quality of the research you do in order to screen the businesses and professionals you send people to. Your credibility depends on people being able to trust the accuracy or your infor-mation and the reliability of those to whom you refer them. Therefore, you must gather enough information so that either you can refer with confidence or the consumer can make an informed decision.

Teddi Kessie, owner of The End Result, a referral service specializing in the building trades in Sherman Oaks, California, personally interviews each tradesperson and checks references, licensing, bonding, and insurance. She advises caution and reliance on personal judgment and intuition. Some referral services specializing in professional services, such as dentistry or therapy, use a review board to approve professionals to be served. You'll also need to drop vendors from your referral list who don't meet your standards or about whom you get complaints that are not solved to the customer's satisfaction.

All you need to start a referral service is a business telephone line and well-organized information. It's basically a database service that requires a com-puter and database software that allows vendors to be listed by the criteria the consumer requests. (Or you can run the business manually if you prefer, but using a computer is far easier.) You'll also need business cards and brochures or flyers suited to the type of vendor you specialize in making referrals to.

For example, let's suppose you are starting a home-repair referral service. Leave flyers with hardware stores and post them on grocery-store bulletin boards, on church bulletin boards, on car windshields, and in mall or boutique parking lots. If you can afford to do so, advertise on the radio and television (it can be cheaper than you think!), in a Pennysaver-type newspaper, and/or in the local newspaper. Such advertising will not only attract calls but also make it easier to sell your services to vendors, because they see you making an investment to reach people who want to use them. You can also write articles for local publications on choosing the right repair person.

Kessie considers herself a combination personal counselor and go-between when problems arise. She adds value to her service by advising homeowners what to expect from various types of repair and remodeling projects. "When you put in a new kitchen floor, it will be higher than the old one; your refrigerator may not fit where it used to, and you won't be able to remove your dishwasher without cutting up the floor." These kinds of tips will save clients unforeseen hassles and keep them coming back to you. On occasion Kessie has also mediated between tradesperson and homeowner when a dispute arose, and once or twice she's covered the (modest) cost of the repair herself when she was unable to effect an agreement.

Franchises in this field are offered by the following firms:

- Family Friend Management, 895 Mount Vernon Highway, N.W., Atlanta, GA 30317; (404) 643-3000

- Homewatch, 2865 South Colorado Boulevard, Denver, CO 80222; (303) 758-7290

- National Tenant Network, Box 1664, Lake Grove, OR 97035; (800) 228-0989. This firm offers computerized tenant-screening services for landlords.

Other resources: *How to Make a Success Out of a Referral Service*, Teddi Kessie, 13061 Hartsook Street, Sherman Oaks, CA 91423. $49.95, plus $5 shipping and handling. Write for brochure, *How to Make Money by Turning Away Customers: An Information Package on Running a Successful Referral Service*, 6407 Irwin Court, Oakland, CA 94609; (510) 655-4296. $75.

■ ■ ■ ■ ■

REPAIR SERVICES

Despite the fact that America is said to be a disposable society, most of us prefer to hold on to what we have if we can keep it working long enough. We don't want to dispose of a vacuum cleaner that falters just after the warranty expires. We don't want to take the lawn mower to the dump just because the engine stops. We don't want to throw out our favorite chair just because it has a rip in the upholstery. But we simply don't know how, nor do we usually have the time to fix things that break down, rip, or tear. That's why there are literally dozens of business possibilities for repair services. We estimate there are 11,311 now in the U.S.

Repair services run the gamut from the jack-of-all trades handyman who does small home repairs and remodeling to specialists who repair small engines, screens, vinyl, furniture and woodwork, china, windshields, telephones, clocks, watches, home appliances, and electrical items like vacuum cleaners and VCRs. (See the entry on Computer Repair and Maintenance for the related specialization in this fast-growing area.) One man who phoned into a radio show on which we were appearing in Chicago told us he was making $60,000 a year gluing things that are broken. He had begun ten years earlier charging $3 an item. Now he charges $75 an hour and specializes in serving antique dealers and collectors.

A repair business can be started on a full-time or part-time basis, and you can either be a generalist or a specialist. You might focus, for example, on repairing old watches and clocks, by contacting antique shops and their customers. A vinyl-repair service mends rips, tears, and color damage to diner seats, automobiles, movie-theater seats, and furniture in sports locations, hospitals, offices, hotels, government agencies, and homes.

Specialized equipment is needed for many types of services, but other than the cost of the necessary equipment, the start-up costs for a repair business are modest: business cards, well-done flyers or simple brochures stating what you do, and multipart forms for quotes or proposals and invoicing. Rates vary greatly, ranging from $15 to $100 per hour, depending on what you repair and your location. You can also increase your income by stocking replacement parts, which you buy wholesale from suppliers, and charging a markup.

Consider what you have for repairing and, if necessary, what training you'll need and where that's available—community colleges, trade schools, home-study courses. If you are concentrating on small jobs, which is what clients usually have the most difficulty finding people to do, keep your travel area as localized as possible to reduce the amount of nonbillable time you spend driving.

Repair work can come from either the front door or the back door. Front door refers to repairs for customers who contact you. The work may be done either on the customers' premises or on your premises. (If you do work on your premises, check your zoning laws if you intend to hang out a sign in front of your house. Many communities do not allow commercial signs in residential areas.) Back door refers to work that is brought into a retailer's repair shop or establishment, which the retailer then subcontracts out to outside repair people who do the work on their own premises.

To get front-door work, you can do any of the following:

- Distribute well-done flyers or simple brochures in your neighborhood. If what you repair is also used in offices (e.g., furniture, leather, vinyl, etc.), leave brochures in office buildings, schools, and businesses.
- Post flyers with tear-off phone numbers at bus stops and on kiosks and bulletin boards.
- Run classified and small display ads in neighborhood publications and local business journals, which reach potential customers at a reasonable cost.
- Advertise in the yellow pages.

Once you have clients, the best marketing method is word of mouth. One handyman we know in Los Angeles is able to work within only a five-mile-square area because word of mouth from satisfied customers generates plenty of new clients on a regular basis.

To get back-door work, contact retailers and repair shops directly. Resources for getting into a repair business include:

Vinyl

The Vinylman Company, 13453 Pumice Street, Norwalk, CT 90650; (310) 921-9993. Provides you with materials to set up a vinyl-repair inventory.

Upholstery

The Foley-Belshaw Institute, 6301 Esplanade, Redondo Beach, CA 95926. Publishes a book that teaches the art of upholstery.

Small Engines

McGraw-Hill's NRI Schools, 4401 Connecticut Avenue, N.W., Washington, DC 20008. Offers a course in small-engine repair that includes a small engine and generator.

Windshields

GlasWeld, P.O. Box 5755, Bend, OR 97708; (800) 321-2597. Offers start-up kits in a range of prices.

Home Repairs

Handyman House Calls, 640 Northland Road, #33, Forest Park, OH 45240; (513) 825-3863. A franchise that provides handymen to do home maintenance and repair. Their fee is $6,250.

■ ■ ■ ■ ■

RESTORATION SERVICES

Consumers today no longer simply cover stained hardwood floors with linoleum; they want the floors sanded, stained, and finished to bring out the old luster, sometimes with modern protections. They don't throw out old rugs and carpets; they want them repaired and restored. They prefer the old enameled iron or porcelain plumbing fixtures to the new plastic variety, and they want someone to refurbish the old finishes. They don't take the old dining table to the dump; they want it carefully hand stripped, and they want the damage repaired and the wood and carvings restored to their original beauty. They sometimes even want to have the furniture stripped and then do the rest themselves. They don't want to rip out and replace old tile work. They want to see cracks and glazing repaired and refinished. They don't tear down old houses; they want to match the detailing that remains and restore old homes to their original appearance.

Both appreciation for what's old and the cost of what's new are making restoring architectural features, plumbing fixtures, floors, and antiques into lucrative businesses that can be started on the side and built into full-time businesses. Each specialty provides a natural market for the skilled craftsperson or someone wishing to develop a skill.

Like many repair businesses, these are based on getting a deposit from the customer to cover parts and materials. It's also important to provide the customer with a written proposal and to get a signed contract so both you and the customer know precisely what work will be done and for what price.

In addition to working with residential clients, you can also work with commercial ones, such as antique shops and interior designers. A business or an apartment or hotel owner can save thousands of dollars by restoring floors, bathrooms, tile, or even quantities of damaged furniture rather than replacing them.

To reach residential customers, you can rely on yellow-pages ads; flyers posted on bulletin boards and kiosks, and in antique shops, hardware stores, and lumber yards; radio advertising; and tear-off pads. It is far easier to reach commercial clients. You can contact them with letters, brochures, and personal selling. Sometimes a single commercial client can become an ongoing source of business, keeping you busy part of each week.

In either case, in addition to a yellow-pages ad, you will want to get as much publicity about your service as possible. Publicity will give you credibility with both consumers and businesses. Your publicity campaign might involve writing articles for the local newspaper or regional magazine on such subjects as how to decide if something is worth restoring, the various types of restoration methods available (including the pros and cons of each), or the ways to prolong the life of wood, tile, enamel, floors, or whatever else your specialty might be. You can also send news releases that focus on a particularly unusual item or location that you have restored to the home-improvement or antiques editor of your local newspaper.

Restoration services are also needed after natural disasters like floods and earthquakes, as well as after fires. For instance, after the Los Angeles earthquake, many people wanted to have their furniture, tile, and rugs repaired.

Although restoration work may be physically demanding, the restoration business is not just for men. Successful bath and kitchen refinishing businesses are owned by women who excel at networking and aggressively market their knowledge and skill. The restoration business can not only be profitable but it also can be enjoyable to see your labor help create a nice-looking, clean, and completely refurbished room or piece of furniture.

Start-up costs for a restoration business depend entirely on the particular type of restoration service you wish to perform. Your costs can range from just a few hundred dollars to purchase supplies (strippers, rags, steel wool, sandpaper, and so on) if you set yourself up in business or you can spend as much as $17,500 to buy one of the many restoration franchises in bathroom and kitchen tile refinishing, carpets, or fixtures. In fact, there are a number of franchises that provide training, tools, and materials for a turnkey business. A few are listed below, but it is wise to read through several business magazines and identify as many franchises as you can, call them to investigate their fees, royalties (if any), and training, and make your decision based on what is best financially for you.

Tile, Bath, and Kitchen Refinishing

Bathcrest, 2425 South Progress Drive, Salt Lake City, UT 84119; (800) 826-6790.

Perma-Glaze, 1638 South Research Loop Road, #160, Tucson, AZ 85710; (800) 332-7397.

Worldwide Refinishing Systems, 500 Lake Air Drive, Waco, TX 76710; (817) 755-8839.

Fixtures

Worldwide Refinishing Systems, 500 Lake Air Drive, Waco, TX 76710; (817) 755-8839.

Carpets

Langenwalter Carpet Dye Concept, 1111 Richfield Rd., Placentia, GA 92670; (800) 422-4370.

Books

Cleaning Consultant Services, Inc., 1512 Western Ave., P.O. Box 1273, Seattle, WA 98111; (206) 682-9748. Publisher of *Cleaning Business Magazine* and many books on topics related to cleaning and restoring, such as *Oriental Rug Repair, Formica Restoration and Repair, Technical Guide to Water Restoration Damage, Fire Restoration and Insurance Work, Wood Furniture Touch-Up,* among many others.

■ ■ ■ ■ ■

REUNION PLANNER

The 1990s will see more twenty-, twenty-five-, and thirty-year high-school and college reunions than any other decade in history. Besides perhaps reviving styles of the 60s and 70s, why is this important? Because reunions provide the basis for a happy kind of service business. In the past, reunions were arranged by people who had more time than today's two-career and single-parent households, so today the staging of reunions is often turned over to paid planners.

The job of a reunion planner is to locate missing class members, mail invitations, take reservations, hire the band or disc jockey, arrange for food, make name tags with yearbook pictures on them, and otherwise coordinate all aspects of the actual reunion. In addition to high-school and college graduating classes, other groups that have reunions include military units, former dormitory residents, former company employees, and families.

What primarily differentiates reunion planners from party or event planners is their ability to locate long-lost class members. The focus of the party is the people, not the event. So it is a highly specialized undertaking, and even the criteria for selecting locations, food, and decorations are different from those associated with other kinds of parties.

Locating classmates involves making telephone calls; searching computer databases; contacting college record keepers, alumni associations, and previous employers; searching telephone directories, birth and marriage records, and voter registration lists; tracking through friends, neighbors, and associates, and even using special tracking companies such as Re-Unite of Florida. The size of this research task is one of the reasons reunion planners start their work a year or more in advance of a reunion.

According to Judy and Shell Norris, founders of Class Reunion, Inc., the first reunion-planning business in the country, this work is seasonal, with the season running from April through Thanksgiving. The Norrises, who employ over twenty home-based researchers and six other people, plan between 85 and 105 reunions per year from their home. But they don't meet with their clients (the reunion planning committees) at home; ordinarily, they meet at the hotel or other facility where the event is going to take place.

Now in their thirteenth year, the Norrises are finding that they're getting a lot of repeat business from groups whose tenth or twentieth reunion they organized ten years ago. "People automatically come back to us because we have all their records," says Shell. In addition, they get a lot of new business, all of which comes from referrals.

The Norrises say some large companies try to coordinate reunions for people in different parts of the country, but they feel a smaller, local reunion-planning business can provide personal service that the big companies can't match.

Reunion planners take their fee from the money paid by each attendee— the more people who show up, the higher the income per reunion. Thus reunion committees do not risk any money, and reunion planners are rewarded for their success in generating large turnouts.

To get started, begin with smaller reunions. Once established, you can set minimums, such as a class having at least 300 members, to get a better return on your time. Annual income from reunion planning can range from a modest sum based on part-time work to six figures.

To get an idea of how many reunions are being held in your area, just count the number of high schools. Each year there are likely to be as many as eight reunions per high school: five-year, ten-year, fifteen-year, twenty-year, twenty-five-year, thirty-year, forty-year, and fifty-year.

To get started, you need business cards, stationery, a brochure, and a computer with database and desktop-publishing software. Much of your business will depend on networking, to make contact with reunion committees. Start with your own high school, or your spouse's, or your children's. Make contact with hotels, printers, display companies (for decorations), florists, caterers, public-address system providers, booking agents, photographers, name-badge suppliers, restaurants, and any other service that might be useful in planning a reunion. Training to become a reunion planner, and further information, can be obtained from Shell and Judy Norris, Class Reunion, P.O. Box 844, Skokie, IL 60076; (708) 677-4949. *Reunion!* software is designed for planning a school reunion.

■ ■ ■ ■ ■

RUBBER STAMP BUSINESS

This business surprised us, but many of the 5,214 people in the rubber stamp business in the United States are earning good money making and selling rubber stamps. People love them and buy them through mail order, at arts-and-crafts shows, and in specialty stores. People are known to sell as much as $2,000 to $5,000 worth of rubber stamps a day at arts-and-crafts shows.

People adorn envelopes and stationery with rubber-stamp impressions of animals, moons, stars, clouds, people, rockets, spaceships, and an endless variety of designs. Using an embossing powder, raised impressions can be created. Metallic and glow-in-the-dark inks humble the customary red and blue stamp pads available in office-supply stores. Special inks enable stamps to be used on fabrics, glossy wrapping papers, foil, and mylar. You can also use rubber-stamping techniques to make badges, buttons, and magnets to be sold as gift items by using a Badge-a-Minit system (Badge-a-Minit, 348 North 30th Road, Lasalle, IL 61301; [800] 223-4103; about $50).

It is not difficult to make your own rubber stamps, and you can use free public-domain clip art, which offers an almost unending supply of subjects. If you like to create your own designs, rubber stamps can be the vehicle for you to be a commercially successful artist, with thousands of people enjoying your creations.

In addition, new technology has made making stamps easier. Instead of using hot-metal type, matrix boards, and a vulcanizer to melt rubber, nowadays you can produce stamps quickly and easily with a personal computer and laser printer used in conjunction with a photopolymer system ($2,800). If you are making art stamps in bulk, however, you will still need to make them from rubber, although you can make the pattern plate with the photopolymer system. If you don't want to invest in the system right away, you can have someone else make the pattern plates for you until you have a good idea what your average volume will be. A washout unit ($3,500) to wash the liquid resin out of the plate is a big advantage, although you can wash by hand with soap and water. The principal source for equipment and supplies is Stewart-Superior, 1800 Larchmont Avenue, Chicago, IL 60613; (800) 621-1205 or (312) 935-6025.

If you make your own stamps, you can sell them at about six times your cost at retail or three times cost at wholesale; if you resell other people's stamps, you can expect to double your money. Bobby Boschan, who as a partner in Stamps, Stamps, Stamps, in Los Angeles, told us many manufacturers sell both retail and wholesale.

Linda Bjorge, owner of L & W Stamps, a home-based manufacturer of business stamps in Onalaska, Wisconsin, says that you need to be an accurate speller with artistic ability and attention to detail. You don't really need technical skills because the suppliers provide excellent technical support.

Resources

Marking Device Association International, 435 N. Michigan Ave., Suite 1717, Chicago, IL 60611-4067; (312) 644-0828.

Marking Industry Magazine, Marking Devices Publishing, 113 Adell Place, Elmhurst, IL 60126; (708) 832-5200. For manufacturers of rubber and photopolymer stamps.

Rubber Stampin' Retailer (magazine), Marking Devices Publishing, 113 Adell Place, Elmhurst, IL 60126; (708) 832-5200. For sellers of art stamps.

Rubberstampmadness (magazine), 408 S.W. Monroe Avenue, Corvallis OR 97330; (503) 752-0075.

SUPPLIERS

Stewart-Superior Corp., 10 Madison Road, #CN 2850, Fairfield, NJ 07004; (201) 244-0505.

Stewart-Superior Corp., 10723 Turbeville Dr., Dallas, TX 75243; (214) 348-9308.

Stewart-Superior Corp., 641 S. Palm St., La Habra, CA 90631; (310) 690-4445.

Louis Melind Co., 7631 N. Austin Ave., P.O. Box 1112, Skokie, IL 60076-8112; (708) 581-2500.

Mounts and handles: M & R Marking, 100 Springfield Ave., Piscataway, NJ 08855-6969; (908) 562-9500.

■ ■ ■ ■ ■

SIGN MAKER

Can you imagine a city or town without signs? Probably not, because signs are everywhere—not just street signs and "house-for-sale" signs, but signs on trucks, storefronts, buildings, short and tall posts, in front of homes and farms, scattered through all parks and zoos—in other words, generally in most places where we work or play. These signs tell us more than the name of the business or individual occupying a building; they give us more than a direction or an instruction. A good sign not only conveys basic information about who or what is located there but also communicates something about the occupants and what they do.

Ken Berry got the idea for a sign-making business when visiting a friend who published a magazine for people selling their own homes. Ken's friend was overwhelmed with work, so when Ken answered the phone for him and discovered people were asking where they could get a good real-estate sign, he went home and started making For Sale by Owner signs that he now sells through retail outlets such as hardware stores. Ken's company, Sign Power, also makes customized signs for realtors, lumber companies, contractors, architects, roofing companies, boat shops, boat owners, and even for other sign makers.

To make good signs, you need to have an eye for design, although sign making now is simpler than it was in the past thanks to computer design programs, scanners, clip art, and special plotters that hold a knife that cuts pressure sensitive films and vinyls. The same process can be used for signs as on trucks, cars, awnings, banners, and T-shirts.

To sell your sign-making services, you need a good collection of samples to show clients. This is so important that when he first started, Berry even made signs for new clients at near cost in order to have them for his portfolio. Another idea is to create custom signs for worthy causes or for highly trafficked locations that will get people talking about your work.

A natural source of customers is people who have signs that need replacing; it just takes observation and shoe leather to find them. Berry says, "The trick is being willing to make sales calls. People will procrastinate about making a sign, so you need to go to them. Then you need to show them enough samples that they become involved in making a choice—not deciding yes or no."

Real estate brokers are a good source of referrals as well as of information on what people are paying for signs and whether they're happy with the quality of the signs they have. Another source of customers is new businesses, which you can find in the listings of new businesses in your city's daily or weekly business journal.

Yellow-page advertising can be expected to more than pay for itself. Research shows that businesses frequently turn to the yellow pages when needing signage.

Start-up costs for a sign business run about $6,000 to $12,000, including a computer, plotter that cuts vinyl, scanner, CD-ROM drive, and supplies. You should also count on periodic investments in new technology to remain competitive, because new processes and equipment are regularly being invented. This equipment allows you to do small runs of signs, but if you have to fulfill a large order of say fifty signs, you'll need to use a printing press to save time and cut costs. A used press will cost $6,000 to $7,000, and you'll need enough space both for the press and for drying racks for the signs. If you don't have a printing press, you can either subcontract the printing to another sign maker or find a printer in your area. Printing on plastic is almost as economical as printing on cardboard, and your customers will be happier.

Small runs of signs made by the 42,827 sign-making firms in the United States sell for $30 to $50 for a one-sided 18-by-24-inch sign and $60 to $100 for a two-sided version. There is an endless market for signs, and more and more clients are looking for unusual and creative designs.

Sign Business Magazine (1008 Depot Hill Road, Broomfield, CO; [303]

469-0424) is the leading publication in this field and contains many articles of interest and ads for equipment and franchises.

Also, Berry sells equipment and does printing for sign makers who do not yet own presses. He can be reached at (206) 283-3414.

■ ■ ■ ■ ■

TRAVEL SALESPERSON/CONSULTANT/ TOUR OPERATOR

Travel is the world's largest industry, employing one out of nine workers, and it continues to grow. People spend more of their leisure time traveling than they do reading, watching sports, pursuing hobbies, or even attending church and cultural events. Leisure accounts for four out of five trips people take. The point is, by addressing people's passion for travel, you can earn a living while fulfilling your own love of travel.

There are three possible paths that a home-based travel devotee can follow: outside travel sales, travel consultant, or tour operator. Here's a brief rundown on each:

Outside Travel Sales.   Although restrictions on airline ticketing prevent your having a full travel agency in your home, you can associate with any travel agency willing to work with you in your community. Your affiliation may run the gamut from simply referring business to them, for which you may get a 10 percent commission, to actually working with your own clients, arranging their travel, making the bookings, and having your agency cut the tickets (because you are not allowed to do so). For this latter kind of work, the agency may give you as much as sixty to seventy percent of the commission. An alternative to working with a local travel agency is to join one of the growing number of networked travel agencies like Leisure Group Limited, which use almost entirely independent home-based sales agents in lieu of in-house staff. You typically pay a small fee such as $50 with Leisure to use their name and official ticketing number for bookings, then fax or mail them the information every time you do a booking for your clients and they cut the tickets for you. (Watch out, though, as some unscrupulous agencies charge thousands of dollars to "allow" you to become an outside sales representative bringing them business!) Outside travel sales can be an interesting foray into the field, although it is difficult to compete with larger, more full-service agencies that can garner the corporate accounts.

Travel Consultant.   Travel agents are usually too busy to provide truly personalized service to people looking for gobs of details and advice for a planned trip. Many agents also simply do not have in-depth knowledge of every conceivable destination. As a result, a new kind of profession is developing: in-depth travel consulting. Consultants typically use their intimate knowledge of a country or region to plan customized tours for discerning clients who are willing to pay for special advice. The consultant might provide a detailed hour-by-hour itinerary, complete with personalized recommendations for romantic restaurants, secluded spots, or exciting nightlife. Consultants also sometimes arrange the bookings, faxing or phoning hoteliers and innkeepers, and then having a local agency cut the tickets. In short, the consultant's services complement rather than substitute for those of travel agents.

Consultants typically charge a flat fee, ranging from $50 to $100 per hour, which varies depending on how detailed a plan you provide. Some travel consultants furnish eighty-page custom-written books supplemented with maps and other helpful information. This business is extremely personal, so you have to interview your clients in-depth and with enough skill that you can understand their needs. You need to be able to pick up on likes and dislikes the client has about traveling. This ability to go right to the heart of the client's needs and make appealing suggestions will also help you get the job in the first place. You have to know the destination like the back of your hand as well, including facilities for special dietary and transportation needs, cultural interests, shopping, and a host of other details. That means you have to visit the destination often, so some of your gross must go to cover your own travel expenses. Some travel consultants have arrangements with local firms, or they set up their own branches, which make bookings for them because they are home based.

Marjorie Shaw, who operates *Insider's Italy* in Brooklyn, New York, and Kajsa Agostini, owner of *Point of View* in Tarzana, California, agree: this is not a business you can delegate. It requires your own personal knowledge, attention, and skill. You must be bilingual if your destination is a non-English-speaking one and you must understand both cultures—ours and that of the destination. That way you know what will appeal to your clients as well as where to find it. It is so important to travel to your destination often that Ms. Shaw estimates your travel expenses will be 20 percent of your gross. Both women were born in the country they now specialize in—Italy in the case of Ms. Shaw, and France for Ms. Agostini.

Tour operators. Tour operators organize and conduct the tours for clients, charging the participants a fee sufficient to cover their costs and make a profit. We estimate there are 10,638 tour operators including those who are home based. Many home-business tour operators cater to highly specialized interests or personal hobbies, such as fitness tours, spiritual tours, tours of English gardens, tours of the great vineyards, and so forth, based on their own personal knowledge and experience. Today, many of the most popular tours involve sports and adventure, such as rock-climbing tours, kayaking tours, bicycle tours, river-rafting tours, and cross-country or downhill ski tours.

If you are a tour operator, you must not only know about uniquely pleasurable locations and excursions, but you must also be able to sell your tours and orchestrate the entire trip for all those who participate. You plan the tour, make the arrangements, and recruit the participants—and sometimes lead the tour yourself or hire others to do so. There are considerable up-front costs involved in undertaking a tour (attractive brochures, direct mail, tour buses, and so forth), so you need to get nonrefundable partial or full deposits to help cover costs. You can set your fees at 40 percent above your costs. So if you package only five tours a year for twenty people each and charge $2,000 for the tour, your gross profits will be $80,000.

To succeed in the tour business, you must have a knowledge of unique places or experiences that you can share with others. For example, if you lead or plan tours to Europe, you need to be fluent in one or more European languages and know the countryside and sites where you will be traveling and/or sending your clients. If you lead rock-climbing expeditions, you must be an expert climber and be familiar with the particular routes you will be covering.

Success as a tour operator depends on three things. You must:

1. Estimate your costs accurately in advance, and then keep within your budget
2. Fill all the openings on your tour
3. Plan and provide appealing, rewarding tours because much of your future business will come from repeat customers

Usually this means finding a specialty or niche that you understand well. For example, Patricia and Ronald Douglas operate Northstar Tours for senior citizens. Another popular type of tour to package is wilderness trips for women over the age of thirty who are inexperienced with the outdoors. Other tour operators specialize in tours for families with children or side trips for business executives attending trade and professional conventions. One tour operator we know, an artist with a French wife, made a nice part-time income taking students to the mountains in France each summer where they studied watercolor and painted to their heart's content, living in houses belonging to his wife's family. Some tour operators specialize in unusual, informative, or entertaining local day, weekend, or evening tours, like Dinner After Dark or the Chocoholics' Shopping Spree.

Computerization is also a factor to take into account in this business. You will likely want to use a database to keep track of your clients and your tour locations, hotels, restaurants, and so on. You can also take advantage of some off-the-shelf commercial mapping software, such as *Zagat-Axxis Cityguide* personal navigation software, which contains maps of major cities and recommendations for hotels, restaurants, and museums.

Some resources to learn more about these professions include the books:

For Fun and Profit: Self-Employment Opportunities in Recreation, Sports, and Travel, Crawford Lindsey, Boulder, CO: Live Oak Publications, 1984.

How to Start a Home Based Travel Agency, Thomas Ogg, Thomas Ogg and Associates, P.O. Box 2398, Valley Center, CA 92082; (619) 751-1007.

Part Time Travel Agent: How to Cash in On the Exciting New World of Travel Marketing, Kelly Monaghan, available from The Intrepid Traveler, P.O. Box 438, New York, NY 10034-0438; (212) 569-1081.

Start & Run a Profitable Travel Agency, Richard Cropp and Barbara Braidwood, Self-Counsel Press, 1704 N. State Street, Bellingham, WA 98225; (604) 986-3366.

You might also call the National Tour Association, Box 3071, Lexington, KY 40596; (800) 682-8886 or (606) 226-4494, if you are involved in the tour industry. Their membership consists of companies who package and sell escorted tours. Another organization is the American Society of Travel Agents, 1101 King Street, Second Floor, Alexandria, VA 22314; (800) 828-2712 or (703) 739-2782, fax (703) 684-6319.

APPENDIX
■■■■■■■■■■■■■■■■■■■■■■■■■■■■
List of Top-10 Best Businesses

Based on the kinds of characteristics people interested in a business that they can operate from home have told us are important to them, we have selected the businesses that possess those qualities to the greatest degree. In most instances, what the following lists describe is obvious. However, a word of explanation about several of the lists is in order.

In one we list what we've called *evergreen* businesses. An evergreen business does work that is always in demand and may well always be. Working alone, one is not apt to get rich or famous at an evergreen. This is a trade-off, for others have tried the way to establish these businesses.

The businesses listed under *Easiest to Enter* are those we think take the least education or experience to enter.

BEST ALL AROUND

Business Plan Writer
Cleaning Service
Consulting of all types
Desktop Video
Mailing List Service
Medical Claims Assistant
Medical Transcription Service
Repair Services
Rubber Stamp Business
Temporary Help

EASIEST TO ENTER

Cleaning Services
Errand Service

Grower of Specialty Foods
Hauling Service
In-Home Health Care
Mailing List Service
Manufacturer's Agent
Pet-Sitting Service
Rubber Stamp Business
Travel Sales

HIGHEST INCOME POTENTIAL

Bill-Auditing Service
Business Broker
Business Plan Writer
Desktop Video
Employee Training
Executive Recruiter

Export Agent
Management Consultant
Manufacturer's Agent
Professional Practice Consultant

BEST-KEPT SECRETS

Association Management Service
Calendar Service
Expert Broker
Image Consultant
In-Home Health Care
Leak Detection Service
Medical Claims Assistance
Mystery Shopping
Rubber Stamp Business
Transcript Digesting Service

FASTEST-GROWING FIELDS

Cleaning Services
Computer Consulting
Computer Programmer
Executive Search
Management Consulting
Medical Transcription
Public Relations
Specialty Consulting
Technical Writing
Temporary Help

HIGHEST DEMAND—EASIEST TO SELL

Bill-Auditing Service
Cleaning Services
Commercial Loan Negotiator
Home Inspector
Leak Detection Service
Medical Claims Assistance
Medical Transcription Service
Scopist
Repair Services
Rubber Stamp Business

MOST RECESSION RESISTANT

Bill Auditing Service
Business Brokering
Collection Agency
Commercial Loan Negotiator
Medical Claims Assistance
Medical Transcription
Scopist
Repair Services
Résumé-Writing Service
Temporary Help

LOWEST START-UP COSTS

Abstracting Service
Bookkeeping Service
Cleaning Services
Family Child-Care Provider
In-Home Health Care
Private Investigator
Professional Organizer
Technical Writer
Transcript Digesting
Wedding Makeup Artist

LOWEST STRESS

Bulletin Board Service
Facialist
Fitness Trainer
Grower of Specialty Foods
Mailing List Service
Pet-Sitting Service
Plant Caregiver
Pool Maintenance Service
Restoration Service
Rubber Stamp Business

EVERGREEN BUSINESSES

Bookkeeping Service
Caterer
Collection Agency
Computer Programmer
Hauling Service

Mailing List Service
Repair Services
Tax Preparation Service
Word-Processing Service

UP-AND-COMING HOME BUSINESSES

Business Plan Writer
Consultants of all types

Desktop Video
Home Inspector
Indoor Environmental Tester
Information Broker
In-Home Health Care
Multimedia Production
Referral Service
Temporary Help

Other Books by Paul and Sarah Edwards

Use the table below to locate other books that contain the information you need for your business interests.

Subject	Best Home Businesses for the 90s	Getting Business to Come to You	Making It on Your Own	Making Money with Your Computer at Home	Working From Home
Advertising		Yes			
Business Opportunities					Yes
Business Planning				Yes	
Children and Childcare					Yes
Closing Sales		Yes	Yes		
Credit					Yes
Employees					Yes
Ergonomics					Yes
Failure			Yes		
Family & Marriage Issues					Yes
Financing Your Business			Yes	Yes	Yes
Franchises				Yes	Yes
Getting Referrals Named		Yes			Yes
Handling Emotional/ Psychological Issues				Yes	
Housecleaning					Yes
Insurance					Yes
Legal Issues					Yes
Loneliness, Isolation					Yes

Managing Information				Yes	Yes
Marketing	Specific techniques by business	Yes—Focus of book	Yes—Attitude	Yes—Technology tools	Yes
Marketing Materials				Yes	Yes
Money			Yes	Yes	Yes
Naming Your Business		Yes			
Networking		Yes			Yes
Office Space, Furniture, Equipment					Yes
Outgrowing Your Home					Yes
Pricing	Yes—Specific			Yes—Specific	Yes—Principles
Profiles of Specific Businesses	Yes			Yes	
Public Relations & Publicity		Yes			Yes
Selecting a Business	Yes			Yes	Yes
Software				Yes	Yes
Speaking		Yes			
Start-up Costs	Yes			Yes	
Success Issues			Yes		
Taxes					Yes
Time Management			Yes	Yes	Yes
Zoning					Yes

Do You Have Questions or Feedback?

The authors of this book, Paul and Sarah Edwards, want to answer your questions. They can respond to you directly, usually within twenty-four hours, if you leave a message for them on the Working From Home Forum on CompuServe Information Service.

If you have a computer and access to CompuServe, simply type "GO WORK" at any "!" prompt; their ID is 76703,242. If you do not now have access to CompuServe, you can obtain a complimentary CompuServe membership and receive $15 of free connect time by calling (800) 524-3388. Ask for Operator 395. You can also obtain a CompuServe starter kit in many stores.

On the forum, you can obtain a copy of the Edwards' bimonthly newsletter *Making It on Your Own* in Library 1. Back issues are available as well for downloading and there is no cost beyond normal CompuServe connect time charges.

If you do not have a computer, you can write to Paul and Sarah in care of "Q&A," *Home Office Computing* magazine, 730 Broadway, New York, NY 10003. Your question may be selected to be answered in their monthly column or they may respond to it on their radio or TV show. However, they cannot respond to every letter.

COMPLETE YOUR LIBRARY OF THE WORKING FROM HOME SERIES BY PAUL AND SARAH EDWARDS

These books are available at your local bookstore or wherever books are sold. Ordering is also easy and convenient. TO ORDER, CALL 1-800-788-6262, prompt #1, or send your order to:

Jeremy P. Tarcher, Inc.
Mail Order Department
PO Box 12289
Newark, NJ 07101-5289

For Canadian orders:
PO Box 25000
Postal Station 'A'
Toronto, Ontario M5W 2X8

		PRICE
_____ The Best Home Businesses for the 90s, Revised Edition	0-87477-784-4	$12.95
_____ Finding Your Perfect Work	0-87477-795-X	$16.95
_____ Getting Business to Come to You	0-87477-629-5	$11.95
_____ Making Money with Your Computer at Home	0-87477-736-4	$12.95
_____ Working from Home	0-87477-764-X	$15.95

Subtotal _____

Shipping and handling* _____

Sales tax (CA, NJ, NY, PA) _____

Total amount due _____

Payable in U.S. funds (no cash orders accepted). $15.00 minimum for credit card orders.
*Shipping and handling: $3.50 for one book, $1.00 for each additional book. Not to exceed $8.50.

Payment method:

☐ Visa   ☐ Mastercard   ☐ American Express

☐ Check or money order

☐ International money order or bank draft check

Card # _____ Expiration date _____

Signature as on charge card _____

Daytime phone number _____

Name _____

Address _____

City _____ State _____ Zip _____

Please allow six weeks for delivery. Prices subject to change without notice. Source key WORK